FOREWORD

The international conference on the 1985 Mexico Earthquakes was organized to coordinate international mutual interest, to report the knowledge gained from early study of the Mexico earthquakes, and to foster cooperative efforts among an international group of engineers and scientists to identify successful practices for earthquake safety. The conference was planned to focus on key issues concerning the 1985 Mexico earthquakes, to provide results of study and analysis specific to the events surrounding that earthquake, and to improve international ties in research and technology-transfer as it addresses the 1985 Mexico earthquakes. Papers published in these proceedings were presented at the Conference to record a comprehensive account of the factors involved in the earthquake disaster and to identify the lessons learned to improve earthquake safety. The conference was held on September 19–20, 1986, in Mexico City just one year after the earthquake event.

This earthquake disaster provides a rare opportunity to test practices in building technology, among other things. In the days and months following the earthquakes, international teams of engineers, scientists, emergency planners, and sociologists joined their Mexican colleagues to study the event. The 1985 Mexico earthquake experience provides an unusually good source of data for study. Available strong motion records combined with structural effects on buildings created a unique natural laboratory. Eighteen strong motion instruments between the coastal area where the earthquakes occurred and Mexico City recorded the earthquake and its aftershocks.

This text presents invited reports and results of study from persons who collected data at the earthquake sites in Mexico and performed study on the effects of the earthquake. Studies reported relate the seismology of the region to expected effects on ground motions and on structural performance. The present scope of earthquake mitigation strategies are evaluated and improvements suggested. These improvements include gaining an understanding of amplification of seismic waves in soil deposits and evaluating anticipated ground motion for estimating response spectra. Improved knowledge of performance of foundations, lifelines and structures during an earthquake and emergency operations for survival and recovery are included.

The conference consisted of eight technical sessions, and a field trip to damage sites in Mexico City. The conference was organized and convened by ASCE under the direction of the Technical Council on Lifeline Earthquake Engineering with the support and cooperation of the ASCE Mexico Section, the Departamento del Distrito Federal (DDF) Mexico, and several technical institutions and Societies. Assistance was also provided by the Earthquake Engineering Research Institute. Dedication of the Conference proceedings was made by Richard W. Karn, past president of ASCE, as a reminder of the painful loss associated with the gain in knowledge for improved earthquake safety.

The conference organizing committee included the following persons: Michael A. Cassaro and Enrique Martinez-Romero, Co-chairmen, Ahmed Abdel-Ghaffar, R. Richard Avent, Reidar Bjorhovde, Jose J. Correa, Charles G. Culver, Nicholas F. Forell, Agustin Navarro Herrera, Francisco J. Serna, and J. Lawrence Von Thun. Dr. Ahmed Abdel-Ghaffar designed the Conference Logo.

Technical sessions were chaired by the following persons:

Session 1—OVERVIEW OF THE EARTHQUAKES—Agustin Navarro-Herrera, President, Mexico Section, ASCE

Session 2—DOMINANT FOUNDATION AND STRUCTURAL FAILURE MODES—Daniel Resendiz, Secretary General, National Science and Technology Council, Mexico

Session 3—DYNAMIC SOIL RESPONSE AND SOIL-STRUCTURE INTER-ACTION—Octavio Rascon-Chavez, Director, Facultad de Ingenieria, UNAM

Session 4—LIFELINES—Leopoldo Lieberman, President, Dela Camara Nacional de la Industria de la Construccion, Mexico

Session 5—PERFORMANCE OF STRUCTURES AND STRUCTURAL COM-PONENTS—Victor Pavon, Sociedad Mexicana de Ingenieria Estructural

Session 6—ANALYSIS OF DAMAGED STRUCTURES—Fernando L. Echegaray, Presidente, Colegio de Ingenieros Civiles de Mexico

Session 7—ANALYSIS OF FOUNDATION FAILURES—Raul Lopez Roldan, President, Sociedad Mexicana de mecanica de Suelos, Mexico

Session 8—ENGINEERING RESPONSE—Fernando Hiriart, Director General, Comision Federal de Electricidad, Mexico

Each of the papers included in the Proceedings has been accepted for publication by the Proceedings Editors. All papers are eligible for discussion in the appropriate journals of ASCE. All papers are eliglible for ASCE awards.

Michael A. Cassaro
Enrique Martinez-Romero
Editors

THE MEXICO EARTHQUAKES-1985
Factors Involved and Lessons Learned

Proceedings of the International Conference
sponsored by the
Mexico Section, ASCE
Technical Council on Lifeline Earthquake Engineering, ASCE
Engineering Mechanics Division, ASCE
Geotechnical Engineering Division, ASCE
Structural Division, ASCE
Earthquake Engineering Research Institute

Camino Real Hotel, Mexico City, Mexico, September 19-21, 1986

Edited by Michael A. Cassaro and Enrique Martinez Romero

Conference Organizing Committee

Michael A. Cassaro, Co-Chairman
Enrique Martinez Romero, Co-Chairman
Ahmed Abdel-Ghaffar
R. Richard Avent
Reidar Bjorhovde
Jose J. Correa

Charles G. Culver
Nicholas F. Forell
Agustin Navarro-Herrera
Francisco J. Serna
J. Lawrence Von Thun

Cooperating Organizations

American Concrete Institute
American Institute of Architects
American Institute of Steel Construction
American Iron and Steel Institute
American Society for Engineering Education
Building Seismic Safety Council
Camara Nacional de la Industria de la
  Construccion
Canadian Society for Civil Engineering
Central United States Earthquake Consortium
Colegio de Arquitectos de Mexico
Colegio de Ingenieros Civiles de Mexico
Cumision Federal de Electricidad, Mexico
Consejo Nacional de Ciencia y Tecnologia
  (CONACYT)

Federal District Department, Mexico
Geological Society of America
International Association for Earthquake
  Engineering
International Association for Bridge and
  Structural Engineering
Institution of Engineers, Pakistan
Instituto Technologico y de Estudios
  Superiores de Monterrey, Mexico
Mexico Society of Soil Mechanics
National Science Foundation
United States Department of Commerce,
  National Bureau of Standards
United States Department of the Interior,
  Geological Survey

Published by the
American Society of Civil Engineers
345 East 47th Street
New York, New York 10017-2398

ABSTRACT

This publication reports initial results of study of the 1985 Mexico Earthquakes, one year after the event. The findings present sufficient depth of analysis to provide an understanding of the causes and effects of earthshaking within Mexico City that results in extensive damage to some buildings and structures. Also reported are the assessment of damage caused by the earthquakes and emergency response including recovery operations. Buildings of different construction types and materials were subject to the earthquake. Performance of their response is analyzed and evaluated.

Topics presented include seismicity associated with the Mexico Earthquakes of 1985. General engineering topics include dynamic soil response, foundation failure, performance of structures and analysis of building failure, analysis of lifelines performance, and emergency response including building code regulations. Specific practical problems addressed include: Modelling of soil motion, modelling of structural behavior, analysis of drift in frame structures, structural pounding, structural stiffness softening due to long duration motion, soil-structure interaction, influence of local soil conditions on building performance, dam behavior, and repair and strengthening of buildings.

Library of Congress Cataloging-in-Publication Data

The 1985 Mexico earthquakes.

Includes index.
1. Buildings—Mexico—Mexico City Region—Earthquake effects—Congresses. 2. Earthquakes—Mexico City Region—Congresses. I. Cassaro, Michael A. II. Martínez Romero, Enrique. III. American Society of Civil Engineers. Mexico Section.
TA654.6.A17 1987 624.1'762'097253 86-32188
ISBN 0-87262-579-6

PROLOG

Introduction

The world is more vulnerable to earthquake disaster today than ever before because of the growing population, its concentration, increased economic and capital investments, and the fragility of lifelines. Every significant earthquake has the potential to provide a valuable learning experience which when studied can help to prevent future earthquake disasters everywhere. The 1985 Mexico earthquakes are being studied to advance international knowledge of earthquakes and improve earthquake safety.

The 1985 Mexico earthquakes experience provides an unusually good source of data for study. Available strong motion records combined with structural effects on buildings create a unique natural laboratory. Eighteen strong motion instruments between the coastal area where the earthquakes occurred and Mexico City recorded the earthquake and its aftershocks. The earthquake energy at Mexico City was far greater than reasonably anticipated by engineers and by the building code. The resulting ground motion spectrum was greater than prescribed by design codes anywhere. The unexpected intensity and the extent of damage were further aggravated by the long duration of strong ground motion and by the unique soil conditions in Mexico City.

The Seismic Event

The 1985 Mexico earthquakes contained at least 20 sustained cycles of vibration with a dominant period of about two seconds. Ground accelerations ranged from 5 to 20 percent of gravity in a period range between 1.5 and 3 seconds. The total duration of sustained shaking continued for about three mintues. The maximum accelerations in the rock were about 3 or 4 percent of gravity. Because of the long duration of shaking, deep soil deposits were excited resulting in amplified ground movements. Historic seismic activity in this region causes Mexico to experience about five times as many major earthquakes as California, with a greater frequency of recurrence.

Mexico City is build partially on alluvial lake deposits that average from 100 to 150 feet (30 to 45 m) thick. At some location within the damaged area, soil deposits extend to depths of about 7500 feet (2300 m). Thus, the earthquakes impacted a teeming city of eighteen million persons upon a treacherous foundation in a land highly susceptible to the occurrence of a great earthquake. More than 10,000 persons lost their lives and at least 100,000 persons were left homeless. More than 400 buildings were destroyed and an additional 3200 were damaged in this most populous city of an earthquake enlightened nation.

The 8.1 Richter magnitude earthquake occurred at 7:19 a.m. on Thursday, September 19, 1985, as the moving mantle of the earth thrust the Cocos plate about six feet beneath the North American plate releasing seismic waves that rocked Mexico City 240 miles (400 km) to the east. On the following day at 7:30 p.m., an after shock of 7.5 magnitude caused additional damage. The movement occurred along a 200 mile (320 km) length in two actions spaced about 26 seconds apart that was responsible for the duration of shaking in Mexico City.

Because of the geotechnical characteristics of the lake bed soil deposits in a portion of Mexico City, an amplification of about 8 with 5% damping was experienced in ground accelerations at some locations. Structures with a natural period of vibration about equal to 2 seconds experienced resonant amplification with the ground motion at these sites. The result produced substantial damage or total collapse of some buildings.

Effects of the Earthquakes

The 1985 Mexico earthquakes presented a different exposure to earth movement than had been expected by experienced earthquake engineers. The results were catastrophic; but knowledge gained of the effects on structures will surely advance understanding of the complexities of earthquakes. The large number and variety of structural types exposed to the earthquake provides a perspective for studying relative effects of construction methods and their impact on strength and performance.

The earthquake shook various types of buildings until they collapsed or were pounded to destruction by blows from adjoining buildings that were also rocked. Small buildings lay crushed beneath taller structures that had toppled. Various types of failure modes resulted including column shear, punching about columns, buildings pounding against each other, buildings overturned, soil subsidence, and foundation failure. A large number of buildings with similar natural periods performed well. Many were located in the same area as others that failed, thus providing an ideal laboratory for comparative structural analysis.

Most of the collapsed buildings were frame structures. Buildings destroyed included concrete frames, flat plates and waffle slabs, structural steel frames and masonry structures. Considering structural height, over 100 buildings less than 5 stories were destroyed, almost 140 buildings between 6 and 10 stories, 27 between 11 and 15 stories, and 3 were greater than 15 stories. Buildings between 6 and 15 stories appeared to sway in resonance with the shaking earth.

Telecommunications and electric power were out after the earthquake. Electric power was restored a few days after the earthquake. Communications were seriously disrupted and slowly restored. Water had been cut off from 6 million persons.

Engineering response required inspection of 6617 buildings. About one half of the buildings inspected were declared too badly damaged to permit further use before reconstruction or demolition.

Factors Involved

Study and analysis of the earthquakes' factors and effects will yield important lessons in building design and city planning. The effects of structure pounding and base rotation including soil-structure interaction caused upper story failures. The disproportionate strength and insufficient ductility of lower floors in some buildings contributed to their failure. These effects were magnified by the long duration of shaking, and the natural period of the ground motion contributed to the resonant character of combined ground-structure motions.

Provisions contained in the 1985 Mexico City Building Code which was applicable during the 1985 event prescribed response spectra in the natural period range from 1.0 to 3.5 seconds. However, the peak acceleration experienced in the 1985 earthquake was more than twice that experienced in any previous severe earthquake in Mexico City. Factors for consideration in any revisions to the building code include dynamic behavior of soil deposits, evaluation of lateral force design coefficients, story drift, and change of natural periods of vibration due to earthquake induced structural decay.

Control of emergency operations should be clear with respect to rescue, shelter for the homeless, lifeline recovery and infrastructure repair. Deployment of volunteer rescue support and forces needed to maintain order, use of rescue equipment, condemnation of damaged buildings, and control of licensing and professional registration for improved standards are considered in the studies following the earthquake.

Expected Learning

How can we maximize learning about earthquake safety from the 1985 Mexico earthquakes? Learning and credibility of the reported results are achieved through an international cooperative effort by scientists and engineers working with the data obtained from the event. Studies of the effects of the earthquakes have begun in all areas of study. These studies evaluate and report on factors that increase public safety during earthquakes. Improvement of our understanding of the societal, economic and political factors is expected.

Study of the 1985 Mexico earthquakes provides a potential for learning about earthquakes never before provided. Knowledge of a natural disaster acquired so painfully is valued and more willingly applied to improve building provisions and city planning policy for reduction of the earthquake hazard.

To study the complete relationship of materials, strength and performance in all cases requires lengthy and careful analysis. This conference provides initial results of a complete range of study on many factors involved in the 1985 Mexico earthquakes. As these and other studies progress, greater understanding will be gained to advance earthquake safety.

We have the technical means to achieve great advances through cooperation and interdependence of nations. Much progress has been made. Cooperative efforts such as this conference and the recent NSF sponsored research program involving Mexican and American engineers and scientists to advance international study of the 1985 Mexico earthquakes will gain the greatest results.

Reduction of seismic vulnerability is a reasonable expectation. The 1985 Mexico earthquakes provide a focus on the influence of building codes and their effect on construction practices, land-use policy, structural design, ability to adequately anticipate ground spectra, and other mechanisms that influence earthquake vulnerability.

Decades of research are able to be compiled through the comprehensive analysis and evaluation of the causes and effects of this great earthquake. Most metropolitan areas are ill prepared for an earthquake of this intensity. Our expectations are to advance that level of preparedness.

Michael A. Cassaro
Enrique Martinez-Romero
Editors

THE 1985 MEXICO EARTHQUAKES
FACTORS INVOLVED AND LESSONS LEARNED

DEDICATION BY RICHARD W. KARN
September 19, 1986

On October 2 last year I received a telephone call from Enrique Martinez-Romero. He was in San Francisco and wanted to meet with me to talk about the disastrous earthquake that occurred just 13 days before in Mexico City. He asked what we could do as civil engineers and as ASCE members to respond to that terrible disaster.

We had dinner that evening and he related some of the terrible experiences and heroic actions that occurred on September 19 and the following days. From that meeting came the idea of arranging a special session on the Mexico City earthquake at the ASCE Annual Convention to be held in Detroit in less than three weeks. The next day I contacted Executive Director Ed Pfrang at ASCE headquarters and we began a whirlwind effort. The program was developed so rapidly that our last speaker, Harry Seed, agreed to participate only a few hours before the session began. The session was a success. It was the best attended meeting at the convention. Everyone was anxious to hear professional engineers analyze the meager information available, and learn what had happened and why.

However, we thought there was a more important contribution to be made. If we could gather together experts from all nations one year later in Mexico City and hear their analyses of the causes and effects of the disastrous event following a year of careful evaluation, we thought we would make a real and lasting contribution for the benefit of all mankind.

Three weeks later in Detroit, we approached the Technical Activities Committee and with support from Chairman George Barnes received their blessing. A Conference Organizing Committee was appointed representing the affected Technical Divisions. Of primary concern to us was that this conference should be designed to impart the most knowledge about this disastrous earthquake for the benefit of a maximum number of people. The conference should not stress just one technical segment, but provide information about all segments and their interrelationships.

When I review the conference program, I conclude that the committee fulfilled that responsibility. The title alone, "An International Conference on the 1985 Mexican Earthquakes—Factors Involved and Lessons Learned," identifies the broad nature of the program and the goal of education. The program ranges from analysis of the seismology of the region through structural, geotechnical and lifeline concerns to the final session which deals with the engineering response. As a result we will all gain from the efforts that have been put forth by the committee and the participants in this conference.

The themes that shall be discussed here between engineers of various countries of Mexican engineers will improve the understanding of the forces of nature. This meeting is a great example of how engineers of the world work together for the benefit of Humanity.

This has been proclaimed a day of mourning and I believe that we should dedicate this conference to the thousands of people here in Mexico who experienced this terrible disaster and whose heroic efforts brought order out of the rubble. We should also dedicate it to the conference participants who will impart knowledge that will aid us should we face a similar disastrous event.

And I think each of you should dedicate yourself to listen and participate so that you may take home with you a better knowledge of what occurred here one year ago and how you may act to lessen the destruction and number of casualties should such an event occur anywhere in the world in the future.

Thus we will have learned from tragedy how to fulfill our Society's objective, which is to advance science and the profession of engineering to enhance the welfare of mankind.

CONTENTS

Dedication
Richard W. Karn ix

OVERVIEW OF THE EARTHQUAKES

Overview of Factors Involved in the Mexico Earthquakes
George W. Housner 1

Review of the Seismicity of Mexico with Emphasis on the September
1985, Michoacan Earthquakes
S. K. Singh and G. Suarez 7

Strong Motion Arrays and Characteristics
Roberto Quaas and Enrique Mena 19

Aspects of Strong Motion
John G. Anderson, James N. Brune, Jorge Prince, Enrique Mena, Paul
Bodin, Mario Onate, Roberto Quaas, Shri Krishna Singh 33

Estimated Strong Ground Motions in the Mexico City Earthquake
Hiroyoshi Kobayashi, Kazuoh Seo and Saburoh Midorikawa 55

Damage Statistics of the September 19, 1985, Earthquake in Mexico City
Gilberto Borja-Navarrete, Manuel Diaz-Canales, Alejandro Vazquez
Vera and Enrique del Valle-Calderon 70

FOUNDATION FAILURE, DYNAMIC SOIL RESPONSE
AND SOIL-STRUCTURE INTERACTION

Geotechnical Notes on the Effects of Mexico's 1985 Earthquakes
Raul J. Marsal 78

Empirical Relationships for Earthquake Ground Motions in Mexico City
Ellis L. Krinitzsky... 96

Effects of the 1985 Earthquake in Lazaro Cardenas, Michigan
Enrique Santoyo and Carlos Gutierrez 119

Earthquake Response of La Villita Dam
Francisco Gonzales-Valencia..................................... 134

Analytical Modelling of Dynamic Soil Response in the Mexico Earthquake of September 19, 1985
Miguel P. Romo and H. Bolton Seed............................. 148

xi

Are the Soil Depositions in Mexico City Unique?
Robert V. Whitman   163

Analysis of Foundation Failures
Pablo Girault D.   178

Soil-Structure Interaction in Mexico City During the 1985 Earthquake
Daniel Resendiz and J. M. Roesset   193

Seismic Design Criteria For Foundations on Control Piles
Enrique Tamez   204

PERFORMANCE OF STRUCTURES AND ANALYSIS OF STRUCTURAL FAILURE

Performance Characteristics of Structures, 1985 Mexico City Earthquake
Charles Scawthorn, Mehmet Celebi and Jorge Prince   217

Preliminary Dynamic Analysis of the Ministry of Agriculture Building
William C. Stone and Ing. Neftali Rodriquez Cueves   233

Implications of Structural Characteristics on Failure
Fernando Fossas R.   255

Observations on Structural Pounding
Vitelmo V. Bertero   264

R/C Frame Drift for 1985 Mexico Earthquake
Mete A. Sozen and Ricardo R. Lopez   279

Evaluation of Performance of Concrete Buildings Damaged by the
September 19, 1985 Mexico Earthquake
Roberto Meli   308

Behavior of Reinforced Concrete Framing Systems
S. K. Ghosh and W. G. Corley   328

Performance of Steel Structures
Robert Hanson   350

LIFELINES

The 1985 Mexico Earthquakes: Effects on Water Supply Systems
Gary M. Lee   364

Effects on Infrastructure
Froylan Vargas-Gomez   368

Summary of the Effects of the 1985 Mexico Earthquake to Power and
Industrial Facilities
S. J. Eder and S. W. Swan   381

ENGINEERING AND EMERGENCY RESPONSE

Seismic Rehabilitation: Why, When and How
Ignacio Martin 396

Damage Assessment and Seismic Behavior of Steel Buildings in Mexico City
Enrique Martinez-Romero...................................... 409

Repairing and Strengthening of Reinforced Concrete Buildings Damaged in the 1985 Mexico City Earthquakes
Jesus Iglesias 426

Emergency Regulations and the New Building Code
Emilio Rosenblueth 440

Thoughts on a Different Approach to Seismic Design Codes
Oscar de Buen 455

The Impact of the Construction of Public Works by the Earthquakes of September 1985
Francisco Norena Casado and Carlos E. Castaneda Narvaes 463

Subject Index.. 473

Author Index.. 474

Overview of Factors Involved in the Mexico Earthquakes

George W. Housner[*], Mem. ASCE

Abstract

The Mexico earthquakes provided many opportunities for learning. New knowledge has been obtained and continuing research will provide additional knowledge. The earthquakes have also demonstrated that there are gaps in our knowledge and that more must be learned. There is a need for better preparation for learning from earthquakes and this preparation must be made in advance of the earthquake. Learning could be much enhanced by stronger international cooperation and the proposed International Decade of Hazard Reduction offers an opportunity.

Introduction

It is appropriate at this point to ask what did we learn from the 19 September 1985 Mexico earthquake and also to ask what more might we have learned and what did we unlearn. The most significant items that we could learn are included in the following topics: 1) Ground motions; 2) Building performance; 3) Foundation behavior; 4) Lifeline functioning, including electric power, water supply, gas supply, sewer system, communications systems, and transportation systems; 5) Emergency management; 6) Disaster mitigation. In all of these we learned something, and from the research projects still underway we can expect to learn more. In this paper I can touch upon only a relatively small number of especially significant items.

In retrospect, looking back at destructive earthquakes such as Tangshan 1976, San Fernando 1971, Nicaragua 1972, Alaska 1964, Niigata 1964 and many others, we see that in most of these we learned something, but much less than we should have learned. In addition, most of these earthquakes brought to light deficiencies in our knowledge and in our understanding of earthquakes. In most of these earthquakes unexpected occurrences demonstrated that we did not know something which we thought we knew. Thus, when a damaging earthquake occurs it not only expands our knowledge but also expands our ignorance. The 1985 Mexico earthquake was no exception.

Ground Motion

The ground motion of the 19 September 1985 earthquake provided us with new knowledge. The remarkable accelerograms recorded on the old lake bed (SCT) showed a dominant period of 2 seconds and the peak

---

*Professor, California Institute of Technology, Pasadena, CA 91125

1

acceleration was an unexpectedly high 20%g. The two 1962 earthquakes
were recorded in Mexico City in Alameda Park and in the basement of the
Latino Americana Tower and the accelerograms showed peak accelerations
of 5%g and a dominant period of 2.6 seconds; but recordings were not
made on firm ground in 1962 and the lack of this information prevented
us from studying the input and response of the soft soft layer. In 1985
the earthquake motions were recorded on the firm ground at the university (UNAM) and these had a peak acceleration of about 4%g and showed no
dominant ground period. This motion on firm ground may be taken to
represent the base motion that excited the old lake bed into oscillation
with 2 seconds period. The response spectrum of the UNAM accelerograms
at 2 seconds period thus enables us to ascertain the unexpectedly small
damping in the clay layer, if we consider the lake bed to vibrate like a
shear-beam. Thus having the motions of both the firm ground and the
soft ground provided valuable new information. In fact, we have learned
enough to see that there are significant gaps in our knowledge, for we
are then led to ask what was the 1985 dominant period in Alameda Park?
Was it again 2.6 seconds, or did the properties of the soft soil change
so that it was stiffer? If the properties of the soil did not change,
it follows that different locations in the city may have different
dominant periods. Then it can be asked, how does the soft soil response
vary over the city? Is the observed period of the ground motion dependent on the causative earthquake fault? That is, will the nature of the
response be different for an earthquake originating in the southeastern
seismic zone, for example, than for an earthquake originating in the
coastal seismic zone? Will the nature of the response be different for
different source mechanisms (subduction fault, strike-slip fault, thrust
fault, normal fault)? It is clear that if the depth of the soft soil
varies over the city, the dominant period in the ground motion, during
an earthquake, cannot vary correspondingly in a continuous fashion.
Undoubtedly, analytical studies will throw some light on this, but we
cannot be certain until ground motions of different earthquakes have
been recorded by an array of instruments dispersed over the city.

Another important piece of knowledge was learned from the ground
motion in the 19 September event. The unusually long duration of
shaking in Mexico City resulted from the occurrence of two consecutive
earthquakes on the causative fault. It was clearly shown by the near-
field accelerograms that the initial fault slip was followed by a second
fault slip approximately 30 seconds later and separated by some miles in
space. In Mexico City, because of the relatively large distance from
the fault, the dispersion of the seismic waves resulted in ground motion
that appeared to be the consequence of a single large event. It has
been observed before that large events, such as the 1964 Alaska M8.4
earthquake, often are not the consequence of a single continuous fault
slip but, rather, the slip hangs up momentarily before progressing to a
neighboring segment of the fault. Thus, a point, P in the near field of
the first fault slip is not in the near field of the second segment of
fault slip and the intensity of shaking at point P from the second slip
is appreciably attenuated. The 19 September 1985 earthquake shows,
however, that in the far field at a point several hundred kilometers
from the causative fault, the seismic waves from the two events overlap
and produce increased intensity and lengthened duration of shaking.
This fact has important implications for situations where M7.5 to M8.5

earthquakes can occur at some distance from cities with highrise
buildings that have periods of vibration in the range of 1 to 5 seconds.

The 1985 earthquake disclosed another gap in our knowledge of ground
motions. If seismologists and earthquake engineers had been asked,
before 19 September 1985, to estimate the peak ground accelerations at a
distance of 350 kilometers from the causative fault of an M8.1 event
their estimates would all have been in the range of 3 to 5%g, thus
agreeing satisfactorily with the actual recorded motions on firm ground
at UNAM. However, if they had been asked to estimate the peak acceleration in the near-field of an M8.1 earthquake, the estimates would have
been in the range of 50% to 100%g, or more. For example, in the United
States, estimates have been made of 75%g for the near-field of an M7.5
event. However, the peak accelerations actually recorded in the near-
field of the 1985 Mexico earthquake were in the range of 15% to 20%g, so
the estimates would have been from 3 to 5 times too large. This discrepancy demonstrates that our knowledge of ground motions is far from
complete.

Performance of Buildings

The 1985 earthquake demonstrated once again that the occurrence of an
earthquake disaster depends upon, 1) the size of the earthquake (a small
earthquake will not generate destructive ground shaking), 2) the existence of a large city close enough to the fault so that damaging ground
motions are experienced (at sufficiently large distances the ground
motions will be attenuated to non-destructive intensity), and 3) the
city must be unprepared for that intensty of shaking. These conditions
were satisfied by the 1985 Mexico earthquake though it might have been
thought that 350 kilometers was too great a distance. The earthquake
caused a disaster, but not a great disaster. The description "great
disaster" must be reserved for earthquakes that greatly damage cities
and/or cause many tens of thousands of casualties. Examples of such
earthquakes are: 1976 Tangshan, China (great damage; 200,000+ deaths),
1923 Tokyo, Japan (great damage; 100,000 deaths), 1908 Messina, Italy
(great damage; 80,000 deaths), 1906 San Francisco (great damage), and
many others. With the population of the world increasing by almost 100
million per year and cities expanding at an even greater rate than the
population, great disasters can be expected more frequently in the
future than in the past, if cities do not take steps to mitigate the
effects of future earthquakes.

Significant engineering lessons have been learned from the 1985
earthquake and further studies will refine these lessons and will, no
doubt, provide new lessons. The one very important lesson that still
needs to be learned is how to design a structure and to calculate
reliably the intensity and duration of ground shaking that would produce
damage just up to the point of collapse. Until this can be done, we
will not be able to specify how safe our cities are for the inhabitants.
Our present state of ignorance is compounded by the fact at present we
cannot be certain about the "maximum possible" intensity of ground
shaking. The 1985 earthquake has provided some information on the

collapse of buildings and on unexpected ground shaking, but much remains
to be learned.

Learning from Earthquakes

The occurrences of earthquakes provides the basic data from which we
learn about earthquake engineering, seismology, disaster mitigation,
etc. Focusing, now, upon learning about engineering, it is important to
recognize that there are two different procedures for learning from
earthquakes. The first of these may be called the research/scientific
approach for which there is needed accurate measurements of such things
as ground motions, building motions, strains in stuctural elements,
behavior of soils and foundations, etc. Statistical analyses, no doubt,
will play an important role in earthquake studies because of our unavoidable lack of knowledge which can only be circumvented by statistical
treatment of the available data.

A second approach to learning from earthquakes may be called the
practical/code approach. We must recognize that the research/scientific
approach develops knowledge slowly and, if the required data are not
available, or the solution of the problem is too difficult, then the
researcher cannot provide the information needed by the practicing engineer. On the other hand, the function of the practicing engineer is to
do, not to research. He must evaluate, design, and construct projects
efficiently. Society demands that engineers provide buildings,
bridges, dams, power plants, etc., even though knowledge is less than
complete. It is the very essence of engineering to do the best job that
can be done with the information that is available. This is often
called using engineering judgment. As a consequence, the practice of
engineering will sometimes run ahead of research, though at other times
practice will fall behind research. The practice/code approach can
learn things from an earthquake that cannot be learned through the
research/scientific approach, because of lack of precise data.   The 1985
earthquake has provided an opportunity for such practical learning. If
a building performs poorly during an earthquake, engineers can identify
why it so performs and can adjust code and practice accordingly.
However, equally valuable information may be learned by studying those
buildings that perform much better than would have been anticipated.
Not only should those buildings that are victims of the earthquake be
studied, but also the outstanding survivors should be studied in depth.

Similarly, in the fields of emergency management and disaster mitigation, studies should be made of the exceptionally good performances as
well as of the exceptionally bad performances.

Preparing to Learn from Earthquakes

The 1985 Mexico earthquake, as well as past earthquakes, emphasized,
once again, the importance of preparing to learn from earthquakes. The
installation and maintenance of accelerographs by UNAM to record ground
motions on the old lake bed and on firm ground is an excellent example
of preparing for earthquakes. Without the information provided by these

instruments it would have been very difficult for engineers to learn
from the earthquake. However, the great value of these records points
out how much more could have been learned if additional instruments had
been installed in selected locations throughout the city, and if appropriate recording instruments had been installed in selected buildings;
and if appropriate instruments had been installed at points in the soft
soil.

Also in preparing for an earthquake it would be desirable to identify
"guinea pig" buildings before the earthquake. This could be done at the
time a building is being designed and constructed so that design calculations, construction drawings, and construction photographs could be
archived. If studies of building performance are only begun after the
earthquake has occurred, then much of the desired information will be
impossible to retrieve. It is clear that there are limits to what can
be done to prepare for earthquakes, for usually optimum networks of
strong motion instruments cannot be installed because of financial
limitations. Neither can all significant buildings, bridges, dams,
etc., be instrumented. There are also limits on how much information
can be archived in anticipation of an earthquake, however, in view of
the potential benefits, much more could be done than has been done in
the past. Perhaps a new field of earthquake engineering should be
developed that could be called Planning for Earthquakes. Courses could
be given at universities, seminars could be held, government agencies
could be advised, etc.

International Cooperation in Earthquake Engineering

The present conference is an example of international cooperation in
learning from earthquakes, though a rather transient and modest example.
Stronger cooperation could be developed, for everyone is interested in
learning from earthquakes in other countries. For purposes of learning,
the occurrences of earthquakes in any single country are too infrequent,
for engineers should not sit and wait for the next earthquake but should
try to improve public safety by upgrading earthquake engineering before
the next earthquake occurs. The earthquake engineering community must
be prepared to learn from earthquakes that occur anywhere in the world
for we cannot claim to really understand earthquakes and earthquake
engineering unless we can understand others´ earthquakes and earthquake
engineering as well as our own. An example of international cooperation
is the formation of the International Association for Earthquake Engineering and the holding of World Conferences. However, a more pur-
poseful cooperation should be established. For example, in each country
preparation could be made in recognition of the fact that, when a significant earthquake occurs, engineers and researchers will come to learn
from it. Relevant data should be made quickly available, such as was
done with the UNAM accelerograms; cooperative research projects should
be planned, instruments for recording aftershocks could be loaned, etc.
In some countries such international cooperation would require government approval, and in these countries it would be desirable for
earthquake engineers to set standards for international cooperation and
to obtain government approval before the earthquake, and not wait until
after the earthquake to begin planning the cooperation.

Better communication between research workers in different seismic
countries should be developed, even though the language barrier poses
difficulties. It would be valuable to know what researchers in other
countries are doing or planning to do and to correlate efforts, instead
of waiting for the research to be completed and published some years
later.

Much better communications should be developed, also, among practicing engineers in different seismic countries. It seems to be a
universal trait among practicing engineers to feel that what they themselves are doing is the best way to do it. In fact, an engineer almost
must feel that way in order to do his job, but it is clear that practicing engineers could, indeed, profit from knowing what engineers are
doing in other countries.

Better international cooperation in research should be developed.
Data should be shared, gaps in knowledge should be identified, cooperative research projects should be undertaken, international visits
between researchers should be made, etc. Educational projects could be
undertaken. In short, earthquakes should be viewed as a world problem,
not as a national problem.

International Decade of Hazard Reduction

At the Eighth World Conference on Earthquake Engineering the Keynote
Address was made by Frank Press, the President of the U.S. National
Academy of Sciences, and a noted seismologist. He proposed that an
International Decade of Hazard Reduction be established. This would
focus on the natural hazards of earthquake, tsunami, wind, flood and
volcano. Efforts are now underway in the U.S.[*], Japan, and some other
countries, to formulate an IDHR. This will require governmental approval and cooperation in all the participating countries. It is
thought that the Decade would be from 1990 to the year 2000, in view of
all the time required for plans and arrangements that must be made to
launch the Decade. It is expected that the United Nations will also
support an IDHR as it has a strong interest in hazard reduction. During
the Decade, it is anticipated that a significantly increased effort will
be made in research, in development, in disaster mitigation, etc. The
IDHR would be an excellent opportunity for developing international
cooperation in earthquake engineering.

---

[*]U.S. National Academy of Engineering has recently issued a report titled:
TOWARD A LESS HAZARD WORLD — A Strategy for International Collaboration
to Reduce Natural Hazards.

Review of the Seismicity of Mexico with Emphasis on the September 1985, Michoacan Earthquakes.

S.K. Singh and G. Suárez *

A review of seismicity of Mexico is presented with emphasis put on the 19 Sept and 21 Sept 1985 Michoacan earthquakes. The earthquake of 19 Sept ruptured a region known as the Michoacan seismic gap, and is the second largest earthquake of this century in Mexico. An examination of seismicity and seismic gaps suggests that, at present, the Guerrero gap has the highest seismic potential. It may rupture in one magnitude 8+ or several smaller earthquakes in next ten years or so. The data suggest that the damage to Mexico City during the 19 Sept 1985 earthquake may not have been due only to the relatively large size and long duration of the earthquake coupled to the explosive growth of the city during the last 40 years, but also caused by the anomalously high radiation of 2 to 5 s waves towards Mexico City.

We also present a brief review of ground motion characteristics in Mexico city. In the lake bed zone of the city ground motions are amplified by up to 50 times with respect to sites in the hill zone. Surprisingly small nonlinear behaviour of clay is found at strains of 0.2% during 19 Sept 1985 earthquake.

Introduction

Large earthquakes ($M_s \geq 7$) along the Pacific coast of Mexico are caused by the subduction of the Cocos or Rivera Oceanic plates beneath the North American plates (Fig. 1). Rivera, a relatively small plate, subducts below the state of Jalisco with a relative velocity of about 2.5 cm/yr. The boundary between Rivera and Cocos plates, although somewhat uncertain, probably intersects the Mexican coast near Manzanillo (19.1°N, 104.3°W). The relative velocity of the Cocos plate with respect to continental Mexico (part of North American plate) increases from about 5 cm/yr near Manzanillo to about 8 cm/yr near Tehuantepec; the vector of convergence has an azimuth of N 35°E (Minster and Jordan, 1978). Large earthquakes also occur in the continent at depths greater than about 40 km (Fig. 1). These earthquakes show a normal faulting mechanism reflecting the breakup of the subducted ocean lithosphere (Singh et al., 1985a). Although relatively infrequent, such earthquakes are known to cause great damage. Finally, less frequent crustal earthquakes ($M_s \leq 7$) also occur within the continental plate. Depending upon the location, such events can cause considerable damage to localized population centers.

* Instituto de Geofísica, U.N.A.M., C.U., 04510 México, D.F.

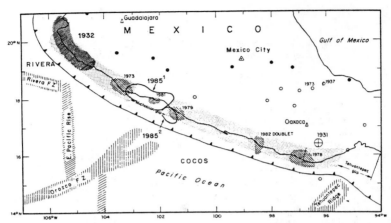

Figure 1. Tectonic setting of Mexico. Large, shallow earthquakes along the
Pacific coast occur because of subduction of Rivera and Cocos
plates below Mexico. Aftershock areas of 19 Sept 1985 earthquakes
are marked 1985[1] and 1985[2] respectively. Aftershock areas of
other, well studied earthquakes are shown cross-hatched. The
stippled band (80 km wide) may be the maximum extent of strong
coupling along the plate interface. Dots: recent volcanoes,
open circle: normal fault earthquakes with M>6.0.

Catalog of Large Earthquakes of Mexico

A catalog of this century's large ($M_s \geq 7$) earthquakes of Mexico
(modified from Singh et al., 1984a) is given in Table 1: The catalog
of last century's earthquakes (Table 2) has been compiled from felt and
damage reports; because of the dearth of population centers along the
Pacific coast this catalog is incomplete and the locations may be
biased.   From Table 1 we note that 34 earthquakes with $M_s \geq 7.0$ and 8
earthquakes with $M_s \geq 7.9$ have occurred in the past 86 years in the region
covered by the catalog.   After the Jalisco earthquake of 1932, the great
Michoacan earthquake of 19 Sept 1985 ($M_s = 8.1$) was the second largest
earthquake this century.

Table 1. Catalog of Large, Shallow Earthquakes ($M_s \geq 7.0$) of Mexico (15°-20°N, 94.5°-
105.5°W) from 1900 to 1985 (Modified from Singh et al., 1984a).

Event	Date	Time h: m: s	Lat(°N)	Long(°W)	Depth km	M_s
1	20 Jan 1900	06:33:30	20.0	105.0	S	7.6
2	16 May 1900	20:12:	20.0	105.0	S	7.1
3	15 Apr 1907	06:08:06	16.7	99.2	S	7.9
4	26 Mar 1908	23:03:30	18.0	99.0	S	7.8
5	27 Mar 1908	03:45:30	17.0	101.0	S	7.2
6	30 Jul 1909	10:51:54	16.8	99.9	S	7.5
7	7 Jun 1911	11:02:42	17.5	102.5	S	7.8
8	16 Dec 1911	19:14:18	16.9	100.7	50	7.6
9	19 Nov 1912	13:55:07	19.93	99.8	S(?)	7.0
10	21 Nov 1916	06:25:24	18.0	100.0	S	7.0
11	29 Dec 1917	22:50:20	15.0	97.0	S	7.1

12	22 Mar 1928	04:17:03.2	16.23	95.45	S	7.7
13	17 Jun 1928	03:19:28.2	16:33	96.70	S	8.0
14	4 Aug 1928	18:28:16.8	16.83	97.61	S	7.4
15	9 Oct 1928	03:01:07.7	16.34	97.29	S	7.8
16	15 Jan 1931	01:50:40.2	16:10	96.64	S	8.0
17	3 Jun 1932	10:36:52.2	19.84	103.99	S	8.4
18	18 Jun 1932	10:12:10	19.5	103.5	S	8.0
19	30 Nov 1934	02:05:15.6	19.00	105.31	S	7.2
20	23 Dec 1937	13:17:58.5	17.10	98.07	S	7.7
21	15 Apr 1941	19:09:51.0	18.85	102.94	S	7.9
22	22 Feb 1943	09:20:44.6	17.62	101.15	S	7.7
23	14 Dec 1950	14:15:49.6	17.22	98.12	S	7.3
24	28 Jul 1957	08:40:10.2	17.11	99.10	S	7.7
25	11 May 1962	14:11:57.1	17.25	99.58	S	7.2
26	23 Aug 1965	19:46:02.9	16.3	95.8	S	7.8
27	2 Aug 1968	14:06:43.9	16.6	97.7	S	7.4
28	30 Jun 1973	21:01:18.0	18.39	103.21	32	7.5
29	29 Nov 1978	10:52:47.3	16.00	96.69	19	7.8
30	14 Mar 1979	11:07:11.2	17.46	101.46	15	7.6
31	25 Oct 1981	03:22:13	17.75	102.25	20	7.3
32	7 Jun 1982	06:52:32.8	16.40	98.54	15	7.0
33	19 Sep 1985	13:17:49.1	18:14	102.71	16	8.1
34	21 Sep 1985	01:37:11.8	17.62	101.82	20	7.5

Table 2. A Catalog of Large 19th Century Earthquakes of Mexico (from Singh et al. 1981)

Event	Date	Region	Epicenter Lat(°N)	Long(°W)	M_s
1	25 Mar 1806	Coast of Colima-Michoacán	18.9	103.8	7.5
2	31 May 1818	Coast of Colima-Michoacán	19.1	103.6	7.7
3	4 May 1820	Coast of Guerrero	17.2	99.6	7.6
4	22 Nov 1837	Jalisco	20.0	105.0	7.7
5	9 Mar 1845	Oaxaca	16.6	97.0	7.5
6	7 Apr 1845	Coast of Guerrero	16.6	99.2	7.9
7	5 May 1854	Coast of Oaxaca	16.3	97.6	7.7
8	19 Jun 1858	North Michoacan	19.6	101.6	7.5
9	3 Oct 1864	Puebla-Veracruz	18.7	97.4	7.3
10	11 May 1870	Coast of Oaxaca	15.8	96.7	7.9
11	27 Mar 1872	Coast of Oaxaca	15.7	96.6	7.4
12	16 Mar 1874	Guerrero	17.7	99.1	7.3
13	11 Feb 1875	Jalisco	21.0	103.8	7.5
14	9 Mar 1875	Coast of Jalisco-Colima	19.4	104.6	7.4
15	17 May 1879	Puebla	18.6	98.0	7.0
16	19 Jul 1882	Guerrero-Oaxaca	17.7	98.2	7.5
17	3 May 1887	Bavispe, Sonora	31.0	109.2	7.3
18	29 May 1887	Guerrero	17.2	99.8	7.2
19	6 Sep 1889	Coast of Guerrero	17.0	99.7	7.0
20	2 Dec 1890	Coast of Guerrero	16.7	98.6	7.2
21	2 Nov 1894	Coast of Oaxaca-Guerrero	16.5	98.0	7.4
22	5 Jun 1897	Coast of Oaxaca	16.3	95.4	7.4
23	24 Jan 1899	Coast of Guerrero	17.1	100.5	7.9

Recurrence Periods of Large Interplate Earthquakes Along the Mexican Subduction Zone

The data in Tables 1 and 2, together with measured and inferred aftershock areas, have been used to determine recurrence periods for some segments of the subduction plate boundary. The results are summarized in Table 3 (modified from Singh et al., 1981). The observed recurrence periods, T_R, vary from 30 to 75 years. Assuming relative plate velocity as $V(cm/yr)$ and the slip during a large earthquake as $D(cm)$, we can write:

$$\eta V T_R = D \qquad (1)$$

where η is a constant to account for aseismic slip. Since D scales as $M_o^{1/3}$ (M_o = scalar seismic moment) we can rewrites (1) (assuming η and V as constants) as:

$$T_R = \frac{D}{\eta V} \propto M_o^{1/3} \qquad (2)$$

Astiz and Kanamori (1984) fitted (2) to Mexican subduction zone earthquake data (Table 3 except for the last two events) and found that:

$$\log T_R = 1/3 \log M_o - 7.5 \qquad (3)$$

Taking an earthquake in 1911 as the last event in Michoacan (Table 3), equation (3) predicts $M_o = 1.3 \times 10^{28}$ dyne-cm for an earthquake in 1985. This seismic moment value is in agreement with the values reported for the 19 Sept, 1985 earthquake by several authors (see later discussion). Note that equation (3) predicts the accumulated seismic moment; for a given segment the moment release may occur in one large event or several smaller events distributed in time.

Table 3. Observed Recurrence Periods of Large, Shallow, Interplate Earthquakes Along the Mexican Subduction Zone. The Data in Brackets are Less Reliable.

Region	Approximate Location Lat(°N)	Long(°W)	Year of Earthquake	Average Period (Yr)
E. Oaxaca	16.2	95.8	1897(7.4); 1928(7.7); 1965(7.8)	34
C. Oaxaca	16.0	96.8	1870(7.9); 1928(8.0); 1978(7.8)	54
W. Oaxaca	16.6	97.7	[1854(7.7)]; [1894(7.4)];1928(7.4); 1968(7.4)	38
Ometepec	16.5	98.5	1950(7.3); 1982(6.9,7.0)	32
San Marcos	16.7	99.2	[1845(7.9)]; 1907(8.0); 1957(7.7)	56
Petatlán	17.3	101.4	1943(7.7); 1979(7.6)	36
Michoacán	18.1	102.5	1911(7.9); 1985(8.1)	74
Colima	18.4	103.2	1941(7.9); 1973(7.5)	32

Seismic Gaps

Kelleher et al. (1973) identified gaps along the Mexican subduction zone with high seismic potential. The earthquakes of Colima (1973; M_s=7.5), Central Oaxaca (1978; M_s=7.8), and Petatlan (1979; M_s=7.6) occurred in gaps outlined by Kelleher et al. Singh et al. (1981) reexamined these seismic gaps incorporating new information. their space-time plot, (Fig. 2) showed Jalisco, Michoacan, Guerrero, Ometepec and Tehuantepec as outstanding gaps. In this figure Tehuantepec and Michoacan regions appeared to have experienced no large earthquakes either in this or in the past century. Singh et al. (1981) suggested that these two gaps were either aseismic, or had anomalously long recurrence periods. A similar conclusion was reached by McNally and Minster (1981). In retrospect it appears almost certain that an earthquake on 7 June 1911 (M_s=7.9) had, in fact, occurred in the Michoacan gap (see UNAM Seismology Group, 1986 for a detailed discussion). The Playa Azul earthquake of 1981 (M_s=7.3) occurred in the middle of the Michoacan gap and an earthquake doublet in 1982 (M_s=7.0,6.9) filled the Ometepec gap. It is worth noting that with the exception of the 21 Sept 1985 earthquake, which extended the rupture area of the 19 Sept 1985 event by about 70km towards the SE, all large earthquakes along the coast since 1973 have occurred in the gaps outlined by Kelleher et al. (1973) by Singh et al.

(1981).

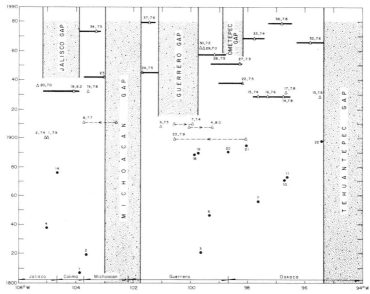

Figure 2.   Space-time plot of large, shallow, interplate earthquakes
along the Mexican subduction zone up to 1980 (from Singh
et al., 1981).   Ometepec and Michoacan gaps are now filled.
The Guerrero gap, at present, has the highest seismic
potential. Note that event numbers beginning 1900 do not
correspond to the numbers given in Table 1.

The September, 1985 Michoacan Earthquakes

The great earthquake of 19 Sept, 1985 ruptured the Michoacan gap
whose seismic potential was previously uncertain. This earthquake
was followed by another major earthquake on 21 Sept (M_s=7.5). At that
time, an array of digital strong-motion stations was in place along
the coast of Michoacan and Guerrero in anticipation of large earthquakes
in the region (Anderson et al., 1986).   The array provided unique strong
motion recordings of both of these events.   Inmediately after the first
earthquake a network of portable seismographs was deployed in the
epicentral area.   The aftershock areas of the two events are shown in
Fig. 1.   The epicentral location of the main earthquake (18.141°N,
102.707°W) was obtained from strong-motion data whereas in the location
of the second earthquake (17.618°N, 101.815°W) both strong motion and
portable seismograph data were used.   The depth of the two events were
constrained to 16 and 20 km, respectively, based on synthetic modeling
of teleseismic long-period (LP) P waves (UNAM Seismology Group, 1986).
The focal mechanisms of both events are nearly the same: dip = 9°,
azimuth = 288°, and rake = 72° (Eissler et al., (1986).

Analysis of teleseismic LP P waves clearly shows that the 19 Sept
earthquake was composed of two subevents separated in time by 27 s, and
that the second subevent occurred about 95 km SE of the first one.
(UNAM Seismology Group, 1986; Eissler et al., 1986). This is also
confirmed by the near-field strong-motion data (Anderson et al., 1986).
The P waves of 21 Sept earthquake can be modeled by a single source.
The source parameters of the two earthquakes are listed in Table 4. In
this table the seismic moments are taken as the average of the values
reported by Anderson et al. (1986) and Eissler et al. (1986). The
Integration of accelerograms (Anderson et al., 1986) and mortality of
intertidal organisms (Bodin and Klinger, 1986) shows a vertical uplift
of about 1 m of the coast in the epicentral area of the 19 Sept earthquake.

Aftershocks of 21 Sept earthquake spill over the rupture area of the
Petatlan earthquake of 1979 (Fig. 1). Projection of the hypocenters of
the aftershocks of 21 Sept and 1979 earthquakes on a vertical plane
oriented N30°E, shows that the 21 Sept earthquake ruptured updip of
the 1979 rupture plane (UNAM Seismology Group, 1986; Valdés et al.,
1982). It follows that the same segment of plate interface along strike
can rupture separately in two large subsegments. This implies that a
seismic gap recently filled by a large earthquake may not be considered
free of seismic potential in the inmediate future. It is not known,
however, how often such cases occur.

Table 4. Source Parameters of the 19 Sept and 21 Sept 1985 Earthquakes

	Origin Time	Location	Depth*	$M_O \times 10^{27}$ dyne-cm	LXW,km^2	$\bar{u}$,cm	$\Delta\sigma^+$,bars
19 Sept 1985 (M_s =8.1)	13:17:49.05	18.141°N, 102.707°W	16km	12.0	170x50	284	25
21 Sept 1985 (M_s =7.5)	01:37:11.75	17.618°N, 101.815°W	20km	3.8	66x33	384	45

* Depth constrained from synthetic modeling of P waves

+ Formula used $\Delta\sigma = \dfrac{8M_O}{3\pi L w^2}$

In the following we note some important features revealed by the
September, 1985 as well as by other large earthquakes along the Mexican
subduction zone:

(a) The September, 1985 earthquakes, in common with all other well
    studied large, thrust earthquakes, occurred near the coast on a
    shallow dipping plane at depths of 16 to 20 km (Chael and Stewart,
    1982; Singh et al., 1984b).

(b) Rupture width, shown by stippled band in Fig. 1, does not exceed
    80 km (Singh et al., 1985a). This, probably, explains relatively
    small rupture lengths (≤220 km) of Mexican earthquakes.

(c) The rupture area of 170x50 km^2 of the 19 Sept 1985 earthquake appears
    to be second only to that the Jalisco earthquake of 1932 (Fig. 1)
    which is estimated as 220x80 km^2 (Singh et al., 1985b).

(d) Mexican earthquakes give rise to an anomalously small number of aftershocks. This follows a remarkably consistent circum Pacific pattern discussed by Singh and Suárez (1985).

(e) Comparison of Galitzin seismograms recorded at De Bilt (Holland) of all large, Mexican interplate earthquakes since 1922 shows that the Oaxaca earthquakes, with very few exceptions, are simple whereas the earthquakes occurring elsewhere along the Mexican subduction zone are complex as well as simple (UNAM Seismology Group, 1986, see also Singh et al., 1984b).

(f) Statistics of earthquakes shows that Gutenberg-Richter's relation logN=a-bM, where N is the number of events with magnitude $\geq$M, is not valid for the Mexican subduction zone; there is a great deficiency of events in the magnitude range $6.4 \leq M_s \leq 7.4$. This evidence of 'characteristic magnitudes' is most impressive for Oaxaca (Singh et al., 1983).

(g) Broad-band teleseismic P wave spectra of some recent Mexican earthquakes (including the Sept 1985 events) similar magnitude, are less energetic at 1 to 10s than subduction earthquakes elsewhere (Houston and Kanamori, 1986).

Items (d) to (g) suggest a relatively homogeneous plate interface and a lack of asperities with scale length of 3 to 30 km along the Mexican subduction zone.

Source characteristics of Sept 1985 Earthquakes in/near Mexico City.

Because of unprecedented damage caused by the 19 Sept 1985 earthquake in Mexico City it has been suggested that the source radiation of this earthquake may have been anomalously more energetic in that direction, at least at frequencies close to the resonant frequencies of the lake bed sites (~2 to 5s). To resolve this issue Singh et al. (1986) have studied Fourier acceleration spectral ratio of 19 Sept to 21 Sept earthquakes at several hard rock sites in and near Mexico City. Fig. 3, taken from Singh et al.(1986), summarizes the results on spectral ratio of the two earthquakes from the acceleration as well as teleseismic data. Since the spectral ratio eliminates the site effect, Fig. 3 reflects the source spectrum ratio and any differences in focal mechanism, directivity, path, and depth of energy release of the two earthquakes.

The spectral ratio increase from the acceleration data in and near Mexico City of about 1 at 1 Hz to about 10 at 0.2 Hz is very surprising since such an increase is not expected from w^{-2} model (Aki, 1967,1972) or Gusev's model (Gusev, 1983; Aki, 1983). At very low frequencies, the ratio is 3 as obtained from the seismic moments of 19 Sept and 21 Sept earthquakes (Eissler et al., 1986; Anderson et al., 1986) and the difference of 0.6 in the M_s values of the two shocks gives a ratio of 4 at 0.05 Hz (20 s) (Figure 3). Houston and Kanamori (1986) present P wave spectra of these two earthquakes from broad-band GDSN data. Spectral ratio measured from their plots is shown in Fig. 3 in the frequency band $0.03 \leq f \leq 1$ Hz (~30 - 1s). Also shown in Fig. 3 is the amplitude ratio in the band 0.04 - 0.2 Hz (25-5 s) calculated from the

spectra of P waves recorded on Galitzin seismograph in DeBilt (DBN).
Finally Fig. 3 shows the expected spectral ratio assuming w^{-2} model
and a constant stress drop, $\Delta\sigma$, of 30 bars. The broad-band P wave
spectral ratio is about equal to the acceleration spectral ratio
between 0.5 and 1 Hz but is much smaller at lower frequencies, being a
factor of 5 less at 0.2 Hz. Note that the broad-band P wave spectral
ratio has been obtained from averaged spectra from stations at different
azimuths (Houston and Kanamori, 1986).

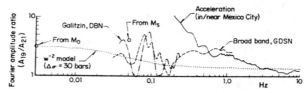

Fig 3. Comparison of Fourier acceleration amplitude ratio of 19 Sept to
       21 Sept 1985 earthquake in/near Mexico City with teleseismic
       spectral ratio (from Singh et al., 1986). At very low frequencies
       the ratio of 3 is obtained from seismic moment ratio of the two
       earthquakes. The difference in M_s value of 0.6 gives a ratio of
       4 at 0.05 Hz (20 s). P wave spectral ratio from broad band GDSN
       stations are taken from Houston and Kanamori (1986). Also shown
       is the P wave spectral ratio from Galitzin seimograms at DBN,
       Holland. Note that the ratio is much higher (5 times at 0.2 Hz)
       in/near Mexico City as compared to broad-band spectral ratio and
       the expected ratio from w^{-2} model (see text).

It appears now, that the 19 Sept earthquake was more energetic
towards Mexico City as compared to the 21 Sept earthquake. Singh et al.
(1986) show that this presumed anomaly is not seen in the epicentral
spectra nor along coastal stations. Although a definitive explanation
for the anomalous ratio towards Mexico City is still not available, two
possible causes, as suggested by Singh et al.(1986), are shallower
depth of energy release for 19 Sept as compared to 21 Sept earthquake
and/or a path effect. A definitive answer is crucial if we are to
realistically evaluate the effects of possible future events in, say,
Guerrero gap. Note that the anomalous nature of the spectral ratio does
not say anything about which of the two events was unusual. In view of
the damage to Mexico City we could perhaps argue that it was the 19
Sept shock which was anomalously more energetic towards Mexico City.

Ground Motion Amplifications in the Lake Bed Zone of Mexico City

It is well known that the ground motions are amplified in the lake
bed zone of Mexico City (e.g., Zeevaert, 1964). This zone consists of
a clay layer of variable thickness with water content of up to 400%,
overlying more resistant sands. The Sept 1985 earthquakes provided
excellent acceleration data to study relative spectral amplification at
some sites in this zone. Fig. 4, from Singh et al.(1986), shows Fourier
relative amplifications at four lake-zone sites with respect to CUP, a
hard site of the hill zone located in the University City. The lake
bed sites are: Secretaría de Comunicaciones y Transportes (SCT), Central
de Abastos, Frigorífico (CAF), Central de Abastos, Oficina (CAO), and
Tláhuac, Bomba (TLA). Note that the relative amplification on NS and
EW for a given station are very similar. Although the vertical (Z)
component is less amplified than the horizontal components, the

frequencies at which these amplifications occur are about the same as those for the horizontal components. The gravest relative amplifications for 19 Sept and the frequencies (f_o) at which they occur on the horizontal components at SCT, CAF, CAO, and TLAH are ($\approx$10 times, 0.45 Hz, EW), ($\approx$8 times, 0.32 Hz, EW), ($\approx$30 times, 0.25 Hz, NS), and ($\approx$20 times, 0.20 Hz, EW), respectively. The shear wave velocity (β) and thickness of clay deposits (H) at SCT, CAF, and (CAO) are (80 m/s, 40 m), (70 m/s, 48 m), and (61 m/s, 58 m), respectively (M. Romo, A. Jaime, Personal Communication, 1986). At these sites $f_o \approx \beta/4H$, suggesting that a one-dimensional model of vertically propagating SH waves is a good first approximation for the observed amplifications (see also Zeevaert, 1964).

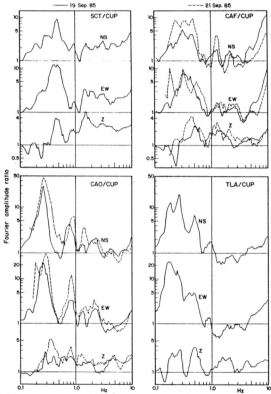

Fig. 4. Relative spectral amplifications at lake bed sites with respect to a hill zone site (CUP), taken from Singh et al. (1986). The frequency at which gravest relative amplification occurs varies from site to site. The ranges of relative amplifications and the associated frequencies are 10 to 50 times and 0.2 to 0.45 Hz, respectively. The relative amplifications are less for 19 Sept as compared to 21 Sept earthquake at CAF and CAO suggesting nonlinear behaviour (see text).

Relative amplifications for 21 Sept (shown by dotted lines in Fig.4) at CAF and CAO are higher than for 19 Sept. The relative amplification

for 19 Sept is about 60% of that for 21 Sept at these sites. This effect
was attributed to nonlinear behavior of the clay during the 19 Sept
earthquake by Singh et al.(1986). This is a surprisingly small nonlinear
effect in view of the strains involved which may explain some of the
damages in the lake bed zone. For 19 Sept the peak to trough displacements at SCT and TLAH at periods of between 2.5 and 5 s were 40 and 80
cm, respectively. For $\beta \approx 75$ m/s, strains were about 0.2%.

Singh et al. (1986) show evidence that with respect to a coastal
site at equal distance from the 19 Sept earthquake, some lake bed sites
may have been amplified by up to 500 times at their fundamental
frequencies. This, to some extent, in supported by M_L calculations of
the 19 Sept earthquake: $M_L \approx 6.0$ on the epicentral zone 7.3 a coastal
hard rock sites at distances ≥ 100 km, and 8.8 in the lake bed zone of
Mexico City.

Normal Faulting Earthquakes in the Subducted Oceanic Lithosphere

Fig. 1 shows locations of normal fault earthquakes $(M \geq 6.0)$ by open
circles. The largest of such earthquakes, shown by circle with a cross,
occurred on 15 Jan 1931 which destroyed the city of Oaxaca (Singh et al.,
1985a). This earthquake appears to have brooken the subducted Cocos
plate. Other examples of recent, destructive normal faulting earthquakes are: Orizaba (29 Aug 1973, $m_b = 6.7$, $M_s = 6.8$, H = 80 km) and
Huajuapan de Leon (26 Oct 1980, $m_b = 6.3$, $M_s \cong 7.0$, H = 65 km). The
destructive earthquake of 1858, Michoacan may represent another example
of lithospheric normal faulting. Such earthquakes, for which the
periods of recurrence are unknown, also constitute an extremely high
seismic risk to population centers of Mexico.

Crustal Earthquakes in Continental Mexico

Shallow crustal earthquakes, with M_s reaching up to 7.0, occur in
the continent. Some examples are: Acambay (19 Nov 1912, $M_s = 7.0$),
Jalapa (4 Jan 1920, $M_s = 6.4$), and Jaltipan (26 Aug 1959, $M_s = 6.4$).
In some cases such earthquakes can be related to mapped geologic
structures. Because such earthquake may occur near populated area, they
also constitute a seismic risk.

Conclusions

Seismic risk to Mexico comes from interplate subduction earthquakes,
normal faulting earthquakes in the subducted oceanic plate, and shallow,
crustal earthquakes in the continent. Of these, the most frequent and
best understood are the interplate earthquakes. At present the Guerrero
gap (Fig. 2) appears to have the highest seismic potential; the last
sequence of large earthquakes ended there about 75 years ago. Equation
(3) suggests that a seismic moment of about 1.3×10^{28} dyne-cm has
accumulated in this region. Whether this moment release would occur in
one, 19 Sept 1985 Michoacan - type $(M_s \approx 8.1)$ earthquake, or several
smaller events is not known. The unprecedented damage to Mexico City
during 19 Sept earthquake appears to be related to the size and
consequent duration of the earthquake as well as to the explosive growth
of the city during the last 40 years. Furthermore, we find anomalously
high radiation towards Mexico City of critical frequencies of 0.2 to 0.5
Hz. It is imperative that we understand the cause of the anomalous

radiation during the 19 Sept 1985 earthquake to properly assess seismic risk of Mexico City for future great earthquakes. Within Mexico City, lake bed sites can get amplified by about 50 times with respect to hill zone sites. The site transfer function appears to be nearly constant for sources at distance ≥200 km, irrespective of their magnitude, azimuth, and depth (Singh et al., 1986).

References

Aki, K. (1967). Scaling law of seismic spectrum, J. Geophys. Res. 72, 1217-1231.

Aki, K. (1972). Scaling law of earthquake source time function, Geophys. J. Roy. Astr. Soc. 31, 3-25.

Aki, K. (1983). Strong motion seismology, in Earthquakes: Observation Theory, and Interpretation, H. Kanamori and E. Boschi, Editors, North-Holland Publ. Co., New York, 223-245.

Anderson, J.G., P. Bodin, J.N. Brune, J. Prince, and S.K. Singh (1986). Strong ground motion and source mechanism of the Mexico earthquake of September 19, 1985 (M_s = 8.1), Science, in press.

Astiz, L. and H. Kanamori (1984). An earthquake doublet in Ometepec, Cuerrero, Mexico, Phys. Earth Planet. Interiors 34, 24-45

Bodin, P. and T. Klinger (1986). Coastal uplift and mortality of intertidal organisms as a result of the September, 1985, Mexico earthquakes, Science, in press.

Chael, E.P. and G.S. Stewart (1982). Recent large earthquakes along the middle American Trench and their implications for the subduction process, J. Geophys. Res. 87, 329-338.

Eissler, H., L. Astiz, and H. Kanamori (1986). Tectonic setting and source parameters of the September 19, 1985 Michoacan, Mexico earthquake, Geophys. Res. Lett. 13, 569-572.

Gusev, A.A. (1983). Descriptive statistical model of earthquake source radiation and its application to an estimation of short-period strong motion, Geophys. J. Roy. Astr. Soc. 74, 787-808.

Houston, H. and H. Kanamori (1986). Source characteristics of the 1985 Michoacan, Mexico earthquake at periods of 1 to 30 seconds, Geophys. Res. Lett. 13, 597-600.

Kelleher, J., L. Sykes, and J. Oliver (1973). Possible criteria for predicting earthquake locations and their application to major plate boundaries of the Pacific and the Caribbean, J. Geophys.Res. 78, 2547-2585.

McNally, K.C. and J.B. Minster (1981). Nonuniform seismic slip rates along the middle America Trench, J. Geophys. Res. 86, 4949-4959.

Singh, S.K., L. Astiz, and J. Havskov (1981). Seismic gaps and recurrence periods of large earthquakes along the Mexican subduction zone: A reexamination, Bull. Seism. Soc. Am. 71, 827-843.

Singh, S.K., M. Rodríguez, and L. Esteva (1983). Statistics of small earthquakes and frequency of occurrence of large earthquakes along the Mexican subduction zone, Bull. Seism. Soc. Am. 73, 1779-1796.

Singh, S.K., M. Rodríguez, and J.M. Espíndola (1984a). A catalog of shallow earthquakes of Mexico from 1900-1981, Bull. Seism. Soc. Am. 74, 267-280.

Singh, S.K., T. Domínguez, R. Castro, and M. Rodríguez (1984b). P waveform of large shallow earthquakes along the Mexican subduction zone, Bull. Seism. Soc. Am. 74, 2135-2158.

Singh, S.K. and G. Suárez (1985). Regional variations in the number of aftershocks ($m_b \geq 5.0$) of large subduction zone earthquakes ($M_w \geq 7.0$), abstract, EOS 66, 958.

Singh, S.K., G. Suárez, and T. Domínguez (1985a). The Oaxaca, Mexico, earthquake of 1931: Lithospheric normal faulting in the subducted Cocos plate, Nature 317, 56-58.

Singh, S.K., L. Ponce, and S.P. Nishenko (1985b). The great Jalisco, Mexico earthquakes of 1932: Subduction of the Rivera plate, Bull. Seism. Soc. Am. 75, 1301-1314.

Singh, S.K., E. Mena, and R. Castro (1986). Some aspects of the source characteristics and the ground motion amplifications in and near Mexico City from the acceleration data of the September, 1985, Michoacan, Mexico earthquakes, Bull. Seism. Soc. Am., to be submitted.

UNAM Seismology Group (1986). The September 1985 Michoacan earthquakes: Aftershock distribution and history of rupture, Geophys. Res. Lett. 13, 573-576.

Valdés, C., R.P. Meyer, R. Zuñiga, J. Havskov, and S.K. Singh (1982). Analysis of the Petatlan aftershocks: Number, energy release, and asperities, J. Geophys. Res. 87, 8519-8527.

Zeevaert, L. (1964). Strong ground motions recorded during earthquakes of May the 11th and 19th, 1962 in Mexico City, Bull. Seism. Soc. Am. 54, 209-231.

STRONG MOTION ARRAYS AND CHARACTERISTICS

Roberto Quaas*, Enrique Mena*

ABSTRACT

Twenty five years of strong motion instrumentation in Mexico led to an important record of the September 19, 1985 earthquakes by an extended accelerograph array. The success in obtaining these records was due to efforts made by the Instituto de Ingeniería at the Universidad Nacional Autónoma de México and close cooperation between Mexican and U.S. institutions.

INTRODUCTION

On September 19, 1985 a magnitude 8.1 earthquake struck the Pacific coast of Mexico and caused extensive damage and casualties in Mexico City. A magnitude 7.5 aftershock followed two days later. Both events were recorded by a broad accelerograph array of analog and digital recorders. Valuable data was obtained from stations along the Pacific coast and rupture area, as well as from sites located in Mexico City and vecinity. The strong motion networks in operation, at the time the Michoacan earthquake occurred, are described and relevant data from most of the accelerograms recorded during the main event presented.

BACKGROUND

Study of seismic activity and instrumentation in Mexico goes back to the beginning of the century when the National Seismologic Service of the Tacubaya Observatory was created in 1910 in Mexico City. The first instruments installed were short period Wiechert seismographs; 76 years later they are still operating and have produced an invaluable catalog of seismologic data.

The magnitude 7.5 earthquake of July 1957 in San Marcos, Guerrero, close to Acapulco, hit Mexico City heavily causing many injuries and damage. The movement was so severe that the pens of the seismographs in Tacubaya came off, losing most part of the record. There was no appropiate instrument available to record such strong earthquakes.

In 1960 the Instituto de Ingeniería (II), of the Universidad Nacional Autónoma de México (UNAM), installed two SMAC B strong motion seismographs in Mexico City. They were among the first recorders of this type in Mexico. One was located at the Alameda Central and the other at

* Instituto de Ingeniería, Universidad Nacional Autónoma de México. Apartado Postal 70-472, Coyoacán, 04510, México D.F., México.

the University campus. Important accelerograms were recorded during the
Acapulco earthquakes of May 1962 (Esteva, 1963). Three AR-240
photographic accelerographs installed later, one in the Tlaltelolco
building complex in Mexico City, another downtown Acapulco and the third
on the Infiernillo dam in Michoacán, recorded the Acapulco earthquake
(M=6.8) of December 1965 (Bustamante et al, 1967).

The interest to further study dynamic responses of soils and
structures under seismic conditions, motivated the II to expand the
strong motion array. By 1970 aproximately 25 strong motion stations were
operating. Most of them were used to measure accelerations on main
hydroelectric dams.

To monitor and record near field seismic activity, a seismic
telemetry system, SISMEX (Prince et al, 1973) was built in 1972. 16
remote stations, located within the Mexico valley and neighbor states
were linked through radio telemetry to a central recording station at
the II, continuously transmitting seismologic and strong motion data.
This network, still in operation, was of great importance during the
September earthquakes.

During the decade of the seventies strong motion stations increased
to 80, covering almost all seismic zones of the country. An extended
catalog of records for engineering purposes has been obtained from major
earthquakes. Studies and research projects derived from this
instumental data contributed to the knowledge of the dynamic behavior of
soils and structures and were of great importance for seismic
engineering in Mexico.

With the appearance of digital seismic recorders by the end of the
past decade, the strong motion network grew substantially. By 1983, 40
digital accelerographs were operating.

In 1985, when the earthquakes of September occurred, approximately
150 accelerographs were installed, fulfilling 25 years of strong motion
instrumentation in Mexico. Designing and maintaining stations and
instruments, as well as data processing and analisis of this broad
strong motion network, have been mainly a responsability of the II, UNAM
and other research institutes like IGPP of the University of California
at San Diego and CICESE of Ensenada, B.C.N. with support from different
government agencies.

Fig 1 shows a map with the location of all strong motion sites
instrumented in Mexico from 1960 to 1985. Type and aproximate number of
instruments installed during this time is also shown. A comparative list
with the technical characteristics of the different instruments used is
given as a reference in table 1.

STRONG MOTION ARRAYS AND THE EARTHQUAKE OF SEPTEMBER 1985

A close up of the central part of the strong motion network with all
its stations which recorded the September 1985 earthquakes is shown in
fig 2. It is actually comprised of two networks, the II array (shown

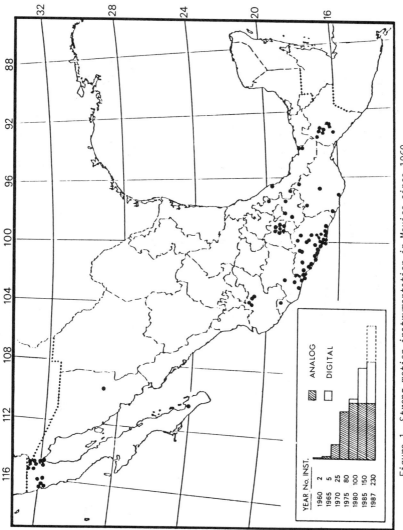

Figure 1. Strong motion instrumentation in Mexico since 1960.

Table 1. General specifications of the instruments used in the strong motion array.

CHARACTERISTIC	SMAC B	AR -240	SMA-1	DCA-310/333	DSA-1
MANUFACTURER	Akashi Seisakusho	United Electro Dynamics	Kinemetrics	Terra Technology	Kinemetrics
TYPE	analog mechanic	analog electro-mechanic	analog electro-mechanic	digital electronic	digital electronic
RECORDING MEDIUM	wax paper	photographic paper	photographic film	digital cassette	digital cassette
TRANSDUCERS (3)	strong motion seismometer	strong motion seismometer	flexure type accelerometer	force balanced accelerometer	force balanced accelerometer
RANGE	1 g	1 g	1 g	2 g	2 g
NATURAL FREQUENCY (Hz)	10	18	25	30	50
DAMPING (% of critical)	0.6	0.6	0.6	0.7	0.7
RECORDING TIME	3 min.	20 min.	25 min.	15 min.	20 min.
SAMPLING RATE	-	-	-	100 sps	200sps
WORD LENGTH	-	-	-	12 bits	12 bits
DYNAMIC RANGE	0.01 - 1.0 g	0.01 - 1.0 g	0.01 - 1.0 g	72 dB	72 dB
TRIGGER	vertical	horizontal	vertical	omnidirec.	vertical
POWER	6V	12V	+/- 6V	+- 12/12V	+/- 12V

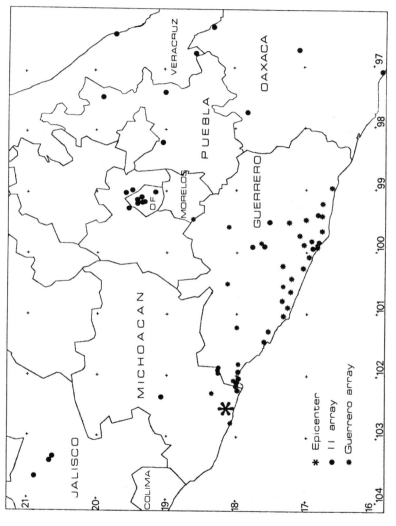

Figure 2. Central strong motion array during the September 1985 earthquakes.

with dots) and the Guerrero array (shown with stars).

The II array includes all the stations located on different types of soil condition in the valley of Mexico, and sites scattered throughout several states. Most are related to highly populated areas like Puebla, Guadalajara, Acapulco and Oaxaca, and some to important structures like dams. Only a few instruments are located in buildings.

A detailed list of the stations and locations are presented in table 2. Different accelerographs were used: analog AR-240 and SMA-1 photographic recorders, and digital instruments DCA-310 and DCA-333. This network is mainly operated by the II and some sites jointly with the Federal Commission of Electricity.

The second network shown in fig 2 comprises the Guerrero array. It was partially installed in 1985 for the purpose of recording strong ground motion on bedrock from large subduction-thrust earthquakes. Instrumentation, site selection and installation has been a joint project of the II, UNAM and IGPP, UCSD (Quaas et al, 1985).

The Guerrero array consists of 30 strong motion stations along the Pacific coast with digital accelerographs DCA-333, DSA-1 and PDR-1. 20 instruments were operating when the September 1985 earthquakes occurred; at the present, 90 percent are installed. All stations are located in free field and built on solid rock. Instruments are contained in steel boxes built into concrete piers, fixed to the underlying rock. Table 3 lists all of the stations in the array.

STRONG MOTION RECORDS

49 instruments of the accelerograph array (fig 2) triggered during the September 19 earthquake. It was the first time that an earthquake M[7.8 has been recorded in Mexico. The extended number of instruments located in the epicentral region and in the valley of Mexico, produced a collection of high quality strong motion records. This event is considered one of the best recorded large subduction thrust earthquakes in history (Anderson et al, 1985).

The stations which recorded the earthquakes are marked in tables 2 and 3. Table 4 lists in alphabetical order, maximum and minimum acceleration, velocity and displacement of all records already processed. This data is the result of the standard processing done at the II, wich includes baseline correction and filtering, and also Fourier and response spectra analysis of each component (Mena et al, 1986).

The maximum acceleration recorded by the array corresponds to the record of El Paraiso, Guerrero, which reached 640 gals in the N-S direction, and 480 gals in the E-W component (Quaas et al, 1986). This record is being analized to determine local effects or amplifications.

Two accelerograms from the epicentral region are shown in fig 3, corresponding to the records obtained at La Villita (VILE), built on

Table 2. Stations of the central II array.

CODE	STATION	SITE DESCRIPTION	LAT(N)	LONG(W)	INSTR.
ACAP *	ACAPULCO PELLANDINI,GRO.	rock	16.840	99.910	SMA-1
ACAS *	ACAPULCO SOP	soil, sand	16.858	99.894	SMA-1
APAT *	APATZINGAN, MICH.	soil, alluvium	19.083	102.350	SMA-1
CALT *	CIUDAD ALTAMIRANO, GRO.	soil, alluvium	18.358	100.658	SMA-1
CARD *	CARACOL MARGEN DER.	rock embank. dam	18.121	99.580	SMA-1
CARI *	CARACOL MARGEN IZQ.	rock embank. dam	18.121	99.580	SMA-1
CDAF *	C. DE ABASTOS FRIG.,D.F.	soft soil, clay	19.368	99.088	DCA-333
CDAO *	C. DE ABASTOS OFIC.,D.F.	soft soil, clay	19.368	99.088	DCA-333
CHIL *	CHILPANCINGO, GRO.	soil, silt	17.553	99.500	SMA-1
CORI *	CERRO DE ORO MI	rock	18.550	96.750	SMA-1
CSER *	CD. SERDAN, PUE.	rock	18.991	97.384	DCA-333
CU01 *	CIUDAD UNIVERSITARIA,DF	rock, basalt	19.330	99.183	DCA-333
CUIP *	I. DE I. PATIO, CU, D.F.	rock, basalt	19.330	99.183	DCA-310
CUMV *	MESA VIBRADORA, CU, D.F.	rock, basalt	19.330	99.183	DCA-333
FICA *	FILO DE CABALLO, GRO.	soil, silt	17.500	99.500	SMA-1
GUA1 *	GUADALAJARA #1, JAL.	soil, silt	20.669	103.398	SMA-1
GUA2 *	GUADALAJARA ZONA IND.	alluvium	20.637	103.352	SMA-1
GUAC	GUACAMAYAS, MICH.	compact clay	18.025	102.204	DCA-310
IN08 *	INFIERNILLO N-080, MICH.	rock embank. dam	18.270	101.900	AR-240
IN12 *	INFIERNILLO N-120	rock embank. dam	18.270	101.900	DCA-310
IN18 *	INFIERNILLO N-180	rock embank. dam	18.270	101.900	DCA-310
INCM *	INFIERNILLO CASA MAQ.	rock	18.270	101.900	AR-240
INMD *	INFIERNILLO MARGEN DER.	rock embank. dam	18.266	101.900	DCA-310
INMI *	INFIERNILLO MARGEN IZQ.	rock embank. dam	18.266	101.900	DCA-310
INPT *	INFIERNILLO POTABILIZ.	rock	18.270	101.900	AR-240
LAB1 *	LAGUNA VERDE #1, VER.	rock	19.683	96.402	SMA-1
LOTA *	LOTERIA NAL. N-24, D.F.	building: roof	19.418	99.140	SMA-1
LOTS *	LOTERIA NAL. SOT., D.F	building: basement	19.418	99.140	SMA-1
MADC *	MADIN CORONA, EDO. MEX.	rock embank. dam	19.536	99.261	SMA-1
MADI *	MADIN MARGEN IZQ.	rock	19.536	99.261	SMA-1

CODE	STATION	SITE DESCRIPTION	LAT(N)	LONG(W)	INSTR.
MADM *	MADIN MEDIA CORT.	rock embank. dam	19.536	99.261	SMA-1
NARJ	NARANJITO, GRO.	soil, sandy silt	17.986	102.156	DCA-310
NONS	NONOALCO ATIZA.SOT,D.F.	building: basement	19.450	99.144	SMA-1
OAXM	OAXACA FAC.MEDICINA	soil: alluvium	17.084	96.716	SMA-1
PESC	PUERTO ESCONDIDO, OAX.	building: basement	15.860	97.103	SMA-1
SCT1 *	SEC. COM. Y TRANSP.,D.F	soft soil, clay	19.393	99.1.7	DCA-333
SMAR	SAN MARCOS,GRO.	soil: alluvium	16.803	99.395	SMA-1
SOLC	SOLEDAD CORONA, PUE.	concrete dam	19.897	97..52	AR-240
SOLD	SOLEDAD MARGEN DER.	concrete dam	19.897	97..52	AR-240
SOLI	SOLEDAD MARGEN IZQ.	concrete dam	19.897	97..52	AR-240
SROC	SANTA ROSA CORONA, JAL.	concrete dam	20.897	103.663	AR-240
SROD	SANTA ROSA MARGEN DER.	concrete dam	20.897	103.663	AR-240
SROI	SANTA ROSA MARGEN IZQ.	concrete dam	20.897	103.663	AR-240
SXPU *	SISMEX PUEBLA, PUE.	soil	19.0.3	98.212	DCA-310
SXVI *	SISMEX VIVEROS, D.F.	soil	19.358	99.171	DCA-310
TACY *	TACUBAYA, D.F.	hard soil	19..03	99.194	DCA-333
TEMD	TEMASCAL MARG. DER.,VER	rock embank. dam	18.300	96.300	SMA-1
TLHD *	TLAHUAC DEPORTIVO, D.F.	soft soil, clay	19.167	99.010	SMA-1
TLHB *	TLAHUAC BOMBA	soft soil, clay	19.167	99.010	SMA-1
TXCL *	TEXCOCO CENTRO, EDO.MEX.	soft soil, clay	19.480	98.991	SMA-1
TXSO *	TEXCOCO SOSA	soft soil, clay	19.580	99.019	SMA-1
VILB *	VILLITA BASE, MICH.	rock embank. dam	18.016	102.205	SMA-1
VILC *	VILLITA CORONA	rock embank. dam	18.016	102.205	SMA-1
VILD *	VILLITA MARGEN DER.	rock embank. dam	18.016	102.205	DCA-333
VILI *	VILLITA MARGEN IZQ.	rock embank. dam	18.016	102.205	DCA-333
YOSO	YOSOCUTA HUAJUAPAN, OAX.	concrete dam	17.827	97.727	SMA-1
ZACA *	ZACATULA, MICH.	compact clay	18.009	102.178	DCA-333

* Station which recorded the September 1985 earthquakes

Table 3. Stations of the Guerrero array (Sep 1985)

CODE	STATION	REC.	SITE	LAT(N)	LONG(W)	INSTR.
ACA2	ACAPULCO	*		*	*	*
ARTG	ARTEAGA	*		18.356	102.293	*
ATYC	ATOYAC,GRO	#	rock	17.211	100.431	DSA-1
AZIH	ZIHUATANEJO	#	rock	17.603	101.455	DCA-333
BALC	EL BALCON	*		18.011	101.216	*
CALE	CALETA DE CAMPOS	#	rock	18.073	102.755	DSA-1
CAYA	CAYACO,GRO	#	rock	17.045	100.266	DSA-1
COMD	LA COMUNIDAD	*		18.124	100.507	*
COPL	COPALA	*		16.605	98.974	*
COYC	COYUCA	#	rock	16.968	100.084	DCA-333
CPDR	CERRO DE PIEDRA	#	rock	16.769	99.633	DCA-333
FIC2	FILO DE CABALLO	*		17.652	99.842	*
LLAV	LA LLAVE	*		17.346	100.792	*
MAGY	LOS MAGUEYES	*		17.377	100.577	*
MSAS	LAS MESAS	#	rock	17.007	99.456	DSA-1
OCLL	OCOTILLO		rock	17.038	99.875	DCA-333
OCTT	EL OCOTITO	#	rock	17.250	99.511	DCA-333
PAPN	PAPANOA	#	rock	17.328	101.040	DCA-333
PARS	EL PARAISO	#	rock	17.344	100.214	DSA-1
PETA	PETATLAN	*		17.5.2	101.271	*
SLUI	SAN LUIS	*		17.272	100.891	*
SMR2	SAN MARCOS	#	rock	16.776	99.408	DSA-1
SUCH	EL SUCHIL	#	rock	17.226	100.6.2	DCA-333
TEAC	TEACALCO	#	rock	18.618	99.453	DSA-1
TNLP	TONALAPA		rock	18.098	99.559	DSA-1
UNIO	LA UNION	#	rock	17.982	101.805	DSA-1
VIGA	LAS VIGAS	#	rock	16.757	99.236	DCA-333
VILE	VILLITA	#	rock	18.016	102.205	DSA-1
VNTA	LA VENTA	#	rock	16.923	99.816	DSA-1
XALT	XALTIANGUIS	#	rock	17.095	99.720	DSA-1

*   Not installed or built by September 1985
#   Station which recorded the September 1985 earthquakes

Table 4. Some main parameters of the accelerograms

STAT	COMP	AMAX	AMIN	VMAX	VMIN	DMAX	DMIN
ACAS	N00E	19.22	-17.70	0.866	-1.413	0.125	-0.107
ACAS	N90W	20.46	-25.17	1.163	-1.219	0.134	-0.110
ACAS	VERT	10.85	-17.47	1.774	-1.374	0.233	-0.223
APAT	N00E	67.38	-68.74	6.180	-6.454	1.881	-1.590
APAT	N90W	81.28	-67.14	7.012	-5.635	2.059	-1.590
APAT	VERT	44.28	-44.63	5.814	-4.187	1.872	-2.205
ATYC	N00E	42.38	-53.88	5.445	-4.907	1.542	-2.036
ATYC	N90E	40.88	-57.94	3.665	-3.147	0.630	-0.891
ATYC	VERT	61.01	-50.19	6.679	-6.040	1.388	-1.611
AZIH	S00E	101.30	-89.59	15.019	-15.863	5.962	-5.770
AZIH	N90W	161.78	-133.10	18.335	-15.130	4.618	-4.175
AZIH	VERT	103.86	-93.30	10.227	-9.659	3.798	-3.004
CALE	N00E	138.49	-128.42	16.696	-16.055	4.630	-5.734
CALE	N90E	137.84	-98.58	9.679	-12.640	3.216	-2.923
CALE	VERT	69.77	-88.34	6.097	-7.109	1.884	-1.864
CARI	N00E	50.24	-49.75	4.044	-4.369	1.790	-1.773
CARI	N90W	55.42	-89.38	5.556	-5.788	2.737	-2.632
CARI	VERT	34.10	-40.78	4.250	-4.315	1.865	-1.395
CAYA	N00E	39.79	-38.79	3.745	-3.102	1.308	-1.019
CAYA	N90E	34.32	-47.96	2.908	-2.589	0.670	-0.677
CAYA	VERT	24.99	-20.61	3.425	-3.811	0.908	-1.315
CDAF	S00E	80.53	-57.91	23.234	-24.845	12.193	-15.021
CDAF	N90W	77.93	-94.62	37.572	-35.028	18.801	-18.885
CDAF	VERT	27.24	-24.97	8.903	-8.874	8.167	-6.337
CDAO	N00E	65.86	-69.16	31.253	-34.985	19.539	-25.018
CDAO	N90E	68.88	-80.40	41.856	-32.999	21.665	-24.670
CDAO	VERT	35.67	-28.01	11.340	-7.965	8.922	-8.547
CHIL	N00E	36.21	-39.99	7.510	-7.368	2.219	-2.336
CHIL	N90W	63.31	-44.12	10.496	-9.709	2.656	-4.114
CHIL	VERT	21.97	-19.64	3.952	-3.355	0.980	-1.145
COYC	S00E	39.99	-42.04	7.041	-7.822	2.827	-1.683
COYC	N90W	33.44	-35.69	2.131	-3.160	1.194	-0.911
COYC	VERT	18.49	-18.84	3.329	-2.268	0.913	-0.688
CPDR	S00E	19.42	-26.58	2.588	-2.568	0.691	-0.524
CPDR	N90W	14.16	-14.51	1.815	-2.522	0.569	-0.461
CPDR	VERT	12.43	-12.93	1.782	-3.070	0.792	-0.576
CU01	S00E	25.47	-28.10	10.205	-8.833	5.543	-5.418
CU01	N90W	33.45	-29.90	9.379	-8.972	7.187	-6.775
CU01	VERT	21.57	-14.89	8.233	-6.895	6.649	-6.310
CUIP	N00E	31.71	-28.42	8.423	-10.251	5.487	-6.165
CUIP	N90W	31.76	-34.65	9.005	-9.370	7.127	-7.709
CUIP	VERT	21.87	-15.65	7.991	-6.528	6.607	-6.282
CUMV	S00E	37.36	-34.14	7.363	-9.194	4.385	-5.702
CUMV	N90W	38.83	-22.69	7.370	-11.011	4.225	-4.451
CUMV	VERT	19.79	-20.14	6.232	-8.402	3.736	-4.573
FICA	N00E	18.06	-16.85	2.026	-2.256	0.551	-0.795
FICA	N90W	16.92	-15.14	2.265	-1.485	0.340	-0.454
FICA	VERT	7.37	-7.25	0.699	-0.780	0.243	-0.261
IN12	LONG	379.36	-330.26	16.475	-16.548	3.552	-2.712
IN12	TRAN	241.01	-294.60	12.205	-11.724	2.823	-2.096
IN12	VERT	249.40	-294.66	9.458	-10.574	2.456	-3.206
INMDa	N65E	98.69	-134.06	5.011	-5.743	1.075	-0.840
INMDa	N25W	85.31	-76.62	7.088	-4.540	1.556	-1.610
INMDa	VERT	77.51	-71.02	4.876	-5.187	1.469	-1.259

Table 4. Continued.

STAT	COMP	AMAX	AMIN	VMAX	VMIN	DMAX	DMIN
MADI	NØØE	7.77	-7.84	1.535	-1.370	0.478	-0.386
MADI	N90W	9.78	-6.89	1.714	-1.579	0.470	-0.681
MADI	VERT	6.15	-4.76	1.132	-1.168	0.417	-0.409
MSAS	NØØE	20.75	-21.63	1.894	-1.899	0.474	-0.508
MSAS	N90E	14.18	-16.90	2.133	-2.837	0.656	-0.499
MSAS	VERT	12.48	-17.45	2.865	-3.853	0.981	-0.948
OCTT	SØØE	48.63	-42.55	5.065	-7.646	1.509	-2.919
OCTT	N90W	55.27	-43.23	4.047	-3.530	1.517	-1.411
OCTT	VERT	20.76	-19.14	2.831	-3.720	1.480	-1.111
PAPN	SØØE	119.03	-156.95	7.364	-9.669	2.848	-1.351
PAPN	N90W	107.35	-113.86	5.013	-6.128	1.573	-1.513
PAPN	VERT	81.59	-71.23	6.039	-8.380	1.812	-1.648
SCT1	SØØE	89.37	-97.97	38.739	-33.185	19.123	-14.310
SCT1	N90W	158.40	-167.92	57.421	-60.499	21.936	-19.066
SCT1	VERT	36.36	-36.64	8.996	-8.056	7.578	-7.227
SUCH	SØØE	103.12	-77.35	11.152	-11.606	2.221	-2.948
SUCH	N90W	81.45	-60.06	6.363	-6.179	1.158	-1.487
SUCH	VERT	38.68	-49.62	5.961	-4.001	1.159	-1.120
SXPU	NØØE	28.64	-29.55	7.021	-7.177	2.987	-3.104
SXPU	N90E	29.23	-32.60	5.876	-6.635	1.952	-2.650
SXPU	VERT	12.78	-15.85	2.838	-4.057	1.407	-1.666
SXVI	NØØE	36.35	-44.11	11.485	-10.670	9.098	-6.630
SXVI	N90E	42.42	-33.64	9.232	-12.196	7.474	-6.842
SXVI	VERT	15.27	-18.15	5.839	-5.196	6.963	-5.700
TACY	SØØE	34.40	-20.62	14.290	-10.425	11.965	-7.775
TACY	N90W	33.22	-24.73	9.810	-9.468	8.619	-6.096
TACY	VERT	16.58	-19.16	8.288	-7.050	7.606	-5.540
TEAC	NØØE	32.00	-51.30	7.381	-7.170	2.823	-3.676
TEAC	N90E	23.55	-24.73	4.744	-3.118	1.361	-1.227
TEAC	VERT	27.14	-27.05	4.407	-3.981	1.620	-1.600
TLHB	NJØE	104.15	-135.88	64.097	-45.897	34.607	-36.610
TLHB	N90W	106.67	-89.25	44.496	-44.606	39.289	-36.168
TLHB	VERT	23.97	-23.70	9.391	-9.375	6.741	-6.784
TLHD	NØØE	117.67	-108.65	34.727	-34.904	16.798	-20.764
TLHD	N90W	111.55	-56.71	36.063	-30.903	21.011	-22.071
TLHD	VERT	52.12	-59.30	17.013	-11.640	6.866	-5.110
TXSO	NØØE	103.04	-87.73	23.395	-29.557	8.437	-9.712
TXSO	N90W	82.28	-102.97	26.658	-26.445	8.685	-8.659
TXSO	VERT	25.05	-25.53	9.171	-6.478	3.139	-3.222
UNIO	NØØE	162.79	-155.70	20.339	-17.542	6.948	-3.758
UNIO	NØØE	135.34	-147.06	11.698	-9.920	4.164	-3.134
UNIO	VERT	120.94	-95.06	8.676	-11.722	2.557	-3.893
VILC	N60E	224.21	-305.39	32.378	-17.737	4.529	-4.611
VILC	S30E	696.17	-322.83	37.900	-45.889	10.782	-13.607
VILC	VERT	201.33	-297.10	12.906	-9.429	1.430	-2.043
VILE	NØØE	120.99	-108.14	16.110	-15.067	6.266	-6.673
VILE	N90E	85.86	-120.87	10.512	-7.830	3.012	-3.772
VILE	VERT	51.04	-57.51	4.743	-4.088	1.208	-1.102
VNTA	NØØE	15.34	-18.23	3.177	-4.297	1.289	-1.074
VNTA	N90E	20.07	-13.13	2.642	-2.218	0.639	-0.876
VNTA	VERT	16.66	-14.24	3.124	-3.199	0.841	-0.975
ZACA	SØØE	264.17	-271.12	30.392	-30.351	11.750	-18.182
ZACA	N90W	181.90	-161.17	13.960	-13.946	8.546	-8.558
ZACA	VERT	144.88	-142.07	11.466	-10.758	9.568	-6.106

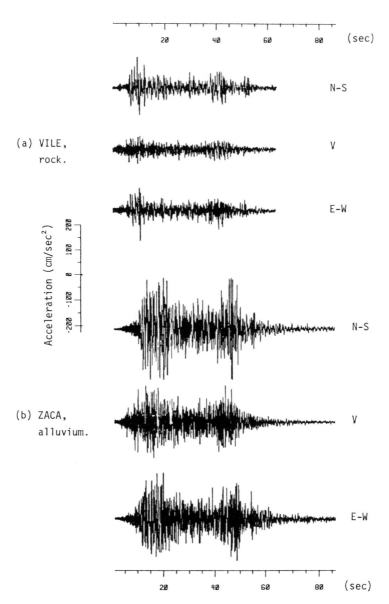

Figure 3. Accelerograms recorded at the epicentral zone.

rock, and at Zacatula (ZACA), which is installed on alluvial soil of the
Balsas river. The approximate distance between both stations is only 10
km. The records show significant differences in amplitude, duration and
frequency content, due only to difference of soil characteristics.

Fig 4 shows three of the most important records of the valley of
Mexico: Tacubaya (TACY), which lays on firm soil on the hilly zone,
Secretaria de Comunicaciones (SCT1) on a 40 m deep clay layer, and
Tlahuac Bomba (TLHB), on a 75 m clay deposit. These last two stations
are located on the lake bed zone. During the 180 seconds long records
shown, the acceleration exceeded several times 100 gals in SCT1 and
TLHB.

Although accelerograph data is still under analysis, some preliminary
results indicate that the waves propagating toward the central part of
Mexico are amplified by a factor of three respect to those travelling
along the coast. Also the records on the lake bed zone of Mexico City
show amplifications between 10 and 50 times within a frequency band of
0.2 to 0.5 Hz, with respect to those of the hilly zone, giving a total
amplification factor of nearly 100. (Singh et al, 1986).

CONCLUSIONS

The earthquakes ocurred on september 1985 and its consequences,
showed the importance of strong motion instrumentation in Mexico.
Although many instruments are already operating throughout the country,
additional efforts should be made to install more accelerographs in
Mexico City, in zones with different soil characteristics, as well as in
buildings and structures which have been scarcely instrumented.

The number and quality of records obtained, is the result of the
continuous effort made by the II and cooperative work with other
institutions.

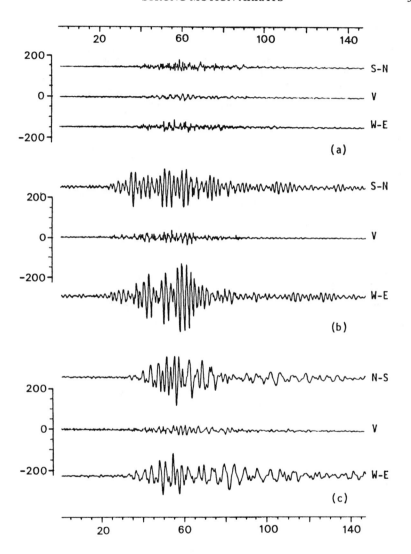

Figure 4. Examples of accelerograms recorded in Mexico City.
(a) TACY, hilly zone; (b) SCT1, lake bed, 40 m thickness clay
layer, and (c) TLHB, lake bed, 75 m thickness clay layer.
Time in seconds, acceleration in gals (cm/seg²).

REFERENCES

Anderson, J.G., J. Brune, J. Prince, et al (1986). Aspects of the
    strong motion from the Michoacán, Mexico Earthquake of
    September 19, 1985. EERI submitted.

Bustamante, J.I., J.López, J. González (1967). Espectros del sismo del
    9 de diciembre, 1965 en Acapulco, El Infiernillo y México. No 140,
    Instituto de Ingeniería, UNAM. México, D.F.

Esteva, L. (1963). Los temblores de mayo de 1962 en Acapulco.
    Revista Sociedad Mexicana de Ingeniería Sísmica, Vol I, No. 2,
    México, D.F.

Mena, E., C. Carmona, R. Delgado et al (1986). Catálogo de acelerogramas
    procesados del sismo del 19 de septiembre de 1985. Parte I: Ciudad
    de México. No. 497, Instituto de Ingeniería, UNAM, México, D.F.

Prince, J., H. Rodríguez, E. Z. Jaworski, G. Kilander (1973). A strong
    motion radio telemetry network. Proceedings V World Conference on
    Seismic Engineering, Rome, Italy.

Quaas, R., J. Prince, J. G. Anderson, et al, (1985). The Michoacan-
    Guerrero, Mexico earthquakes of september 1985: Preliminary
    description of the strong motion accelerographic array.
    Report GAA-1B, Instituto de Ingeniería, UNAM, Mexico, D.F.

Quaas, R., D. Almora, J.M. Velasco et al (1986). Registros del sismo de
    septiembre de 1985 obtenidos en la estación de El Paraíso, Guerrero
    y calibración del acelerógrafo. Report GAA-1D, Instituto de
    Ingeniería, UNAM, México, D.F.

Singh, S.K., E. Mena, R. Castro (1986). Some aspects of the source
    characteristics and the ground motion amplifications in and near
    Mexico City from the acceleration data of the september, 1985,
    Michoacan, Mexico earthquakes. Bull. Seis. Soc. Amer. submitted.

ASPECTS OF STRONG MOTION

John G. Anderson[1], James N. Brune[1], Jorge Prince[1], Enrique Mena[2] Paul Bodin[1],
Mario Onate[2], Roberto Quaas[2], Shri Krishna Singh[2]

ABSTRACT

Strong motion accelerograms from the Mexico earthquake of September 19, 1985 provide the most complete picture to date of the damage-producing motions of a magnitude 8+ earthquake. The success in obtaining these records was significantly enhanced due to close cooperation between the fields of seismology and earthquake engineering, and also between U.S. and Mexican scientists.

INTRODUCTION

Strong motion accelerographs are operating in Mexico as the result of two major sources of support. The first general category is instruments installed and maintained entirely from any of several Mexican sources for funds. The agency in Mexico which maintains all of these instruments is the Instituto de Ingeniería (II), at the Universidad Nacional Autónoma de México. Instruments in this category include all accelerographs in Mexico City and many digital and analog accelerographs scattered throughout Mexico. The second category includes the Guerrero accelerograph network, described here, and the Baja California accelerograph network (Anderson et al., 1982) has been installed with support from the U.S. National Science Foundation in a cooperative effort between II personnel and personnel at the Institute of Geophysics and Planetary Physics, at the University of California, San Diego.

GUERRERO ARRAY

The Guerrero array consists of 30 digital accelerographs which were installed for the specific purpose of obtaining strong motion records from a large ($M > 8$) earthquake. The array was strategically located in Guerrero and Michoacan, Mexico, in two seismic gaps, with the expectation, obtained from seismological research, that these locations were high probability areas for such a large earthquake. Figure 1 shows a space-time diagram of Mexico to illustrate that prior to the 1985 events, the Michoacan region was a seismic gap. This was the basis of the placement of the accelerographs in that location. Actually, prior to the September 1985 earthquakes, we were uncertain about the seismic potential of the Michoacan region, where there were no certain prior earthquakes. In the Guerrero gap, in contrast, there were several large earthquakes at about the turn of the century (1899, 1908, 1909, 1911).

Table 1 lists all of the stations in the Guerrero array. The 1985 earthquakes occurred at a time when installation of the array was about 65 percent complete. Therefore there are only 16 accelerograms for the earthquake from that array.

Figure 2 shows the locations of instruments in the Guerrero array which recorded the 1985 earthquakes. Most of the units are in the Mexican state of Guerrero, in the Guerrero gap, but several instruments were located in Michoacan, and were in the immediate vicinity of rupture during the September 1985 event.

[1]Institute of Geophysics and Planetary Physics, University of California, San Diego, La Jolla, California, U.S.A.

[2]Instituto de Ingeniería, Universidad Nacional Autónoma de Mexico, Mexico City, Mexico

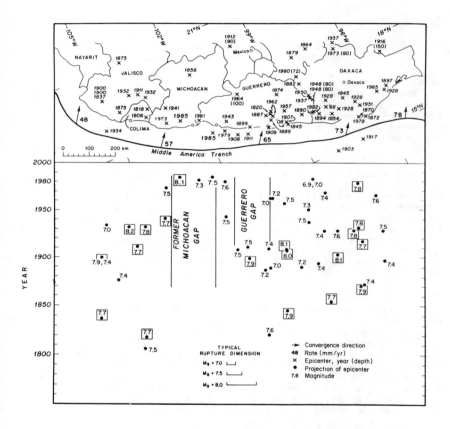

Figure 1. Top: map of Mexico with epicenters of large historical earthquakes identified by year, and depth in parentheses when event is known to be deep.

Bottom: Space-time diagram in which epicenters are projected down and plotted at year of occurrence. Deep events and events located far inland and thus not clearly related to subduction are deleted. Larger events are highlighted. Guerrero gap and former Michoacan gap are illustrated.

Table 1.
Accelerograph Stations in the Guerrero Array Which Were
Installed Prior to the September 19, 1985 Earthquake

Station	Location Lat.° N	Long.° W	Instrument Type	S/N	Geology
Caleta de Campos	18.0727	102.7552	DSA-1	261	metavolcanic
La Villita	18.0475	102.1840	DSA-1	260	gabbro
La Union	17.9824	101.8054	DSA-1	259	Metavolcanic
Zihuatenejo	17.6030	101.4550	DCA333	106	tonalite
Papanoa	17.3278	101.0399	DCA333	111	weathered plutonic
El Suchil	17.2258	100.6418	DCA333	109	plutonic
Atoyac	17.2113	100.4309	DSA-1	256	weathered plutonic
El Paraiso	17.3444	100.2145	DSA-1	257	plutonic
El Cayaco	17.0452	100.2664	DSA-1	258	
Coyuca	16.9967	100.0900	DCA333	107	schist/gneiss
El Ocotillo	17.0378	99.8749	DCA333	110	weathered gabbro
Xaltianguis	17.0950	99.7201	DSA-1	253	granodiorite
El Ocotito	17.2500	99.5106	DCA333	104	weathered plutonic
La Venta	16.9129	99.8159	DSA-1	252	granitic gneiss
Cerro de Piedra	16.7692	99.6326	DCA333	112	weathered gneiss
Las Mesas	17.0070	99.4565	DSA-1	254	weathered granitic/gneiss
San Marcos	16.7760	99.4077	DSA-1	255	granitic gneiss
Las Vigas	16.7560	99.2359	DCA333	108	plutonic
Tonalapa	18.0975	99.5594	DSA-1	249	met. shale
Teacalco	18.6174	99.4528	DSA-1	248	volcanic tuff

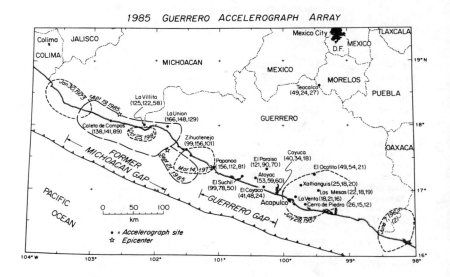

Figure 2. Map of coastal Mexico, epicenters and aftershock zones of 1985 events, and locations of strong motion stations in Guerrero array on September 19, 1985. Short dashed lines show limits of aftershocks of large earthquakes in this region since 1951. Peak accelerations, in cm/sec^2, are given for each station, for the north, east, and vertical components, respectively, in parentheses. (Figure from Anderson et al., 1986, p. 1044; copyright 1986 by the AAAS)

MEXICO CITY ACCELEROGRAPHS

Table 2 lists   Mexico City vicinity accelerographs which recorded the September earthquake and Figure 3 shows the locations of those which were located in Mexico City in more or less free field conditions. The soil conditions in Mexico City vary widely, from relatively firm soils or volcanic flows in the hills zone to soft clay in the lake zone as indicated in Table 2 and Figure 3.

SEISMOLOGICAL CHARACTERISTICS

Before discussing the strong motion it is useful to review some seismological characteristics of the Sept. 1985 Mexico earthquake. Several parameters are listed in Table 3. For comparison, Table 3 also shows some of the characteristics of the March 3, 1985 Chile earthquake. The Chile earthquake is important for being about the same size, and also for producing strong motion records from near the faulting.

Figure 4 is modified from Scholz (1982). It shows the relationship of two parameters from several earthquakes which have occurred in a strike slip environment and several which have occurred in subduction thrust zones, such as in Mexico. According to all purely elastic models, for a long earthquake which ruptures the entire width of the seismogenic zone the seismic moment is proportional to the product of the rupture length, L, and the rupture width, W, squared. The constant of proportionality is the stress drop, which may vary from one earthquake to another. This figure shows that the stress drop appears to increase as the seismic moment increases. The Mexico and Chile earthquakes have been added to the figure. These two earthquakes are not anomalous based on Figure 4. The point for the Mexico earthquake is a little low (ie, stress drop appears to be a little higher than other events of the same size), but considering the uncertainties in interpretation of rupture width which have not yet been resolved, it is consistent with the other points.

In contrast to this result, Houston and Kanamori (1986) have looked at the spectrum of teleseismic P-waves in the frequency range of 0.05 to 1 Hz. While these spectra are similar at frequencies less than 0.1 Hz, from 0.1 to 1.0 Hz the Mexico earthquake spectra are depleted relative to Chile and relative to a worldwide average. The lower amplitudes in Mexico appear to correlate with a less complex rupture process than that found for the Chile event.

STRONG GROUND MOTION

Levels of Peak Motions

Table 4 lists all peak accelerations, peak velocities, and peak displacements for the main shock from the Guerrero array. Table 5 lists peak accelerations, velocities, and displacements which are available from the Mexico City vicinity. Figure 5 shows peak accelerations which were recorded in the Chile and the Mexico earthquakes. The peak values in the Mexico earthquake are much less scattered than in Chile, and except for the points in Mexico City, the Mexico points almost seem to provide a lower bound to the Chile points. These peak accelerations are at a higher frequency than the frequencies which were studied by Houston and Kanamori (1986), but if it is allowable to extrapolate between the two frequency bands, the lower peak accelerations may be consistent with the teleseismic results.

There is however one other factor which is important in evaluating these peak accelerations, namely site effects. The site conditions in Michoacan and Guerrero are uniform. All stations were placed on the most competent rock outcrop consistent with the target location. Only one station (El Cayaco) was not sited on rock. Compressional wave velocities measured from rock samples taken at many of the sites have a median value of about 4 km/sec, with the variation among sites sampled to date ranging from a low of 1.6 km/sec to a high of 5.6 km/sec. The high value in this preliminary set was obtained from the site at La Villita. Samples from the other stations above the source zone are not completed yet, but the rock samples are similar to others which have measured about 4 km/sec.

Table 2.
Accelerograph Statons in the Vicinity of Mexico City

Station	Code	Lat.° N Long° W	Type/N0.	Accelerograph Comp.	Nat. Freq.	Damp G.	Site Description
Cd. Univ. D.F.	CU01	19.330 99.183	DCA333 -121	S00E VERT N90W	33.0 31.0 32.0	0.64 0.66 0.70	Rock basalt. 1st floor of 3-story Idel main Ibldg. Hilly zone
Idel Patio	CUIP	19.330 99.183	DCA310 -154	N00E VERT N90W	31.0 31.3 31.4	0.73 0.66 0.68	Rock, basalt. Free field. Idel yard.
Mesa Vibra-dora C.U.	CUMV	19.330 99.183	DCA333 -145	S00E VERT N90W	31.0 31.0 30.0	0.70 0.66 0.75	Rock, basalt. Shaking table, Free field.
Sismex Puebla	SXPU	19.043 98.212	DCA310 -148	N00E VERT N90E	32.0 32.0 31.0	0.71 0.77 0.74	Hard soil, sand and gravel. Free field. Puebla Valley.
Tacubaya, D.F.	TACY	19.403 99.194	DCA333 -168	S00E VERT N90W	30.0 30.0 30.0	0.70 0.70 0.70	Hard soil. Free field. Hill zone, D.F.
Sismex Viveros	SXVI	19.358 99.171	DCA310 -133	N00E VERT N90W	30.4 32.0 33.0	0.66 0.80 0.78	Soft soil, clay. Free field. Transition zone, D.F.
C. de Abastos Frigorifico	CDAF	19.368 99.088	DCA333 -114	S00E VERT N90W	31.0 31.0 31.0	0.70 0.70 0.70	Very soft soil, Free field. Texcoco lake bed zone, D.F.
C. de Abastos Oficina	CDAO	19.368 99.088	DCA333 -115	S00E VERT N90W	31.0 31.0 31.0	0.70 0.70 0.70	Very soft soil, clay. 1-story bldg. Texcoco lake bed zone, D.F.
Secretaria de Comunicaciones y Transportes	SCTI	19.393 99.147	DCA333 -144	S00E VERT N90W	30.0 30.0 30.0	0.75 0.66 0.70	Very soft soil, clay. Free field. Texcoco lake bed zone, D.F.
Tlahuac Bombas	TLHB	19.279 99.008	SMA1 -4590	N00E VERT N90W	18.3 19.0 18.5	0.60 0.60 0.60	Soft soil, clay. Free field. Xochimilco lake bed zone
Tlahuac Deportivo	TLHD	19.293 99.035	SMA1 -4591	N00E VERT N90W	18.3 19.0 18.5	0.60 0.60 0.60	Soft soil, clay. Free field. Xochimilco lake bed zone

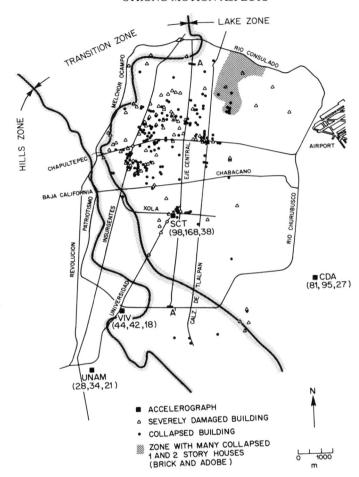

Figure 3. Mexico City map showing free-field accelerograph stations, generalized soil classification, and sites of worst building damage from Instituto de Ingeneria (1985) preliminary report. Peak accelerations (cm/sec²) for the north, east, and vertical components, respectively, are given in parentheses by each station. (Figure from Anderson et al., 1986, p. 1044; copyright 1986 by the AAAS)

Table 3.
Characteristics of Mexico and Chile Earthquakes

Event	Michoacan	Michoacan	Chile
Date	Sept. 19, 1985	Sept 21, 1985	Mar. 3, 1985
Time	13:17	01:37	22:46
M_S	8.1	7.5	7.8
M_0 (dyn-cm)	$0.9-1.5 \times 10^{28}$	1.4×10^{27}	1.1×10^{28}
L (km)	170	70	125
W (km)	50	40	90

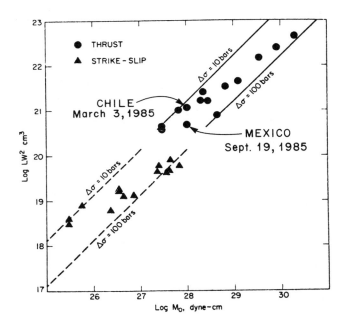

Figure 4. Plot of log LW^2 versus log M_0 for the large interplate earthquakes from the data set of Sykes and Quittmeyer (1981). The lines of slope 1 are constant stress drop lines, assuming $C=0.6$ for the thrust events, and 0.3 for the strike-slip events (after Scholz, 1982).

Table 4.
Strong Motion Data from the Guerrero Array
Sept. 19, 1985 Mexico Earthquake ($M_S = 8.1$)

Station	$R1$	$R2$ (1)	Trigger (2)	Dur. (3)	Comp. (4)	A_{max} (5)	V_{max} (6)	D_{max} (7)	V_{max} (8)	D_{max} (9)
Caleta	22.7	0.0	13:17:	49.4	N	138	25.9		16.70	5.73
de		0.0			W	141	19.5		12.64	3.22
Campos		0.0			DN	89	16.9		7.11	1.88
		0.0	13:18:	25.6	N	40	4.1	4.4		4.04
		0.0			W	51	4.8	3.2	5.96	1.18
		0.0			DN	24	3.3	2.0	2.91	0.88
La Villita	43.7	0.0	13:18:	64.0	N	125	25.9		16.11	6.67
		0.0			W	122			10.51	3.77
		0.0			DN	58	11.0		4.72	1.21
La Union	84.0	0.0	13:18:	62.8	N	166	28.0		20.34	6.95
		0.0			W	148	14.4		11.70	4.16
		0.0			DN	129	17.7		11.72	3.89
Zihuatenejo	134.6	8.0	13:18:	71.8	N	103	20.8	34.9	15.86	5.96
		8.0			W	161	17.9	17.2	18.34	4.62
		8.0			DN	105	14.6	22.1	10.23	3.80
Papanoa	187.9	63.0	13:18:	59.5	N	162	14.0	21.2	9.67	2.85
		63.0			W	117	7.7	12.9	6.13	1.57
		63.0			DN	84	10.4	14.6	8.38	1.81
El Suchil	230.4	112.0	13:18:	60.0	N	102	16.0	17.5	11.61	2.95
		112.0			W	81	7.1	7.9	6.36	1.49
		112.0			DN	51	6.8	9.2	5.96	1.16
Atoyac	251.1	135.0	13:18:	42.2	N	53	8.0	13.9	5.44	2.04
		135.0			W	59	4.6	5.5	3.67	0.89
		135.0			DN	60	8.3	8.6	6.68	1.61
El Paraiso	266.3		13:18:		N					
					W					
					DN					
El Cayaco	275.0	152.0	13:18:	25.6	N	41	5.2	10.0	3.75	1.31
		152.0			W	48	3.5	2.3	2.91	0.68
		152.0			DN	24	5.4	9.0	3.81	1.32
Coyuca	294.1	175.0	13:18:	38.8	N	42	9.0	12.4	7.82	2.83
		175.0			W	35	3.6	5.3	3.16	1.19
		175.0			DN	19	4.2	7.8	3.33	0.91
La Venta	324.3	206.0	13:18:	10.2	N	18	5.5	2.7	4.30	1.29
		206.0			W	21	3.6	1.5	2.62	0.88
		206.0			DN	16	3.3	1.5	3.20	0.98
Cerro de	348.9	225.0	13:18:	25.5	N	27	5.9	9.2	2.59	0.69
Piedra		225.0			W	15			2.52	0.57
		225.0			DN	13	3.8	7.1	3.07	0.79
Las Mesas	354.9	237.0	13:18:	14.1	N	22	4.6	5.1	1.90	0.51
		237.0			W	18	3.2	3.3	2.84	0.66
		237.0			DN	19	4.5	3.3	3.85	0.98
Xaltianguis	325.3	207.0	13:18:		N	25				
		207.0			W	18				
		207.0			DN	20				
El Ocotito	340.2	223.0	13:18:		N	49			7.65	2.92
		223.0			W	54				
		223.0			DN	21			3.72	1.48
Teacalco	332.5	244.0	13:18:	38.4	N	49	9.4	12.6	7.38	3.68
		244.0			W	24	5.4	6.0	4.74	1.36
		244.0			DN	27	5.8	10.3	4.41	1.62
El Ocotillo	312.7									
San Marcos	370.0									
Las Vigas	387.5									

Tonalapa   318.3

NOTES

1. Epicentral distance (km), based on epicenter at 18.182° N, 102.573° W, origin time 13:17:47.8.

2. Closest distance to outline of aftershock zone (km).

3. Origin time of accelerogram.

4. Duration (seconds) of accelerogram.

5. Orientation, while nominal, is expected to be accurate.

6. Peak acceleration (cm/sec^2).

7. Peak velocity (cm/sec). This is obtained from an integration which did not employ a high-pass filter at low frequencies, made possible because the accelerograph is digital. There are some uncertainties in this, however, and these values are preliminary.

8. Peak displacement (cm). Obtained from the unfiltered velocities. The same notes apply. For some records, the peak velocity and peak displacement are reduced merely because the instrument did not run long enough to recognize their presence.

9. Peak velocity (cm/sec). To obtain these values, a high pass filter with a corner at about 0.015 Hz has been applied. The much lower values present in this case result because there are very strong low frequency signals period about 20 seconds) which have been filtered out from the records. The low frequencies are physically meaningful, and can be shown to correlate from one accelerogram to the next along the coast.

10. Peak displacement (cm). Filtered records. See note 9.

TABLE 5.
Strong Motion Data from Mexico City and Vicinity
Sept. 19, 1985 Mexico Earthquake ($M_S = 8.1$)

Station	$R\,1$ (1)	$R\,2$ (2)	Trigger (3)	Dur. (4)	Comp. (5)	A_{max} (6)	V_{max} (7)	D_{max} (8)	V_{max} (9)	D_{max} (10)
Teacalco	332	244	13:18:	38.4	N	51.3	9.4	12.6	7.38	3.68
		244			W	24.7	5.4	6.0	4.74	1.36
		244			DN	27.1	5.8	10.3	4.41	1.62
CU01	379	289		60.0	S	28.1			10.20	5.54
					W	33.5			9.38	7.19
					UP	21.6			8.23	6.65
CUIP	379	289		60.0	N	31.7			10.25	6.17
					W	34.7			9.37	7.71
					UP	21.9			7.99	6.61
CUMV	379	289		60.0	S	37.4			9.19	5.70
					W	38.8			11.01	4.45
					UP	20.1			8.40	4.57
SXPU	469	379		85.3	N	29.6			7.18	3.10
					E	32.6			6.63	2.65
					UP	15.9			4.06	1.67
TACY	380	290		156.0	S	34.4			14.29	11.96
					W	33.2			9.81	8.62
					UP	19.2			9.29	7.61
SXVI	381	291		60.0	N	44.1			11.48	9.10
					E	42.4			12.20	7.47
					UP	18.2			5.84	6.96
CDAF	389	299		60.0	S	80.5			24.85	15.02
					W	94.6			37.57	18.88
					UP	27.2			8.90	8.17
CDAO	389	299		180.0	N	69.2			34.98	25.02
					E	80.4			41.86	24.67
					UP	35.7			11.34	8.92
SCT1	385	295		180.0	S	98.0			38.74	19.12
					W	167.9			60.50	21.94
					UP	36.6			9.00	7.58
TLHB	394	304		150.0	N	135.9			64.10	36.61
					W	106.7			44.61	39.29
					UP	24.0			9.39	6.78
TLHD	392	302		150.0	N	117.7			34.90	20.76
					W	111.6			36.06	22.07
					UP	59.3			17.01	6.87

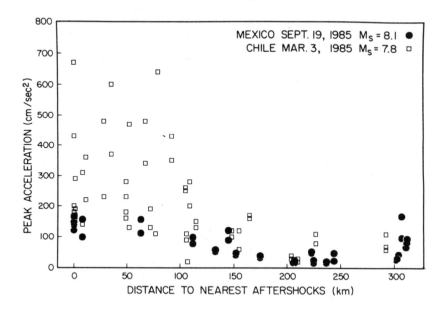

Figure 5. Peaks of horizontal components of acceleration plotted against distance outside the boundary of the aftershock zone (Figure 2). (Figure from Anderson et al., 1986, p. 1046; copyright 1986 by the AAAS)

In contrast to this situation, the site conditions in the Chilean data set are not uniform, and are not yet as well documented. Conditions described in Bolt and Abrahamson (1986) are evidently obtained from geological maps of the area rather than field inspection. Some of the accelerograms which are nominally listed as coming from rock sites show apparent ringing, probably caused by local site conditions. Therefore it is likely that to some extent the lower levels obtained near the faulting in Mexico are the result of differing site conditions.

From the Mexican data alone, there is clear evidence that the site conditions are important. The accelerations in Mexico City were unambiguously amplified by local site conditions. In addition, an II accelerograph, Zacatula 4.3 km from the La Villita accelerograph recorded peaks in acceleration of 1.5 to 2.5 times those recorded at La Villita. Peak velocities at Zacatula were also amplified by a similar amount. The Zacatula station is situated on a river terrace deposit of probable Quaternary age. The deposit is an indurated cobble conglomerate with a high density of cobbles ranging in size mostly from 5 to 25 cm.

Appearance of Accelerograms

Figure 6 shows the north-south component of all accelerograms from the Guerrero array. Figure 7 shows the east-west acceleration from those Mexico City sites which are shown in Figure 3. At the stations above the faulting (Caleta de Campos, La Villita, La Union) the duration of strong shaking is fairly long (over 30 seconds) but at stations farther to the southeast, the duration is shorter. This is because the rupture on the fault propagated to the southeast during the event, so that the arrivals in that direction are compressed in time. In Mexico City, the durations are much longer than in the source region. At the station CDA and SCT, the strong shaking lasted over 60 seconds (only the most significant part of these records is shown), and the total duration of these accelerograms exceeds 180 second.

Anderson et al. (1986) have demonstrated that above the fault, the accelerograms can be integrated to obtain a permanent offset. The offset obtained is consistent in magnitude and direction with that expected from the earthquake mechanism. Vertical offsets are also apparently consistent with observed uplift along the coast.

Figures 8 to 13 show a selection of accelerograms and response spectra from the Guerrero array. These records have been filtered at low frequencies, with the cutoff in the vicinity of 0.15 Hz, so the static displacements are not visible. Figures 14 to 16 show the same information for a selection of records from the Mexico City vicinity.

Because ot the unprecedented building damage in Mexico City for the earthquake and because the damage was in large part caused by amplified 2 second energy, an important question is whether or not the earthquake source energy at 2 second period was anomalous compared, for example, with previous large Mexico earthquakes. A survey of the velocity and displacement records outside of the Mexico City basin (Figures 8—13) shows obvious high amplitudes at these periods, e.g. espeially records from Caleta de Campos, La Villita, Papanoa, Teacalco, and CUIP. Some records from the coast show local maxima in the response spectra at 2 seconds (e.g. Caleta de Campos and La Villita) but at all stations closer than El Cayaco (Figure 2) the response spectra also attain even higher values of periods shorter than 2 seconds. The highest peaks with velocity response spectra near 2 second period on the near-source stations Caleta de Campos and La Villita (~60 cm/sec) for zero damping are smaller than the response spectra peaks near the same period for 1971 San Fernando (Pacoima Dam > 150 cm/sec, near 1.5 second period) and 1940 Imperial Valley (El Centro > 110 cm/sec, near 2.0 second period) (EERL 72-80, 73-81). Thus there does not appear to be any clear indication of anomalously high source energy near 2-second period, but a final conclusion awaits a more thorough comparison with other Mexico earthquakes. Earth structure effects (e.g. energy focusing) also might have been partly responsible for the unusual damage for the earthquake.

CONCLUSIONS

Earthquake hazards are distributed widely around the world, and the need to measure the strong motion in the vicinity of strong earthquakes is an international problem. The success in

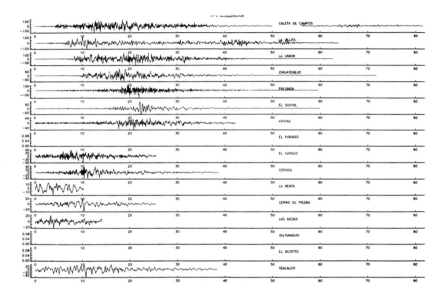

Figure 6. North-south component of acceleration for stations above the aftershock zone. Vertical separation of traces is proportional to separation of the projection of stations onto the trench. Time, T_0, is the origin time of the earthquake.[1] The clock correction at Caleta de Campos is uncertain.

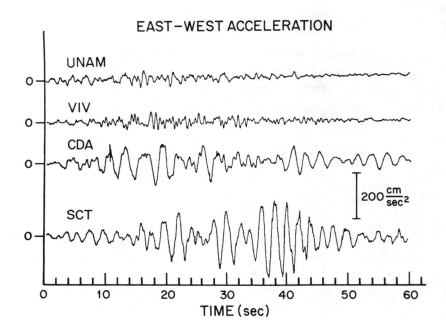

Figure 7. Most significant one-minute segments of the east-west acceleration recorded on the free-field accelerographs in Mexico City. Complete accelerograms are longer 100 sec of motion preceded the segment of the SCT record shown here. No time correlation exists among these traces. (Figure from Anderson et al., 1986, p. 1048; copyright 1986 by the AAAS)

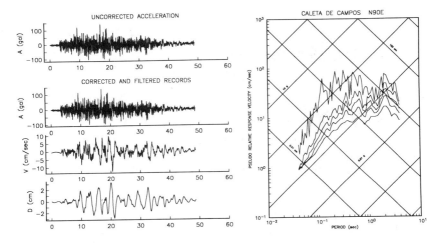

Figure 8. East west acceleration, velocity, displacement, and pseudo relative velocity response at Caleta de Campos, September 19, 1985

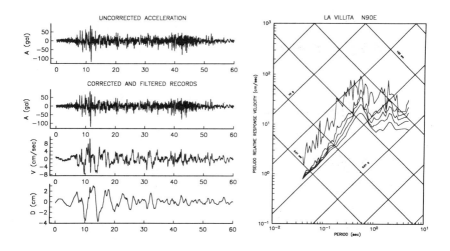

Figure 9. East west acceleration, velocity, displacement, and pseudo relative velocity response at La Villita, September 19, 1985

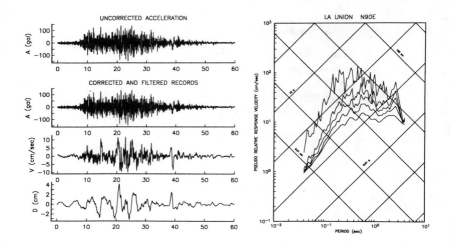

Figure 10. East west acceleration, velocity, displacement, and pseudo relative velocity response at La Union, September 19, 1985

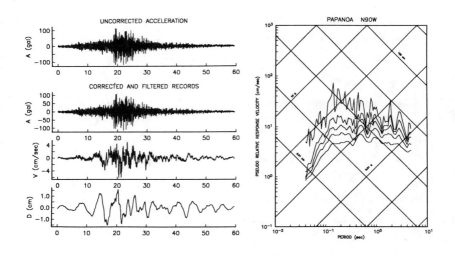

Figure 11. East west acceleration, velocity, displacement, and pseudo relative velocity response at Papanoa, September 19, 1985

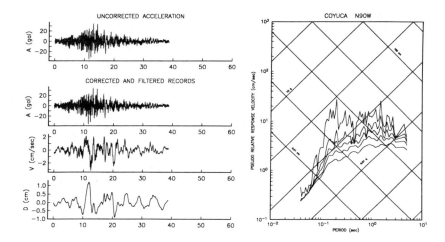

Figure 12. East west acceleration, velocity, displacement, and pseudo relative velocity response at Coyuca, September 19, 1985

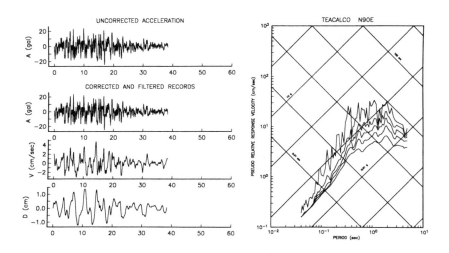

Figure 13. East west acceleration, velocity, displacement, and pseudo relative velocity response at Teacalco, September 19, 1985

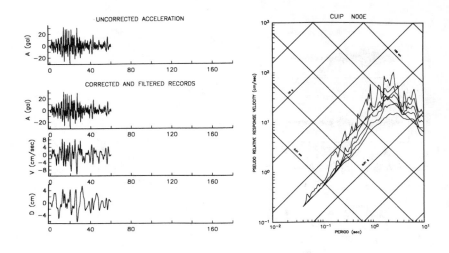

Figure 14. East west acceleration, velocity, displacement, and pseudo relative velocity response at Instituto de Ingenieria patio, September 19, 1985

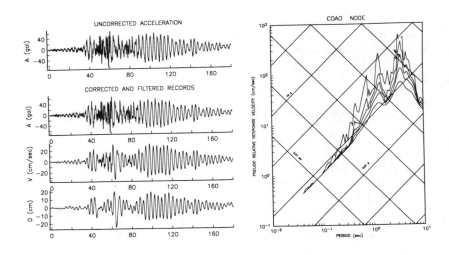

Figure 15. East west acceleration, velocity, displacement, and pseudo relative velocity response at C. de Abastos Oficina, September 19, 1985

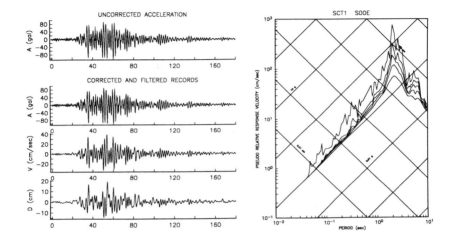

Figure 16. East west acceleration, velocity, displacement, and pseudo relative velocity response at Secretaria de Comunicaciones y Transportes September 19, 1985

obtaining accelerograms from the epicentral area of the Mexico earthquake is a result of application of seismological information about the relative likelihood of earthquakes, and international cooperation to put the instruments in one of these locations.

ACKNOWLEDGMENTS

This research was supported by National Science Foundation grants CEE82-19432 and ECE-13489.

REFERENCES

(1) Anderson, J.G., J.N. Brune, J. Prince, and F.L. Vernon III, Preliminary report on the use of digital strong motion recorders in the Mexicali Valley, Baja California, *Bull. Seism. Soc. Am.*, *73*, 1451-1468, (1983).

(2) Anderson, J.G., P. Bodin, J. Brune, J. Prince, S. Singh, R. Quaas and M. Onate, Strong ground motion of the Michoacan, Mexico earthquake, *Science, 233*, 1043-1049, (1986).

(3) Bolt, B. And N. A. Abrahamson, Seismological features of the March 3, 1985 Chile earthquake, *in Earthquake Spectra 2*, 253-272, (1986).

(4) EERL, Analyses of strong motion earthquake accelerograms, Vol. III - Reponse Spectra, Part A - Acclerograms IIA001IIA020, Earthquake Engineering Research Laboratory, Calif. Institute of Technology, Pasadena, Calif. 272 pp., (1972).

(5) EERL, Analyses of strong motion earthquake accelerograms, Vol. III - Reponse Spectra, Part C - Acclerograms IIC041IIC055, Earthquake Engineering Research Laboratory, Calif. Institute of Technology, Pasadena, Calif. 191 pp., (1973).

(6) Houston, H. and H. Kanamori, Source characteristics of the 1985 Michoacan, Mexico earthquake at short periods, (Geophys. Res. Letters, in press), (1986).

(7) Instituto de Ingeniería de la Universidad Nacional Autónoma de México, El temblor del 19 de septiembre de 1985 y sus efectos en las construcciones de la Ciudad de México, Informe Preliminar Instituto de Ingeniería, UNAM, Mexico City, (1985).

(8) Scholz, D. H., Scaling laws for large earthquakes, consequences for physical models, *Bull. Seism. Soc. Amer. 72*, 1-14 (1982).

(9) Sykes, L. and R. Quittmeyer (1981). Repeat times of great earthquakes along simple plate boundaries, in D.W. Simpson and P. G. Richards, eds., *Earthquake Prediction: an International Review,* 217-247.

ESTIMATED STRONG GROUND MOTIONS IN THE MEXICO CITY

by

Hiroyoshi KOBAYASHI*, Kazuoh SEO** and Saburoh MIDORIKAWA***
Presentation: Yoshitaka YAMAZAKI****

1. DAMAGE OF BUILDINGS IN THE MEXICO CITY DUE TO THE EARTHQUAKE

Most remarkable damage due to the Michoacan, Mexico Earthquake of September 19, 1985 is severe damage of high rise buildings in the Mexico City, in spite of long epicentral distance of 350 km. According to the report of the *Instituto de Ingenieria, Universidad Nacional Autonoma de Mexico* (UNAM)[1], 265 buildings were damaged severely or collapsed. That were 101 of lower than 5 storied building, 134 of 6 to 10 storied, 27 of 11 to 15 storied, 3 of higher than 15 storied building. Damaged buildings were reinforced concrete structures, steel structures, steel reinforced concrete structures and masonry structures. Especially reinforced concrete structures suffered most severe damage. By these damages, about 6000 persons were killed.

In generally, reinforced concrete structures are used for buildings in the Mexico City. These structures have few shear walls, and their rigidity is not sufficient for antiseismic design. They were designed rather simplly on planning and elevation.

In order to know the general dynamic behavior of building structures, authors performed measurements of structural vibrations due to microtremor, and determined the natural period and damping coefficient of undamaged buildings in the Mexico City. For these measurements, they developed a compact system of analyzer with seismometer. This system consists of two seismometers, amplifiers, A/D converter, and a portable computer, EPSON HC-20.[2]

Measured 20 buildings were reinforced concrete structure, steel reinforced concrete structure or steel structure. In Fig.1, they showed the location of measured buildings. The results of the measured period were shown in Figs.2 and 3. Fig.2 showed relation between natural period T of horizontal sway fundamental mode of building and number of stories N of the building. Mark of square is steel structure and others were reinforced concrete structure or steel reinforced concrete structure. For reinforced concrete structures of 5 to 30 storied building, it was concluded that T = 0.105 N sec, and for tall steel structures, T = 0.1 N sec. In case of Japan, reinforced concrete or steel reinforced concrete structures have a relationship of T = 0.05 N sec and steel structures have a relationship of T = 0.1 N sec. So the reinforced concrete structures have a large difference between Mexico and Japan, on the horizontal rigidity. In Fig.3, they showed relationship between natural torsion period of the buildings and number of stories.

* Professor of Earthquake Engineering, ** Associate Professor,
*** Research Associate, **** Graduate Student
Graduate School at Nagatsuta, Tokyo Institute of Technology

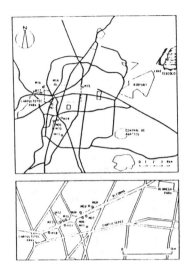

FIG.1 LOCATION OF BUILDINGS WHOSE
VIBRATIONAL CHARACTERISTICS
WERE MEASURED

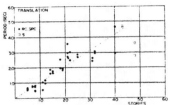

FIG.2 RELATION BETWEEN NUMBER OF
STORIES AND NATURAL PERIOD

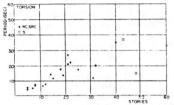

FIG.3 RELATION BETWEEN NUMBER OF
STORIES AND NATURAL PERIOD

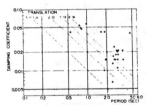

FIG.4 RELATION BETWEEN NATURAL
PERIOD AND DAMPING
COEFFICIENT

    This system is also available for determination of structural
damping coefficient. On the fundamental mode of sway oscillation,
relationship between natural period T and damping coefficient h was
shown in Fig.4. In case of Mexico City, the predominant period of microtremor of ground surface is rather long and it could be very close to
the natural period of the structure. In not a few cases, the separation
of ground motion and structural vibration on spectrum was difficult.
Then the determination of the damping coefficient are not sufficient for
all measured buildings. In the figure, they showed broken lines of
h·T = 0.01, 0.02, 0.03, 0.04. These lines correspond to case of soil
category I, II, III, IV of Building Code of Japan, which were determined
by the similar measurements. Category I and IV mean firm and very soft
ground, respectively. The case of Mexico City showed larger value than
that of category IV of Japan.

    From these results of undamaged buildings on natural period and
damping coefficient, the buildings, which have natural period of from
0.5 sec to 2.0 sec and damping coefficient of h = 0.05, suffered most
severe damage.

2. DAMAGE CONCENTRATED ZONE IN MEXICO CITY

According to the report of UNAM, distribution of damaged buildings is as shown in Fig.5.[1] Dots in the figure showed the location of damaged buildings, and these points were concentrated in the central part of the city. In the figure, also showed damage concentrated zone of the case of the earthquake of 1957 by broken line and the case of the earthquake of 1979 by dotted line. In spite of difference of the source zone of the earthquakes, center of the damaged zone of these three cases were same part of the city, that is *Roma* Area to *Alameda* Park. These earthquakes were different each other on source mechanism and distance. However, the patterns of damage distribution are very similar, it can be considered that, the predominant period and intensity amplification of the ground motions were caused by the characteristics of the soil structures, mainly.

3. STRONG GROUND MOTIONS DURING THE EARTHQUAKE

UNAM had succeeded the measurement of strong ground motions during the earthquake, at eight stations in the city, five of them were installed on hilly zone, and other three were on the old lake zone.[3] [4],[5],[6] The former are UNAM (1,2,3), *Viveros de Coyoacan* and *Tacubaya*, the latter are *Secretaria de Comunicaciones y Transportes* (SCT) and *Central de Abastos* (Office, Freezing House). Surrounding area of SCT is suffered severe damage, but other stations are not so. See Fig.6.

On peak acceleration and maximum velocity, seismograms showed 39 gal and 11 kine at UNAM, 168 gal and 61 kine at SCT, and 95 gal and 42 kine at *Central de Abastos*. As examples of the time historical record,

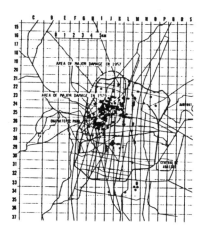

FIG.5 DISTRIBUTION OF COLLAPSED OR   FIG.6 LOCATION OF STRONG-MOTION
      HEAVY DAMAGED BUILDINGS   ACCELEROGRAPH SITES IN
                                            MEXICO CITY

they showed seismograms of SCT in Fig.7, and of *Central de Abastos*
(Office) in Fig.8. In case of Fig.8, later phase of 4 seconds period
is significant, this might be considered as surface waves generated by
the soil structure in the Mexico Valley.

4. SUBSOIL CONDITIONS OF THE MEXICO CITY

        The Mexico City is located on the south-west part of the Mexico
Valley. Its surrounding mountains of the valley are volcanoes. The
geological basin of the valley lied 1.5 km under ground surface, and its
P-wave velocity is 4.5 km/sec. P-wave velocity of the layer of from 1.5
km to 0.5 km in depth is 2.9 km/sec, and shallower than 0.5 km is 1.7
km/sec.[7] Shallow part of the soil is compressible layers, and still
now continue the subsidence. Velocity of the subsidence is 5 m per 30
years. S-wave velocity of the top clayey soil is 50 to 80 m/sec and its
thickness is 10 to 20 m. At ancient time, the area of the city was in
the lake, after that the lake was reclaimed, and developed to the city.
Downtown of the city shows heaviest subsidence and severest earthquake
damages. West and south part of the city are hilly zone and covered by
lava flow and very thin top soil layer. Most of the city is covered by
thick deposit of clayey layers, and the thickness of the deposit of east
part is larger than that of west part. Fig.9 showed the contour line of
the thickness of clayey deposit [1], and it can be assumed that the

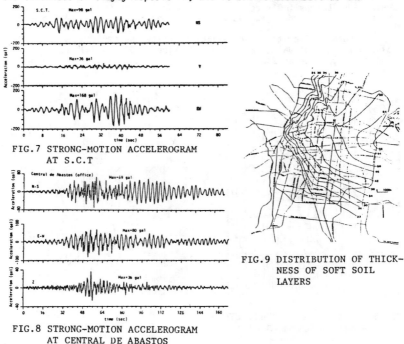

FIG.7 STRONG-MOTION ACCELEROGRAM
       AT S.C.T

FIG.8 STRONG-MOTION ACCELEROGRAM
       AT CENTRAL DE ABASTOS
       (OFFICE)

FIG.9 DISTRIBUTION OF THICK-
       NESS OF SOFT SOIL
       LAYERS

deeper soil layers will show similar trends. In such situations, facilities and building structures of the city have been subsided before the
earthquake, and tilted buildings and uneven roads are usual. And main
pipes for water services also suffered some damage by usual subsidences.

5. MICROTREMORS

Authors measured microtremors at ground surface in and around the
city, to collect the information of soil structures.[8] Natural period
of the seismometer is 1 sec in mechanically, and it is enlarged to 5 sec
electrically. Maximum magnification of the system is 4700 volt/cm, and
overall characteristics of the system was shown in Fig.10.

As shown in Fig.11, they selected 95 points for the measurement of
microtremor. These 95 points covered almost whole area of the city, and
included the sites of strong motion seismometer. On 19 points of east-
west line, which is shown in Fig.11, they showed time histories of NS-
component of the microtremor record in Fig.12, and also showed Fourier
spectra in Fig.13. Measured points No.1 to No.4 and No.19 are on hilly
zone of the valley, and amplitude of the microtremor is very small and
predominant period is rather short. (5 seconds period component is
superposed.) Nos.5 to 10 are in downtown area and many damaged buildings
exist, and predominant period is 1.0 to 2.5 sec, that correspond to the
natural period of the collapsed buildings. At Nos.11 to 15, predominant
period is much longer, 4 to 5 sec, and *Central de Abastos* is also
included in this zone.

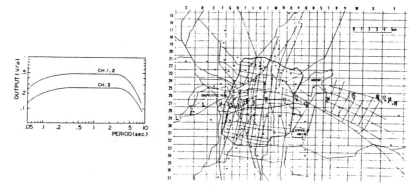

FIG.10 OVER-ALL RESPONSE CURVE   FIG.11 LOCATION OF OBSERVATION
     OF OBSERVATION SYSTEM   POINTS OF MICROTREMORS
                                  IN AND AROUND MEXICO D.F.

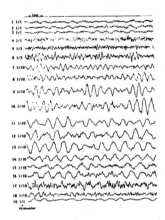

FIG.12 TIME HISTORY RECORDS
OF MICROTREMORS
ALONG EW-LINE

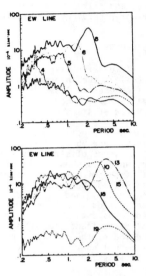

FIG.13 FOURIER VELOCITY SPECTRA
OF MICROTREMORS ALONG
EW-LINE

6. MICROTREMOR AT THE SITES OF STRONG MOTION SEISMOMETER

At the sites of strong motion seismometer, authors compared the
acceleration response spectra (h = 0.05) of the main shock [6] with the
Fourier velocity spectra of the microtremor. As shown in Figs.14 a, b,
c, d, e and f, they showed good agreements in spectral shape, except
Central de Abastos (Office), As it would be considered empirically
that the Fourier velocity spectra of the microtremors reflect the transfer function of S-wave in layered soil ground, the agreements suggest
that the characteristics of response spectra are strongly influenced by
the transfer function. The spectral ratio of acceleration response spectrum of the main shock to Fourier velocity spectrum of microtremor would
be equivalent to the acceleration response spectrum of incident waves
from seismic bedrock during the main shock. Then products of this spectral ratio and Fourier spectrum of microtremor at individual site, will
indicate the inferred acceleration response spectrum of the main shock
at the ground surface. As mentioned previously, case of *Central de
Abastos* (Office), shown in Fig.8, would not be same as the other
strong motion records, because of surface waves generated by the layered
soil structure, which has surrounding boundary of mountains or
topography under ground. But by the lack of geological information in
this moment, this problem should be discussed later, therefore it was
omitted from present study.

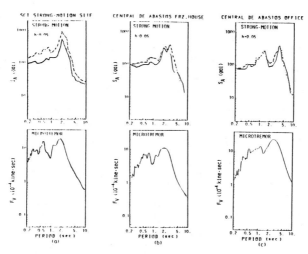

FIG.14 (a)-(c) COMPARISON OF SPECTRA OF STRONG-MOTION RECORDS
AND MICROTREMORS

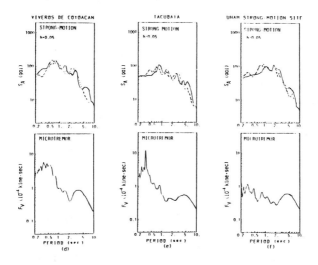

FIG.14 (d)-(f) COMPARISON OF SPECTRA OF STRONG-MOTION RECORDS
AND MICROTREMORS

On the microtremor of hilly zone, especially on the lava flow, the conditions might not be equal to those of flat deposit in plain. So authors divided problems into two groups, one is for hilly zone and the other one is for old lake zone. On individual zone, authors made the spectral ratio of acceleration response spectrum of main shock to Fourier velocity spectrum of microtremor and showed in Figs.15 and 16. As mentioned before, these figures can be considered as acceleration response spectrum (h = 0.05) of seismic incident waves from seismic bedrock. They took mean value of individual figure and showed by thick line. Fig.15 presents the results on hilly zone, that are UNAM, *Viveros de Coyoacan* and *Tacubaya*, and Fig.16 presents the results on old lake zone, that are SCT and *Central de Abastos* (Freezing House).

7. INFERRED GROUND MOTIONS DUE TO MAIN SHOCK

Acceleration response spectra of main shock were estimated at individual site, where microtremor was measured, as the product of mean value of acceleration response spectrum of incident wave and Fourier velocity spectrum of measured microtremor. For hilly zone, Fig.15 was used and for old lake zone Fig.16 was used as the response spectrum of incident wave. Several examples of inferred response spectrum (h=0.05) of ground surface in severe damaged zone were shown in Fig.17. Using these response spectra, authors picked up the response values of individual point on the period of 0.5 sec, 0.7 sec, 1.0 sec, 1.5 sec, 2.0 sec, 2.5 sec, 3.0 sec, 4.0 sec and 5.0 sec, and made contour map of response acceleration of 5 % damping at each period, as shown in Figs.18 to 26. In these figures, shaded area is the area of highest response value at each period.

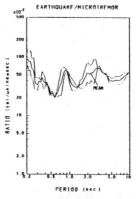

FIG.15 RATIO OF ACCELERATION RESPONSE SPECTRUM OF STRONG -MOTION RECORD TO FOURIER VELOCITY SPECTRUM OF MICRO- TREMOR (UNAM, TACUBAYA, VIVEROS DE COYOACAN)

FIG.16 RATIO OF ACCELERATION RESPONSE SPECTRUM OF STRONG -MOTION RECORD TO FOURIER VELOCITY SPECTRUM OF MICRO- TREMOR (CENTRAL DE ABASTOS (FREEZING HOUSE), S.C.T.)

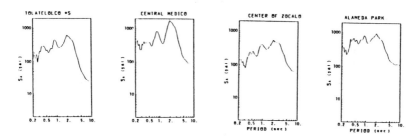

FIG.17 EXAMPLES OF ESTIMATED ACCE-
LERATION RESPONSE SPECTRA
(h=0.05)

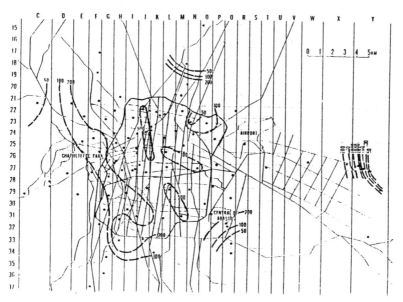

FIG.18 CONTOUR MAP OF ESTIMATED ACCELERATION RESPONSE
(T=0.5 sec, h=0.05, UNIT;gal)

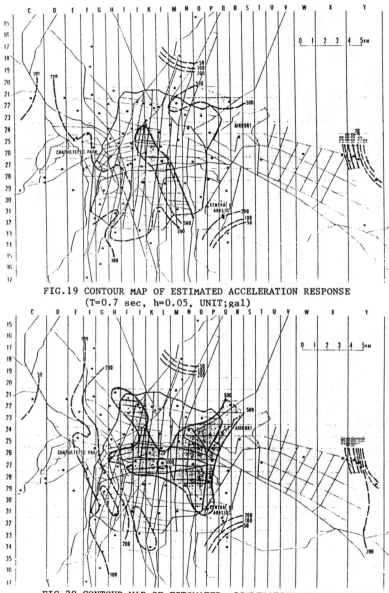

FIG.19 CONTOUR MAP OF ESTIMATED ACCELERATION RESPONSE
(T=0.7 sec, h=0.05, UNIT;gal)

FIG.20 CONTOUR MAP OF ESTIMATED ACCELERATION RESPONSE
(T=1.0 sec, h=0.05, UNIT;gal)

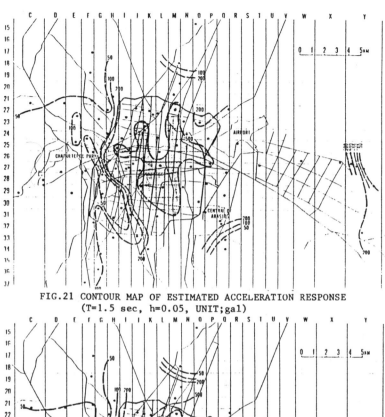

FIG.21 CONTOUR MAP OF ESTIMATED ACCELERATION RESPONSE
(T=1.5 sec, h=0.05, UNIT;gal)

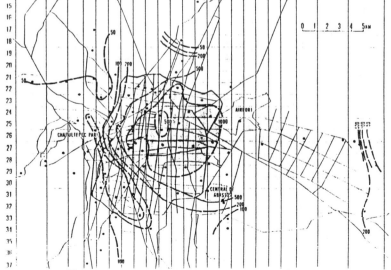

FIG.22 CONTOUR MAP OF ESTIMATED ACCELERATION RESPONSE
(T=2.0 sec, h=0.05, UNIT;gal)

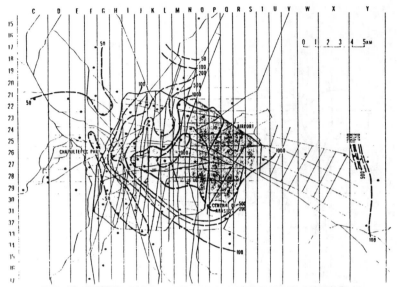

FIG.23 CONTOUR MAP OF ESTIMATED ACCELERATION RESPONSE
(T=2.5 sec, h=0.05, UNIT;gal)

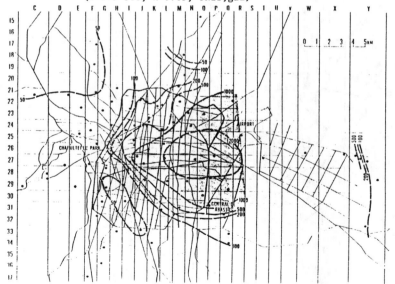

FIG.24 CONTOUR MAP OF ESTIMATED ACCELERATION RESPONSE
(T=3.0 sec, h=0.05, UNIT;gal)

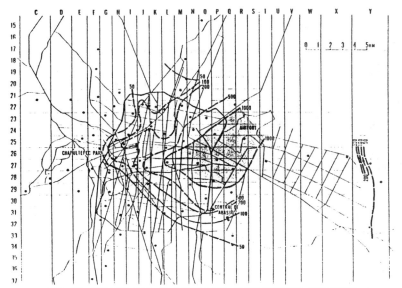

FIG.25 CONTOUR MAP OF ESTIMATED ACCELERATION RESPONSE
(T=4.0 sec, h=0.05, UNIT;gal)

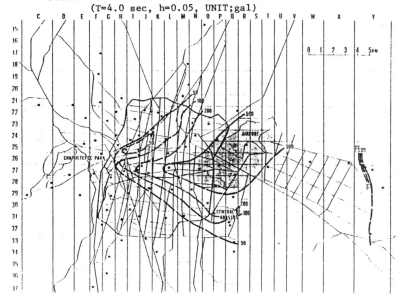

FIG.26 CONTOUR MAP OF ESTIMATED ACCELERATION RESPONSE
(T=5.0 sec, h=0.05, UNIT;gal)

8. CONCLUDING REMARKS

As the concluding remarks, authors pointed out several results as following;
(1) Difference between the hilly zone and old lake zone on response acceleration is very clear. In case of period range of 1 sec to 2 sec, the response acceleration in downtown of the Mexico City is 10 times larger than that of UNAM. Thus, it corresponds to three degrees of M.M. seismic intensity scale.
(2) On period range of 1.0 sec to 1.5 sec, area of high acceleration response is fitted to the area of severe damage to buildings.
(3) Contour lines of period range longer than 2 sec are similar to those of basement of top clayey layers. Thus it means these rather longer period component were produced by rather shallow sediments.
(4) Oldest part of the city, Zocalo, shows low acceleration response.
(5) From the acceleration response contour maps, authors confirmed that, undamaged buildings used for the measurement of natural period and damping didn't suffere so strong ground motions.

ACKNOWLEDGEMENTS

Tokyo Institute of Technology dispatched the investigation team for cooperation to UNAM by the support of the Fund for International Academic Cooperation, Tokyo Institute of Technology. On measurements of microtremor, Prof. Cinna Lomnitz and staffs of UNAM cooperated with them. And also on the vibration test for buildings, Prof. Cinna Lomnitz, Mexico Branch of Nissho Iwai Co. LTD. and Nippon Kokan Co. LTD. helped them. Mr. Shun'ichi Kataoka, Shimizu Construction Co. LTD., worked together in field survey and data analyses of microtremor. Mr. Masayoshi Matsubara and Mr. Hiroyuki Matsuzaki, graduate students of Tokyo Institute of Technology, also cooperated them on data analyses. Authors wish to express their sincere gratitudes to all of them.

REFERENCES

1) Instituto de Ingenieria de la Universidad Nacional Autonoma de Mexico: "El temblor del 19 de Septiembre de 1985 y sus efectos en las construcciones de la Ciudad de Mexico", Sept. 30, 1985.
2) Hiroyoshi Kobayashi et al.; "A portable Measurement System on Vibrational Characteristics of low-rised Building", Summaries of Technical Papers of Annual Meeting, Architectural Institute of Japan, Vol. Structure I, pp.467-468, 1985.
3) J. Prince et al.; "Acelerogramas en Ciudad Universitaria del sismo del 19 de Septiembre de 1985", Informe IPS-10 A, Instituto de Ingenieria, UNAM, Sept. 20, 1985.
4) E. Mena et al.; "Acelerograma en El Centro SCOP de la Secretaria de Comunicaciones y Transportes, sismo del 19 de Septiembre de 1985", Informe IPS-10 B, Instituto de Ingenieria, UNAM, Sept. 21, 1985.
5) R. Quaas et al.; "Los dos acelerogramas del sismo de Septiembre 19 de 1985, obtenidos en la Central de Abastos en Mexico D.F.", Informe IPS-10 C, Instituto de Ingenieria, UNAM, Sept.23, 1985.
6) J. Prince et al.; "Espectros de las componentes horizontales registradas por los acelerografos digitales de Mexico D.F. sismo del 19 de Septiembre de 1985, acelerogramas en Viveros y en Tacubaya", Informe IPS-10 D, Instituto de Ingenieria, UNAM, Oct.1, 1985.

7) R. J. Marsal and R. Graue: "The Subsoil of Lake Texcoco", The Subsidence of Mexico City and Texcoco Project, pp.167-202, 1969.
8) Hiroyoshi Kobayashi et al.; "Measurement of Microtremors in and around Mexico D.F.", Report on Seismic Microzoning Studies of the Mexico Earthquake of September 19,1985, Part 1, Tokyo Institute of Technology, Jan. 1986.

Note that the results shown in Figs. 15 to 26 are preliminary and the results with minor modification will appear in another article.

DAMAGE STATISTICS OF THE SEPTEMBER 19, 1985 EARTHQUAKE
IN MEXICO CITY

Gilberto Borja-Navarrete,+
Manuel Díaz- Canales,++
Alejandro Vázquez-Vera,+++
Enrique del Valle-Calderón,*

Introduction

Several studies have been made to assess the type and magnitude of the damage caused by the earthquake that shook Mexico City on the mor-- ning of september 19, 1985. Grupo ICA has participated in all stages of the actions and analisis of the effects of this quake aimed at taking advantage of this disastrous experience and has prepared a complete stu dy that includes seismicity aspects, characteristics of the earthquake, geological aspects, existing instrumentation, evolution of the codes, definition and behavior of structures and damage evaluation backed by photogrametric studies and direct inspection of buildings; this paper resumes part of the study and describes the types of structures that exist in the City and how they were affected by the quake. An important feature of the study is that and inventory of all the existing buil- dings in the zone of maximum damage was obtained, taking into account the type of structure, materials used and number of levels, in order to compare damaged buildings against existing ones to obtain the res- pective statistics.

Geological Aspects and Characteristics of the Motion

From the stratigraphical point of view, Mexico City is founded upon three different types of soils: very soft and wet clays typical of the ancient lake area; compact sands and silts characteristic of the hill's zone and transition soils constituted by soft clay with less water content, interbedded with lenses of sands and gravels.

It was found that the zone of maximum damage was located entirely in the ancient lake bed zone, see fig. 1. Acceleration values in the different types of soil ranged from about 20% gravity in the lake zone, exceeding considerably desing accelerations specified by the code, to 40% gravity in the zones of firm soil.

Largest destruction that occurred in the lake zone was mainly due to the fact that filtering and amplification of the seismic waves - -

+ President, Grupo ICA,
++ Executive vice president,
+++ General Director, Engineering firms,
* Consultant.

coming from the distant epicenter, resulted in an almost harmonic movement with dominant periods of 2 seconds, with large amplitudes of motion
and long duration, fig. 2; the intense phase of the motion in that zone
lasted for about 45 seconds, affecting mainly those buildings which had
oscillation periods in the vicinity of 2 seconds, which were close to
resonance, as shown in fig. 3, where the design spectrum for the soft
soil zone of the city is compared with the response spectrum obtained
for that zone from the E-W component of the accelerograph records shown
in fig. 2, for a damping value of 5% of critical.

The earthquake caused undulations and permanent pledging of the
surface as well as bending of rails, something never before observed in
the city. There was also cracking of underground pipes and sudden
settlement of some buildings and overturning of some others, caused by
soil or piles failure.

Structural Behavior and Damage Evaluation

Types of existing structures. There are six basic types of structures
in the city as shown in fig. 4; the first one correspond to old buildings, and consists of very thick masonry bearing walls and floor systems with wood or steel beams and brick or wood floors or stone vaults
and arches. The second one is a modern version of the other, with
thinner masonry bearing walls, reinforced with vertical and horizontal
concrete elements and with concrete floor systems. These two types
are mainly used for housing buildings with a maximum of 6 to 8 stories
high; as they have many walls in both directions they are rather stiff
and their periods of vibration are relatively small, usually less than
0.5 sec; therefore, their dynamic response in the soft soil zone was
small and they suffered little damage, in general, as will be seen later.

The third and fourth types of structure are framed systems with
deep beams and slabs for the third type, or waffle slabs for the
fourth, connected to columns to conform rigid frames; partition or facade walls have no theoretical structural function. They are mainly
made of reinforced concrete, but in some cases, for the taller buildings, steel is used. The number of levels varies from 2 or 3 to more
than 40, as in the well known Latino-Americana Tower, and are used for
housing or office buildings. These two types were the most affected
by the earthquake, as their periods of vibration, in many cases, were
close to those of the motion and their displacements were large.

Type of structure fifth or sixth, have additional stiffening elements
as concrete or masonry shear walls or diagonal bracings, either of concrete or steel, placed in some bays to reduce displacements and improve
the general behavior of the structure. Few buildings with these systems were damaged.

Types of damage commonly found

Concrete was found to be the predominant material in the structures
that were seriously affected. Few steel buildings were damaged, mainly
because this materials is used in taller buildings whose dynamic respon

se was lower because their periods of vibration are longer than those
of the soil. There was only one 21 story steel building that collapsed; its measured period before the earthquake was 2 seconds, therefore, it was certainly a case of resonance.

Main types of failure found in concrete buildings were: diagonal
cracking in beams, columns and walls due to shear; cracking and loss of
concrete in beams and columns due to compressions caused by flexure or
a combination of axial forces and flexure, with buckling of the reinfor_
cing bars; shear failures in waffle slabs around columns with several
cases of punching.

As will be seen later, there was a larger incidence of failures in
buildings from 6 to 15 stories high, mainly with structural systems of
types 3 and 4 described before. A large number of failures in upper
or intermediate levels were due to pounding with adjacent buildings,
changes in stiffness and/or mass, or excessive loads. A large number
of corner buildings suffered heavy damage due to torsional oscillations
produced by collaboration of asymetrical non-structural walls, as the
deformations caused by the quake exceeded the gap left between the
structure and non-structural brick walls, forcing them to take seismic-
forces. Buildings with waffle slabs and columns, forming "equivalent"
frames, had twice as much failures than buildings with deep beam and
columns constituting rigid frames. "Soft" first story caused by the
existence of non- structural walls in upper levels of apartment buildings, with parkings without walls at the base, was also the reason of
some partial or total collapses.

Statistics of Damaged Buildings

In order to make a rapid evaluation of damage just after the earth_
quake, aerophotogrammetric surveys, to back up direct observation of
damaged buildinos, were made. The most affected zone has an approximate
surface of 43 square kilometers and is limited by the Circuito Interior
to the north and west, by the avenues Eugenia and División del Norte to
the south and by Calzada de la Viga to the east, see fig. 5; this zone
was divided in 10 sectors. It is worth to mention that the whole metro_
politan area has a surface of 1100 squake kilometers.

For a preliminary evaluation three types of damage were considered; total collapse, partial collapse and severe structural damage. Fig. 6
shows that in the 10 sectors mentioned above there are 53 368 constructions, from which only 757 had those types of damage, representing only
1.4% of the existing buildings; 133 presented total collapse, 353 partial collapse and 271 heavy structural damage; sectors 1 thru 4 had 86%
of the total number of cases.

A very interesting statistic was obtained in relation with the number
of levels of the affected buildings, as shown in fig. 7. The observed
failures, with respect to the total number of each type of building
that existed in the 10 sectors ranged as follows: 1% of the structures
of 1 to 2 levels, 1.3% of the ones with 3 to 5 levels, 8.4% of those
with 6 to 8 levels, 13.5% of the ones with 9 to 12 levels and 10% of

the buildings with more than 12 levels; actually the number of buildings with more than 15 levels with severe damage is very small; this
confirms that the most affected types of structure were those with vibration periods close to the predominant periods of the soil motion. It
is surprising that these averages for the 10 sectors change very much
from sector to sector; for example the percentage of damaged buildings
against those existing in the range from 9 to 12 stories in sector 2 is
as high as 67%, probably due to soil conditions. This will be investiga
ted in future work.

Although the number of 1 to 2 levels housing buildings affected is
relatively large, with 46% of the total number of cases, it was found
that most of them were seriously deteriorated before the earthquake, by
lack of maintenance.

Regarding its use, fig. 8 shows that 55% of the damaged buildings
were of housing type, 23% private office type, 9% public office buildings and 13% of different uses: factories, schools, hospitals, hotels,
recreational,commercial, banks or religious buildings.

Certainly there were many other buildings less seriously affected.
Official records mention more than 3300 affected buildings, but more
than half of them had only non-structural damage and may be easily repaired.

Conclusions

The earthquake that occurred on september 19, 1985 with a Richter
magnitude of 8.1 and maximum intensities in the modified Mercalli Scale
of IX and X in Mexico City, caused the largest historical recorded destruction. Considering the severity of the motion in the zone of soft
soil of the city and the peak of the response spectrum for structures
whose vibration period is near or equal to two seconds, it is surprising that the number of severily damaged buildings was not larger, as
design code accelerations were exceeded considerably, as shown by fig.
3. This suggests that actual ductility and damping in many buildings
was larger than the currently assumed values. This should be investigated.

The marked influence of the soil upon which a building is constructed
will modify previous concepts regarding microzonation of the City. Also, the large amplifications of the soft soil will be of concern, as
there are other earthquake prone cities in the world with soft soils.

Future buildings should include stiffening elements in some bays,
in order to reduce lateral deformations and obtain a better performance
under strong earthquakes.

It is convenient to increase the number of accelerographs installed in the city, to measure the effects of future earthquakes in the
different types of soil, and improve microzonation.

Partially affected buildings should be carefully studied by highly qualified specialists who will design the necessary retrofit and rehabilitation that guarantee their safety.

Acknowledgements

The study realized by Grupo ICA was possible thanks to the collaboration of a large number of engineers, architects and technicians who work in the different engineering firms of the group; mainly ISTME, GEOSISTEMAS and AEROFOTO; they performed the field surveys, the inventory of existing buildings, organized the information to be processed by computer, made the drawings to illustrate the study and many other jobs necessary to make the study a reality.

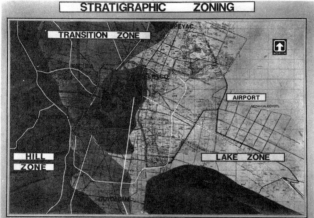

Fig. 1

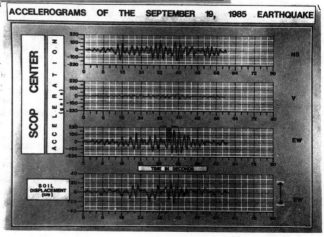

Fig. 2

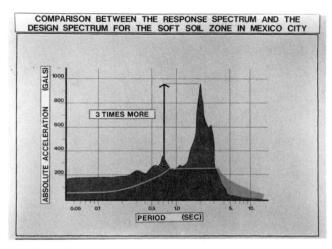

Fig. 3

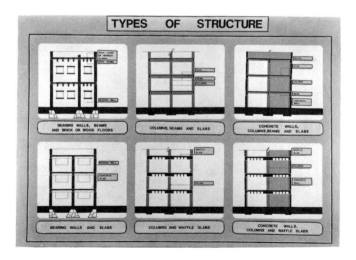

Fig. 4

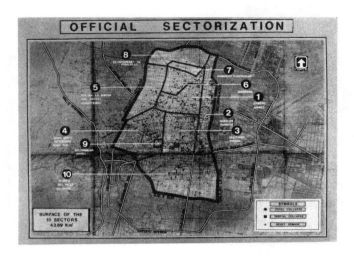

Fig. 5

Fig. 6

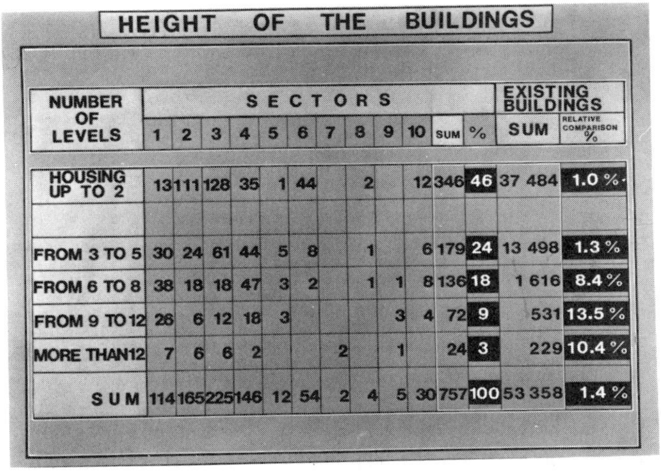

HEIGHT OF THE BUILDINGS

NUMBER OF LEVELS	1	2	3	4	5	6	7	8	9	10	SUM	%	EXISTING BUILDINGS SUM	RELATIVE COMPARISON %
HOUSING UP TO 2	13	111	128	35	1	44		2		12	346	46	37 484	1.0 %
FROM 3 TO 5	30	24	61	44	5	8		1		6	179	24	13 498	1.3 %
FROM 6 TO 8	38	18	18	47	3	2		1	1	8	136	18	1 616	8.4 %
FROM 9 TO 12	26	6	12	18	3			3		4	72	9	531	13.5 %
MORE THAN 12	7	6	6	2		2		1			24	3	229	10.4 %
S U M	114	165	225	146	12	54	2	4	5	30	757	100	53 358	1.4 %

Fig. 7

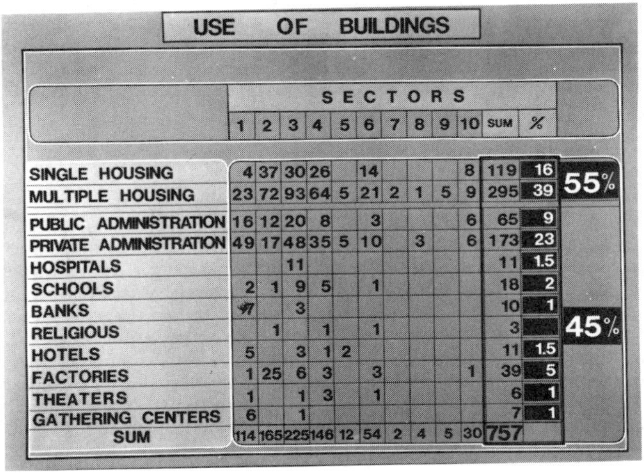

USE OF BUILDINGS

	1	2	3	4	5	6	7	8	9	10	SUM	%	
SINGLE HOUSING	4	37	30	26		14				8	119	16	55 %
MULTIPLE HOUSING	23	72	93	64	5	21	2	1	5	9	295	39	
PUBLIC ADMINISTRATION	16	12	20	8		3				6	65	9	
PRIVATE ADMINISTRATION	49	17	48	35	5	10		3		6	173	23	
HOSPITALS			11								11	1.5	
SCHOOLS	2	1	9	5		1					18	2	
BANKS	7		3								10	1	
RELIGIOUS		1		1		1					3	1	45 %
HOTELS	5		3	1	2						11	1.5	
FACTORIES	1	25	6	3		3				1	39	5	
THEATERS	1		1	3	1						6	1	
GATHERING CENTERS	6	1									7	1	
SUM	114	165	225	146	12	54	2	4	5	30	757		

Fig. 8

GEOTECHNICAL NOTES ON THE EFFECTS OF
MEXICO'S 1985 EARTHQUAKES

By Raúl J. Marsal,[1] F. ASCE

ABSTRACT: The present notes briefly describe the most relevant effects of the September 19 and 20, 1985 earthquakes on shallow and deep foundations used in Mexico City, which is located at about 400 km (249 miles) from the seismic foci on the Pacific coast. For the sake of comparison, an account of the observations made at the port of Lázaro Cárdenas and at the adjacent industrial complex built on the heterogeneous delta deposits of the Balsas River, close to the subduction zone of the Cocos plate and the continent, is also included. From the aforesaid observations in Mexico City, several lessons were learned and preliminary conclusions derived.

INTRODUCTION

The major earthquakes that struck Mexico on September 19 and 20, 1985, provided a unique opportunity to assess the behavior of different constructions subjected to unusually strong accelerations (Ref. 11). These notes cover a brief description of the most conspicuous effects induced by the seismic forces on the foundations of buildings in Mexico City, located at a distance of 400 km (249 miles) from the epicenter, as well as relevant observations recorded in the vicinity of the port of Lázaro Cárdenas, only 35 km (22 miles) away from the subduction zone of the Cocos plate and the Continent (Refs. 2 and 3).

BEHAVIOR OF FOUNDATIONS IN MEXICO CITY

Background.- In order to analyze the events that happened in Mexico City as a result of the macroseisms of September, 1985, as far as the behavior of foundations is concerned, it is necessary to recall: (1) The particular subsoil conditions brought about by the stratigraphy and properties of the lacustrine clay deposits; (2) the regional subsidence induced by pumping of water from the aquifers within the boundaries of the urban zone; and (3) the occurrence of intense earthquakes with epicenter laying in the vicinity of the Valley (earthquake of Acambay) or at the subduction zone on the Pacific coast at a distance from 250 to 400 km (155 to 249 miles).

The three factors mentioned above have a decisive influence on the design of foundations in Mexico City. On the other hand, some other factors of common occurrence in the City

---

[1] Advisor to the Directorate of Comisión Federal de Electricidad
(Federal Commission of Electricity, Mexico), Ródano 14, 06598-México, D.F., MEXICO

should be also considered, such as the behavior of adjoining buildigns supported by different types of foundation and the previous history of the building site itself. In addition, it is worthwhile noting that one of the consequences of the subsidence, as recorded during the past decades, is the development of cracks in the ground; this phenomenon implies the existence of tensile states of stress within the subsoil. The prediction of such a phenomenon poses some difficulty as a result of the irregular distribution of the hydraulic head losses at the pervious horizons and of the stratigraphical differences in the subsoil profiles of the urban zone.

Stratigraphy (Refs. 7, 9 and 13).- The stratigraphical zoning of Mexico City, based on borings performed at different times to depths of up to 100 m (328 ft) is depicted in Fig. 1. Three zones can be observed, namely lake bed, transition and hill (firm ground). The first zone contains thick deposits of lacustrine clay interbedded with firm strata at different depths. A typical soil profile of this zone is presented in Fig. 2 where it can be noted that the natural water content (w_n) of the clays ranges from 100 to 500%, whereas the value of w_n in the sandy clayey or silty dense or cemented strata is equal to approximately 50%; the firm layer found at a depth from 30 to 35 m (98 to 115 ft) has been used as the supporting material of point-bearing piles for heavy buildings foundations. This firm layer is underlain by another deposit of lacustrine clays with a thickness ranging from 9 to 15 m (30 to 50 ft). At depths in excess of 55 m (180 ft) dense or heavily consolidated deposits of sand, silt or clays are encountered.

One of the various possible stratigraphical distributions in the transition zone is illustrated in Fig. 3; the lacustrine clay deposits ($50 < w_n < 300\%$) are only 10-m (33-ft) thick, and they are bounded by surface sandy and clayey layers and a sequence of predominantly sandy interspersed deep strata.

The soils at the hill zone correspond to weathering of volcanic tuffs or to eroding processes of such rocks. The topography is rough; eolian, fluvial or man-made deposits may be encountered at small valleys, showing a heterogeneous composition and variable compaction. The soils corresponding to this zone are in general hardly compressible and they show a relatively high shearing strength, with the exception of some sites where construction materials were mined in past times.

Subsidence of the City (Refs. 1, 7, 9 and 13).- Due to the extraction of water from the subsoil by means of municipal and private wells within the urban area, it became evident in 1930 that the City was subsiding (Ref. 5). As indicated in Fig. 4, the rate of progress of the phenomenon increased during the period 1940-1960, reaching settlement values from

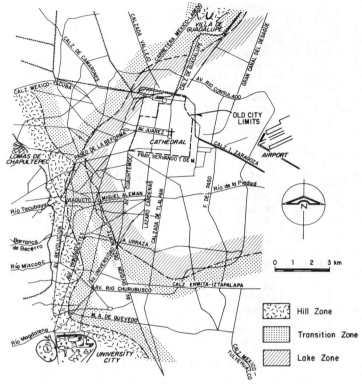

FIG. 1.- Stratigraphical Zoning of Mexico City (1 km = 0.62 miles)

5.5 to 7.2 m (18 to 24 ft) at the Cathedral and at the monument to Charles IV, respectively; subsequently, and as a
result of the prohibition of exploiting the aquifers (1953),
the subsidence radically diminished and at present it increases at a rate of 7 to 10 cm/year (3 to 4 in./year) in
the downtown area of the City; however, the population boom
(from 3 to 9 million people from 1960 to 1985) has extended
the urban area towards the south and the east of the Valley,
covering "virgin" ground and making it necessary to install
municipal wells to supply drinking water to the new settlements. The ensueing result is a strong local subsidence and
a severe impact in the drainage system and on the buildings
of such modern sections of the City. In Fig. 5 it is shown
the contours of equal sinking recorded from 1891 to 1966
which reveal differential subsidence, partly due to changes
in the stratigraphical sequence of the subsoil and partly
to the distribution of the water wells.

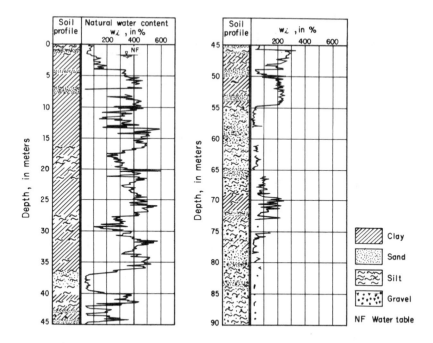

FIG. 2.- Continuous Boring Pc 143 at the Lake Zone (1m = 3.3 ft)

In 1948, Nabor Carrillo correlated the subsidence phenomenon with the consolidation of the soft clay deposits induced by the drop of hydraulic head in the underground aquifers. This theory was subsequently corroborated by means of piezometric measurements in different parts of the City. The pore pressure distribution for two consolidation times is sketched in Fig. 6 denoting that the pressure also varies at the relatively pervious strata; the rate of variation of the settlement as a function of depth and time is also presented in the figure. Both graphs point to problems faced by the designer of foundations resting on either friction or point-bearing piles.

The occurrence of a phenomenon closely related to the regional subsidence has been observed in the last decades, namely, the development of cracks in the ground at different parts of the lake zone and at the boundaries of the hill and transition zones.

Seismicity of the Valley of Mexico.- Another factor which influences the foundation design of buildings located in Mexico City, is the incidence of strong earthquakes; based on the statistical instrumental data of these events, 33 ground

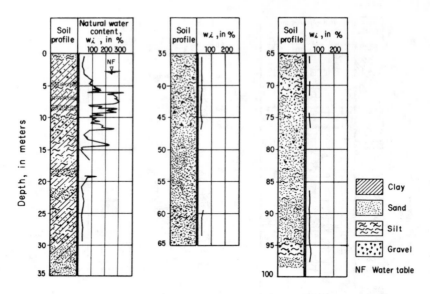

FIG. 3.- Continuous Boring Pc 190 at the Transition Zone (1m = 3.3 ft)

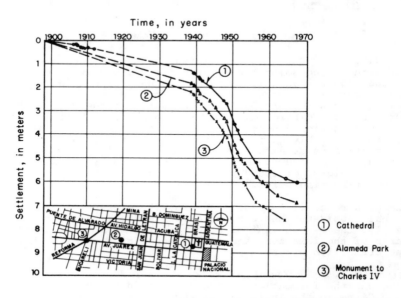

FIG. 4.- Time-Settlement Curves from 1898 to 1966 (1m = 3.3 ft)

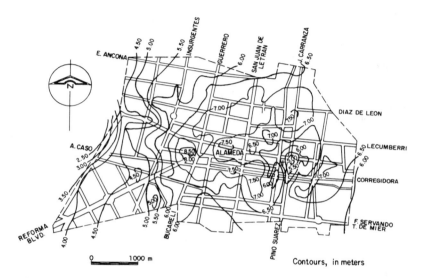

FIG. 5.- Contours of Equal Sinking from 1891 to 1966 (1m=3.3 ft)

shakings have been recorded during this century, with a magnitude (Richter) ranging from 7.0 to 8.4 (Ref. 12); most of them have originated in the Pacific coast as a result of the subduction phenomena of the Cocos plate, and other important earthquakes are related to active faults in the NW of the City at distances in the order of 100 km (62 miles). The characteristics of the earthquakes in the lake zone of the City can be consulted in Ref. 10, whereas the experimental reports on the dynamical properties of the lacustrine clays and of the intermediate hard strata are found in Refs. 7, 8 and 13.

With the information summarized herein, it will be possible to discuss the main topic of this Conference, in what refers to the behavior of foundations in Mexico City as a result of the 1985 earthquakes.

Influence of the Stratigraphical Sequence. The approximate boundaries of the zones sustaining heavy damage during the earthquakes of July 28, 1957 and September 19, 1985 have been plotted on a plan of the urban area shown in Fig. 7. When such boundaries are superimposed on the plan of Fig. 1, it is observed that damage concentrates in the lake and the transition zones; no major losses were reported at the hill zone and they seem to have been apparently less important towards the eastern part of the City where low rise dwellings and structures can be found. Earthquakes of minor intensity (March 1979 and October 1981) caused damages in a similar array to that of Fig. 7, although smaller in scope.

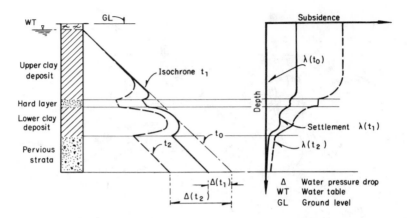

FIG. 6.- Pore Pressure and Settlement Distribution with
Depth due to Pumping of the Subsoil Aquifers

Consequently, the case histories described in the next sections
correspond to constructions located at the lake and the
transition zones.

Underground Structures.- This group comprises structures
such as the subway system and the deep sewage collectors.
The former correspond to reinforced concrete cut and cover
box structures very close to the ground surface, with a dead
weight smaller than the own weight of the soil displaced
(overcompensation); the latter are composed of reinforced
concrete conduits advanced in tunnels excavated at depths
varying from 10 to 30 m (32 to 98 ft) and 2.50 to 5.0 m
(8 to 16 ft) in diameter and these structures also imply an
unloading of the ground along their length. At the concrete
boxes, and particularly around the subway stations, the
emersion induced by unloading becomes important and as a consequence of the 1985 earthquake longitudinal cracks were
observed in several stretches; on the contrary, movements
related to the collectors were minimal. The structural behavior of both types of underground facilities was satisfactory. However, damage was recorded at the water supply
mains and at the shallow drainage system [1 to 2 m (3 to
6 ft) in depth], regardless of the stratigraphical zoning.
The effects of the surface seismic waves were conspicuous
along some streets and boulevards of the City (buckling of
tramway tracks and sidewalks, and ground waving).

Footings and Rafts.- This type of shallow foundations is
quite common in low rise buildings (two or three stories
high) constructed in the lake and the transition zones. Cases
of poor behavior during the earthquakes of September 1985
have been reported; specific investigations have shown the
existence of masonry footings with no tying reinforced con-

crete beams whatsoever, resting on top of loose fills or in areas with land cracking. These remarks are important since they correspond to the most numerous buildings in the City.

Partially Compensated Foundations.- A case history is described involving two similar buildings [nine stories, street level and basement; approximately 13 by 40 m (43 by 131 ft) in plan; depth of excavation, 3.9 m (13 ft); and a slenderness ratio of the structure equal to 3.5], founded on concrete boxes and beams constructed in trenches under the foundation slab; the effective pressure increment at the base is from 4 to 5 ton/m^2 (5.7 to 7 psi) and both structures are located in the lake zone at sites previously occupied by constructions one to two stories tall. Building A underwent the collapse of the superstructure although the

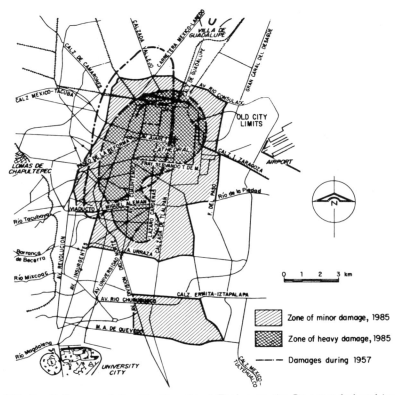

FIG. 7.- Influence of the Stratigraphical Zoning on the Damages Induced by the Earthquakes of July 1957 and September 1985 (1 km=0.62 miles) (See Fig. 1)

foundation did not suffer appreciable total or differential deformations, whereas the other one (B) sank approximately 1 m (3 ft) with respect to the surrounding ground, tilting along the transversal direction (4.2%) and sustaining minor damages in the superstructure. Mention should be made that the latter building had already subsided and was inclined (1.2%) prior to the September 1985 earthquakes.

The structural collapse during the first seismic shocks of building A, or construction problems during the excavation of building B, may explain the difference in behavior. Note that both buildings did not follow the provisions established by the Building Code approved in 1976 as far as long term settlements is concerned, due to the magnitude of the effective mean pressure increment established when the foundations were designed.

Compensated Foundations.- In contrast with the case described in the previous section, the following case history will refer to a multistory office building, 12 stories high, street floor and basement, rectangular in plan measuring 10 by 37.5 m (33 by 123 ft) and formed by a very regular reinforced concrete structure and substructure with the base slab at a depth of 6 m (20 ft); the slenderness ratio of this building is equal to 5.

The geometry of the building is shown in Fig. 8 together with the subsoil stratigraphy and a graphical comparison of the effective vertical stresses (p_o) with depth, the preconsolidation loads (p_c) determined from standard consolidation tests, and the stress increments ($\Delta\bar{\sigma}$) transmitted by the foundation slab. The right part of Fig. 8 also depicts the time-settlement curve after concreting of the substructure and during the first eight years of operation. The structure was designed in 1950 in accordance with the Building Code of 1942.

During the earthquake of July 28, 1957, the behavior of the building was satisfactory (no damages or differential settlements were reported). However, as a result of the 1985 earthquakes, 35 years after completion of the structure, the building exhibits a large differential settlement with an inclination towards the NE corner of about 60 cm (24 in.) as well as important structural damages; the neighboring building to the south, very old and lacking maintenance, sustained total collapse. There is evidence of pounding between both constructions.

The most plausible hypothesis brought forward is that the overturning moments generated by the earthquakes of September 1985, which exceeded by far the intensity provisions of the 1942 Code and had a prevailing period of 2 sec, were of such a magnitude that the maximum stresses under the foundation became of the same order of magnitude than the bearing capacity of the underlying soil and caused a local shear

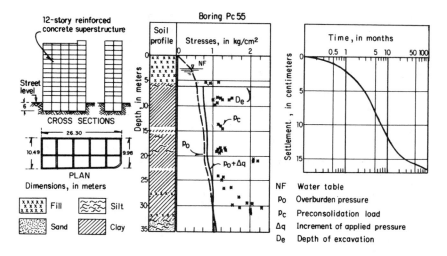

FIG 8.- Compensated Foundation at the Lake Zone
(1 m = 3.3 ft ; 1cm = 0.39 in. ; 1 kg/cm² = 14.22 psi)

failure. Other slender buildings constructed in the same section of the City, also showed tilting and important settlements.

Pile Foundations.- Two solutions commonly used in Mexico City will be discussed, namely friction piles and point-bearing piles.

Friction Piles.- In view of the difficulties encountered when excavating to great depths [in excess of 4 m (13 ft)] unless special procedures are used to avoid large expansions due to ground unloading and to the seepage forces, as well as to hinder the bottom failure, it has been quite common during more than two decades to adopt a solution which combines partial compensation of loads with the use of friction piles.

Although most of the 6 to 12 stories high buildings with this type of foundation has shown a satisfactory behavior during the earthquakes of September 1985, several cases were documented covering from large settlements [of up to one meter (3 ft)] to complete collapse due to overturning; these cases have prompted discussions about the validity of the soil-pile adhesion to carry the dynamic forces and of the criteria applied to the design of this type of foundation. On this respect the Building Code enforced before the seismic event referred to above, specifies in its complementary provisions that in addition to satisfying the limiting service requirements, the compatibility of the loads transmitted by the foundation slab to the subsoil and the loads carried by the friction piles should be verified for the most unfavorable loading conditions (static and dynamic). Note that this type of foundation was developed to avoid the emergence of the building due to ground subsidence.

What did we know about the behavior of friction piles when the solution described was implemented? On those days the real concern related to the effects of the so-called negative skin friction acting on the point-bearing piles, which could represent an additional load on the piles as important or even higher than the load transmitted by the permanent actions of the building. Pull-out tests on wood and concrete piles were carried out in order to measure the adhesion with the soil at different intervals following the driving and at several rates of displacement. Some of the results obtained are presented in Fig. 9. The curve pull-out load (P) versus displacement (δ) exhibits a linear pattern up to a maximum value (P_{max}) and then it falls down until reaching an asymptotic minimum value (P_{min}); in general terms the ratio P_{min}/P_{max} is approximately equal to 0.5. The most significant variable in this type of tests is the pulling-out rate ($\dot{\delta}$); for the case of wood piles, a threefold increase of P_{max} was measured when $\dot{\delta}$ rose from 10^{-4} to 10 cm/min (0.0004 to 4 in./min). The tests were performed on virgin ground and some of them included cycles of loading and unloading at a very slow rate (1 cycle/day); the cumulative effects of the deformations on the adhesion, for conditions likely to happen under seismic forces, were not contemplated in this study.

In addition to the uncertainties related to the soil adhesion, the design of friction piles become more involved due to the ground subsidence. This is not a static phenomenon since it depends on the consolidation of the clay deposits surrounding the piles. The piles are subjected to positive adhesion while carrying the load transmitted by the building and to a negative adhesion-induced load which can be also developed at the upper portion of the piles; the pile length corresponding to each of these two effects changes with time and is a function of two factors: (1) The consolidation rate of the clays above the firm layer; and (2) the increase in soil adhesion caused by this consolidation.

Point-Bearing Piles.- Since the decade of the forties, the heaviest buildings have been founded on piles driven to the firm layer at an approximate depth of 30 m (98 ft) (Ref. 7). Wood piles were used and they were designed to carry a load from 20 to 25 tons each; the offset from the vertical was practically beyond control due to the length and splices of the component poles [20 to 25 cm (8 to 10 in.) in diameter], No consideration was given neither to the forces induced in the structure due to earthquakes nor to the effects of the soil-pile adhesion. Save for a few particular cases, the emersion of this type of foundation triggered by the subsidence of the City, was of moderate magnitude during the fifties, since the phenomenon was concentrated mainly on the clay deposits underlying the firm stratum (see the isochrone t_1 in Fig. 6). When the consolidation progressed towards the upper clay strata as a result of the pressure head drop in the firm layer (isochrone t_2, in Fig. 6), the rate of subsidence of the ground not only increased but also the effect of the adhesion on the piles became stronger, thus increasing notably the negative friction load (Fig. 9, curves P vs. δ). This compound action, which has attenuating effects as far as the emersion of piles is concerned, together with the geometric and structural characteristics of this discontinuous poles, lead to a series of documented case histories with a very complex behavior as revealed by the effects on the adjoining ground or on the adjacent buildings. The impact of the earthquakes of September 1985 resulted in settlements of the sidewalks with respect to the buildings, and an increase of the tilting or of the differential deformations, whichever is the case; no collapse of structures has been reported as a result of failure of the wood piles driven to the firm layer.

The unfavorable behavior just described, the conspicuous emersion of the piles resulting from the progressive development of the subsidence phenomenon toward the soft clay deposits overlying the firm layer, the substitution of wood

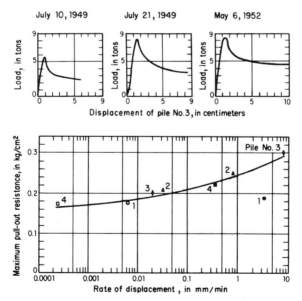

FIG. 9.- Pull-Out Tests on Wood Piles at the Lake Zone
(1cm=0.39 in.; 1mm/min=0.04 in./min; 1kg/cm² = 14.22 psi)

piles for reinforced concrete piles with welded splices, and the comprehensive geotechnical studies of the subsoil of the City, prompted important changes in the criteria applicable to the design of this type of foundations (Refs. 9 and 13). The number of piles was appreciably reduced when allowable loads per pile increased to 50 tons with due account of the negative skin friction, and control measures have been improved to keep vertical the pile during driving. The satisfactory behavior of the concrete piles (with or without welded splices, precast or cast in situ) during the earthquakes of September 1985, represents a positive progress in this field. The emersion is still a shortcoming due to its implications: (1) The effects on adjacent structures; and (2) the need to design the piles to carry the lateral forces induced by ground shaking. To lessen such effects, special devices have been developed to: (1) Control the load on the pile while allowing the sinking of the foundation; (2) make the pile penetrate into the firm layer; (3) reduce the transmission of lateral loads; etc.; their operation and efficiency is still subject to evaluation.

EFFECTS OF THE EARTHQUAKES IN THE VICINITY OF THE EPICENTERS

Background.- The following discussion will concentrate on the principal effects observed in the zone of the industrial port of Lázaro Cárdenas, following the earthquakes of September 1985. For the sake of brevity, no mention will be made of the impact of such events on the cities of Ciudad Guzmán, in Jalisco, Zihuatanejo, in Guerrero, and other important towns of this region of Mexico.

The port of Lázaro Cárdenas, situated where the Balsas River meets the Pacific Ocean, comprises an important industrial complex of recent development which includes steel mills, metalmechanic factories, fertilizer plants, petroleum related installations, etc. Most of the industrial plants have been sited upon delta deposits which were progressively filled with materials coming from the dredging of the navigable channels for the port zone.

The heterogeneity of the recent deposits in what refers to the quality of the materials (gravel, fine sand, silt and clay, peat) and to its random distribution (lenses and paleochannels), constitutes the predominant geotechnical characteristics; this fact together with the circumstance of being a zone subjected to earthquakes and hurricanes, and additionally to possible floods from the Balsas River, partially controlled by the El Infiernillo and La Villita dams, integrate a complex and conflicting physical environment.

The foci of the earthquake of September 1985 lay in front of Lázaro Cárdenas and it was triggered when the displacements of the Cocos plate with respect to the continent were reactivated along a stretch of 170 km (106 miles), at a distance from 30 to 40 km (19 to 25 miles) from the coast, and at a depth of approximately 18 km (11 miles); the magnitude M_s of this compound event due to the rupture of the Michoacán Gap was 8.1 (Ref. 11).

The most conspicuous effects observed in the region are summarized in what follows. The location of the industrial complex, the port of Lázaro Cárdenas, the dams of El Infiernillo and La Villita, and the epicenters, are shown in Fig. 10.

Sand Boiling at Isla de Enmedio (Fig. 10).- In this island of the river delta there exists a particular stratigraphical sequence which has favored the occurrence of the sand boiling phenomenon during the seismic events discussed herein as well as during previous earthquakes (1979, 1981). The subsoil comprises a layer of uniform fine sand in loose state, 1 m (3 ft) in thickness, overlaid by clayey or silty deposits upon which artificial fills have been placed in order to rise the ground surface to elevation + 3.5 m (+ 11 ft);

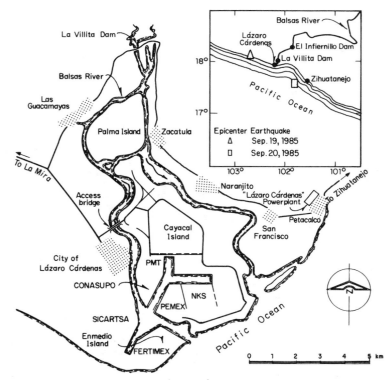

FIG. 10- General Layout of Lázaro Cárdenas Industrial Port and Vicinity

the sand layer in turn is underlaid by interspersed strata
of clays, silts, peat and a very dense sand, the latter
being very thick (Ref. 6).

During the earthquake of September 19, 1985, sand boils were
produced at different parts of a fertilizer plant then under construction (FERTIMEX), as a result of the pore pressures induced in the relatively loose, upper layer of fine
sand and of the subsequent hydraulic fracturing of the clay
deposits and of the landfills. Due to this reason, settlements were recorded at the surface which buckled pavements,
sidewalks and gutters; the main structures of the chemical
complex, founded upon concrete piles driven to dense sand
at depths from 10 to 12 m (33 to 39 ft), were hardly scathed,
save for cracking of walls tied to steel frames and floor
subsidence; one of the railroad tracks went out of alignment and settled due to the same reason.

At the foundry, forging and machining plant of NKS sited on
top of salt marshes filled with granular material recovered
for the port zone, an unexpected phenomenon occurred: part
of the site was flooded by the flow of water rushing from
the subsoil [phreatic level at elev 0.00 and the ground surface at elev + 4.0 m (13 ft)]; within a few hours the ground
became dry again and the whole area was left covered by a
very thin layer of fine sand; no cracks or sand boils were
detected. Presumably, high pore pressures in a loose sand
stratum underlying the artificial fill caused seepage of
ground water to the surface. This phenomenon induced settlements varying from 10 to 40 cm (4 to 16 in.). The principal structures of this plant are founded on concrete piers
resting at a depth of 12 m (40 ft); however, the secondary
columns around the perimeter carrying light steel trusses
as well as the sheet metal walls, transmit their load to
the ground by means of individual footings. As a result of
the settlements mentioned before, most of the secondary columns of the foundry and steel mill aisle detached from their
concrete bases when the anchor rods were sheared off. Un-
leveling of the floor slabs was also noticed. Damages caused
by the seismic events can be considered as slight and they
were repaired in less than three months.

At other important industrial plants such as that of SIDERMEX,
the effects induced by the earthquakes of September 1985
as far as sand boiling and settlements is concerned were
of minor consequences and they only affected canal linings,
pavements and some light-weight structures.

Tsunami and Damages Along the Shoreline.- The sea wave generated by the seismic action flooded low lands along the
shoreline, eroding the bases of three transmission towers
of the 230-kV line La Villita-FERTIMEX as well as the embankment of the railroad along a 300-m (985 ft) long stretch.
According to a limnigraph located at the entrance of the
port of Lázaro Cárdenas, the wave height was equal to 1 m

(3 ft) above the tide level, corresponding to approximately
half the height recorded at the village of San Francisco
(Fig. 10) situated at about 5 km (3 miles) from the Balsas
River mouth.

Urban Constructions.- The visual inspection of buildings
and dwellings at the city of Lázaro Cárdenas and neighboring towns revealed that damage was rather minor (cracks in
walls, failure of concrete braces and detaching of façade
elements). No collapse occurred; only two movie theaters
which had been already damaged during previous earthquakes,
were in the process of being demolished.

Roadways and Railways.- With the exception of failures at
the approach embankments and the column breakage at the twin-
bridge crossing the right branch of the Balsas River, no
other major damages were observed at the roads constructed
in the delta area. Some stretches of the railroad from
Apatzingán to Lázaro Cárdenas were affected by settlement
or displacement of the tracks. The landslides at cuts or
slopes were minimal at both the delta region and along the
reservoir of La Villita Dam.

La Villita and El Infiernillo Dams.- These earth and rockfill embankments constructed across the Balsas River for
power generation, are located at a distance of 15 and 55 km
(9 and 34 miles), respectively, from Lázaro Cárdenas. Notwithstanding the closeness to the source of the major earthquake, damages reported (cracking at the crest and settlements) were in fact moderate. Along this line, a comprehensive report has been prepared (Ref. 3) covering instrumental records taken after the earthquakes of September 1985
and comparing them with the effects of other events of this
type occurred during the life span of both dams (about 20
years of operation) (see also Ref. 4).

CONCLUDING REMARKS

The information presented herein and the exchange of observations with investigators and engineers in the fields of
geology, geophysics, geotechnical and structural engineering, and seismic risk analysis have led to the following
comments and conclusions.

1. There exists a positive correlation between the stratigraphical zoning of Mexico City's subsoil (Fig. 1) and
   the location of the buildings damaged by earthquakes
   (Fig. 7). The areas mostly affected by the seismic events
   correspond to the transition and lake zones, which are
   underlaid by soft lacustrine clay deposits of variable
   thickness (Figs. 2 and 3). Due to their fabric and high
   natural water content, they show a nearly linear behavior
   (weak damping, $\zeta < 5\%$) when subjected to the shearing
   stresses induced by the earthquakes. If in addition the
   seismic waves have a high energy level in the range from

0.5 to 2 sec, a serious problem of amplification of the seismic forces comes into being because: (1) The natural periods of vibration of the lacustrine clays fall in such an interval; and (2) the fundamental periods of slender and tall buildings of Mexico City become of the same order of magnitude if special provisions are not taken to stiffen the structure. Apparently, this set of circumstances are likely to explain the disastrous consequences brought about by the earthquakes of September 1985 at the zones shown in Fig. 7.

2. A fact that undoubtedly affected the behavior of the damaged buildings, was the actual condition they kept prior to the earthquake of 1985. The change in the use of the buildings from its intended purpose and the insufficient maintenance; the effects of the regional subsidence and cracking of the ground; the differential settlements in the buildings themselves or those induced by adjacent structures; the construction of slender buildings with no base enlargement and dwellings set on heterogeneous dumped fills, constitute a list of factors which, although contemplated in the 1976 Building Code, were not duly implemented.

3. The observations recorded at the Balsas River delta (Fig. 10), revealed that the impact of the September 1985 earthquake in this region located close to the epicenter was smaller than in Mexico City. This conclusion is impressive if one takes into account that: (1) The harbor facilities and buildings of the industrial complex are founded upon an erratic subsoil comprised by clay deposits, loose fine sands and artificial fills recently constructed to rise the ground level; (2) sand boiling was observed at a zone close to the coastline, with the resulting settlements and damages to light structures and communication facilities; (3) waving of the ground caused side displacement of the railroad tracks, an indication of a strong activity of the superficial seismic waves; (4) structural and façade damages were inflicted to important buildings at the city of Lázaro Cárdenas, although without collapsing; and (5) scouring effects were noticed at the bases of transmission towers and at the coastal railroad embankment as a result of the tsunami [maximum wave height of 1 m (3 ft)]. However, all those incidents can be considered as tolerable, given the large amount of energy released by the rupture of the Cocos plate in the Pacific gap near the mouth of the Balsas River.

ACKNOWLEDGEMENTS

The writing of these notes was sponsored by the Comisión Federal de Electricidad (CFE) of Mexico. The author is indebted to Messrs. Fernando Hiriart for his critical review of the manuscript and to Raúl Esquivel for his assistance in the preparation of this paper.

APPENDIX.- REFERENCES

1. Carrillo, N., "Influence of Artesian Wells on the Sinking of Mexico City", Proceedings of the 2nd International Conference on Soil Mechancis and Foundation Engineering, The Netherlands, 1948.

2. Comisión Federal de Electricidad, "Efectos de los sismos de septiembre en el delta del Balsas" (Effects of the Earthquakes of September 1985 on the Balsas River Delta), in Spanish, internal report, Mexico, 1985(a).

3. Comisión Federal de Electricidad, "Comportamiento de las estructuras de las centrales José Ma. Morelos y El Infiernillo, Mich., durante los sismos de septiembre de 1985" (Behavior of the Structures of La Villita and El Infiernillo Dams During the Earthquakes of September 1985), in Spanish, preliminary report, Mexico, 1985(b).

4. Comisión Federal de Electricidad, "Behavior of Dams Built in Mexico (1974-1984)", Vol. II, Contribution to the 15th International Congress on Large Dams held in Laussane, Switzerland (English-Spanish), Mexico, 1985(c).

5. Gayol R., "Breves apuntes relativos a las obras de saneamiento y desagüe de la capital de la República y de las que, del mismo género, necesita con grande urgencia" (Brief Notes Related to the Water Supply and Drainage of Mexico City and to Similar Works Urgently Needed), in Spanish, Revista Mexicana de Ingeniería y Arquitectura, Vol. II, Mexico, 1929.

6. Jaime, A., Montañez, L., Zavala, J. and Santoyo, E., "Estudio de licuación del subsuelo del complejo industrial de fosforados, FERTIMEX, S.A., Lázaro Cárdenas, Mich." (Study of subsoil liquefaction at the industrial fertilizers complex of FERTIMEX, S.A., Lázaro Cárdenas, Mich.), in Spanish, report submitted by Instituto de Ingeniería, Universidad Nacional Autónoma de México, Mexico, 1979

7. Marsal, R.J. and Mazari, M., "The Subsoil of Mexico City" (Spanish-English), published by Facultad de Ingeniería, Universidad Nacional Autónoma de México, Mexico, 1959.

8. Rascón, O.A., "Estudios encaminados a la predicción de espectros de temblores en el Valle de México" (Studies of the prediction of earthquake spectra in the Valley of Mexico), in Spanish, Boletín de la Sociedad Mexicana de Ingeniería Sísmica, Mexico, 1965.

9. Reséndiz, D., Springall, G., Rodríguez, J.M. and Esquivel, R., "Información reciente sobre las características del subsuelo y la práctica de la ingeniería de cimentaciones en la Ciudad de México" (Recent Information on the Subsoil Characteristics and the Practice of Foundation Engineering in Mexico City), in Spanish, Vol. I, Proceedings, V Reunión Nacional de Mecánica de Suelos, Mexico, 1970.

10. Rosenblueth, E. and Elorduy, J., "Characteristics of Earthquakes on Mexico City Clay" (Spanish-English), in Nabor Carrillo - El Hundimiento de la Ciudad de Mexico y Proyecto Texcoco, pp. 287-328, Secretaría de Hacienda y Crédito Público, Mexico, 1969.

11. Rosenblueth, E. and Meli, R., "The 1985 Earthquake: Causes and Effects in Mexico City", Concrete International, May 1986, pp. 23-34, U.S.A.

12. Singh, S.K., Rodríguez, M. and Espíndola, J.M., "A Catalog of Shallow Earthquakes of Mexico from 1900 to 1981", Instituto de Geofísica, Universidad Nacional Autónoma de México, Mexico, 1983.

13. Zeevaert, L., "Foundation Engineering for Difficult Subsoil Conditions", Van Nostrand Reinhold, New York, U.S.A., 1972.

EMPIRICAL RELATIONSHIPS FOR EARTHQUAKE GROUND

MOTIONS IN MEXICO CITY

by

Ellis L. Krinitzsky,[1] M. ASCE

Abstract

The information that has been developed from earthquakes felt in Mexico
City show characteristics that are highly site dependent. However, horizontal
accelerations for hard sites in Mexico City for subduction zone earthquakes
appear to be very closely relatable to values from Japanese data. This relationship may be extended to allow for magnitude of earthquake, distance from
source and dispersion in the data, whether mean values, mean + σ, etc. For
other motions than acceleration, and for all motions on soft sites, the site
dependent relationships observed in Mexico City should be used in combination
with the above accelerations for hard sites. Missing, however, are motions
that may be expected from shallow earthquakes with sources near Mexico City.
Their characteristics are certain to be different from those originating in
the subduction zone. Their values can be estimated from existing charts from
other parts of the world.

Introduction

Let us begin by considering what was special about the 19 September 1985
Mexico earthquake in its effects on Mexico City. Essentially they were:

a. Greatly amplified ground shaking in the soft lake deposits of the
   Valley of Mexico. These were almost monochromatic wave forms having
   predominant periods of two to five seconds and with durations
   (≥ 0.05 g) of about one minute.

b. A concentration of damage within restricted portions of the lake bed
   deposits.

---

[1] Geologist, Geotechnical Laboratory, Waterways Experiment Station, Corps of
Engineers, Vicksburg, Mississippi 39180, USA.

c. Foundation failures that resulted from severe weakening of lake bed clays and structural failures resulting from the powerful long period shaking.

A question that we may ask ourselves is how can we with our present knowledge model earthquake ground motions that are appropriate for the Valley of Mexico?

Observations

In the Valley of Mexico, the 19 September 1985 earthquake produced peak horizontal accelerations of 0.04 g on rock and nearly 0.2 g on lake soils. The maximum contrast is about 5X between soil and rock.

Amplifications of this order were observed in Mexico City during past earthquakes. Faccioli and Flores (1975) show comparisons of peak accelerations for three earthquakes. These are contained in Table 1. Note that the amplifications of acceleration on the soft soil vary from 1.79X to 5.23X. Thus, the 5X amplification during the 1985 earthquake could have been fully expected. What obviously was not expected was the severity of the shaking.

Figueroa (1963) published a set of reliable and well-documented isoseismal contours for 22 major earthquakes in Mexico that occurred between 1887 and 1963. None of these earthquakes had significant effects in Mexico City. The severest effect that was cited by Figueroa was a localized MM Intensity of VII in Mexico City. Adjacent areas were MM VI. These intensities resulted from a magnitude M_s = 7.5 earthquake in Acapulco on 28 July 1957. Intensity VII is below the threshold of damage to well built structures, however, hundreds of buildings were damaged in Mexico City during that earthquake presumably because of poor construction.

The Acapulco earthquake of 1957 was taken as the basis for earthquake design in Mexico City on the assumption that it recorded the worst that could happen in Mexico City.

Using a catalogue of earthquakes in Mexico from the beginning of this century to 1968, Esteva (1970) prepared probabilistic contour maps for Mexico in terms of acceleration and velocity for 50-, 100- and 500-year return periods. His values for the area of Mexico City are:

Return Period Years	Peak Acceleration cm/sec^2	Peak Velocity cm/sec
50	80	12
100	100	15
500	200	30

Esteva's values were for ground that is very little deformable, such as compact conglomerates, or ground that we will discuss later as hard sites.

Esteva cautioned in his paper that even the 500-year recurrence values are not conservative enough for use with nuclear power plants or other constructions for which possible failure would be enormously costly.

There was valuable information at hand that pointed to the long predominant period of 2 sec that was experienced in most areas of Mexico City during the 19 September 1985 earthquake (see Prince, et al., Informe IPS-10D, 1985). Rascon and others (1977) published the response spectra for a series of earthquakes that were recorded in Mexico City between 1961 and 1968. These earthquakes, with their predominant periods and site conditions, whether soil or rock, are listed in Table 2. The preponderance of a predominant period of 2 to 3 seconds on the soil sites is striking. On rock, the predominant period also contains motions of two seconds but those are part of a wider range of values from 0.6 to 2 sec. Thus, there is a strong site dependence for the predominant period of earthquake shaking in Mexico City in which the shorter periods seen in the rock are quickly attenuated and the long periods are accentuated. Changes in the horizontal directional components (E-W versus N-S, etc.) did not affect the predominant periods significantly.

During the 28 August 1973 earthquake, a predominant period of 5 sec was measured at the Palacio de los Depaxtes (see Faccioli and Flores, 1975). The record had about 10 cycles of sinusoidal and monochromatic wave forms. For the 19 September 1985 earthquake, the largest recorded predominant period was 3.5 to 4.5 sec at the principal office of the Central de Abastos. These two records are the only ones that recorded predominant periods of 4.5 to 5.0 sec. Elsewhere, the recurrence of 2 sec periods for earthquakes of different magnitudes, different focal depths and different distances from their sources

Table 1

Peak Accelerations (cm/sec^2) in Mexico City on Soil and Rock

Faccioli and Flores (1975)

Date	Rock			Soil			Amplification Factor	
	Site	Component		Site	Component			
		EW	NS		EW	NS	EW	NS
6/7/64	University City	14.43	20.45	Nonoalco-Tlatelolco (Patio Hidalgo Bldg.)	42.72	36.68	2.96	1.79
8/23/65	University City	2.78	4.04	Nonoalco-Tlatelolco (Basement Atizapan Bldg.)	9.29	21.16	3.34	5.23
2/8/68	University City	11.24	14.37	Nonoalco-Tlatelolco (Patio Atizapan Bldg.)	44.07	30.68	3.92	2.13

Table 2

Predominant Periods of Earthquakes Recorded in Mexico City,
1961-1968 from Rascon and Others (1977)

Date of Earthquake	Location of Record in Mexico City	Predominant Period Horizontal Motion sec	Site
10 Dec 61	Central Alameda	2-3	Soil
11 May 62	" "	2-3	Soil
19 May 62	" "	2-3	Soil
30 Nov 62	" "	0.7-2	Soil
6 Jul 64	Manuel Gonzalez Bldg	2-3	Soil
	Patio, Hidalgo Bldg	2-3	Soil
	Basement, Hidalgo Bldg	2-3	Soil
23 Aug 65	Basement, Atizapan Bldg	2-3	Soil
	University	0.6-2	Rock
9 Dec 65	Basement, Atizapan Bldg	2-3	Soil
1 Jul 68	Patio, Atizapan Bldg	2-3	Soil
	Basement, Atizapan Bldg	2-3	Soil
2 Aug 68	Patio, Atizapan Bldg	2-3	Soil
	Basement, Atizapan Bldg	2-3	Soil
	University	2-3	Rock

suggests a strong site dependence in the period that very likely would prevail at these two sites as well.

The locations for strong motion records in Mexico City made during the 19 September 1985 earthquake are shown in Fig 1. The Universidad locations are on hard volcanic rock. Tacubaya is in an area of an alluvial fan but is founded on hard material. Víveros de Coyoacán is on 10 m of soft alluvial soils overlying rock. SCT and Central de Abastos are on soft clays of the lake deposits. The peak accelerations and velocities recorded at these sites on 19 September 1985 are shown in Table 3. Tables 4 and 5 show the amplification factors respectively for accelerations and velocities. Amplification factors for accelerations vary from 1.17 to 4.72. They were lowest at Víveros de Coyoacán and highest at SCT. The amplification factors for velocities were 1.20 to 6.20 and these followed the pattern set for the accelerations.

The above mentioned variations in predominant period between rock and lake bed deposits appears to result from a filtering action when wave motions enter the soil from the rock. The most pronounced monochromatic and long period waves in the lake bed soils are associated with the thickest deposits. There may be an effect noted here that is brought on by the shape of the basin.

The evidence is that motions in the Valley of Mexico from future earthquakes will result in effects similar to those already experienced. Specifically, the soils in the lake bed will experience an amplification of up to 5X the peak acceleration and velocity values in rock and the wave forms in the soils will be monochromatic with predominant periods of 2 to 5 sec and possibly more.

Modelling of Earthquake Ground Motions

On the basis of the foregoing observations, we have a starting point for modelling earthquake ground motions in the Valley of Mexico. The principles apply also to analogous situations elsewhere.

Since we are modelling subduction zone earthquakes, it is appropriate to bring in data from other parts of the world where there are many more records. Our comparison will be with data from subduction zone earthquakes in Japan. A group of charts showing earthquake magnitude (M_s), and distance from source

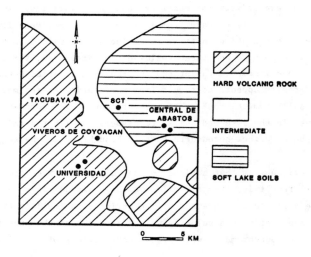

FIG. 1.-General Site Conditions and
Location of Strong Motion Instruments
in Mexico City

Table 3

Site Conditions, Peak Accelerations and Velocities in Mexico City
for the 19 Sep 1985 Earthquake

Site	Installation	Peak Hor Accel, cm/sec^2		Peak Hor Vel, cm/sec	
		E-W	N-S	E-W	N-S
Universidad:	Mesa Vibradora	39	34	11	9
Volcanic rock	Jardin	35	32	9	11
(Hard)	Laboratorio	35	28	9	10
Tacubaya:		33	34	10	14
Alluvial fan					
(Hard)					
Viveros de Coyoacán:		42	44	12	12
10 m alluvial soil on rock					
(Soft)					
SCT: Lake deposits (Soft)		170	98	62	37
Central de Abastos:	Oficina	80	69	42	35
30 m + clay	Frigorifico	95	81	38	25
(Soft)					

Table 4

Amplification Factors for Peak Accelerations (cm/sec^2) in

Mexico City on Soil and Rock for the 19 Sep 1985

Earthquake

Rock			Soil			Amplification Factor	
	Component			Component			
Site	E-W	N-S	Site	E-W	N-S	E-W	N-S
Universidad-Tacubaya Average	36	32	Viveros de Coyoacán	42	44	1.17	1.38
			SCT	170	98	4.72	3.06
			Central de Abastos Average	88	75	2.44	2.34

Table 5

Amplification Factors for Peak Velocities (cm/sec) in Mexico City

on Soil and Rock for the 19 Sep 1985 Earthquake

Rock			Soil			Amplification Factor	
	Component			Component			
Site	E-W	N-S	Site	E-W	N-S	E-W	N-S
Universidad-Tacubaya Average	10	11	Viveros de Coyoacán	12	12	1.20	1.09
			SCT	62	37	6.20	3.36
			Central de Abastos Average	40	30	4.00	2.73

for parameters of horizontal motions is in the process of being prepared by
E. L. Krinitzksy, Frank K. Chang and Otto W. Nuttli. These are based on a
selected collection of 229 accelerograms. The charts shown here are preliminary. The data will be published later.

A distinction to keep in mind is that the motions recorded for subduction zone earthquakes are generally different from those of shallower earthquakes. A separation can be made in terms of focal depths. Subduction zone
is taken here to be with a focal depth of 20 km or greater. Shallow plate
boundary earthquakes are those with focal depths of 19 km or less.

Our experience is that the shallower earthquakes have higher peak values
near their sources and their motions attenuate more rapidly with distance than
do the subduction zone earthquakes.

Comparison of Subduction Zone Earthquake Ground Motions and Those of Shallow Plate Boundary Earthquakes

A comparison of horizontal acceleration from Mexico City (19 September
1985) with those of subduction zone earthquakes in Japan for M_S = 7.0 to 7.8
is shown in Fig 2.

There is a large interdispersion of data from hard and soft sites in
Japan.

Hard is taken to be rock and stiff soil that is 16 m or less in thickness over rock. Soft is soft to medium stiff clay and all deep cohesionless
soils greater than 16 m in thickness. The boundary between hard and soft is
at a shear wave velocity of 400 m/sec.

The Mexico City data falls within the range of dispersion observed in
Japan. There is a comparable case also for velocities as shown in Fig 3.

The Mexico City data is distinctive in the spread that it shows between
hard and soft sites. What appears to be the case in Mexico City is a predictable site dependence that is not as apparent in Japan because of the nature of
the data collection.

Fig 4 shows hard site horizontal accelerations in Mexico City compared
with the Krinitzsky-Chang-Nuttli charts for subduction zone earthquake motions
at hard sites with values of mean + σ or 84 percent of the spread in the data.
The Mexico data fit excellently for M = 8.0 at a distance of 400 km from the

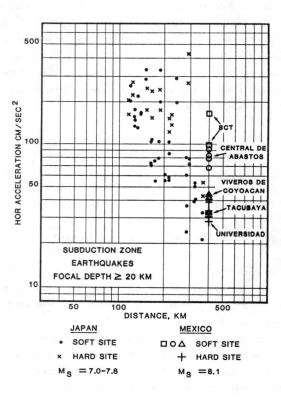

FIG. 2.-Comparison of Horizontal
Accelerations versus Distance from
Source in KM for Subduction Zone
Earthquakes, Japan and Mexico City

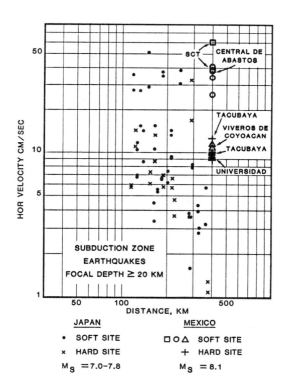

FIG. 3.-Comparison of Horizontal
Velocities versus Distance from Source
in KM for Subduction Zone Earthquakes,
Japan and Mexico City

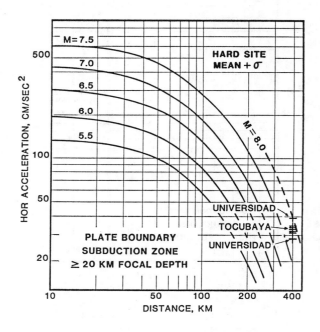

FIG. 4.-Hard Site Accelerations in
Mexico City Compared with Krinitzsky-
Chang-Nuttli Charts for Subduction
Zone Earthquakes

source. Fig 5 shows the same values for shallow plate boundary earthquakes.
Note that the Mexico City values lie considerably off the curves.

Fig 6 shows that the fit noted for subduction zone accelerations at hard
sites does not extend to soft sites. There is a large spread in the data from
Mexico City that is not suitably evaluated in these charts. A comparison for
soft sites of shallow plate boundary accelerations in Fig 7 is even more
greatly different.

Figs 8 and 9 show comparisons of the horizontal velocities in Mexico City
with hard site subduction zone and shallow earthquakes respectively. In these
cases the velocities do not fit the charts. Figures 10 and 11 show comparable
comparisons for soft sites. The velocities for soft sites in Mexico City are
even more greatly unrelated to the data in the charts.

Modelling Peak Earthquake Ground Motions
for the Valley of Mexico

At this point, an empirical working relationship can be proposed for
assigning earthquake motions for the Valley of Mexico.

We may observe that horizontal accelerations for hard sites for the Valley of Mexico corresponds to values from Japan. Horizontal accelerations for
soft sites are higher but are within the range of indicated dispersion in the
data. When we come to the velocities, we observe higher values in Mexico, but
here again they are within the range in dispersion of such data and the Mexico
earthquake is of a greater magnitude (M_S = 8.1) than the recorded events in
Japan (M_S = 7.0 - 7.8). Also there is a site dependence in the Valley of Mexico. The site dependence appears to be predictable from one earthquake to the
next.

Thus, we can relate Mexico City predictably to charts for hard site
accelerations from subduction zone earthquakes. Based on that relation, we
can use the site dependent observations in Mexico City to shape the accelerations for soft sites and the velocities for both hard and soft sites.

Missing however, are the effects of nearby earthquakes with shallow
focal depths should they occur. Such earthquakes would introduce motions that
are significantly different from those with sources in the subduction zone.

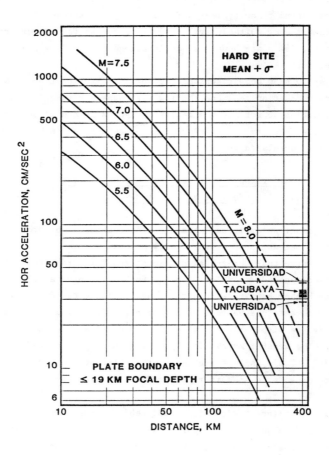

FIG. 5.–Hard Site Accelerations in
Mexico City Compared with Krinitzsky–
Chang–Nuttli Charts for Shallow
Plate Boundary Earthquakes

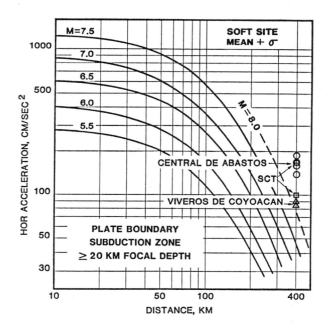

FIG. 6.-Soft Site Accelerations in
Mexico City Compared with Krinitzsky-
Chang-Nuttli Charts for Subduction
Zone Earthquakes

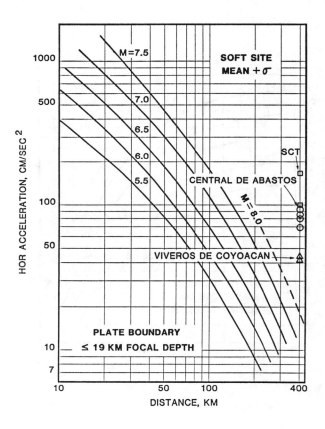

FIG. 7.-Soft Site Accelerations in
Mexico City Compared with Krinitzsky-
Chang-Nuttli Charts for Shallow
Plate Boundary Earthquakes

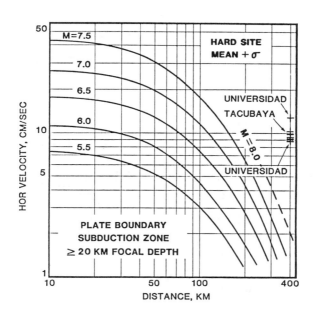

FIG. 8.-Hard Site Velocities in Mexico City Compared with Krinitzsky-Chang- Nuttli Charts for Subduction Zone Earthquakes

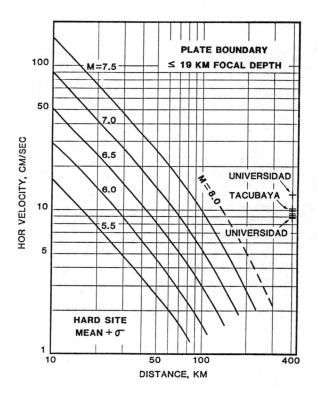

FIG. 9.–Hard Site Velocities in
Mexico City Compared with Krinitzsky-
Chang-Nuttli Charts for Shallow
Plate Boundary Earthquakes

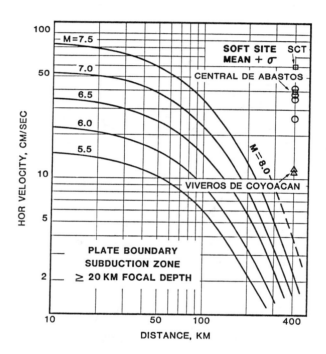

FIG. 10.-Soft Site Velocities in
Mexico City Compared with Krinitzsky-
Chang-Nuttli Charts for Subduction
Zone Earthquakes

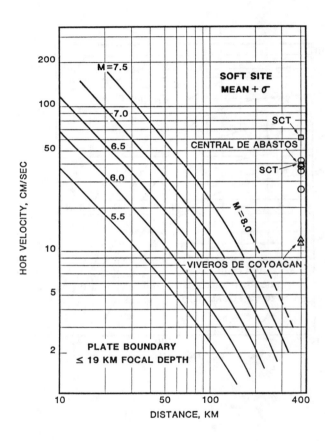

FIG. 11.-Soft Site Velocities in
Mexico City Compared with Krinitzsky-
Chang-Nuttli Charts for Shallow
Plate Boundary Earthquakes

Conclusions

Motions in Mexico City can be related dependably to charts for horizontal accelerations at hard sites for earthquake magnitude and distance from source that are being developed from Japanese subduction zone data. For velocities at hard sites, and for all motions on soft sites, there are known site dependent relationships in Mexico City that should be used to shape predicted peak motions.

Earthquakes with shallow focal depths and sources near to Mexico City may provide motions that are significantly different from those of subduction zone earthquakes. Potentials for these shallow earthquakes need to be evaluated.

REFERENCES

Esteva M., Luis, 1970, Regionalizacion Sísmica de Mexico para Fines de
Ingeniería, No. 246, Instituto de Ingeniería, Universidad Nacional Autonoma de
Mexico, pp 229-246.

Faccioli, Ezio, and Jorge Ramirez Flores, 1975, Respuestas Sísmicas Maximas
Probables en las Arcillas de la Ciudad de Mexico, No. 359, Instituto de
Ingeniería, Universidad Nacional Autonoma de Mexico, 34 pp.

Figueroa A., Jesus, 1963, Isosístas de Macrosísmos Mexicanos, No. 67,
Instituto de Ingeniería, Universidad Nacional Autonoma de Mexico, pp 45-67.

Prince, J., and R. Quaas, E. Mena, L. Alcántara, D. Almora, A. Barreto,
C. Carmona, R. Carrera, G. Chavez, R. Delgado, S. Medina, M. A. Oñate,
P. Pérez A., M. Torres, R. Vázquez, J. M. Velasco. 1985. Espectros de las
Componentes Horizontales Registradas por los Acelerografos Digitales de Mexico
D. F. Sismo del 19 de Septiembre de 1985. Acelerogramas en Viveros y en
Tacubaya, Informe IPS-10D, Instituto de Ingeniería, Universidad Nacional
Autonoma de Mexico, 26 paginas.

Rascon, O., M. Chavez, L. Alonzo, V. Palencia. 1977. Regístros y Espectros
de Temblores en las Ciudades de Mexico y Acapulco, 1961-1968, No. 385,
Instituto de Ingeniería, Universidad Nacional Autonoma de Mexico,
Figures 77-122.

EFFECTS OF THE 1985 EARTHQUAKE IN
LAZARO CARDENAS, MICH.

By Enrique Santoyo[1] and Carlos Gutiérrez[2]

ABSTRACT: An account is presented of a geotechnical survey made shortly after the major earthquake of September 19, 1985 (magnitude 8.1) at the industrial port of Lázaro Cárdenas in the state of Michoacán, Mexico, to assess the damage and the behavior of foundations and structures, particularly those at El Cayacal and Enmedio islands and at the urban zone. Remedial measures are suggested.

INTRODUCTION

On Thursday September 19, 1985 a very strong earthquake occurred with a Richter magnitude of 8.1 and an epicenter located across the coast of Michoacán state, close to the mouth of the Balsas River in the Pacific coast. The focus was traced 30 km offshore from the port of Lázaro Cárdenas. The most important aftershock of this earthquake took place on September 20 with a magnitude of 7.5.

In order to perform a geotechnical survey of the effects induced by the earthquake on the industrial complex of Lázaro Cárdenas, a field trip was made on September 28 and 29, 1985 covering the islands of El Cayacal and Enmedio and the urban zone of Lázaro Cárdenas (Fig. 1). A summary of the report is presented herein.

LOCAL GEOTECHNICAL FEATURES

Stratigraphy.- The geotechnical studies carried out at El Cayacal and Enmedio islands in the mouth of the Balsas River, have shown that the gravel and boulder content of the subsoil is larger than the percentage determined at the site of the steel mill of SICARTSA; when compared with the zone of SICARTSA, it has been found that at both islands the superficial sitly sands, deposited in more recent times, tend to be less dense, and close to the shoreline they are found predominantly in a loose state.

---

[1] General Manager, TCG Geotecnia, S.A., Manuel M. Ponce No. 143, 01020-México, D.F., MEXICO

[2] Senior Engineer, TGC Geotecnia, S.A.

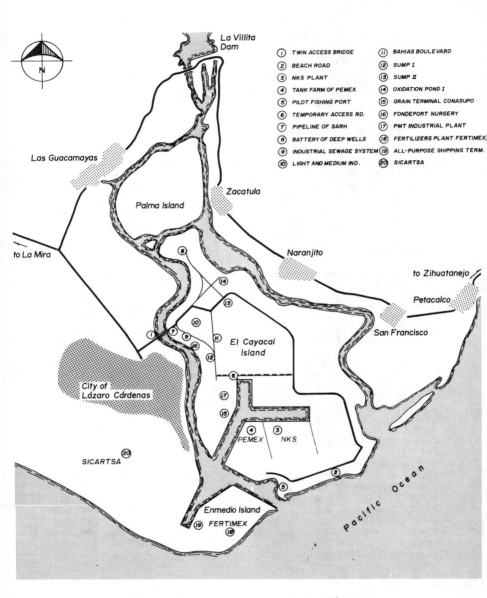

① TWIN ACCESS BRIDGE	⑪ BAHIAS BOULEVARD
② BEACH ROAD	⑫ SUMP I
③ NKS PLANT	⑬ SUMP II
④ TANK FARM OF PEMEX	⑭ OXIDATION POND I
⑤ PILOT FISHING PORT	⑮ GRAIN TERMINAL CONASUPO
⑥ TEMPORARY ACCESS RD.	⑯ FONDEPORT NURSERY
⑦ PIPELINE OF SARH	⑰ PMT INDUSTRIAL PLANT
⑧ BATTERY OF DEEP WELLS	⑱ FERTILIZERS PLANT FERTIMEX
⑨ INDUSTRIAL SEWAGE SYSTEM	⑲ ALL-PURPOSE SHIPPING TERM.
⑩ LIGHT AND MEDIUM IND.	⑳ SICARTSA

FIG. I.- General Layout of Lázaro Cárdenas Industrial Port, and Vicinity

An important geotechnical feature is constituted by the dumped fills formed by dredged materials on top of which the industrial complex has been built. Generally speaking, these landfills were placed with no compaction control whatsoever, thus leaving behind the coarse particles like boulders, gravel and coarse sand close to the discharge points of the pipes carrying the dredged materials whereas the fine sands, silts and clays flowed towards the tidelands. Subsequently, when these tidelands were filled with granular materials, isolated lenses of soft and loose deposits became trapped under the fill.

Dynamic Behavior of the Soils.- The stratigraphical sequence found at the site suggests that settlements are likely to occur due to the rearrangement of the particles constituting the granular fills when an earthquake strikes, and to an eventual liquefaction of the natural deposits of saturated loose silty sand found at shallow depths.

These phenomena were observed at the industrial fertilizers plant of FERTIMEX as a result of an earthquake of March, 1979. However, at that time it was not possible to assess the magnitude of the settlements induced due to the lack of a reliable benchmark; only an account was made of the cracks and sand boils from which water, sand and clay lumps from the dredged material erupted.

During the reconnaissance of the effects induced by the September 1985 earthquake, additional settlements of the granular fills and local evidences of liquefaction were observed at the islands of Enmedio and El Cayacal, as well as at the second stage of the SICARTSA plant construction; this liquefaction phenomenon was more conspicuous close to the shoreline of both islands.

SEISMIC EFFECTS

The effects of the earthquakes were appreciated in the whole area of Lázaro Cárdenas. At the FERTIMEX plant permanent deformations of the ground surface can be noticed from which it can be inferred that the seismic waves were 45 to 60 m (148 to 197 ft) in length, with an amplitude of about 20 cm (8 in.) and a horizontal displacement in the order of 50 cm (20 in.).

The regional subsidence of the natural ground surface could be estimated to be of no less than 3 cm (1 1/4 in.) if the dislodging of the supports for the deep well pumps of the Ministry of Agriculture and Hydraulic Resources (SARH) is taken as a reference point. On the other hand, maximum settlements of 30 cm (12 in.) were observed at a zone underlaid by the loosely compacted dumped fills of granular material, with respect to the structures supported by deep foundations.

At the earth and rockfill dam of La Villita, located at a
distance of about 13 km (8 miles) from the mouth of the
Balsas River, settlements recorded at the crest were of
about 20 cm (8 in.) and appreciable deformations of the
rockfill slopes were observed, particularly at the upstream
slope, as evidenced by the emergence of 30 to 40 cm (12 to
14 in.) of the piezometer standpipes.

Another earthquake-induced phenomenon was the encroachment
of land by the sea; the wave height recorded at Lázaro Cárdenas was about 1 m (3.3 ft) and it was sufficient to
cover about 200 m (656 ft) along the sea shore, with tree
trunks and debris.

The main effects caused by the earthquake on the infrastructure works and industrial plants of the zone are described in what follows; the location of all the structures
referred to is shown in Fig. 1.

El Cayacal Island

Access Bridge to El Cayacal Island.- The twin bridge shows
the following structural damages: (1) The approach embankments on the island side are longitudinally fissured, and
water and sand boiled from the fissures (Fig. 2); (2) the

FIG. 2.- *Pavement Failure
of the Approach
Road to El Cayacal
Island Bridge*

slopes protecting the abutments failed; (3) the coupling of several columns with their capitals failed, apparently due to flexocompression; (4) the ends of the beams have slight fractures probably due to the pounding between them; and (5) some of the protruding edges of the capitals are damaged.

The inspection of the structure as a whole suggests that the foundation did not settle appreciably and consequently it seems reasonable to strengthen the structure by means of pouring new annular columns around the old ones and to join them structurally with their capitals. It will be necessary to check the structural integrity of the columns with respect to their foundation footings.

Beach Road .- This important road embankmemt was constructed by filling a tideland without excavating the full depth of the underlying soft and loose deposits; it will be the access road to the plants of NKS and PEMEX (Fig. 1). On one side of the embankment a provisional pipeline of raw water was placed and on the opposite side there runs the high voltage transmission line. At the eastern end of this beach road there is a 300-m (984-ft) long stretch where important longitudinal cracks were produced as well as appreciable settlement of the crest. This behavior can be related to the liquefaction of the fine sand stratum underlying the embankment, a phenomenon which was confirmed by the sand boils along the cracks and by the lateral displacement of the slopes (Figs. 3 and 4). The raw water pipeline placed superficially was completely dislodged due to the movements of the embankment.

FIG. 3.- *Failure of the Beach Road*
Besides a Tideland

FIG. 4.- Close-Up of the Liquefaction Phenomenon at the Embankment Shortly After the Earthquake of September 19, 1985

The uncoupling of the pipes used as perpendicular drains to the embankment could be appreciated through the cracks, thus rendering them useless.

The foundation elements of several transmission towers underwent differential settlements that made them out of alignment; in addition, the sand and gravel placed at each tower platform settled up to 20 cm (8 in.). These deformations were in part due to the sea encroachment which affected some of the transmission towers.

Industrial Plant of NKS. - The main structures of this plant are suppported by piers (Fig. 5) whereas the largest and heaviest equipment sit on top of concrete box foundations. The light machines and equipment are founded upon superficial rafts. This variety of foundation types and of the stresses transmitted to the soil, together with the heterogeneity of the subsoil, can explain the occurrence of differential settlements of up to 30 cm (12 in.) (Fig. 6). It is evident that the recompaction of the loose fill and the liquefaction of the superficial sand were the source of the settlements.

As a result of these effects, the equipment with shallow foundations and that resting on top of concrete boxes or shallow piles, suffered settlements which will make it necessary in some cases to level them up and eventually to

FIG. 5.- Heavy Equipment Supported by Piers Showing no Damage. Industrial Plant of NKS

FIG. 6.- Differential Settlement Between the Concrete Box Foundation and the Surrounding Floor Caused by the Earthquake Inside an Aisle of the NKS Plant

underpin them; the couplings between machinery supported by different types of foundations were dislodged or sheared off.

The roofs of asbestos sheets were unscathed; however those sheets placed vertically were almost totally broken due to the lateral displacements induced by the earthquake.

Tank Farm of Petróleos Mexicanos (PEMEX).- The concrete floor slabs surrounding the tanks showed small movements in both the horizontal and vertical directions; however, they were sufficient to dislodge the slabs and their joints through which water and liquefied sand sprouted.

Pilot Fishing Port.- The wharf has no apparent damages; there only exist faint evidence of liquefaction of the ground behind the structure.

Temporary Access Road.- This road connects the first construction stage of the main boulevard with the beach road; only a few minor cracks were observed.

Pipeline of SARH.- This raw water pipeline is formed by concrete pipes 1.8-m (72-in.) in diameter with bell joints and Neoprene O'Rings and it suffered settlements large enough to dislodge the joints (Fig. 7). However, it can

FIG. 7.- *Pipeline of SARH (1.8 m (72 in.) Dia meter), Dislodged by the Seismic - In duced Movements*

be assumed that this type of problem occurred predominantly at the crossings with river channels and at the zones with poorly compacted fills, particularly if the pipeline was empty when the earthquake struck.

Battery of Deep Wells and Pipeline.- Three wells, representative of the battery of deep wells, were inspected; it could be observed that the pedestals of the three pumps had evidence of regional subsidence of about 3 cm (1 1/4 in.) thus inducing tensile stresses in the horizontal pipes which in turn tilted the motors of the pumps.

Along the line collecting the water from the wells (manifold), settlements occurred at the fill covering the trench excavated for the pipeline; this fact is of no importance unless it induces rupture of the pipeline.

Industrial Sewage System.- Three manholes of the sewage system corresponding to the first stretch of the Boulevard across Sump No. 1 were inspected; it was observed that the water level is above the pipeline and it probably coincides with the phreatic level. A survey was made of the ground surface to check for evidences of problems in the subsoil; only small fissures were detected through which small amounts of liquefied sand erupted, although at points randomly distributed.

Park for Light and Medium Industries.- The site where this industrial park will be developed is at present a barren land covered with granular fills, where no buildings have yet been constructed; for this reason no significant observations are available at this site.

"Bahías" Boulevard and Railroad Embankment.- Longitudinal fissures were observed at the side berms as well as settlement of the trenches excavated for the pipelines crossing the Boulevard.

Sumps I and II.- The crest of the slopes of the excavations made for constructing both sumps, shows fissures evidencing an incipient failure; since at present the excavations reach only a shallow depth, their eventual failure would be hardly important.

Oxidation Pond No. I.- The site has been completely cleared and construction of the peripheral dyke has started. No evidence of either fissuring or liquefaction was observed at the ground surface; however, should the dyke had been already completed, it is possible that some damages could have occurred as concluded from the geotechnical studies made for oxidation ponds I and II.

Grain Terminal of CONASUPO.- Structural failures of the lower columns of the tower built on top of the silos were observed (Fig. 8), as well as at the supports of the conveyor (Fig. 9) and at the joints between column and girders of the structure for grain handling (Fig. 10). It was not possible to inspect the interior of the terminal and therefore no assessment of the foundation conditions could be made.

FIG. 8.-   *Grain Terminal of CONASUPO. A Complete Floor*
Collapsed Between the Silos and the Tower Due
to Column Failure

FIG. 9.-   *Collapse of the Structure Supporting*
the Conveyor Belt

FIG. IO.- *Seismic Effects on Columns with Cold Construction Joints and Absence of Stirrups. Grain Terminal of CONASUPO*

FONDEPORT Nursery .- This site is of particular interest because a good number of fissures were observed due to the loose state of the superficial material and to its closeness to the river.

PMT Industrial Plant and Educational Facilities. The PMT Plant and the buildings for the education institution "Centros de Capacitación Marítima Portuaria y de Estudios Tecnológicos del Mar" were only inspected from the outside and no evidence of structural damage was observed.

Enmedio Island

Fertilizers Plant of FERTIMEX.- The most conspicuous effects of the earthquake were observed at the site of this plant, particularly in the zone close to the beach; the liquefaction phenomenon affected the ground in the vicinity of the office building and at the access roads to the expansion site of the plant, where permanent deformations in both the vertical and horizontal directions were evident, the former with a magnitude of about 20 cm (8 in.) and the latter of up to 50 cm (20 in.) (Figs. 11 and 12).

It should be mentioned that as a result of the earthquake of March 1979 when the construction of this plant was under way, ground liquefaction also occurred, mostly concentrated on where at that time was still a tideland; this zone was

FIG. 11.-   Pavement Cracks and Settlement of the Shallow
            Foundation of a Light-Weight Structure, with
            Evidences of Liquefaction. Notice the Ground
            Waving. FERTIMEX Plant

FIG. 12.- Waving of the Railroad Tracks at the
           Entrance to the FERTIMEX Plant

subsequently filled and at present it is part of the site
where the plant will be expanded. During the earthquake
of 1985 sand boils were again observed specially near the
beach (Fig. 13) either isolated or associated to the fissures, whereas inland the sand boils always appear as a
result of the ground cracking. On the other hand, there is
scarce evidence of liquefaction effects within the plant
itself founded upon piles, a fact which demonstrates that
the pile driving increased the relative density of the sand
and reduced the susceptibility to liquefaction. In spite
of this reasoning, differential settlements are evident
between the structures and the equipment supported by different pile groups, particularly if they are compared with
the equipment resting on shallow foundations.

FIG. 13.- *Typical Sandboil at the Expansion Site of the*
FERTIMEX Plant Close to the Shoreline

During the earthquake of 1979 and once again as a consequence of the last seismic event of 1985, some fasteners of
the secondary structural elements of the truss members
failed and consequently many asbestos roof sheets were
broken; in addition, fissuring of pavements, dislodging of
sewer mains and the collapse of trenches dug for cables and
ducts was also observed.

All-Purpose Shipping Terminal.- The docks supported by
piers did not show any apparent damage; on the contrary,
the container yard had a general subsidence of about 40 cm
(16 in.) with maximum values of 60 cm (24 in.) (Fig. 14).
At the port warehouse, having a steel structure resting on

shallow foundations, the end walls constructed with mortar
blocks and of reinforced concrete frame, were broken.
Another type of damage suffered by this harbor facility,
was the large deformations of the railroad tracks which in
some stretches will require complete reconstruction.

*FIG. 14.- Subsidence of the Container Dock at the All-Purpose
Terminal, Induced by the Earthquake. Enmedio Island*

Urban Zone of Lázaro Cárdenas.- Several buildings in the
city collapsed, whereas others had structural damages, including a hotel which was also damaged during the earthquake of 1979. Generally speaking, it can be observed that
the structural failures were caused primarily by the lack
of transversal reinforcing steel, and to a large degree to
the absence of stirrups at the intersection of the columns
with the girders, as well as to the insufficient wind
bracing in buildings three-stories high or taller. (Fig. 15)

CONCLUSIONS

As a result of the earthquake of September 19, 1985, it
could be observed once again at the zone of the industrial
port of Lázaro Cárdenas, Mich. the local effects of liquefaction and subsidence of the granular fills, particularly
in the vicinity of the shoreline of the islands of Enmedio
and El Cayacal, as evidenced by the occurrence of cracks
and sand boils.

On what refers to the behavior of structures constructed at
the site, settlements of the ground surface and of the

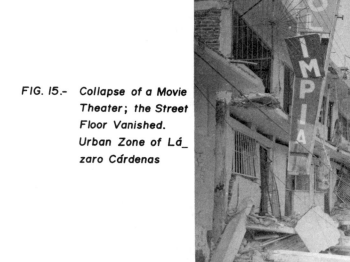

FIG. 15.- *Collapse of a Movie Theater; the Street Floor Vanished. Urban Zone of Lá_zaro Cárdenas*

granular fills and embankments, were induced in the earth-work by poor compaction procedures. Structural damages are evident at some of the industrial plants, although most of the damages can be repaired to restore them to their origi-nal operating conditions. However, the reconstruction works should be carefully supervised, particularly those related to the infrastructure and to public services such as access roads, electricity, water and sewage systems.

ACKNOWLEDGEMENTS

Grateful appreciation is due to the "Fondo Nacional para los Desarrollos Portuarios" (FONDEPORT), Mexico, for its permission to publish the material contained in this paper.

EARTHQUAKE RESPONSE OF LA VILLITA DAM

By Francisco González-Valencia[1]

ABSTRACT: Due to the recent industrial and housing developments at the port of Lázaro Cárdenas, located 13 km (8 miles) downstream of La Villita Dam, at the mouth of the Balsas River, the hazard of a dam failure due to the seismic activity in the zone in analized based on instrumental data of the dam behavior recorded after several strong earthquakes.

INTRODUCTION

The earth and rockfill embankment of La Villita Dam is 60-m (196.8-ft) high, with a crest length of 420 m (1377.6 ft), a slightly curved axis and external slopes of 2.5:1. The maximum cross section and the type and zoning of materials constituting the dam are depicted in Fig. 1.

The subsoil at the damsite comprises formations from the Tertiary constituted by pseudo-stratified layers of andesite and andesitic breccias showing a NE-SW strike and a pronounced dip towards the SE. These strata have a thickness varying from a few centimeters to several meters; they are affected by a strong fissuring along a general NE-SW direction and dip towards the NW (Fig. 2). The thickness of the weathered foundation material is conspicuously greater at the left bank and the zone has been subjected to strong tectonic stresses. The alluvial deposit at the river bottom reaches a thickness of 70 m (230 ft) and it is formed by boulders, gravel, sand and silt.

Construction of the dam was concluded in 1967 and since then it has been instrumentally monitored; its behavior has been reported elsewhere (Refs. 2, 3, 10 and 11). However, the structural safety of the embankment evolves with time not only due to environmental factors and to the evolution of the material properties but also as a result of the criteria and methods of analysis used. The response of the structure when subjected to strong earthquakes is presented herein and the hazard of a dam failure is discussed.

SEISMIC EXPERIENCE AT THE DAMSITE

The damsite lies at a distance of 13 km (8 miles) from the mouth of the Balsas River at the Pacific Ocean, in the southwestern part of Mexico (coordinates 18.04°N and 102.18°W).

---

1 Head, Data Processing Office, Comisión Federal de Electricidad (Federal Commission of Electricity, Mexico), Augusto Rodin 265, 03720-México, D.F., MEXICO

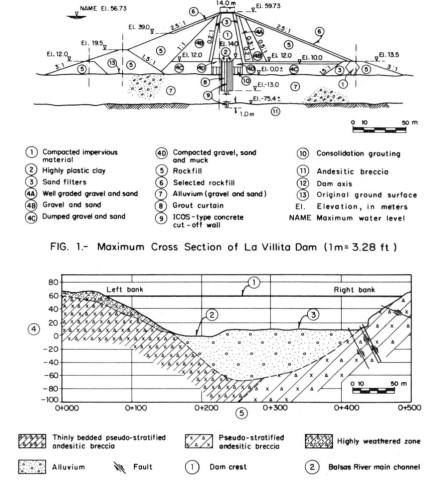

FIG. 1.- Maximum Cross Section of La Villita Dam (1m= 3.28 ft)

FIG. 2.- Geological Profile of La Villita Damsite (1m= 3.28 ft)

The zone is highly seismic due to the subduction phenomenon of the Cocos Plate thrusting under the North American Plate along Mexico's Pacific coast. Assuming a square area 4° on each side centered around the dam, the average recurrence of earthquakes with a magnitude $M_s \geq 7$

is slightly over 13 years whereas for temblors with a magnitude $M_s \geq 5$ is of only nine months, which represents a frequency one and a half times higher than at Southern California (Ref. 2).

Table 1 presents the number of seismic events recorded at a distance of less than 100 km (62.15 miles) from the dam and it can be observed the variation of the earthquake activity in the vicinity of the dam since 1975.

TABLE 1.- Number of Earthquakes Recorded in the Vicinity[a] of La Villita Dam from 1975 to 1985[b]

Year	Richter magnitude				Number of annual events
	$M_s \leq 3$	$3 \leq M_s \leq 4$	$4 \leq M_s \leq 5$	$M_s \geq 5$	
1975	1	1	4	3	9
1976	0	6	26	5	37
1977	0	10	28	9	47
1978	3	8	21	9	41
1979	0	14	77	13	104
1980	1	28	21	2	52
1981	21	84	36	3	144
1982	2	55	9	0	66
1983	0	21	5	1	27
1984	1	25	2	0	28
1985	79	291	28	4	402
TOTAL	108	543	257	49	957

a   Between latitude 17.5° N and 18.5° N, and longitude 101.5° W and 102.5° W.
b   Source : Ref. 4.

A summary of the most conspicuous seismic parameters recorded at the dam is shown in Table 2 and they will be analyzed in what follows. The detailed description of these events can be consulted in Refs. 2 and 9.

The strongest earthquake in the history of the dam corresponds to S5

TABLE 2.- Parameters of Major Earthquakes Occurred in the Vicinity of La Villita Dam

Earthquake denomination	Date	Richter[a] magnitude	Duration (sec)	Focal depth (km)	Distance[b] from the dam (km)	Accelerations recorded[c] (gals)		
						Crest	Base	Right bank
(1)	(2)	(3)	(4)	(5)	(6)	(7)	(8)	(9)
S1	Oct 11, 1975	4.9	14.1	33	52	343	82	72
S2	Nov 15, 1975	5.9	19.5	33	10	209	85	39
S3	Mar 14, 1979	7.6	31.3	60	121	371	133	17
S4	Oct 25, 1981	7.3	71.6	33	31	423	_d	_d
S5	Sep 19, 1985	8.1	76.1	30	58	696	_e	120
S6[f]	Sep 21, 1985	7.5	63.9	33	61	212[g]	_e	41[g]

a   Source : PDE Bulletin : periodic publication of the NEIS.
b   Calculated from data published in Ref. 4.
c   Transversal component (river direction).
d   Data not presented due to lack of reliable records.
e   Instrument removed.
f   Assumed to be the main aftershock of seism S5.
g   Preliminary data. Source : E. Mena, Institute of Engineering, UNAM, personal communication.
Note : 1 km = 0.62 miles

(September 19, 1985) in Table 2. The accelerograms recorded at the dam crest during this temblor are shown in Fig. 3 and the damped response spectra in Fig. 4. During this event, five instrumental stations placed near to the dam in extremely competent bedrock, recorded accelerations ranging from 120 to 150 gals whereas at the Zacatula Station, located 3 km (1.9 miles) downstream from the dam on a dense silty clay formation, a maximum acceleration of 271 gals was registered (Refs. 1 and 7).

Unfortunately not all the records of the accelerographs installed at the dam were available and therefore it was not possible to assess the effects of the local geology on the damping and/or amplification

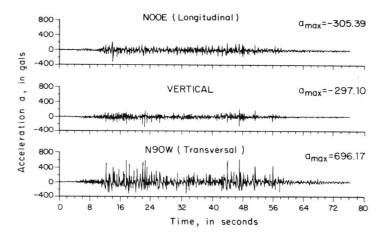

FIG. 3.- Acceleration vs. Time of the Three Accelerogram Components Recorded at the Dam Crest. Earthquake of September 19, 1985

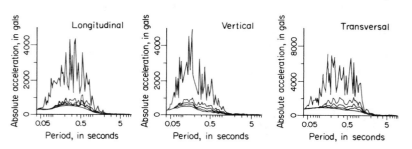

FIG. 4.- Damped Response Spectra at 0, 2, 5, 10 and 20 % of the Three Accelerogram Components Recorded at the Dam Crest. Earthquake of September 19, 1985

phenomena, although it is evident that at the damsite the maximum accelerations registered reached about 150 gals at the sound rock, approximately 270 gals at the alluvial deposits, and 696 gals at the dam crest. These magnitudes confirm the results obtained by Itobayashi et al. (Ref. 5) in the sense that earthquake motions which have different intensity and frequency characteristics could occur at the same site, subjecting the dam to a complex pattern of dynamic loading which is difficult to take into account in the present methods of theoretical analysis.

DAM BEHAVIOR

The instrumentation installed at the dam during construction consisted of 188 devices and several rows of surface reference points, placed at different cross sections parallel to the river, as shown partially in Fig. 5.

Periodical measurements taken at the instruments have enabled the determination of the magnitude and orientation of the permanent displacements occurred at the dam and these results can be consulted in detail in Refs. 3 and 11. The effects induced by the earthquakes listed in Table 2 have been quite important and they represent the largest percentage of such movements.

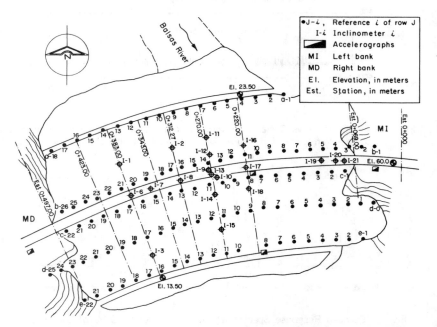

FIG. 5.- Location of Accelerographs, Inclinometers and Surface Reference Points   (1 m = 3.28 ft)

Settlements.- Vertical displacements measured at Rows B and C of surface reference points are depicted in Fig. 6 where it can be noticed that the maximum recorded value at the upstream shoulder is equal to 71.5 cm (28 in.) out of which 44% (31.8 cm or 12.5 in.) corresponds to the effects induced by earthquakes S5 and S6. At the downstream slope the maximum value reached 45.2 cm (17.8 in.) out of which 48% (21.8 cm or 8.6 in.) is due to these two earthquakes. An asymmetry can be observed in the distribution of the settlements and the effect of submergence of the granular materials becomes evident in the upstream shell where larger movements exist. It can be noticed in Fig. 7 that the magnitude of the surface settlements decreases steadily as the height of the embankment decreases. Measurements taken at the inclinometer casings in what refers to settlements are quite similar to those surveyed at the surface reference points (Fig. 8) and the distribution pattern shows that the peak values occur at the upper end and that the movements decrease rapidly with depth down to the elevation corresponding to the contact with the alluvium (or with the ICOS cut-off wall) and at greater depths the settlements are of small magnitude and uniformly distributed on the average. It can also be observed in Fig. 8b that the loss of free board from the end of construction to date has been equal to approximately 53 cm (21 in.) from which 37% correspond to the effects of the earthquakes included in Table 2 particularly to temblors S5 and S6 (21%).

Displacements.- The horizontal displacements are obviously associated to the vertical movements and they are of smaller magnitude than the latter (Ref. 3). In this case it is also true that the largest displacements have been recorded at the crest and that they decrease in magnitude with the embankment height. Generally speaking, the upstream shell moves towards upstream whereas the downstream shell displaces along a downstream direction. Fig. 9 shows the displacements measured at two rows of surface reference points close to the dam crest, following the occurrence of seisms S5 and S6; it should be pointed out that since the time elapsed between earthquakes S5 and S6 was too short, only one measurement could be made of the displacements at the points of Row C (Fig. 9b) and the results demonstrate that the deformations induced by event S6 were rather small.

HAZARD ANALYSIS

The potential hazards to a dam from earthquake loading not only depend on the characteristics of the earthquake but also on both the geometry and the mechanical properties of the structure.

Considerable judgment is involved in assessing the seismic hazard at a damsite; however, earthquake S5 can be deemed as the maximum credible earthquake (MCE) to be used for the dynamic analyses performed for La Villita Dam.

The main hazards to a dam under seismic loading are:

- Slope failure
- Overtopping
- Core cracking
- Foundation failure

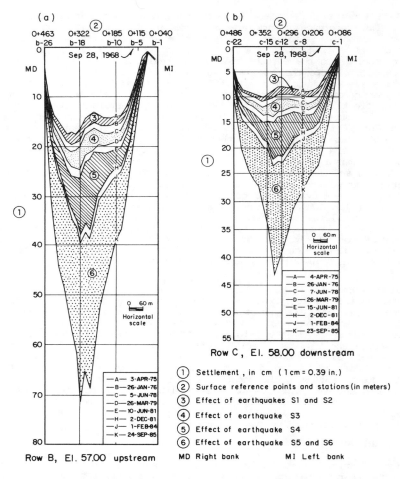

FIG. 6.- Vertical Movements of Surface Reference Points Close to the Dam Crest (1 m= 3.28 ft)

Slope Failure.- For design purposes, the slope stability of the maximum cross section of the dam was analyzed with the Swedish method of slices thus obtaining a minimum safety factor of 1.66 for the upstream slope for the case of sudden drawdown and of 1.07 for the downstream slope, after assuming a constant horizontal force induced by an acceleration of 150 gals acting at the base and under full reservoir (Ref. 10). This pseudo-static method of analysis was during the sixties the standard procedure and at present it is only acceptable for static computations. Nowadays the Finite Element Method (FEM)

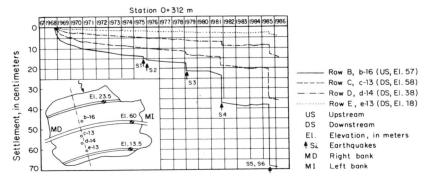

FIG. 7.- Vertical Displacements Measured at Different Rows of Surface Reference Points (1m = 3.28 ft; 1cm = 0.39 in.)

is used for modeling the dynamic response of dams; however, if the uncertainties involved in the mechanical properties of the materials and their variation not only with time but also due to the seismic effects are taken into account, the use of sophisticated methods of analysis is questionable, since their complexity not necessarily leads to a better estimate of the embankment behavior. In view of this fact, simplified methods of analysis have been developed based on the approach suggested by Newmark (Ref. 8) where he assumes that the deformation of the slope comes as a result of the displacements occurred along well defined sliding planes, although this mechanism is rarely encountered in reality; therefore, it will be still necessary to do a considerable amount of research in order to provide adequate tools for analysis. For the case of La Villita Dam, the fact that there was no slope failure gives assurance that the cross section is stable when subjected to the forces induced as intense as the MCE.

Overtopping.- This cause of failure of earth and rockfill dams has been considered at the forums of ICOLD as the most important one and it can develop due to excessive deformation of the embankment or by seiches in the reservoir created by either landslides or ground motions.

In 1980, Romo et al. (Ref. 2, Chapter 7) performed a deformation analysis of La Villita Dam acted upon by the dynamic loading imposed by earthquake S3, by means of the simplified methods of Newmark (Ref. 8), Makdisi-Seed (Ref. 6) and Reséndiz-Romo. With the first method losses of free board equal to 0.04, 2.04 and 5.5 cm (0.016, 0.8 and 2.17 in.) were obtained for ground accelerations of 300, 500 and 700 gals, respectively. With the method of Makdisi-Seed practically no settlements are induced by an acceleration of 370 gals. With the method proposed by Reséndiz-Romo, a loss of free board equal to 26, 33 and 38 cm (10, 13 and 15 in.) was obtained for accelerations of 200, 300 and 350 gals, respectively. If it is assumed that the acceleration at the crest during earthquake S3 was equal to 371 gals and that the settlements recorded were of 2 and 3.4 cm (0.78 and 1.34 in.) at the

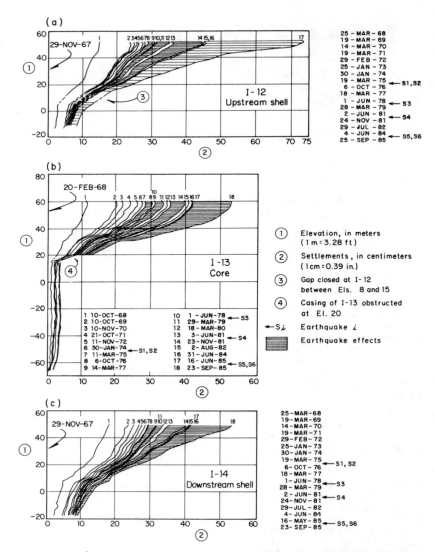

FIG. 8.- Settlements Measured at Inclinometer Casings of Station 0+270

crest and at the upstream shell, respectively, the results obtained with the two first methods are on the unsafe side and those of the third method are too conservative.

As it can be observed in Table 2 and Figs. 6 and 8, the deformations

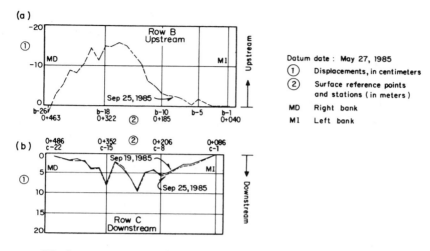

(a)

(b)

Datum date : May 27, 1985
① Displacements, in centimeters
② Surface reference points and stations (in meters)
MD Right bank
MI Left bank

FIG. 9.- Horizontal Displacements (in River Direction) of Two Rows of Surface Reference Points (1 cm = 0.39 in.)

occurred at the dam are directly proportional to the acceleration and duration of the earthquakes, which in fact could be expected. Based on this evidence and on the values recorded after the earthquakes S1 to S6, the graphs plotted in Fig. 10 were prepared from which it is possible to calculate the maximum expected deformations during a seism of less or equal magnitude than the MCE. If it is considered that the geometry and material properties have a slight variation after each earthquake, it is to be expected that the results obtained from such type of graphical presentations are not accurate enough although they provide the order of magnitude of the phenomenon, which can be further evaluated and improved in the future.

The original free board of La Villita Dam was equal to 2.5 m (8.2 ft) considering the flood level at elevation 56.73 m (186 ft), and as it was mentioned before, the loss of free board since construction has been of 59.2 cm (23.3 in.), including the effect of MCE; therefore, it can be concluded that the risk of overtopping due to deformation of the embankment is very low and it can remain at that level provided the original elevation is restituted after a severe earthquake.

On the other hand, no unstable zones have been detected at the river banks upstream from the dam since construction, and no landslides have been recorded in the reservoir area.

During the occurrence of MCE, waves in the reservoir formed with a maximum amplitude of 50 cm (20 in.) and at that time the actual free board was equal to approximately 8.5 m (28 ft) because the reservoir was then at elevation 50.2 m (165 ft) and therefore overtopping due to seiches is not very likely to take place.

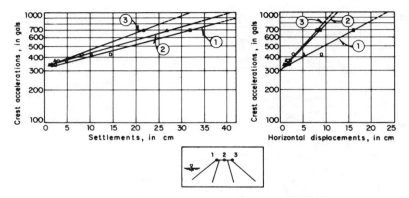

FIG. 10.- Maximum Vertical and Horizontal Displacements Due to Seismic
Action on La Villita Dam   (1 cm = 0.39 in.)

Core Cracking.- The dam core was constructed with a highly plastic
clayey material (w_L = 56%, w_p = 24% on the average) compacted in
layers 15-cm (6-in.) thick, achieving a degree of compaction equal to
96% with respect to the Standard Proctor Test.

In addition to the horizontal and vertical displacements described
before, earthquake S5 (MCE) induced the formation of longitudinal
cracks as long as 100 m (328 ft), following an almost parallel direction to the dam axis and close to both the upstream and downstream
parapets; they coincided approximately with the contact between the
impervious core and the granular shells. The toppling of nine panels
of the parapet between Stations 0+270 and 0+310 (Fig. 11) was also
observed. The opening of the cracks varied from 0.5 to 5 cm (0.2 to
2 in.) for the upstream ones and from 1 to 15 cm (0.4 to 6 in.) for
the downstream cracks, and differential settlements from 1 to 20 cm
(0.4 to 8 in.) were measured. From the excavation of exploratory pits
it could be determined that the depth of the cracks was equal to the
thickness of the base for the road built along the crest (60 cm or
24 in. approximately) and that they vanished when reaching the filter
materials. The pattern of distribution and location of the cracks is
similar to that observed following earthquake S3 (Ref. 3) as a result
of the larger subsidence of the granular shells with respect to the
core.

No evidence exists of the development of transversal cracks which
might have induced piping phenomenon, and no seepage has been observed
at the downstream slope. In addition, the zoning of materials shown
in Fig. 1 provides an adequate self healing mechanism of eventually
open cracks as Dr. Terzaghi once suggested; it can be therefore
concluded that the risk of core cracking and piping failure due to the
embankment deformation is quite low.

Foundation Failure.- The main hazard imposed by the foundation
refers to the development of surface faulting under the dam and the

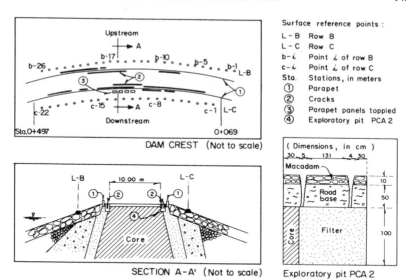

FIG. 11.- Cracks Produced by the September 19, 1985 Earthquake on La Villita Dam (1 m = 3.28 ft ; 1 cm = 0.39 in.)

pervasive ground deformations associated with nearby existing faulting. During the geological exploration no evidence of major faulting under the dam was observed (Ref. 11) and at present there are no indications that faulting has been formed due to the effects of seismic activity in the region, a fact which can be corroborated by the small magnitude of the horizontal and vertical displacements measured at the toe of the embankment.

In view of the great thickness and gradation of the alluvial deposits underlying the embankment, it was feared that a partial liquefaction of them could occur during an earthquake; for this reason, a large scale in situ test was performed during construction by means of explosive charges. From the results of this test such a possibility was abandoned (Ref. 11) and this decision has been verified subsequently during the occurrence of earthquakes.

Although the foundation rock is sensibly sound, the risk of formation of new major faulting under the dam due to seismic action cannot be disregarded; however, it is reasonable to assume that the risk of a foundation failure is of little concern.

CONCLUSIONS

Although the risk of failure of a dam cannot be considered to be naught notwithstanding the safety margins, controls and engineering provisions taken into account, the performance of La Villita Dam after being subjected to severe seismic loading has been quite satisfactory and it is to be expected that the response of the dam when acted upon by such strong earthquakes as those recorded to date will be equally reliable.

The hazard analysis carried out leads to the conclusion that the risk of failure of La Villita Dam is very low when subjected to seisms as strong as the maximum credible earthquake (MCE).

Continuous instrumental records of the dam have made it possible to evaluate the hazard of La Villita Dam failure and they constitute an invaluable information for the evaluation and development of improved analytical methods for the dynamic design of dams. It will be necessary to complement these data with the proper assessment of the dynamic properties of the materials constituting the embankment and of their changes with time as a result of the occurrence of earthquakes. These requirements imply the need for further research work.

APPENDIX.- REFERENCES

1. Anderson, J., Brune, J., Bodin, P., Prince, J., Quaas, R., Oñate, R., Almora, D., and Pérez, P., "Preliminary Presentation of Accelerogram Data from the Guerrero Strong Motion Accelerograph Array, Michoacán-Guerrero, Mexico, Earthquakes of 19 and 21 September 1985", Instituto de Ingeniería, UNAM, Mexico, October 1985.

2. Comisión Federal de Electricidad, "Performance of El Infiernillo and La Villita Dams Including the Earthquake of March 14, 1979", Publicación No. 15 (English-Spanish), Mexico, February 1980.

3. Comisión Federal de Electricidad, "Behavior of Dams Built in Mexico (1974-1984)", Vol. II, Publication No. 47, contributed to the 15th International Congress on Large Dams held in Laussanne, Switzerland (English-Spanish), Mexico, 1985.

4. Instituto de Ingeniería, UNAM, "Información sísmica preliminar" (Preliminary Seismic Information), in Spanish, periodic publication from 1975 to date, Mexico.

5. Itobayashi, Y., Matsumoto, N., and Kondo, S., "Characteristics of Observed Earthquake Motions on Rock Foundation and Seismic Safety Evaluation of Existing Dams in Japan", Proceedings of the 14th International Conference on Large Dams, ICOLD, Q. 52, R. 3, pp. 39-59, Rio de Janeiro, 1982.

6. Makdisi, F.I., and Seed, H.B., "Simplified Procedure for Estimating Dam and Embankment Earthquake-Induced Deformations", Journal of the Geotechnical Engineering Division, ASCE, Vol. 104, No. GT7, Proc. Paper 13898, July 1978, pp. 849-867.

7. Mena, E., Carmona, C., Alcántara, L., and Delgado, R., "Análisis del acelerograma 'Zacatula' del sismo del 19 de septiembre de 1985" (Analysis of the "Zacatula" Accelerogram of the Earthquake of September 19, 1985), in Spanish, Instituto de Ingeniería, UNAM, Mexico, October 1985.

8. Newmark, N.M., "Effects of Earthquakes on Dams and Embankments", Géotechnique, London, England, Vol. 5, No. 2, June 1965.

9. Prince, J., "Estudio de los pulsos en los acelerogramas registrados en la corona de La Villita" (Study of the Pulses in the Accelerograms Recorded at the Crest of La Villita Dam), in Spanish, Informe Proyecto 4706, Instituto de Ingeniería, UNAM, Mexico, February 1986.

10. Secretaría de Recursos Hidráulicos, "Presas de México" (Dams in Mexico), in Spanish, Vol. I, Mexico, 1969, pp. 393-413.

11. SRH-CFE-UNAM, "Behavior of Dams Built in Mexico", Vol. I, Contribution to the 12th International Congress on Large Dams held in Mexico City (English-Spanish), Mexico, 1976.

Analytical Modelling of Dynamic Soil Response in the
Mexico Earthquake of Sept. 19, 1985

Miguel P. Romo[1] and H. Bolton Seed[2]

Abstract

Accelerograph records and damage distribution show that local soil
conditions had a major effect on the intensity of ground motions in different parts of Mexico City in the earthquakes of September 19 and 20,
1985. This paper reviews the effects of subsoil conditions on the
ground motions at the recording stations and presents the results of
analytical studies to determine whether the observed effects could be
evaluated by somewhat simplified wave propagation studies.

Introduction

One of the most dramatic aspects of the earthquake effects in
Mexico City in the earthquake of Sept. 19, 1985 (Magnitude 8.1) was the
enormous differences in intensities of shaking and associated building
damage in different parts of the city. In the south west part of the
city, ground motions were moderate in intensity and damage was minor.
However in the northern part of the city, ground shaking had high intensity and catastrophic damages occurred. Similar behavior has been
observed in previous earthquakes and the differences attributed to the
differences in soil conditions in the different parts of the city. In
the 1985 earthquake these differences appear to be somewhat more accentuated than in other earthquakes in the past 40 years.

It is the purpose of this paper to describe how the recorded
ground motions varied with the soil conditions in different areas of
Mexico City and to present the results of some preliminary studies of
the extent to which the observed differences in shaking intensities
could be predicted by somewhat simplified analyses of ground response.

Soil Conditions in Mexico City

The soil conditions in Mexico City have been the subject of many
investigations in the past 50 years and are reasonably well established.
The city is located on the edge of an old lake bed; thus while the
western part of the city is underlain by rock and hard soil deposits, the
eastern part of the city is located on soft clay deposits filling the

---

[1] Research Professor, Institute of Engineering, National Autonomous
University of Mexico, Mexico, D.F.

[2] Professor of Civil Engineering, University of California, Berkeley, CA.

former lake bed. An east—west profile showing this variation in soil
conditions (after Zeevaert, 1972) is shown in Fig. 1. Between the hard
formations in the west and the deep clay deposits in the east, there is
a "transition zone" where the soils have generally stiff characteristics
but may also involve some limited depths of clay.

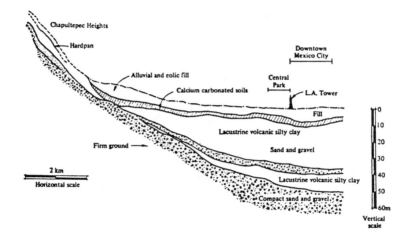

Figure 1   East—West Soil Profile — Basin of Valley of Mexico
(after Zeevaert, 1972)

In the lake-bed area, the clay deposits are underlain by very stiff
and hard formations with shear wave velocities comparable to those of
soft rock. Contours showing the approximate depths of soils (mostly
involving a surface layer of sand fill and an underlying deep layer of
soft clay with interbedded thin layers of sand and silt) which overlie
very stiff and hard formations are shown in Fig. 2.

Damage surveys show that virtually all the structures which
collapsed or suffered major damage in the earthquake of September 19,
lie within the zone bounded by the soil depth contours of 30 m and 48 m
as indicated in Fig. 2. Surveys also show that the major damage in this
area occurred to structures with story heights ranging from about 6 to
15 stories.

Ground Motions in the Sept. 19, 1985 Earthquake

Strong motion records of the earthquake motions in the city were
obtained at several locations including:

1.   Three sites located on the rock and stiff soil area at the
     University of Mexico (UNAM).

2.   One site on the rock and stiff soil area at Tacubaya (T).

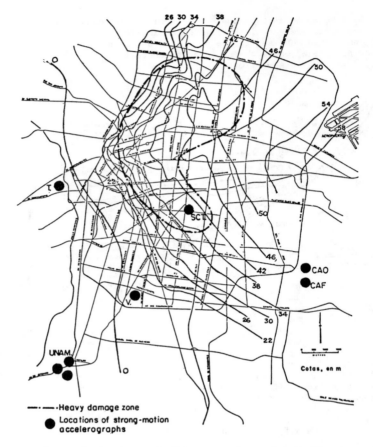

Figure 2   Depths to Hard Layer at Base of Soil Deposits
(modified after Resendiz et al., 1970)

3. One site located on the transition zone at Viveros (V).

4. One site (the SCT Building) on the clay deposits near the
    southern boundary of the heavy damage area; the depth of soils
    overlying the hard formations at this site is about 35 m.

and 5. Two sites about 0.8 km apart on the deeper clay deposits in
         the Central Market area: at one site (CAF) the soil depth was
         about 45 m and at the other site (CAO) the soil depth was
         about 57 m.

The locations of the recording stations are shown in Fig. 2.

The records of the earthquake motions obtained at the various sites indicate that:

1. Motions recorded at the University sites and at Tacubaya on the rock and hard soil deposits had generally similar characteristics with peak ground accelerations of the order of 0.04g, peak spectral accelerations (5% damping) of about 0.11g, and a predominant period of about 2 seconds.

2. There was a major amplification of the motions by the soft clay deposits underlying the SCT and Central Market sites. At the SCT site, where the soil conditions are more closely comparable to those in the heavy damage area to the north, the peak ground acceleration was about 0.17g and the peak spectral acceleration for 5% damping was about 1.0g at a period of about 2 seconds.

3. There were significant differences in the ground motions recorded at the SCT building site and at the Central Market sites, with the Central Market sites showing lower peak accelerations and maximum spectral amplifications at higher periods than at the SCT site. Thus at the CAO site, where the depth of soil was about 55 m, the peak ground acceleration was about 0.09g, and the peak spectral acceleration (5% damping) was about 0.35g at a period of about 3.5 seconds.

A comparison of representative average spectra for the SCT Building site, the Central Market site (CAO) and for sites in the rock and stiff soil zones is shown in Fig. 3. It is readily apparent from this comparison why damage was negligible in the rock and stiff soil zones but very severe in the central part of the city underlain by clay layers with depths ranging between about 30 to 45 m.

It is interesting to note that one day after the main shock, the city was subjected to a major aftershock of Magnitude 7.5. Ground motions were also recorded at the same stations in the aftershock; the motions were somewhat lower in intensity during the aftershock, as evidenced by the comparison between the response spectra for main shock and aftershock motions at the CAO site shown in Fig. 4. It is noteworthy that the forms of the response spectra at this site were remarkably similar for the two events, although the spectral peaks occurred at slightly lower periods in the aftershock, suggesting that the strains induced during the September 19 event were high enough to produce some small non-linear effects in the ground response.

Details of Soil Conditions at Recording Stations

(1) SCT SITE

The subsoil conditions at the SCT site are fairly representative of those in the more heavily damaged zone of the city. The stratigraphy broadly consists of a compact 4 m thick layer of mixed sand, clay and silt, followed by a 27 m thick clay layer with interbedded seams of silty sand, volcanic glass, fly ash, sand and silts; the water content

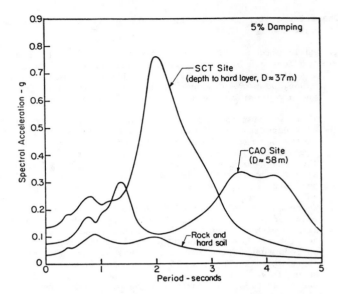

Figure 3   Average Acceleration Response Spectra for
Motions Recorded on Different Soil Conditions

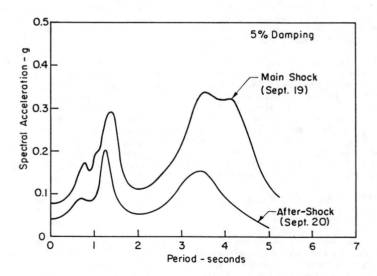

Figure 4   Average Response Spectra at CAO Site for
Main Shock and Strongest Aftershock

in the clayey materials ranges from about 100% to 450% and the undrained shear strength varies from 0.25 to 0.8 kg/cm^2. Underlying this layer there is a very compact, lightly cemented stratum 3 m thick of sandy silt (locally known as the hard layer), followed by a 4 m thick layer of very stiff clay overlying the so called deep deposits composed of a very hard and stiff layer (more than 100 SPT blows/ft) of cemented silty sand which is usually considered as the base of the soil profile.

(2)   CAO Site

The subsoil conditions at the CAO site consist of a layer of silty sand 5 m deep followed by a 37 m thick clay layer with interbedded seams of silty sand, fly ash, volcanic glass, and silts; the water content in the clayey soils varies from some 150% to 500%, and the undrained shear strength from 0.2 to 0.6 kg/cm^2. Underneath this clay layer are a series of intercalated strata of sandy silts and silty clays about 10 m in thickness, followed by a 4 m thick layer of stiff clay which overlies the deep hard deposits.

(3)   CAF Site

The CAF site is located about 0.8 km south of the CAO site. The upper 15 m of the soil profiles at the two sites are very similar, but the clay layer at the CAF site seems to be slightly stiffer and about 13 m less in thickness; thus the hard deposits are encountered at a depth of about 45 m at the CAF site.

Although the stiffness of the clay varies slightly from one site to another, other aspects of the dynamic properties seem to be reasonably constant. Representative average relationships for modulus attenuation ratio and damping ratio with strain, as determined by tests performed in earlier studies (Leon et al., 1974) and in recent studies by Romo and Jaime (1986) are shown in Fig. 5.

Analytical Studies of Ground Motions in Mexico City

Because of the fact that the heavy damage zone in Mexico City is located in the area of the lake-bed deposits, mainly to the north of the SCT Building, it is desirable to develop procedures for evaluating the characteristics of the earthquake ground motions in those parts of the city where no records were obtained but which are never-the-less of major interest for damage evaluation purposes. Accordingly some preliminary analyses have already been made of the potential influence of different depths and stiffnesses of the clay on the nature of the ground motions.

Such analyses are made possible by:

1. The existence of information such as that shown in Fig. 2, which provides general information on the depth of the clay and sand deposits forming the soil profile above the hard formations in this part of the city.

2. Available information concerning the dynamic properties of the soils, especially the clay, obtained from both previous studies and laboratory studies made since the earthquake. Thus for example, the shear wave velocity of the clay deposits is known to be in the range of 60 to 80 m/sec and data concerning the dynamic properties of the clay are shown in Fig. 5.

3. The clay deposits are very thin compared with their lateral extent and thus in most cases, the dynamic response can be evaluated by one-dimensional wave propagation analyses.

4. Previous studies (Herrera and Rosenblueth, 1965; Seed and Idriss, 1969) have shown that one-dimensional ground response analyses, as illustrated in Fig. 6, can provide values of ground surface motions in good agreement with values recorded in previous earthquakes, and that most of the amplification of motions takes place in the soil deposits overlying the hard layer.

Thus, assuming that the ground motions recorded on the hard formations in the University area and at Tacubaya are representative of those developed in the hard formations underlying the lakebed area, it has been possible to make simplified preliminary analyses of the motions likely to be developed at the ground surface in areas underlain by clay deposits.

In making the analyses it is necessary to select a rock motion to represent the characteristics of the motions developed on the hard sites in Mexico City in the Sept. 19 earthquake. Such a motion can be selected in two ways:

1. By selecting a representative record obtained on a hard site in the Sept. 19 earthquake, or a motion with a representative spectrum for motions recorded on hard sites in this event.

2. By selecting an earthquake record from a previous earthquake and modifying it to have generally the same characteristics as the motions developed on the hard deposits at UNAM and Tacubaya. Thus for example, the Pasadena recording of the 1952 Kern County, California earthquake (Magnitude ≈ 7.6) can be modified to produce a motion having a response spectrum generally similar to that of the recorded motions.

Both procedures have been used in order to explore the effect of the form of the rock motion records on analytical results.

In view of the preliminary nature of the studies at this stage of the investigation, it was considered reasonable to perform the analyses using a simplified representation of the actual soil profiles. Thus a homogeneous layer with average properties was considered for each soil profile investigated. The average stiffnesses were first determined from the natural frequencies of the sites, evaluated directly from the Fourier spectra of the recorded motions. The resulting values compared well with shear moduli determined from resonant column and cyclic

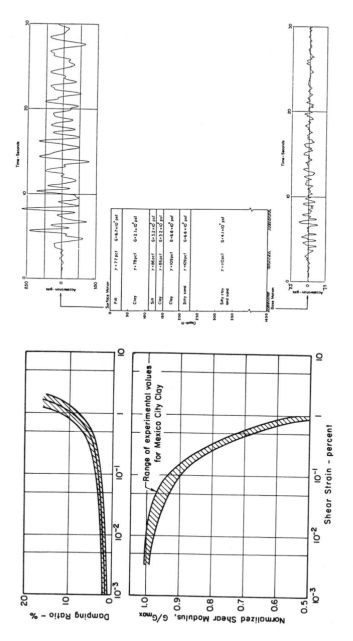

Figure 5   Strain-Dependent Shear Moduli and
Damping Ratios for Mexico City Clay
(after Leon et al., 1974 and
Romo and Jaime, 1986)

Figure 6   Ground Response Analysis for Mexico City
(After Seed and Idriss, 1969)

triaxial tests (Romo and Jaime, 1986) on clay samples having similar water contents and undrained shear strengths. On this basis the following properties were selected for use in the analyses:

Site	Depth	Shear Wave Velocity	Unit Weight
SCT	35 TO 40 m	75 to 80 m/s	1.2 t/m^3
CAO	58 m	65 to 75 m/s	1.2 t/m^3
CAF	45 m	70 m/s	1.2 t/m^3

Using these characteristics, in conjunction with the soil properties shown in Fig. 5, analyses were made using two procedures: (1) a probabilistic or random analysis procedure and (2) a deterministic procedure. In both procedures the non-linear properties of the soil were taken into account using the equivalent-linear approximation (Seed and Idriss, 1969). Details of the analytical procedures and the results obtained are presented below.

Random Analysis Procedure

This method of analysis was developed by Romo (1976) and basically consists in solving iteratively the following equation:

$$P_r (\omega) = \left| H (\omega) \right|^2 P_i (\omega) \tag{1}$$

where $P_i(\omega)$ is the power spectral density of the input stationary random process, $P_r(\omega)$ is the power spectral density of the response, and $H(\omega)$ is the complex transfer function of the system and is determined numerically by the finite element method. Details of the procedure may be found elsewhere (4).

The input motion was defined from the accelerograph records obtained during the September 19 event on the stiff deposits at the UNAM sites. At the time of the main shock all three of these stations recorded the ground motions. Using the six horizontal components an average motion was defined. The acceleration response spectrum for this motion is shown in Fig. 3. The maximum acceleration for the motion is 0.037g.

It is worthwhile to note that in using directly the average motion as input it is implicitly assumed that the ground motion characteristics of the hard deposits in the UNAM area and those of the deep deposits elsewhere are the same. It is to be expected that there will be some differences in the motions; however at this stage there are no sound bases to define what these differences might be.

The results of the response analyses are presented in Figs. 7, 8 and 9 where the spectra for the computed surface motions are compared with the average response spectra of the recorded motions.

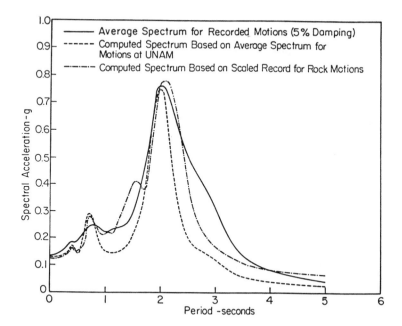

Figure 7   Comparison of Spectra for Recorded and
Computed Motions at SCT Site

The response spectrum of the motion computed at the SCT site (average v_s = 80 m/s) is compared in Fig. 7 with the average spectrum of the two recorded orthogonal horizontal motions. It may be seen that the main features of the actual motion are reproduced well and the peak spectral values are about the same.

Figure 8 shows a comparison of the response spectra for the computed and recorded motions at the CAO site (average v_s = 66 m/s) for the September 19 earthquake. The agreement between computed and recorded motion spectra is very good. Similarly good agreement is shown in Fig. 9, which compares response spectra for computed and recorded motions at the CAF site (average v_s = 70 m/s). Analyses have also been made for the aftershock motions with similarly good results.

Deterministic Analysis Procedure

Deterministic analyses of ground response were made using the one-dimensional. vertical wave propagation analysis procedure (Seed and Idriss, 1969; Schnabel et al., 1972) to explore whether the amplifying effects of the clay deposits could be evaluated using a reasonable representation of the motions developed in the rock and hard soil deposits, other than those recorded in the actual earthquake. These

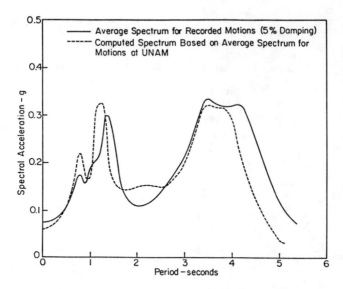

Figure 8   Comparison of Spectra for Recorded
and Computed Motions at CAO Site

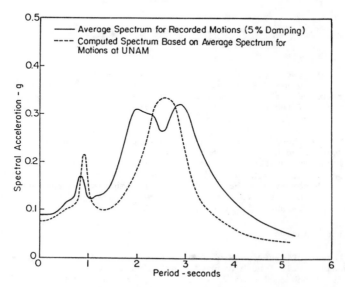

Figure 9   Comparison of Spectra for Recorded
and Computed Motions at CAF Site

studies were made for the following conditions at the SCT site:

1. Assuming the soil at the site to have an overall average shear wave velocity of 75 m/sec.

2. Assuming the modulus attenuation curve for the soil to be the same as that shown in Fig. 5.

3. Assuming that the motions developed in rock and hard soil had a peak ground acceleration of 0.035g, a predominant period of 2.0 seconds and could be represented by an appropriately scaled version of the Pasadena record of the 1952 Kern County earthquake. The response spectrum for the assumed motions in the rock and hard soil layer is shown in Fig. 11.

The acceleration response spectrum for the computed ground surface motions at the SCT site is shown in Fig. 7 where it is also compared with the average acceleration response spectrum for the motions recorded at this site. It may be seen that the spectra for the computed and recorded motions are again in generally good agreement.

The results of a similar analysis of the motions likely to develop at the Central Market (CAO) site (soil depth ≃ 55 m) are shown in Fig. 11.

Since the results of the ground response analyses seem to provide a reasonable basis for determining the ground motions at the three locations (SCT site, CAO site and CAF site) where motions were recorded, it seems reasonable to conclude that they are likely to provide a good basis for evaluating the motions at other locations of major interest, such as the heavy damage zones of the city. To this end analyses have been made for conditions similar to those described above for the SCT site, but for soil deposits ranging from 20 m to 70 m.

The results of these analyses are shown in Figs. 10 and 11. Figure 10 shows the computed values of peak ground acceleration along a typical soil profile. It may be seen that there is a very significant amplification of peak ground acceleration for soil depths of 30 to 40 m

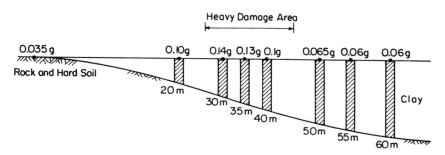

Figure 10   Computed Distribution of Peak Ground Surface Accelerations for Typical Soil Profile

but much smaller amplifications for soil depths exceeding about 50 m. The locations where values of peak ground acceleration are highest correspond well with the parts of the city where heaviest earthquake damage occurred.

Figure 11 shows a comparison of the response spectra for the assumed rock motions and those for the computed motions for soil depths of 35 m and 55 m. It is interesting to note the great similarity between the relative spectral values for the analytically derived motions and those for the recorded motions previously presented in Fig. 3.

Finally the computed spectra for all soil depths ranging from 20 to 70 m are shown in Fig. 12. Since the soil depths in the heavy damage area range mostly from about 30 to 50 m, it is possible to estimate from these results a representative average spectrum for the heavy damage zone in Mexico City in the September 19 earthquake. A reasonably conservative estimate of such a spectrum is shown by the dashed line in this figure. Since analyses provide the only basis for extrapolating the recorded motions to determine representative motion characteristics in other areas of the city, it is believed that a representative spectrum similar to that shown in Fig. 12 may provide the most reasonable basis for assessing the building damage caused by the earthquake in relation to the motions responsible for its occurrence.

Conclusion

The preceding pages present the results of some preliminary studies of ground response in different parts of Mexico City in the Sept. 1985 earthquakes. It is clear that local soil conditions had a major effect on the intensity of ground motions in different parts of the city and that there was considerable variation in motion characteristics even within those parts of the city underlain by clay, due to the different depths of clay. It seems reasonable to conclude that the characteristics of the motions in different parts of the city can be determined with a satisfactory accuracy for many engineering purposes by ground response analyses using one-dimensional wave propagation methods which take into account the strain-dependence of shear modulus and damping ratios by the equivalent linear approach. Thus the results of such analyses may provide a useful basis for assessing the ground motion characteristics in the heavy damage area of the city, even though there were no recording instruments in that zone, and for developing seismic risk maps and site dependent design spectra for the Valley of Mexico.

Acknowledgements

The authors gratefully acknowledge the support of CONACYT (the Consejo Nacional de Ciencia y Tecnologia) of Mexico and the National Science Foundation in the U.S.A. in making the studies described in this paper. Appreciation is also expressed for the cooperation and help provided by numerous colleagues.

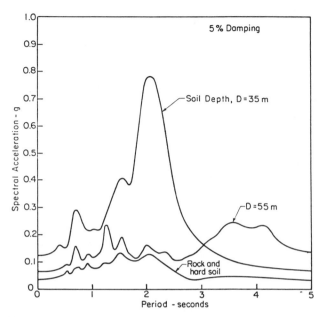

Figure 11   Acceleration Response Spectra for Computed Motions for
             Different Soil Conditions

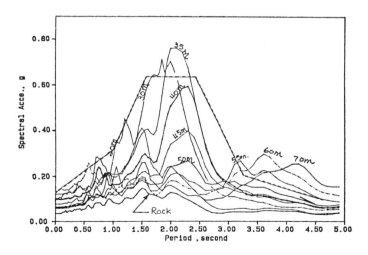

Figure 12   Spectra for Computed Motions for Different Soil Conditions
             with Representative Average for Heavy Damage Area

14   Romo/Seed

References

1. Herrera, I. and Rosenblueth, E., "Response Spectra on Stratified Soil," Proceedings, III World Conference on Earthquake Engineering, New Zealand, Vol. I, pp. 44-60, 1965.

2. Leon, J. L., Jaime, A., and Rabago A., "Dynamic Properties of Soils-Preliminary Study," Institute of Engineering, UNAM, 1974 (in Spanish).

3. Resendiz, D., Springall, G., Rodriquez, J. M., and Esquivel, R., "Recent Information About Subsoil Characteristics and Foundation Engineering Practice in Mexico City," V Reunion Nactional de Mecanica de Suelos, Mexico, D.F., November, 1970 (in Spanish).

4. Romo, M. P., "Soil-Structure Interaction in a Random Seismic Environment," Ph.D. Dissertation, University of California, Berkeley, November, 1976.

5. Romo, M. P., Chen, J. H., Lysmer, J., and Seed, H. B., "PLUSH: A Computer Program for Probabilistic Finite Element Analysis of Seismic Soil-Structure Interaction," Report No. UCB/EERC-77/01, University of California, Berkeley, September, 1980.

6. Romo, M. P. and Jaime, A., "Dynamic Characteristics of Some Clays of the Mexico Valley and Seismic Response of the Ground," Technical Report, DDF, April, 1986 (in Spanish).

7. Schnabel, P. B., Lysmer, J., and Seed, H. B., "SHAKE: A Computer Program for Earthquake Response Analysis of Horizontally Layered Sites," Report No. EERC/72-12, University of California, Berkeley, December, 1972.

8. Seed, H. B., "The Influence of Local Soil Conditions on Earthquake Damage," 7th International Conference on Soil Mechanics and Foundation Engineering, Specialty Session 2, Mexico, pp. 33-66, August, 1969.

9. Seed, H. B. and Idriss, I. M., "The Influence of Soil Conditions on Ground Motions During Earthquakes," Journal of the Soil Mechanics and Foundations Engineering Division, ASCE, Vol. 94, No. SM1, pp. 93-137, January, 1969.

10. Zeevaert, Leonardo, "Foundation Engineering for Difficult Subsoil Conditions," Van Nostrand Reinhold Company, 1972.

ARE THE SOIL DEPOSITIONS IN MEXICO CITY UNIQUE?

Robert V. Whitman, F.ASCE[*]

Abstract: The answer clearly is: YES! However, the amplification
and soil-structure interaction effects observed in Mexico City are
important considerations - even if they may not be so severe -in may
other major cities of the world. The use of microzonation to
account for local soil conditions is reviewed in the light of the
experiences in Mexico City, and suggestions concerning future
directions are offered.

Introduction

My answer to the question posed in the title is - for practical
purposes - YES! I cannot tell you with certainty that there are not
other locations where volcanic ash has settled into a lake to produce
soils with:

* Water contents that reach 300% to 400%.
* Shear wave velocities as low as 40 m/s.
* Nearly linear behavior to large dynamic strains.

but I cannot think of another major city where such conditions exist.
Fig. 1 compares typical shear wave velocity profiles in several cities
where local soil conditions are thought to influence the nature and
intensity of earthquake ground motions, and clearly the situation in
Mexico City is unique.

However, this uniqueness of the soils in Mexico City is not really
the important question. What we really want to ask is: Are the
soil-related events observed in Mexico City - wide variation in
recorded ground motions with location; concentration of damage in a
localized area, strong amplification of motions by the soil; uplifting
and overturning - unique? Now, just as clearly, the answer is NO!
There have been localized areas of damage during every major
earthquake; San Francisco 1906, Tokyo 1923, Concepcion and Valdivia in
Chile 1960, to mention just a few. There have been a number of cases
where structures of longer periods, and founded upon a signficant depth
of less than firm soils, have responded quite strongly to distant
earthquakes. To cite a few examples: Caracas 1967, Sacramento during
earthquakes in Nevada, and even in Boston as a result of an earthquake
in Eastern Canada earthquake in 1925.

*Professor of Civil Engineering, Department of Civil Engineering,
Massachusetts Institute of Technology, Cambridge, MA 02139.

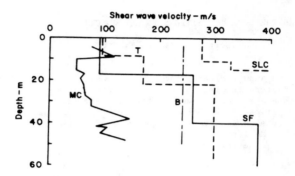

FIG.1 - Comparison of Shear Wave Velocities from Several Cities:
MC-Mexico City (18); T-Tokyo, composite from several sources (5, 14);
B-Boston (15); SF-San Francisco (16); SLC-Salt Lake City (4)

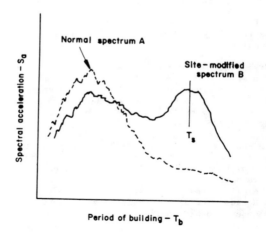

FIG.2 - Schematic of Normal and Site-modified Response Spectra.

These are significant, practical problems with which engineers and
code writers have wrestled for several decades. The experiences in
Mexico City during the Michoacan Earthquake of 1985 have provided very
dramatic examples of the great importance of these problems. It is
thus an appropriate time to re-examine current and future practice
concerning these matters — especially in regard to the problem of
microzonation.

Effects of Local Site Conditions

Fittingly, the first comprehensive discussions of the effects of
local site conditions upon earthquake-caused damage were presented here
in Mexico City — during a Specialty Session on Soil Dynamics during the
7th International Conference on Soil Mechanics and Foundation
Engineering (9, 11). An excellent monograph has been published by the
Earthquake Engineering Research Institute (12). There are several
different ways in which local site conditions can manifest themselves.

Ground failures: In this category are problems of liquefaction and,
in hilly terrain with steep slopes, landsliding. Liquefaction, which
can occur where there are loose-to-medium dense saturated granular
soils, is generally the greater potential problem. It can cause slope
failures, bearing capacity failures, lateral spreading of slightly
inclined ground, excessive ground oscillation, settlement and sand
boils. All of these aspects of liquefaction can cause great damage to
structures — even sand boils, which can come up through light slabs on
grade. The subject of liquefaction has been reviewed in detail in a
recent report (6). Fortunately, this was one problem that Mexico City
did not experience in the 1985 earthquake, although it did occur in the
epicentral region along the Pacific Coast.

Dynamic ground response: This phrase refers to the modification of
ground motions as they pass upwards through a soil column. Usually
there is amplification of some aspect of the motion — peak acceleration or peak velocity — but in many cases peak acceleration may
actually be diminished. Often there is a concentration of the energy
in the motion within a range of frequencies related to the fundamental
period of the soil.

This aspect has been especially marked in Mexico City during a
series of major earthquakes and its manifestations during the 1985
earthquake will be reviewed in other papers presented to this
Conference. The phenomenon has been discussed extensively in the
literature, and numerous methods for calculating dynamic soil response
have been proposed. One important unresolved question is the
importance of considering non-linearity in the response of soil. Such
non-linearity may cause peak surface acceleration to be decreased
(relative to that at some depth) during strong shaking while being
amplified during weak shaking, and may increase the natural period of
the site as the strength of shaking increases. On the basis of
laboratory tests, these non-linear effects should be quite important,

but field observations have not always been consistent with this
expectation. There have been indications that Mexico City clay behaves
in a more linear manner than many other soils, and that this behavior
has contributed to the very strong observed amplification effect.

Focussing effects: This phrase refers to the concentration of
ground shaking in localized regions because of horizontal variations in
the subsurface soil profile. For example, during some earthquakes,
damage has been greatest along the margins of a valley where soils lie
against steeply sloping rocks. Increased ground motions have been
observed in such regions, at least during weak-to-moderate shaking.
Focussing is actually one aspect of the behavior discussed under the
previous heading, being a 2-and 3-dimensional phenomenon whereas
dynamic ground response often is analyzed considering only one
dimension.

While there have been numerous theoretical studies that emphasize
the potentially important effects of focussing, knowledge concerning
this problem is still diffuse and unorganized.

Effects of topography: Here we refer to the effects of rapid
variations in surface elevation in hilly and mountainous terrain. Once
again theoretical computations have indicated that the effects may be
quite important, with certain frequency components of motion being
amplified at the crests of hills or at the edges of plateaus. There
is also field evidence: the greater than average damage in Guatemala
City in 1976 to houses located at the edges of cliffs, and the severe
damage to apartment buildings constructed on the ridges of the Canal
Beagle area above Viña de Mar, Chile, in 1985.

Additional aspects: Other explanations have been offered for
greater-than-average damage experienced by buildings founded over soft
soils – such as the possibility that such buildings had already
experienced some cracking before the earthquake because of static
settlements. It is also important to keep in mind that factors having
nothing to do with local site conditions can have major influences upon
the intensity and frequency content of ground motions – even for a
fixed magnitude and hypocentral distance: e.g. details of the rupture
process, direction of rupture propagation, and the paths of
transmission from rupture zone to site. Uncertainties associated with
these factors may, in some cases, obscure the effects of local site
conditions.

These considerations all apply when selecting the ground motion(s)
to be used for the design of a facility so important that special
exploration and analyses are justified. They also apply in the less
specific problem of microzonation – toward which the remainder of this
paper is aimed.

Damage Vs. the Natural Period of Soil

From both theory and actual recordings of motions, we know that topography and soil amplification, including focussing, can concentrate energy in a more or less narrow range of frequencies. This feature of local site effects is often portrayed using elastic response spectra, as in Fig. 2. The period T_s, about which the hump on the soil-modified spectra B is centered, is considered to be the fundamental period of the site. It is then argued that a building whose fundamental period T_b coincides with T_s will be especially strongly affected by the earthquake.

This clearly is true if one considers solely elastic response. However, most buildings are designed with the expectation that they will yield during a major earthquake. As yielding occurs, the effective period of the building increases. Thus if the elastic period T_b coincides with T_s, during a major earthquake the building will tend to "slide off the peak" of the elastic response spectrum, and the response may not be so severe as supposed. Conversely, if a building with T_b less than T_s yields during an earthquake, its effective period increases toward T_s and the response may be greater than would be indicated by the elastic response spectrum.

These ideas have been understood in general terms for some time. At least one quantitative study has been performed (10, 17), the results of which will be summarized briefly. This study concentrated primarily upon the response of single-degree-of-freedom (1-DOF) systems with elastic-plastic force-deformation characteristics. Two types of ground motions were used as input: "normal motions" whose elastic response spectra had no predominant site-related peaks, and "site modified motions" – both actually-recorded motions, including an early record of motion in central Mexico City, and motions computed from normal motions using one-dimensional dynamic soil response theory together with a range of assumed site characteristics. The study was structured around the concept of smoothed inelastic response spectra (8). The ordinates are related to the peak acceleration, the peak velocity and the ductility (ratio of peak distortion to distortion at yield) developed in the 1-DOF system.

Several types of comparisons were made between the response to "normal" and "site-modified" motions. Fig. 3 shows the ductility ratios developed in a 1-DOF system with an elastic natural period $T_b=0.93s$ and viscous damping ratio of 5%, as the level of shaking, represented by the ratio of peak input acceleration to response yield acceleration, increases. Motion A2 is a "normal motion"; motion D2 is a "site modified motion" whose spectra has a broad, predominant peak at about $T_s=0.9s$. As the intensity of shaking increases, motion D2 is the first to cause yield (=1). However, at stronger shaking, say $a/a_y=3$ or more, much the same ductility ratio is developed by both motions.

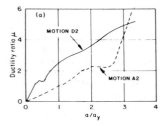 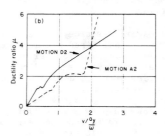

FIG. 3 − Ductility Ratio Versus Strength of Ground Motions for $\tau = 0.93$
       sec, Using Site-Modified (Motion D2) and "Normal" (Motion A2)
       Ground Motions.

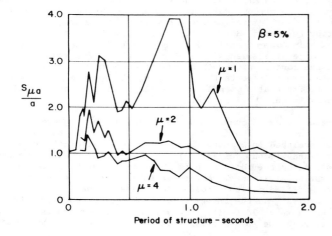

FIG. 4 − Elastic and Inelastic Response Spectra for Ground Motion D2.

Fig. 4 plots the yield resistance required to hold the developed ductility ratio μ to certain specific values, as a function of the period T_b of the 1-DOF system. The required yield resistance is expressed as the response acceleration at yield in ratio to the peak acceleration of the input motion, which is the "site modified motion" D2. The curve for μ=1 is just the normalized elastic response spectrum, and shows the predominent peak centered at about T_s=0.9s. However, this peak disappears for μ=4; this curve has a shape very similar to inelastic response spectra computed from normal motions.

Results such as those in Fig. 4 can be used to compute the spectral response ratios (for 5% viscous damping ratio) $S_{\mu am}/a$ and $S_{\mu vm}/V$, where $S_{\mu am}$ is the maximum ordinate of the inelastic acceleration response spectrum, for a ductility ratio μ, $S_{\mu vm}$ is the corresponding maximum ordinate of the inelastic velocity response spectrum and a and v are respectively the peak acceleration and peak velocity of the input motion. Averaging the results for the several "site-modified" ground motions used in the study, for μ in the range of 2 to 4, these ratios are 1.12 and 0.65. These values compare to 1.0 and 0.5, respectively, computed by Newmark and Hall using "normal motions".

All of these results show, quantitatively, that the response of ductile structures to "site-modified" motions is relatively insensitive to the actual predominant period T_s, and that the increase in response is much smaller than is indicated by an elastic response spectrum. When coupled to estimates of the effect of site conditions upon peak acceleration and peak velocity, such results permit construction of inelastic spectra for use in design. For example, Fig. 5 compares inelastic acceleration spectra at μ=4 for firm ground and several depths of a medium clay site. The decrease at low periods results from a decrease in peak acceleration up through the clays. The increase at large ordinates is about 60%

The aforementioned study also considered force-displacement relations with other than elasto-plastic characteristics, and with generally similar results. These additional studies did emphasize the importance of detailing for ductility ratios of at least 4. Multi-DOF systems were not studied. Obviously it would be premature to draw firm conclusions on the basis of these results alone.

Strategies for Microzonation

Microzonation, in the context of this discussion, involves the subdivision of a city or region into smaller areas within which different seismic design requirements are mandated.

An area might be microzoned to account for fault zones or for steep terrain in which landslides or rockfalls potentially cause excessive damage to any construction. These primarily geological aspects of the problem will not be considered here.

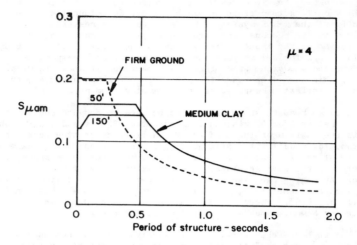

FIG. 5 - Inelastic Spectra for Site Where a = 0.2 g and v = 6 in/sec
(0.15 g/s) on Firm Ground.

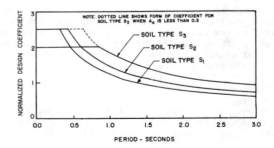

FIG. 6 - Normalized Lateral Design Force Coefficients (A$_a$ = A$_v$ = 1.0)
(1)

Microzonation also should consider the potential for liquefaction
failures. For regions where there has been an areawide study of
liquefaction potential, maps can be developed delineating sub-areas
where special attention must be given to the possibility of
liquefaction. For other regions, curves of standard penetration
resistance vs depth, for different depth of ground water, may be used –
as in the Massachusetts Building Code – as a screening test to identify
when a site must be reviewed for the possibility of liquefaction.
Special attention may mean: more detailed site-specific study,
improvement of a site, special design of structures and/or foundations,
or – from the standpoint of planning – restrictions upon land usage.
The potential for liquefaction may well be the most important reason
for microzoning a city or region, and is a major topic in its own right
(6) – but it is not the main subject matter for this paper.

Rather, we are here primarily concerned with microzonation as
regards differences in the character and intensity of ground motions –
and especially with the appropriate strategies for this purpose. A
discussion of methods that might be used to evaluate and analyze a
particular site or sites can become quite technical. However, I
believe the major obstacle to practical microzonation – at least within
the United States – is lack of a sound, agreed-upon strategy for
specifying the geographical variation of design requirements.

Some general principles: Paradoxically, the primary general
principle that should govern "microzoning" is that one should not, if
at all possible, establish zones! Boundaries across which there is
a step change in requirements are almost certain to lead to trouble
as regards to both adoption and compliance. One can understand the
difficulties that arise if requirements differ on opposite sides
of the same street or within a block. There may be exceptional cases
where soil conditions do change abruptly, such as at the edges of a
steep-sided valley. In general, however, subsurface conditions change
with distance in a continuous manner and so too should the effects of
local site conditions upon ground motions.

This makes undesirable an otherwise sensible strategy for dealing
with local site effects. I refer to requiring greater ductility in
structures whose fundamental period equals, or is somewhat less than,
an expected very predominant period in the ground motions. Required
changes in ductility are almost inherently incremental in nature, and
hence any such policy would violate the principle stated in the
previous paragraph.

It then follows that the level of forces considered in the design of
buildings must be varied to account for local site conditions. The
appropriate geographical variation may be prescribed either by:

* Maps giving contours for one or more parameters related to ground
  motion or design forces. Specific rules for interpolating
  between contours must be set forth. Just what parameters might
  be mapped, and how such maps might be constructed, will be
  discussed subsequently.

* Rules for evaluating soil factors on a site-by-site basis.
Examples are soil factors dependent upon a calculated fundamental
period of the soil (as in the 1982 version of the Uniform Building
Code) or soil factors related to word descriptions of site
characteristics (as in the ATC-3/NEHRP recommended design
provisions (1,2) and in the newest version of the Uniform Building
Code).

The second approach is undesirable, since such rules are subject to
different interpretations by different engineers. Soil factors related
to word descriptions also imply step changes in requirements, thus
violating the first principle stated above. However, these are the
only approaches possible where the effort required to produce maps is
not justified.

A final principle is that the less detailed and complete the review
of plans by building officials, the more precise the microzonation
restrictions should be. That is, some leeway for interpretation may be
allowed to owners/architects/engineers if there is to be a thorough
review of plans. Unfortunately, this principle and those discussed in
the previous paragraph generally are not consistent.

Lateral force coefficients: In the usual building code format,
"equivalent" static lateral forces are prescribed for purposes of
design. For example, in the ATC-3/NEHRP recommended provisions, the
base shear coefficient C is given by:

$$C = \frac{1.2A_2S_b}{RT_b^{2/3}} \text{ but not to exceed } 2.5\ A_1S_a/R$$

where A_1 and A_2 are macro ground motion parameters given by zoning
maps, R is a factor related to the ductile capacity of the structure,
T_b is the fundamental period of the structure and S_a and S_v are soil
factors. S_a varies between 0.8 and 1.0, the smaller value applying
when soft ground is shaken strongly. S_v ranges from 1.0 for firm
ground to 1.5 for deep, soft ground. (A maximum factor of 2 is now
being recommended to the Uniform Building Code.) These requirements
are displayed in graphical form in Fig. 6.

This format does not show the "hump" which can appear in elastic
response spectra where there are strong dynamic soil response effects.
Indeed, in the original ATC-3 study the requirement for soft soil was
arrived at, in part, by averaging typical spectral shapes, as shown in
Fig. 7. Thus, it might seem that the requirements are non-conservative
regarding what might happen at any one site. However, from the results
presented in the section Damage vs. Natural Period of Soil, we see that
this is not necessarily true for ductile structures. The use of a
maximum soil factor of 1.5 has various historical origins. Despite
knowing that local site amplifications can reach and exceed a factor of
3, a maximum factor of 1.5 was retained for the ATC-3 study. The
writer remembers agreeing to this only because Protonotarios's results
(10) showed this to to be reasonable – for ductile structures.

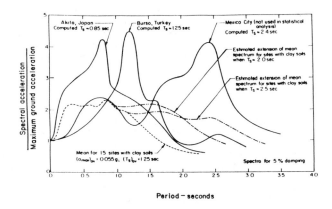

FIG. 7 – Comparison of Mean Spectra with Actual Spectra for Sites with Soft to Medium Stiff Clay (13)

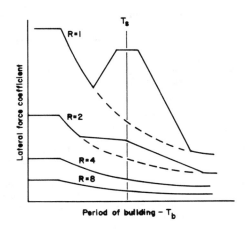

FIG. 8 – Sketch of Lateral Force Coefficients for Given Site, as a Function of Ductility Factor

This discussion implies that soil factors really should be different for different categories of structures, depending upon the degree of ductility assigned to that category. Moreover, as the presumed ductility decreases, the "hump" related to local soil conditions should reappear. Thus, for a given site, there would be a set of curves for different R-factors, somewhat as shown in Fig. 8. In the limit for R=1, the curve would be essentially an elastic response spectrum, modified to account for the role of higher natural modes of the structure.

Thus, while the soil factor format introduced in the ATC-3/NEHRP recommended provisions is reasonable for ductile structures, it would seem too simple for a wide range of categories of structures. Hence, there may be merit in returning to a soil factor which varies with period, as in the recent Uniform Building Codes; that is, soil factors described by a formula or graph and related to a characteristic period of a site. Now the formula or graph must include the ductility factor for the structure; the nature of the soil factor might be somewhat as shown in Fig. 9. More study will be required to determine the most appropriate form for the relationship. At least one parameter – the characteristic period T_s – and perhaps a second one – the maximum amplification S_{max} at a ductility factor of unity – must be specified. Ideally these parameters would be mapped continuously over the area being microzoned.

Specifications for dynamic analysis: It is difficult to see how the selection of recorded ground motions can be prescribed in a way that ensures a continuous variation of input over an area being microzoned. Hence it would seem that the specification of input for dynamic analysis must use elastic response spectra (or possibly Fourier spectra). Of course recorded ground motions deemed compatible with the spectra appropriate to a specific site might, with suitable blessing from a building official, be used for the actual analysis.

It should be possible to develop some relatively simple spectral shape – for an example, see Fig. 10 – describable by a few parameters whose variation over an area can be mapped.

Mapping: This is not a simple task, even though I may have made it sound as though it were. In few if any cities or regions is there, today, enough information such that microzonation maps can be developed with total confidence. Data from past earthquakes – patterns of damage and ground motion recordings – form the best basis for mapping; indeed, it can be said that any microzonation map will be rather unsatisfactory unless some such data are available. Based upon recent experience in Chile, measurements of ground motions at numerous stations during small, barely-felt earthquakes provide extremely valuable supplemental data (3). Theoretical ground response calculations are very useful in guiding the interpretation of actual data. Judgement in the application of data and theory will be essential.

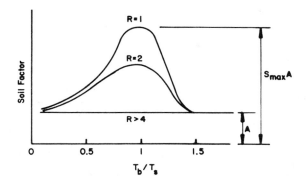

FIG. 9 - Sketch of Possible Curves of Soil Factor

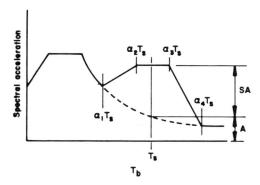

FIG. 10 - Sketch of Possible Site Modified Response Spectrum

I am reminded of George Housner's remarks concerning the preparation of zoning maps. He observed that, from the standpoint of scientists, it is impossible to prepare such maps; our knowledge simply is insufficient. However, if you bring together experts and tell them they must finish the task, they will produce a useful and reasonably reliable product. But, he also remarked, you must not expect them to explain exactly why the product has the form that resulted. Certainly the same is true for microzonation maps.

Conclusions

While the appropriateness and need for microzonation has been evident for some time, there have been very few efforts to do so - other than to account for possible ground failures. Now that the 1985 tragedy in Mexico City has forcibly reminded us about this problem, it is timely to devote more effort to the task. Even though the clay in Mexico is unique, the problems exposed by the earthquake are not unusual. A first step is to develop a logical, workable strategy for microzonation. This paper has discussed the questions that must be faced and has suggested some approaches that appear most useful.

References

1. Applied Technology Council, Tentative Provisions for the Development of Seismic Regulations for Buildings, ATC Publication 306, National Bureau of Standards Special Publication 510, U.S. Government Printing Office, Washington, D.C., June 1978.

2. Building Seismic Safety Council, NEHRP Recommended Provisions for the Development of Seismic Regulations for New Buildings. Part 1. Provisions, Prepared by BSSC for FEMA, Washington, D.C., 1985.

3. Celebi, M., "A Feature of the 3 March 1985 Chile Earthquake-- Topographical and Geological Amplification," 4th Chilean National Conference on Earthquake Engineering, Viña del Mar, Chile, 1986, pp. C1-19.

4. Donovan, Neville, Personal communication, 1986.

5. Kawasumi, H, Shima, E., Ohta, Y., Yanagisawa, M., Allam, A., and Miyakawa, K., "S. Wave Velocities of Subsoil Layers in Tokyo. 1." Bulletin of the Earthquake Research Institute, Tokyo, Vol. 44, 1966, pp. 731-747.

6. National Research Council, Liquefaction of Soils During Earth- quakes," Report by Committee on Earthquake Engineering, NRC, 1985.

7. Newmark, N.M. and Hall, W.J., "Seismic Design Criteria for Nuclear Reactor Facilties," Proceedings of the 4th World Conference on Earthquake Engineering, Vol. 2, 1969, pp. B-4 37-50.

8. Newmark, N.M. and Hall, W.J., Earthquake Spectra and Design, Earthquake Engineering Research Institute, Monograph Series, Berkeley, California, 1982.

9. Ohsaki, Y., "Effects of Local Soil Conditions upon Earthquake Damage," Soil Dynamics, Proceedings of the Specialty Session 2, 7th International Conference on Soil Mechanics and Foundation Engineering, R.V. Whitman, ed.; Woodward-Clyde Consultants, Oakland, California, 1969, pp. 3-32.

10. Protonotarios, J.N., "Linear and Non-linear Response to Site-Affected Earthquake Ground Motions," Ph.D. Thesis, Department of Civil Engineering, Massachusetts Institute of Technology, 1974.

11. Seed, H.B., "The Influence of Local Soil Conditions on Earthquake Damage," Soil Dynamics, Proceedings of the Specialty Session 2, 7th International Conference on Soil Mechanics and Foundation Engineering, R.V. Whitman, Ed.; Woodward-Clyde Consultants, Oakland, California, 1969.

12. Seed, H.B. and Idriss, I.M., Ground Motions and Soil Liquefaction During Earthquakes, Earthquake Engineering Research Institute, Monograph Series, Berkeley, California, 1982.

13. Seed, H.B., Ugas, C. and Lysmer, J., "Site Dependent Spectra for Earthquake Resistant Design," University of California, Berkeley, Report No. EERC 74-12, Nov. 1974.

14. Shima, E, Ohta, Y, Yanagisawa, M., Allam, A., and Kawasumi, H., "S Wave Velocities of Subsoil Layers in Tokyo. 2." Bulletin of the Earthquake Resaerch Institute, Tokyo, Vol. 46, 1968, pp. 759-772.

15. Trudeau, P.J., Whitman, R.V., and Christian, J.T., "Shear Wave Velocity and Modulus of a Marine Clay," Journal of the Boston Society for Civil Engineers, 1974, pp. 12-25.

16. Warwick, R. E., "Seismic Investigation of a San Francisco Bay Mud Site," Bulletin of the Seismological Society of America, Vol. 64, No. 2, 1974, pp. 375-385.

17. Whitman, R.V., and Protonotarios, J.N., "Inelastic Response to Site-Modified Ground Motions," Journal of the Geotechical Engineering Division, ASCE, GT10, 1977.

18. Zeevaert, L., Foundation Engineering for Difficult Subsoil Conditions, Van Nostrand Reinhold Co., New York, NY, 1972.

ANALYSES OF FOUNDATION FAILURES

By Pablo Girault D
*Member ASCE

ABSTRACT: During the earthquake of September 19th, 1985, many
buildings tilted and underwent settlements, sometimes of very
large magnitudes. This paper describes and analyzes these   -
settlements.
The characteristics of ground motion that took place in several
zones of Mexico City are presented and related to damages to
foundations. Mat, friction and end bearing pile foundations
that settled are described, as well as other types of damages
in Mexico City. Some damages near the epicenter are also   -
presented here.

INTRODUCTION

The very long, destructive earthquake that struck Mexico on Septem
ber 19th, 1985 produced much damage, especially in Mexico City where
hundreds of buildings were totally destroyed and thousands damaged.

The peculiar characteristics of ground motions that took place in
certain areas of Mexico City were responsible for the large damages.

This paper describes and analyzes the damages that foundations of
buildings underwent during the earthquake. Bearing capacity failures
produced settlements and tilting of buildings.

Description of other damages related to the subsoil for Mexico City
and towns near the epicenter is also included.

EARTHQUAKE CHARACTERISTICS

The epicenter of the earthquake was located at latitude 17.68°North
and 102.47° West Longitude, in the Pacific Ocean, some 30 Km away from
the West Coast of Mexico (Fig. No. 1) (Ref. No. 1).

The earthquake took place at 7:18 a.m. (13:18 Greenwich time) on   -
Thursday September 19th, 1985. It was classified as of intensity of
8.1 in Richter's scale. However Richter's classification does not   -
describe the destructiveness of the earthquake in the "Lake Zone" of
Mexico City, because of the peculiar ground motion it produced.

The earthquake was caused by the sudden release of elastic energy
during the subduction of the "Cocos" Crustal Plate under the North Ame
rican Continental Crustal Plate. Mexico City is located 400 Km North-
east of the epicenter and thus, far away.

The aftershock, on September 20, produced no damages.

Other details of the earthquake are given in other sessions of this
conference.

*Consulting Engineer
Agustín Ahumada # 319
México 11000,D.F.

GROUND MOTION NEAR EPICENTER

Many strong motion measuring instruments were located along the
Pacific Coast and near the epicenter. They recorded maximum accelerations of the ground of approximately 16% of gravity (g) in
the horizontal direction (Figure No. 1) (Ref. No. 1).

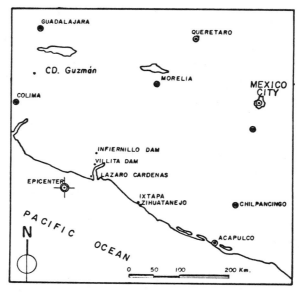

FIG. I MAP SHOWING EPICENTER

All of these instruments were located on subsoil of rather low
compressibility.

GROUND MOTION IN MEXICO CITY

The ground motion in Mexico City was very much influenced by the
type of subsoil that prevails under each zone of the City. Several
accelerograms of the earthquake were obtained in different parts of
the City.

In figure No. 2, in a map of the City, the location of the strong
motion instruments is shown: on firm soil, one at the University
City facilities (C.U.) on the southern part of the City, and one at
Tacubaya (TAC).

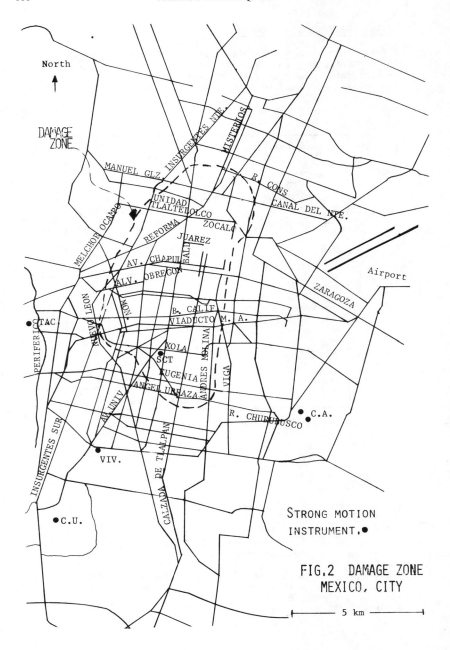

FIG.2 DAMAGE ZONE
MEXICO, CITY

Other instruments recorded the earthquake on soft ground, at the Secretaria de Comunicaciones y Transportes (S.C.T.) in the southern part of the City, and at the Central de Abastos on the eastern part of the City (C.A.) (Figure No. 2).

The ground motion of hard subsoil may be represented by the accelerogram recorded at C.U. and shown in Figure No. 3. At this place, instead of the Volcanic Mexico City clays, there are cemented sands and silts of low compressibility. The peak horizontal acceleration recorded at this location was 4% of gravity.

Figs. Nos. 3 & 4 - Acceleration Measured, Sept. 19 Earthquakes. Ref. 1

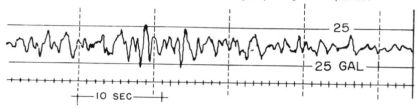

Fig. No. 3. E-W Component, at C.U.

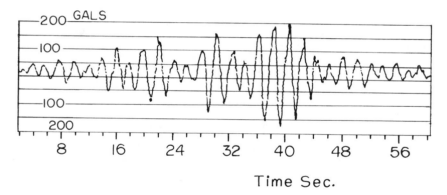

Time Sec.

Fig. No. 4 Computed Component for N30E - S60E from N-S and E-W Records, at S.C.T.

However in the "Lake Zone of the City", where much damage to foundations and structures, and collapse of buildings took place, the vibrations of the ground arriving from the epicenter were transformed, filtered and amplified by the clay layers and a very peculiar ground motion was recorded at the surface of the ground: the accelerations within the strong part of the earthquake may be represented by a harmonic motion with variable amplitudes, with a remarkable uniformity in the period of vibration (Fig. No. 4). This period is of two seconds at S.C.T., and it is believed that many structures came into resonance because their fundamental natural period of vibration was near that value (Fig. No. 4).

The East-West component of motion was 70% stronger than the N-S. In the Fig. No. 4 component, the acceleration amplitude remains higher than 5% of gravity during 15 complete oscillations of two second period, and five peaks are greater than 15%. So many cycles of this harmonic strong motion produced the collapse of many buildings between 9 and 16 stories because resonance occurred. This record is believed to be representative for the area where most of the damages to buildings occurred with slight variation in the length of the period of vibration.

At the Central de Abastos, on the Eastern part of the City, the predominant ground period was 3.6 seconds and the peak acceleration of 9.5% of gravity. Here the depth of the clay layers is much larger and this is why the period of vibration was longer.

Little damage was observed within this part of the City because the predominant ground motions would damage buildings over 25 stories high; there were no buildings this tall in this area. The harmonic motions recorded were produced by the clay layers vibrating horizontally in simple shear (Fig. No. 6) in their fundamental mode: if we compute the value of G (modulus of rigidity) from the formula for the fundamental period of vibration of the soil strata vibrating in shear:

$$T_1 = \frac{4\,H}{v_s} \quad \text{where the shear volocity } v_s = \sqrt{\frac{G}{\rho}} \text{ and } H = 40 \text{ m, the}$$

value of G would be near 80 Kg/cm^2 , which is in the order of magnitude for México City subsoil.

Other type of vibrations of the clay layers are assumed to have been small and vertical components of vibration, produced maximum accelerations of 4% throughout the City, irrespective of subsoil type.

The double amplitude of displacement was calculated to be of 50 and 42 centimeters at the surface, in the Lake Zone, from the integration of the accelerograms recorded at the Central de Abastos and S.C.T., respectively. Reference 1.

The ground horizontal fundamental period of vibration varies linearly with the thickness and inversely with the square root of the stiffness of the clay layers throughout the City. Towards the edges of the "Lake Zone", the thickness of the clay decreases and the stiffness decreases, and out of phase vibrations of the subsoil are produced, resulting in compressions and extensions of the surface of the ground. (Figure 6).

DAMAGES

There were practically no damages to foundations, structures of buildings or facilities on stiff soil. The zones with stiff soil are located to the West and Southwest of the City (Fig. No. 2).

The damaged buildings were located, in 90% of the cases, within that part of the City called the "Lake Zone" which is underlain by very thick deposits of the typical Mexico City Volcanic Clay.

There was little damage to buildings located in the Western and Southwestern "Transition" areas of the city where the clay layers extend to depths less than approximately 39 meters. This depth includes what are called the "Top and Bottom Volcanic clay layers and the First Hard Layer". Bedrock is at depths near two thousand meters under the City. The stratigraphy is described in detail in another paper to this conference.

Important damages were restricted to the area (Damage Zone) where the stratigraphy included clay layers of thickness from about 39 to 50 meters depth. Remarkably, little damage occurred for areas on the East side of the City, where the depths to stiff soils are greater than 50 meters, but there are practically no tall structures there.

The Damage Zone is shown in Figure No. 2, with the location of the strong motion instruments.

The Eastern and Northern boundaries could move out, if tall buildings are there, in future earthquakes. Most of the damages were in the buildings structures and only a small percentage in their foundations.

DAMAGES TO FOUNDATIONS

Mat Foundations

About 17 mat foundations, without piles, sank during the earthquake, as much as 1.2 meters. Table I. The magnitude of the settlements depend on the value of the static net pressure applied to the mat and the slenderness of the building, which influenced the pressure increments due to the overturning seismic moments.

TABLE I
Maximum Settlement of Some Buildings on Mat
Foundations after the Earthquake.

Building	Number of Stories	Length and Width (m)		Foundation Depth (m)	Settlement (cm)
MER 59 y DUR	7	17,	13	1.20**	120
MER 61	8	17,	13	1.50**	95
MER 65	7	17,	14	1.50**	80
CA NO	7	30,	25	1.80	120
CUPJ	10	48,	10	6.0	50
NA 28	10	21,	8.3	5.3	44
School C-14*	4	50,	12	1.0**	40
H. A CE*	4.3	35,	9	1.0**	80
H. DR	4	30,	19	0.2	50

*   On footings?
** Estimated

The first four buildings in Table I had higher than allowable net pressures and had undergone large settlements before the earthquake (Photo No. 1). These buildings had slenderness ratios (H/W) near 1.0 or less and thus their foundations did not receive large increments of load due to the earthquake. Their settlement during the earthquake is explained because of large static bearing pressures.

A building on a mat foundation, with no piles, located at the South western limit of the Damage Zone had a differential settlement of 44 cm after the earthquake. The building is very slender, 30 meters tall and 8.3 meters wide and was tilted before the earthquake.

Photo 1. Buildings on Mat Foundations sank,
during Earthquake.

For a seismic overturning moment corresponding to a seismic shear
coefficient of 6% of gravity, applied at 0.66 times the height, dis-
garding vertical accelerations, the bearing capacity of the subsoil at
the edge of the foundation is exceeded 1.5 times in 2/3 of the length
of the building and 2.2 times in the rest of the length. Because of
the foundation depth of 5.3 m the volcanic clays influence the bearing capacity of this building.

During the earthquake the bearing capacity of the subsoils was
most probably exceeded, as 6% is a conservative seismic shear coefficient for this earthquake, but the cyclic nature of the earthquake's
acceleration and the energy absorption due to settlements may have
prevented overturning of this building.

It is remarkable that the foundations of the last three buildings
listed on Table I, failed, as they are only four stories high. The
last building has a mat at sidewalk level. The other two are probably
on footings. In the four-story school building, tilting was accompanied
by horizontal movements of eight centimeters.

All the buildings listed in Table I, failed because of poor foundation design except for the 10 story CUPJ, where resonance might have
influenced its behavior.

Friction Piles

Some 25 buildings on mat foundations also supported on friction
piles, suffered sudden, and in cases, large settlements during the
earthquake (Table II), with large differential settlements and tilting. These buildings tilted practically as rigid blocks.

Previous tiltings due to static loads were increased during the
earthquake. Previous settlements are included in Table II. Penetration of the friction piles during the earthquake and simultaneous shear
failure of the volcanic clay under the mat, produced the settlements.

Photographs No. 2 and 3 show buildings that settled very much
during the earthquake. Bulging of the pavement around some of these

buildings was noted; the amount of heaving was relatively small. The
soil under the mat displaced laterally and upwards around the buildings in a much larger area, and thus the bulging is difficult to notice
and also to measure; this was also true for mat foundations.

Photo No. 2

Building on Friction
Piles after earth-
quake.

It is suspected that the bearing capacity of the friction piles
during the earthquake was decreased somewhat because the clay layers
were vibrating in shear, at strain rates with double amplitude values of
the order of one percent, as an average; thus degradation of the shear
modulus might have taken place. However, the failure of friction piles
in foundations, was mostly produced by the extremely large increments
of load that they received during the earthquake, because of seismic
overturning moments, larger than what they were designed for.

In two of these buildings, the mat foundations failed structurally:
In one 20-story building, the 35 cm thick reinforced concrete slab,
failed in shear while the bottom reinforcing bars remained anchored
to the underlying foundation beams, thus there was splitting of the slab
horizontally, near the supports (Fig. No. 5). After the earthquake, the
slabs supported the soil pressures, working as catenaries with deflections near 20 cms. at the center. The friction piles located under the
foundation beams of this building penetrated during the earthquake and
differential settlements after the earthquake were of 55 cms.

It is believed that the energy spent by the earthquake in breaking
and bulging this foundation mat and producing the subsoil shear failures, saved this building's superstructure from severe damage or even
collapse.

TABLE II

Maximum Settlements of some Buildings on -
Friction Piles after the earthquake.-

Building	Number of Stories	Length and width (m)	Approx. Maximum Settlement cm
DI 20 NO	15	50, 28	130
ZA 74	9	37, 13	120
VERT	10	14	100
RE Y AV	10	70, 22	100
AL OB 151	16	40, 18	60
LI	15	21, 15	60
AR BE* △	20	40, 40	60
JU*+	16	46, 34 & 60	55
CO 84	11	28, 18	50
JUZ	12	53, 17	30
QUE	10	29, 13.5	30
FRON	13	29, 12	16
ZA Y M			15

* Foundation slab broke
+ Piles with "penetrating" point
△ With "B" piles

For earthquakes like the one in September 19th, 1985, the criterium in seismic structural design is oriented to avoid partial or total collapse of the building and accept large damages. It is therefore much better to end up with a building tilting, than having its collapse.

In another similar case, the building settled 55 cm and the foundation slab heaved 1.5 meters reducing the basement height to crawling space; in this case, the slab concrete failed in tension at the top of the underlying foundation beams.

A building within the heart of the "Damage Zone", was recently checked to have enough friction piles to support the earthquake specified by the building Code. This building suffered differential settlements with a maximum of 30 cm. In spite of its tilting, the building's foundation behaved well considering the earthquake's magnitude. The superstructure was not damaged: absorption of energy because of the settlements helped to decrease the superstructure's response.

A ten story building overturned when its concrete mat foundation, supported on friction piles, failed in shear. The foundation did not cover all of the area of the 12 by 17 meters lot.

The stronger component of the earthquake, according to the S.C.T. record, acted along the minimum moment of inertia of the foundation. The fundamental period of vibration was lengthened by rocking of the foundation and the building most probably vibrated into resonance.

Photo No. 3.
Settlement of Building after earthquake.

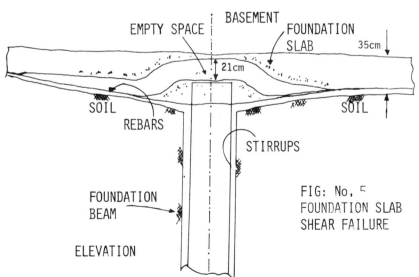

BASEMENT

EMPTY SPACE

FOUNDATION SLAB

35cm

21cm

SOIL

SOIL

REBARS

STIRRUPS

FOUNDATION BEAM

FIG: No. 5
FOUNDATION SLAB SHEAR FAILURE

ELEVATION

As it overturned, the west corner sank some six meters into the soil, displacing soil backwards and upwards forming a bulge in its backyard. Piles were pulled out of the ground as the back part of the foundation rose out of the ground almost three meters. Other piles broke under tension at their head.

Overturning of a building under a random cyclic motion is difficult because the motion is reversed before the structure overturns and the absorption of energy of the incipient shear failure, diminishes the response of the building.

In the case of resonance, overturning is a possibility.

Many buildings' foundations on friction piles in a range of 10 to 16 stories performed well, in the Damage Zone, but their superstructures were badly damaged during the earthquake.

End Bearing Piles

End bearing piles performed better than friction piles in the earthquake. However, there are less buildings on end bearing piles nowadays, and the design factor of safety is near three.

Settlements due to penetration of this type of pile were much smaller and the author knows of only three failures of these pile foundations:

The piles under a concrete shear wall in a tall building sank about 50 cm. breaking the foundation. This shear wall received overturning moments much larger than what it was designed for, during the earthquake.

An old, slender 14 story building, increased its inclination during the earthquake.

In a building in the Southern part of the City, and away from the damage zone, piles were broken in shear at their top when, because of regional subsidence, the piles' heads were not surrounded by soil anymore, loosing their embedment.

"Controlled" piles

Many buildings were supported on end bearing piles which had load limiting "control" devices on their heads; the piles were designed to penetrate freely through holes in the foundation slab. The devices were of two types: a) two inch wooden cubic blocks placed in layers of about 20 blocks per layer in approximately four layers; compression of the blocks is supposed to take place at a constant predetermined load. The wooden blocks compressed very much on the first oscillations of the buildings depriving the foundation slabs (mats) from the load carrying capacity of the piles during the earthquake. Many slender buildings suffered large tilting when supported on these devices.

The other type of load limit device used commonly, is a sheet metal flat jack, filled with oil. The load is measured by means of a pressure gage and limited by hand, during periodic inspections. In slender buildings in the damage zone, many of these devices burst open due to over-pressures generated by the overturning seismic moments.

MECHANICS OF SETTLEMENTS

The final settlements of buildings are known, but it is not known how the buildings settled gradually during the earthquake. Most probably the progression of the small shear failures and the corresponding settlements, was of increments during the large oscillations of the buildings which may have been from 10 to 20; the movement was downwards in every case because upheaval of the part of the foundation where pressures decreased in that oscillation, seems unlikely, unless surrounding areas were heavierly loaded.

Practically all of the buildings that suffered large settlements had concrete or brick shear walls or load bearing walls. The walls conveyed greater seismic overturning moments to the foundations.

RESONANCE

In other recorded earthquake, some regularity in the period of vibration had been observed (Reference No. 2) but the intensity and duration, were not strong or long enough, to establish a steady state of resonance, both in the subsoil and in structures.

Apparently, the Sept. 19, 1985 earthquake had enough energy in a band near the two second period to set into vibration, in simple shear, the upper subsoil layers. This happened in the "Damage Zone" producing a uniform period ground movement which acted like a harmonic forced vibration on all structures and when the ground and building's fundamental period were near, resonance occurred and oscillations of buildings tended to infinity, limited only by the capacity of the structure to dissipate the ingoing earthquake energy.

The fundamental period of vibration of the building depends on the stiffness of the structure, its weight and on the rocking and sliding stiffness of the foundation. It is believed that buildings from about 9 to 16 stories had, or acquired, periods of vibration near two seconds: when building structures became overstressed in the latter part of the earthquake and worked in the plastic range, or there was rocking and/or sliding of their foundations, their period of vibration increased.

Many buildings in the resonance period range, remained standing after the earthquake, even though they were severely damaged, because they had many partition or infilling walls made of brick. The breaking of brick absorbed large amounts of energy and the earthquake could not build up large excursions of the structure. As long as buildings kept enough of these walls within their frames and the breakage of brick was possible still, near the end of the earthquake, they remained standing.

Displacing the subsoil in small alternating shear failures requires much energy.

Absorption of energy at foundations, in a controlled and limited way, seems to be very attractive to protect buildings from collapse, in future earthquakes. Seismic shear coefficients specified for foundations, in building codes must be smaller than for structures of buildings, for this reason.

OTHER TYPES OF DAMAGES

Sidewalks in the "Damage Zone" were badly cracked and displaced due to differential horizontal movements of the surface of the ground: many sidewalks buckled in compression, and cast iron sewer inletes were

crushed alonq curbs. The displacements took place even though no
buildinqs were near them, like in front of empty lots. Asphalt
pavements crushed into the slabs of concrete pavements indicating
differential horizontal movements during the earthquake.

The stone facing of the edge of sidewalks came off due to horizontal
accelerations at ground level.

Some cracks were observed on the surface of the ground, due to
compression in horizontal directions caused by out of phase vibrations
of the subsoil: street car tracks no longer in use and buried in the
pavement, buckled at these places (Photo No. 4). (Fig. No. 6 b).

The earthquake produced much damage to water pipes that were buried
in the areas where most damages to buildings occurred; the water system
suffered very much. The author inspected a 12 inch steel pipe failed
under compression at a joint, next to where track rails buckled.

Grabens were formed on the surface of the qround at three places
known to the author; the largest was about 40 by 120 meters and 0.80 m
deep; it sank under streets and one and two story homes, where the
clay layers extend to depths approximately 60 meters, near the airport.
One possible explanation is: out of phase simultaneous outward shear
vibration of the clay layers at the graben edges, leaving a soft clay
"column" unsupported laterally for a couple of seconds and permitting
its lateral expansion and consequent vertical compression (Fig. No.
6 c). The outward movement was approximately 25 centimeters each way
during about 1.8 seconds (half the natural period of vibration).

Photo No. 4. Buckled and broken, buried rail and cracking of
pavement in background.

Horizontal openings of sidewalk slabs was observed at the graben
boundaries.
   A large reinforced concrete water conduit in an old river bed that
crosses the "Damage Zone" along Viaducto M.A. (Fig. No. 2). underwent
slight compression spalling of the concrete at the construction joints.
This rigid conduit extends westwards into a zone where less movement
of the ground took place: the subsoil slipped under it, as it vibrated
at double amplitudes of 40 cms and bumps 15 cms high. rose on the
parallel adjoining roadways every 100 meters, where the surface soil
buckled due to the friction against the conduit.
   The subway ("Metro") concrete "box", built one meter under the
street level, rose two inches along some streets. This structure is
overcompensated by about 2.5 ton/m^2 and its behavior is typical of
overcompensated buildings during earthquakes. This concrete structure
suffered no damage, nor did the elevated tracks.
   Utilities were damaged as they entered the buildings that underwent
sudden settlements during the earthquake.
   The deep, five meter diameter, sewer system, at 30 meters depth under the "Damage Zone", performed very well during the earthquake.
   A peculiar phenomenon was the sinking of steel electric power posts
during the earthquake. These posts sank four meters during the earthquake and are located approximately one block away from each other.
The vibrations decreased the friction in the buried portion of the
post.
   Telephone cables suffered no damage during the earthquake: the
concrete telephone conduits are placed with some clearance at the
joints to absorb differential settlements: these spaces probably
saved the conduits from breaking in compression. However, the long-
distance-telephone Central Building collapsed partially. destroying
communications in and out of the City.

DAMAGES NEAR EPICENTER

   Towns near the epicenter are small. Some damages were observed:
   The roadway, on the approaches to a bridge, cracked open due to
licuefaction of soils in the river terrace under the highway embankment; several longitudinal cracks, about six inches wide, opened
over a length of half a mile, crisscrossing the pavement.
   A water pipe, 2.1 meters in diameter, crossing under the roadway
at this place, suffered a lateral displacement of several inches due
to licuefaction of soils under the embankment.
   Some licuefaction of sands took place also, under some rather recent
sandfills in several industrial plants, in the town of Lázaro-Cárdenas,
near the epicenter. In some cases, the typical sand cones appeared
at the surface and in other water ran out of cracks and deposited
fine clean sand in thin layers, with no sand cone forming.
   An embankment for a road failed by spreading out during the earthquake. The subsoil under the embankment is peat. This embankment cros-
sed a lagoon's outlet to the ocean.
   Tsunamis were produced after the Sept. 19 and 20 earthquakes at Ixta-
pa, a resort 150 Km away from the epicenter (Fig. No. 1). Sea water
reached the ground floor of most hotels along the beach, with damages
to furniture only.

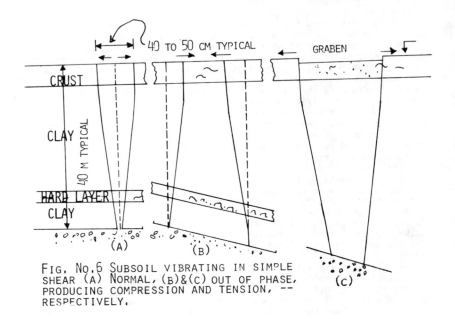

FIG. NO.6 SUBSOIL VIBRATING IN SIMPLE
SHEAR (A) NORMAL, (B)&(C) OUT OF PHASE,
PRODUCING COMPRESSION AND TENSION, --
RESPECTIVELY.

o o o o o o o

REFERENCES

1.) "Accelerograms at C.U., C.A.. T.A.C., S.C.T., Viveros and La
Villita. September 1985. Instituto de Ingeniería.
U.N.A.M. Mexico City.

2.) Zeevaert L. "Pile design Problems in Earthquake Areas". Fig.
No. 3. Pile Talk Seminar. Assoc. Pile & Fitting Corp.
March 1977. Clfton, N.J.

SOIL-STRUCTURE INTERACTION IN MEXICO CITY DURING THE 1985 EARTHQUAKES

by

Daniel Reséndiz*, M. ASCE and J.M. Roesset**, M. ASCE

Abstract

The effects of the flexibility of the soil and the foundation on the seismic response of structures, by opposition to clear foundation failures, cannot be easily identified from a simple observation of buildings after an earthquake, requiring either records of the motions (both translational and rotational components) at the base (and other levels), or detailed analytical studies. Although neither of these are available at this time, it is still possible, using relatively simple models, to make preliminary estimates of the types and magnitudes of the effects in Mexico City for different types of buildings and foundations. This paper presents a basic discussion of the nature of soil structure interaction effects and their possible importance in Mexico City, identifying some of the key aspects that should be taken into account, and recommends various topics where further research would be desirable.

Introduction

The purpose of this paper is to review some of the basic concepts of seismic soil structure interaction and their applicability to the case of Mexico City, to present preliminary estimates of the possible nature and magnitude of the effects, and to identify some lessons to be learned from the 1985 earthquake through appropriate future research.

The effects of local soil conditions on the characteristics of the seismic motions at the base of a building are normally studied in three separate phases[12]:

1. Before any structure is built the amplitude and the frequency content of the seismic motions at the free surface or at any depth within a soil deposit are functions of the soil properties in the linear elastic and inelastic ranges, as well as the types, relative amplitudes and frequencies of the waves arriving at the site. This effect is commonly known as soil amplification although in reality there is an amplification of the motions over some frequency ranges and deamplification over others. There has been in the past some controversy as to the nature and magnitude of amplification effects, the validity of the one dimensional theory (which assumes body waves propagating vertically), and our ability to predict site specific motions (particularly for average soil deposits). However, the geometric and mechani-

---

*Secretary General, National Council for Science and Technology (CONACYT), México, D.F.
**Professor, The University of Texas at Austin

cal properties of Mexico City's subsoil have always represented the
ideal example to illustrate these soil effects and to explain them
with the simplest theories. Figure 1 shows the response spectrum of
the motion recorded in the lake zone at site SCT[7], where large amount
of damage took place during the earthquakes of September 1985[9]. The
soil at the site has a depth of 35 m (115 ft) a relative mass density
of 1.30 (unit weight of 12,750 N/m[3] or 81 lb/ft[3]) and a shear wave velocity of 70 m/sec (230 ft/sec)[2,10]. Hence the one dimensional linear
theory yields a fundamental period of 2 seconds (a frequency of 0.5
cps) which agrees very well with the main peak in the response spectrum. The second and third natural frequencies, if the soil layer had
homogeneous properties, would be 1.5 and 2.5 cps. It can be seen in
Figure 1 that there is an additional peak in the spectrum around this
second frequency but that a third peak occurs at a frequency slightly
above 3 cps, indicating that while the simple one dimensional theory
assuming a homogeneous soil layer with constant properties cannot re-
produce all the details of the motion it can explain the main features.
The same predictability has been shown to hold true for other sites in
Mexico City where ground-motions were recorded[10]. A more detailed
discussion of the dynamic soil response of the Mexico City Valley lies
out of the scope of this paper and is presented in another session.

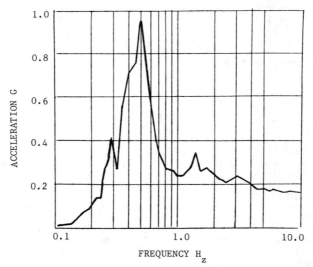

Figure 1. Response spectrum of motion at SCT. 5% Damping

2. The motion of a massless foundation before any structure is
built, or if the structure had no mass, would be different from that
recorded at the free surface or at any depth within the soil deposit
(including the level of the foundation). The differences will consist
in general of an averaging of the translational motions (a decrease of
their amplitude) and the occurrence of rotational components of motion.
The only case where this effect would not be present is for a surface

foundation and vertically propagating seismic waves in a uniform soil deposit.

3. Once the structure is built, or when its mass is taken into account, the inertia forces generated by the structural vibrations will give rise to base shears, an axial force and overturning and torsional moments. Unless the soil is extremely stiff, these base forces will result in additional deformations which will alter the motion of the foundation. The acceleration at the base of the structure will thus be different from the one that would be recorded in the free field (at the surface or at the foundation level) and from the one that the foundation would experience by itself.

Effects 2 and 3 are commonly known as soil structure interaction. The first one is sometimes called kinematic interaction (function of the geometry of the foundation and the types of seismic waves propagating through the soil), while the second is referred to as inertial interaction (caused by the inertia forces in the structure).

While this division into three separate phases is convenient from a conceptual point of view, it is important to remember that the effects are very closely related and take place simultaneously.

It is common trying to relate the damage and general performance of buildings during an earthquake, at a site where soil effects are important, to the proximity of the structures' natural period and that of the soil deposit. This approach ignores not only the characteristics of the buildings and the quality of their design, but also the effects of nonlinear structural behavior and soil structure interaction. For a soil deposit with a fundamental period of 2 seconds, corresponding to the response spectrum of Figure 1, one would thus conclude that buildings with periods between 1.4 and 3 seconds, and particularly around 2 seconds, would experience the strongest motions. In fact, since the depth of the clay deposit in the area of heaviest damage varies from 25 to 50 meters (natural periods of 1.5 to 2.9 seconds) the same argument would suggest that depending on the location within this area the buildings most affected by the earthquake would be those with roughly 15 to 29 stories (assuming a natural period of 0.1 seconds per story, which is a good approximation for the case of buildings in Mexico[6]). However, considering soil structure interaction effects as well as nonlinear structural behavior, it can be shown that somewhat stiffer buildings with fundamental elastic periods on a rigid base of 0.7 to 1.8 seconds (say 7 to 18 stories) would be more seriously affected by the characteristics of the Mexico City earthquakes. This shows better agreement with the actual height of the buildings more severely damaged (6 to 16 stories).

Out of some 330 severely damaged buildings inspected by teams from the Instituto de Ingeniería of the Universidad Nacional Autónoma de México (UNAM) in the area of heavy damage, 13% had some foundation distress, although not all of them could be properly considered as foundation failures. Aside from a few cases in which relatively slender buildings on shallow foundations or friction piles completely overturned, a more common type of damage resulted from settlements leading in some cases to permanent leaning of the structures. While these types of failures are immediately apparent, others require a more detailed inspection of the foundation with possible excavation of the surrounding soil. The structural damage resulting from foundation failures or differential settlements (occurring during or after the earthquake due to dissipation of excess pore pressures) fall clearly within the category of soil structure interaction effects. Even so most dynamic soil structure interaction analyses concentrate on the effect of the soil flexibility on the dynamic response of the structure assuming an adequate performance of the foundation, linear soil behavior (with equivalent properties consistent with the levels of strains) and perfect bonding between the foundation and the surrounding soil (although separation effects are sometimes included). Identification of this type of effects is impossible from visual observation of the buildings, since it requires records of the motions (both translational and rotational components) at the base, in the free field, and possibly at other floor levels, or detailed analytical studies. Such records are not available in Mexico City and no theoretical studies have been completed to date. Even so, it is possible to estimate with relatively simple models the types of effects, their approximate magnitude and the performance of various types of buildings and foundations.

Kinematic Interaction

When dealing with a surface foundation and seismic waves propagating at arbitrary angles of incidence, the main two effects will be an averaging of the translational motion and the appearance of rotational components. Figure 2 shows the ratios of the amplitudes of the translational motion at the center of a rigid mat and the torsional component of the horizontal motion at the edge, to the amplitude of motion at the free surface of the soil in the free field for horizontally propagating shear waves in an elastic half space[12]. The results are a

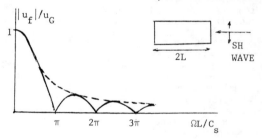

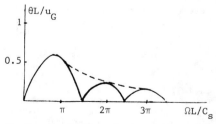

Figure 2.   Transfer functions for translation and torsion of foundation. Horizontally propagating SH waves

function of $\Omega L/c_c$ where Ω is the frequency in radians/second and c_c is the apparent velocity of propagation of the waves. It can be seen that the translational motion of the foundation decreases with increasing frequency (filtering or averaging effect) but that the torsional component becomes significant over an extended range of frequencies.

In assessing the potential importance of these effects in the case of Mexico City the key parameter is the apparent velocity of propagation of the waves in the horizontal direction **c**. Most soil structure interaction analyses with travelling waves assume values of **c** of 2 to 3 km/sec (6,000 to 10,000 ft/sec) corresponding to wave velocities in rock. This assumption is justified by theoretical considerations (clearly body waves travelling at any angle through rock would have nearly vertical incidence when propagating through a soft soil deposit) as well as by experimental determination of apparent horizontal velocities from records obtained with instrumental arrays (on firm ground). For these values of **c** one would conclude that torsional effects due to kinematic interaction would be negligible in Mexico City. On the other hand, given the epicentral distance, one might expect that the 1985 earthquake would have a significant content of surface waves. The question then is whether Love waves could be generated in the clay deposit of the valley. For values of the apparent velocity **c** of 70 to 100 m/sec (230 to 330 ft/sec) and periods of 1.5 to 2 seconds (values of Ω of π to 1.3 π) important torsional effects would be present in the excitation of foundations with a length 2L of 70 to 100 m. While the translation of the middle of the slab might be reduced by 30%, the motion of the edge combining the rigid body translation and torsional rotation might increase by 20 to 25%. The importance of these effects would depend then on the configuration and characteristics of the structure. These effects would be even more significant for spread footings since in this case the occurrence of torsional components would not be partly offset by a continuous mat through averaging of the translational motion, and to some degree for pile foundations if the pile heads are not connected by a rigid slab (although the nature of these effects for pile foundations is far more complicated).

Similar considerations can be made for Rayleigh waves except that in this case the filtering of the translational motion (for a rigid mat) would be accompanied by rocking components of motion.

When dealing with embedded mat foundations there will be kinematic effects even for vertically propagating waves[2, 3]. Figure 3 shows the ratio between the amplitudes of the translational and rotational motions of a rigid box foundation (the rotation is multiplied by the radius yielding the vertical displacement at the edge) and the amplitude of the translation at the free surface of the soil in the free field. It can be noticed that as the amplitude of the translation decreases the magnitude of the rotation increases. The most significant parameter in the definition of these curves (which are valid for embedment depths larger than half of the foundation radius) is the natural frequency f_0 of the embedment layer. For Mexico City, with a shear wave velocity of the soil of 70 m/sec (230 ft/sec), this frequency would be 17.5/E where **E** is the embedment depth in meters and f_0 is in $\sec^{-1}$. High frequency components of motion (of 2 cps or larger) would experience a substantial reduction in amplitude for embedment depths of only 3 to 5 m (10 to 15 ft). On the other hand the main component of the earthquake with a frequency of 0.5 cps (a period of 2 sec) would only experience significant reductions in amplitude for embedment depths of

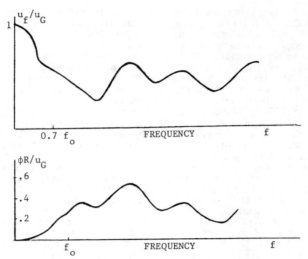

Figure 3. Transfer functions for translation and rocking of
foundation. Vertically propagating waves

15 m (45 ft) or more. Short, stubby buildings would benefit from even
moderate embedment of their foundations but these are the buildings
which are not likely to be in trouble for an earthquake with the characteristics of the Mexico City motions. More flexible buildings with
fundamental periods of 1.5 to 2 seconds when accounting for the flexibility of the soil (inertial interaction) would require the deeper em-
bedments. For a slender structure, on the other hand, the rotational
component may offset in part the reduction in translational acceleration at the base and result in increased displacements in the upper
levels.

There have been very few studies conducted to estimate kinematic
effects on pile foundations[1,4]. For a single pile the amplitude of
motion at the pile head is esentially equal to that at the same level
in the free field. There is the possibility of a slight increase in
motion over the range of small frequencies (long periods) and a substantial amount of filtering for very high frequencies but little effect overall for the range of frequencies of common interest. When
dealing, on the other hand, with a complete pile foundation consisting
of a large number of piles, filtering effects may start to take place
at lower frequencies, particularly for end bearing piles. The effect
will be larger for an embedded foundation on piles even if it is assumed that the mat is not in contact with the soil. In this case
moreover the rotational component of motion will not be of any consequence when dealing with end bearing piles penetrating a hard soil
stratum or rock. It should be noticed that kinematic interaction
analyses for pile foundations are needed not only to estimate the
foundation motions but also to compute the forces in the piles caused
by the seismic waves, which must be combined with those resulting from
the vibration of the structure.

Identification of some kinematic interaction effects is not easy unless detailed analyses are conducted to separate them from the effects of inertial interaction. Structures will experience, for instance, torsional vibrations due to an irregular distribution of masses and stiffnesses (leading to eccentricities between the centers of mass and stiffness of the floors) even if the motion at the foundation from kinematic interaction does not have a torsional component. Similarly rocking motions will always exist due to the overturning moments at the base caused by the inertia forces and will be combined with those resulting from the base input for embedded foundations.

Inertial Interaction

The inertial interaction, or modification of the base motion due to the structural vibration, is the most commonly associated with the name soil-structure interaction. Although the effect of kinematic interaction may be equally important, or even more so in some cases, the inertial interaction is of significance not only in seismic design, but also in cases where the dynamic excitation is applied directly to the structure.

Two different approaches can be used to estimate inertial interaction effects in the seismic case. The first one, similar to that used in the other two phases, is to determine the changes in the base motion in order to arrive at a design earthquake, including all soil effects, which can be used for the dynamic analysis of the structure on a rigid base. The second, easier to understand and implement, is to modify the structural model to include the effect of soil flexibility.

To estimate inertial interaction effects it is convenient to consider a single degree of freedom system consisting of a mass **M** at a height **h** over the foundation base and an axial or shear spring with a stiffness **k**. This system can be selected so as to represent the behavior of the structure in its first, fundamental mode, or so as to represent an equivalent system for an assumed deformed shape of the structure[12]. If T_o is the fundamental period of the structure on a rigid base and x_i are the modal or assumed displacements of level i with mass m_i, at a height h_i

$$M = (\Sigma \ m_i \ x_i)^2 / \Sigma \ m_i \ x_i^2 \qquad k = 4 \ \pi^2 \ M/T_o^2 \qquad h = \Sigma \ m_i \ x_i \ h_i / \Sigma \ m_i \ x_i$$

If the soil and the foundation are reproduced as a first approximation by a horizontal spring and dashpot ($k_x \ c_x$) and a rocking spring and dashpot ($k_\phi \ c_\phi$), which are functions of frequency, the effective undamped natural period of the soil structure system is

$$T = T_o \ \sqrt{1 + k/k_x + kh^2/k_\phi} \qquad (1)$$

The effective damping of the system at a frequency Ω can be expressed approximately as

$$D = D_{st}(T_o/T)^2 + D_s[1 - (T_o/T)^2] + \frac{1}{2} \ \Omega \ (\frac{T_o}{T})^2 \ [\frac{c_x}{k_x} \cdot \frac{k}{k_x} + \frac{c_\phi}{k_\phi} \cdot \frac{kh^2}{k_\phi}] \qquad (2)$$

where D_{st} is the internal damping in the structure, D_s is the internal soil damping and the third term represents radiation damping.

From the consideration of this highly simplified model it can be concluded that inertial interaction will have two main effects: an increase in the effective natural period of the system and a change (in general an increase) in the effective damping. It should be noticed that these effects are similar to those associated with nonlinear structural behavior. When both soil structure interaction and nonlinear structural response occur simultaneously their effects are compounded although not additively (as the structure softens due to inelastic behavior the interaction with the soil decreases).

The key parameters to estimate the magnitude of inertial interaction effects are the values of k/k_x, kh^2/k_ϕ, c_x/k_x and c_ϕ/k_ϕ. For a circular mat foundation on the surface of an elastic half space the dynamic stiffnesses may be expressed in the form[5]

$$k_x = \left[8GR/(2-\nu)\right]k_1 \qquad c_x = \left[8GR^2/(2-\nu)c_s\right]c_1 \atop k_\phi = \left[8GR^3/3(1-\nu)\right]k_2 \qquad c_\phi = \left[8GR^4/3(1-\nu)c_s\right]c_2 \right\} \qquad (3)$$

where G is the shear modulus of the soil, c_s its shear wave velocity and ν its Poisson's ratio, R is the radius of the foundation and k_1, k_2, c_1, c_2 are functions of frequency. Figure 4 shows the variation of these coefficients for a half space[11].

When dealing with a layer of soil of finite depth the terms k_x, c_x increase by a factor $1 + 0.5$ R/H, where H is the depth of the stratum and the terms k_ϕ, c_ϕ by $1 + 0.16$ R/H. In addition, as shown also in Figure 4, the dynamic coefficients show some marked oscillations due to the natural frequencies of the soil. More importantly, the terms c_1 and c_2 become virtually zero below the natural frequency of the soil layer.

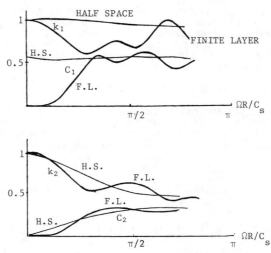

Figure 4. Dynamic stiffness coefficients.
           Circular mat foundations

Magnitudes of interaction in Mexico City

In the case of Mexico City, for the soil properties mentioned before and a stratum depth of 35 m (115 ft) whose natural period is 2 sec, assuming that buildings have a natural period of 0.1 seconds per story, a unit weight of 2,400 to 3,000 N/m^3 (15 to 20 lbs/cu ft) and **h** equals 0.7 times the building height, eq. (1) becomes approximately

$$T = T_o (1 + \frac{1}{2\lambda} + \lambda)^{1/2} \qquad (4)$$

where λ is the slenderness ratio of the building (ratio of its height to its base diameter).

This indicates that the effective natural period of buildings with slenderness λ between 1 and 5 may increase in Mexico City by a factor of 1.6 to 2.5 over that computed on a rigid base. This increase in the period was thus clearly detrimental during the 1985 earthquakes for buildings with initial periods (on a rigid base) of 1 to 1.5 seconds (even somewhat smaller periods if one accounts for nonlinear structural behavior).

Moreover, it should be noticed in Figure 4 that as the effective period approaches or exceeds 2 seconds the radiation damping (which would be benefitial) decreases strongly, since c_1 and c_2 tend to cero. Interaction effects would be larger in this range for slender buildings for which the rocking motion would control. On the other hand buildings with initial periods of the order of 2 seconds or larger would benefit from the elongation of the effective period, although they would not be able to count on radiation damping.

Embedment of the foundation would increase the values of k_x and k_ϕ, reducing therefore the shift in the effective period[3]. It would also increase substantially the values of c_x and c_ϕ but only above the natural frequency of the soil layer (for effective periods smaller than 2 sec). Foundation embedment would thus be beneficial from the dynamic point of view for structures with natural periods of 0.7 to 1.2 seconds but it would not help (and might harm) buildings in the range from 1.5 to 2 seconds.

The stiffnesses of pile foundations depend on the number of piles, their spacing and their end conditions[4]. The horizontal stiffness is likely to be of the same order than that of a mat. The rocking stiffness would also be similar to that of a mat foundation (or smaller depending on the number of piles) for floating piles, but could be much larger for end bearing piles. Thus the same type of comments made for surface foundations would apply generally to floating piles while end bearing piles would behave more like deeply embedded foundations.

For buildings with slenderness ratios greater than 1 on surface or shallow mats, spread footings or floating piles, rocking motions would be the predominant effect of inertial interaction. One could expect therefore larger settlements in the outside piles or footings, and in extreme cases permanent leaning or even overturning. All of that was abundantly observed in Mexico City during the 1985 earthquakes[9].

These are, clearly, topics on which more detailed studies should be conducted in specific cases to determine the foundation stiffnesses, the structural characteristics and the importance of interaction effects.

Lessons to be learned from the 1985 earthquakes

To learn from the experience of the 1985 earthquake it would be de-

sirable to:
1. Conduct two dimensional wave propagation analyses of the Mexico City Valley to determine the types of waves that can propagate through the clay and to assess the possible importance of kinematic interaction effects (such as torsional components of motion for long buildings).
2. Conduct a careful inventory of damaged buildings with regard to their structural and foundation characteristics to verify whether simple models and analyses as those suggested in the previous pages would predict reasonably the observed behavior. In this case recommendations could be made for the most desirable types of foundations in various areas of the city for different buildings.
3. Perform additional research on the seismic behavior of pile foundations, including both kinematic interaction and determination of the foundation stiffnesses. These studies should account for nonlinear soil behavior, separation and gapping effects, initial states of stress and the build up and dissipation of excess pore pressures. They are perhaps more important for floating piles.

Some of these studies are already being conducted at the Instituto de Ingeniería of UNAM. Others are being started under joint research projects sponsored in part by the National Science Foundation. One such effort which addresses the last two points will be conducted by Professors Bielak and Christiano of Carnegie Mellon University in collaboration with the first author.

Conclusions

While the importance of soil amplification effects in Mexico City has long been recognized, the above considerations indicate that soil-structure interaction and type of foundation can also influence significantly the dynamic response of structures, particularly in the range of 7 to 15 stories.

The strongest detrimental effect of soil-structure interaction in Mexico City seems to occur for structures whose fundamental period on a rigid base is 2/3 to 2/5 that of the soil at the building site, i.e. for buildings with a fundamental period from 0.7 to 1.8 seconds. On the other hand, buildings with rigid-base periods of about 2 seconds or larger would clearly benefit from soil-structure interaction in the conditions of Mexico City.

The type of foundation would also increase or reduce the interaction effects depending on the building height or fundamental period.

Additional studies under progress will add to the lessons learned from the 1985 earthquakes.

References

1. Blaney, G.W., Kausel, E. and Roesset, J.M., "Dynamic Stiffness of Piles", 2nd Int. Conference on Numerical Methods in Geomechanics, ASCE, Blacksburg, Virginia, 1976
2. Domínguez, J., "Response of Embedded Foundations to Travelling Waves", Research Report R78-24, M.I.T., August 1978
3. Elsabee, F. and Morray, J.P., "Dynamic Behavior of Embedded Foundations", Research Report R77-33, M.I.T., September 1977
4. Kaynia, A.M. and Kausel, E., "Dynamic Stiffness and Seismic Response of Pile Groups", Research Report R82-03, M.I.T., 1982
5. Kausel, E., "Forced Vibrations of Circular Foundations on Layered

Media", Research Report R74-11, M.I.T., January 1974
    6. Kobayashi, H. et al, Report on the characteristics of microtremors in Mexico City, The Graduate School of Nagatsuta, Tokyo Institute of Technology, Yokohama, Japan, 1986
    7. Prince, J., et al., Informes Preliminares IPS-10A to IPS-10E, Instituto de Ingeniería, UNAM, September-October 1985
    8. Reséndiz, D., Springall, G., Rodríguez, J.M. and Esquivel, R., "Información reciente sobre las características del subsuelo y la práctica de la ingeniería de cimentaciones en la Ciudad de México", V. National Meeting on Soil Mechanics, México, 1970
    9. Reséndiz, D., "El sismo del 19 de septiembre 1985 en la Ciudad de México: Aspectos geotécnicos y de cimentaciones", México, 1985
    10. Romo, M.P. y Jaime, A., "Características dinámicas de las arcillas del Valle de México y respuesta sísmica del suelo". Primera parte, Informe Interno, Instituto de Ingeniería, UNAM, México, D.F., 1986
    11. Veletsos, A.S. and Wei, Y.T., "Lateral and Rocking Vibrations of Footings", Journal of the Soil Mechanics and Foundations Division, ASCE, September 1971
    12. Wolf, J.P., "Dynamic Soil Structure Interaction", Prentice Hall, 1984

SEISMIC DESIGN CRITERIA FOR FOUNDATIONS ON CONTROL PILES

By Enrique Tamez [1]

ABSTRACT: Control piles have been widely used in Mexico
City for underpinning buildings with excessive settlements
caused by the consolidation of the soft clay deposits, and
as a foundation solution for structures supported by point
bearing piles driven to a firm stratum through the clay
deposits, with the aim of preventing the buildings from
emerging due to the regional subsidence. An analysis is
presented of the mechanism governing the interaction effects
of the different component parts of the control system (box-
type concrete foundation, deformable pile control device,
point-bearing pile, surrounding compressible soil, firm
supporting layer and regional subsidence), including seismic
forces not contemplated in the original design of the system,
and recommended design criteria are suggested to guarantee
a satisfactory behavior of the control piles.

INTRODUCTION

The so-called "control piles" were developed by the late
engineer Mr. Manuel González Flores as a solution for underpinning buildings with excessive settlements due to consolidation of the soft clay deposits of Mexico City as well
as to prevent the emersion of structures founded on point-
bearing piles resting on firm material, resulting from the
regional subsidence caused by the extraction of water from
the subsoil aquifers; this type of foundation is illustrated
in Fig. 1. By allowing the pile head to cross the foundation slab, the latter will be supported by the subsoil and
it will settle at the same rate as the soil, thus preventing
the building from sinking or emerging with respect to the
surrounding ground surface.

As originally conceived, the control device of the piles
was installed to operate under the static load of the
structure, part of which is transmitted to the head of the
piles through the deformable cells, whose capacity is
adjusted empirically, based on the settlement monitoring of
the building with time, but without following suitable
criteria to determine neither the bearing capacity of the
piles nor the optimum relationship between the loads transmitted by the deformable cells and those of the foundation
slab.

---

[1] Director TGC-Geotecnia, S A, Manuel M Ponce 143 01020 México, D F

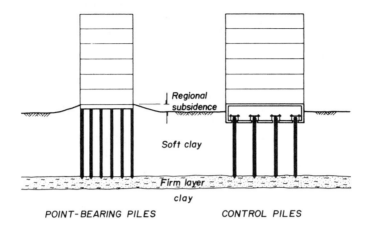

POINT-BEARING PILES   CONTROL PILES

**FIG. I.- Control Piles. An Answer to the Problem of
Settlement and Emersion of Buildings**

The occurrence of very strong earthquakes has subjected the
control piles to dynamic conditions not contemplated in the
original design; these in turn have induced the development of deformation, oftentimes excessive, in the control
devices, leading to sudden differential settlements. The
structural effects brought about by such deformations are
added to those induced by the seismic forces.

With the aim of contributing to a better understanding of
the performance of this type of foundation, under both
static and dynamic (seismic) loading conditions, this paper
describes and analyzes the mechanism which makes it possible
to explain the interaction effects among the different
component parts of the control system comprising the box-
type concrete foundation, the deformable cell, the surrounding soil, the firm layer where the pile tip rests upon, the
regional subsidence of the city and the seismic forces.
From such analysis, design criteria for this type of foundation is proposed.

STATIC CONDITIONS

A vertical cross section along one of the internal control
piles of a pile group is depicted in Fig. 2 together with
the elements comprising the control system and the forces
acting on each of them.

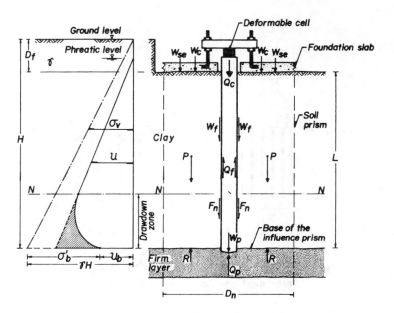

FIG. 2.- Distribution of Vertical Stresses

Static Net Load.- The static net load (W_{ne}) is produced by
the dead weight of the structure (W_m) plus the static live
load (W_{ve}) and part of the accidental live load defined by
the building code of Mexico City in terms of a <u>reduced live
load</u> (W_{vr}) and substracting the total weight of the soil
excavated down to the foundation elevation of the slab, W_c
(compensated load), as indicated by the following equation:

$$W_{ne} = W_m + W_{ve} + W_{vr} - W_c \qquad (1)$$

The net load is responsible for inducing compressive and
shear stresses in the soil and the piles in addition to the
in situ original stresses existing within the soil mass
prior to the construction of the foundation; consequently,
it is the main cause for the development of deformation in
the soil-pile system. This net load can be divided into
two components: one of them (Q_c) is transmitted to the pile
head through the deformable cell, and the other (W_{se}) to
the soil in contact with the foundation slab, according to
this expression:

$$W_{ne} = Q_c + W_{se} \qquad (2)$$

The load W_{se} transmitted to the prism of soil of diameter D_n (Fig. 2) surrounding the pile imposes on the soil a downwards movement, thus inducing a relative displacement between it and the pile driven to the firm layer; this relative displacement generates a downwards skin friction force (W_f) equal in magnitude to W_{se}, in such a way that the load applied by the slab to the soil is transferred, finally, to the pile through friction; therefore, Eq. 2 can be rewritten as follows:

$$W_{ne} = Q_c + W_f \qquad (2')$$

Negative Skin Friction.- Once the pile has been driven and its adhesion with the surrounding soil has been re-established, the regional subsidence of the city starts showing its effects on the prism of soil in the influence area of the pile. The lower part of the prism, located below the horizontal plane N-N, undergoes a progressive consolidation due to the loss of pore pressure induced by the extraction of water from the deep aquifers underlying the clay deposits. The pressure distribution of the water filling the voids of the clay shown at the left of Fig. 2, is representative of the piezometric conditions prevailing at present in a large part of Mexico City; it can be observed that above plane N-N, the pore pressure u corresponds to the hydrostatic pressure whereas below such plane N-N, it is smaller than the hydrostatic, thus proving that nowadays the process of regional consolidation is only influencing the lower part of the prism of soil (u_b). This fact means that such a lower part shrinks with time while the upper zone moves downward as a rigid body. Since the tip of the pile rests against the firm layer, the downward movement of the soil prism with respect to the pile induces a downward frictional force (F_n) in addition to force W_f. This force F_n is known as <u>negative skin friction</u>; however, it has the same direction and orientation than W_f, and therefore both components add together to arrive at a total negative frictional force the magnitude of which has a limiting value, namely, the frictional bearing capacity of the pile, Q_f. This limiting condition is expressed as follows:

$$Q_f = W_f + F_n \qquad (3)$$

or

$$Q_f = W_{se} + F_n \qquad (3')$$

Assuming that the prism of soil shown in Fig. 2 acts like a free body, its equilibrium is given by the following equation:

$$W_c + W_{se} + P = R + Q_f \tag{4}$$

where:

W_c = load compensated by the excavation to a depth D ;

W_{se} = net static load transmitted to the soil by the foundation slab;

P = total weight of the soil prism;

R = total reaction of the firm layer against the base of the prism;

Q_f = limiting frictional bearing capacity of the pile.

Substituting Eq. 3' into Eq. 4:

$$W_c + W_{se} + P = R + W_{se} + F_n$$

After simplifying terms:

$$W_c + P = R + F_n$$

Finally:

$$F_n = W_c + P - R \tag{4'}$$

If the area of the base of the prism is A,

$$W_c = \gamma D_f A$$

$$P = \gamma L A$$

$$R = u_b A + R'$$

where R' is the effective reaction (intergranular) exerted by the firm layer and L is the thickness of the clay deposit below the foundation slab (Fig. 2).

Substituting these values into Eq. 4':

$$F_n = \gamma D_f A + \gamma L A - u_b A - R' = \gamma (D_f + L)A - u_b A - R'$$

or

$$F_n = (\gamma H - u_b)A - R' \tag{5}$$

If it is assumed that the prism has a square base with each side dimension equal to D_n, the area A will be D_n^2; substituting this value in Eq. 5 and solving for R':

$$R' = (\gamma H - u_b)D_n^2 - F_n \tag{5'}$$

where H is the total thickness of the clay deposit.

This equation shows that upon development of the negative skin friction F_n, the effective reaction of the firm layer (R') decreases correspondingly. When F_n reaches a magnitude necessary to satisfy the condition of limiting static equilibrium expressed by Eq. 3', Eq. 5' indicates that the value of R' will depend in this case on the dimension D_n of the soil prism; consequently, the minimum dimension of the base of the prism $(D_n)_{min}$, will be such that the value of reaction R' becomes zero; this means that:

$$0 = (\gamma H - u_b)(D_n^2)_{min} - F_n$$

Therefore:

$$(D_n)_{min} = \sqrt{\frac{F_n}{\gamma H - u_b}} = \sqrt{\frac{Q_f - W_{se}}{\gamma H - u_b}} \qquad (6)$$

When this limiting condition is developed, the upper face of the soil prism which is in contact with the foundation slab, will move downwards at the same rate than the ground surface adjacent to the building and therefore the building as a whole will sink together with the ground.

Minimum Pile Spacing.- Eq. 6 provides the minimum spacing between piles of a common group, necessary to guarantee that sufficient negative skin friction is developed to make the soil prism move downwards thus preventing the building from emerging, and at the same time satisfying the limiting condition given by Eqs. 3 and 3'. In order to have a certain margin of safety, it is recommended to have a pile spacing S, 25% greater than the minimum spacing, that is to say:

$$S \geq 1.25(D_n)_{min}$$

$$S \geq 1.25\sqrt{\frac{Q_f - W_{se}}{\gamma H - u_b}} \qquad (6')$$

Limiting Bearing Capacity.- If Eqs. 3 or 3' are satisfied, the maximum static load transferred to the pile top will be:

$$W_{pem} = Q_c + W_f + F_n = Q_c + Q_f \qquad (7)$$

or

$$W_{pem} = Q_c + Q_f = Q_u \qquad (7')$$

Q_u being the limiting bearing capacity of the control system comprising the deformable cell, the foundation slab, the pile and the surrounding soil.

Point Bearing Capacity.- The point bearing capacity of the pile should be, at least, equal to Q_u times a safety factor if the tip is to be restrained from penetrating the firm layer; this implies that:

$$Q_p \geq Q_u \cdot FS_p \geq (Q_c + Q_f)FS_p \qquad (8)$$

A safety factor $FS_p = 2$ is recommended, and therefore the minimum value of the point bearing capacity will be:

$$Q_p = 2(Q_c + Q_f) \qquad (8')$$

In this expression, Q_p and Q_f vary as a function of the soil mechanical properties and of the pile dimensions, whereas Q_c can be freely assumed by the designer within certain practical boundaries, since such a selection affects the point bearing capacity and consequently the pile dimensions as indicated below.

Load Applied to the Deformable Cell.- If Q_c is written in terms of Q_f,

$$Q_c = nQ_f \qquad (8'')$$

which if substituted into Eq. 8' gives:

$$Q_p = 2(1 + n)Q_f \qquad (9)$$

By assigning arbitrary values to n, the magnitude of Q_p is obtained.

On the other hand, for a circular pile (Ref. 2):

$$Q_p = \frac{\pi}{4} B^2 q_c \qquad (10)$$

and

$$Q_f = \pi BL\overline{f} \qquad (10')$$

where:

B   = diameter (or side dimension) of the pile;

q_c = cone penetration resistance of the firm layer;

L   = pile length;

$\bar{f}$ = mean frictional strength of the clay.

Substituting Eqs. 10 and 10' into Eq. 9:

$$\frac{\pi}{4} B^2 q_c = 2(1 + n) \pi BL\bar{f}$$

Solving for B:

$$B = \frac{8(1 + n)L\bar{f}}{q_c} \tag{11}$$

By assigning arbitraty values to n, those corresponding to
B are obtained. From these values the most suitable one
from the point of view of construction and installation is
selected.

The most common diameters used for underpinning with control
piles vary from 0.45 to 0.60 m (18 to 24 in.).

It becomes evident that the diameter (or side) of a pile
likely to provide a balanced design of the factors involved
in Eq. 9 not only depends on the ratio $n = Q_c/Q_f$ but also
on the pile length and on the shearing strength of the
surrounding clay and of the firm layer. These design parameters are obtained in a reliable, fast and economic manner
by means of the cone penetrometer with electric recording
(Ref. 1).

Load-Settlement Curves.- Fig. 3 shows graphically the
relationship between the static load transmitted to the
cell-slab-soil-pile system and the settlement ρ_ℓ of the
foundation slab. Curve (a) corresponds to the behavior of
the deformable cell which always carries its maximum load
Q_c and therefore continuously behaves within its plastic
range. Curve (b) depicts the relationship between the
settlement ρ_ℓ and the frictional force transmitted to the
pile by the surrounding soil, being such load composed of
the static component W_{se} induced in the soil by the slab,
and of the negative skin friction (F_n) produced by the
regional subsidence; the addition of both component reaches
the magnitude of the limiting frictional bearing capacity
of the pile (Q_f) and consequently this part of the system

also operates within the plastic range. Curve (c), corresponding to the combination of the two previous diagrams, represents the total system, the limiting bearing capacity of which Q_u, is the sum of the limiting capacities of the cell and of the pile; for this reason the whole system operates at its limiting capacity when the building settles at the same rate as the regional subsidence.

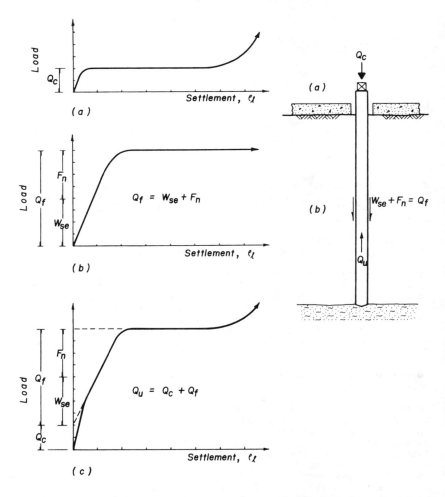

FIG. 3.-   Load-Settlement Relationships : (a) Of the Deformable Cell; (b) of the Subsystem Slab-Soil-Pile; and (c) of the Entire System

SEISMIC CONDITIONS

Seismic Effects.- An earthquake induces in the foundation an increase of the vertical load which modifies the limiting equilibrium conditions acting on the control system under static loads (see Fig. 3c). This limiting condition corresponds to point E in Fig. 4. The increase of the dynamic load due to an earthquake, W_{sd}, applied to the system shown in Fig. 2, is fully transmitted to the soil prism through the foundation slab, because the deformable cell is not able to carry the additional load. Since the frictional force Q_f developed between the soil and the pile is also at a limiting condition, a displacement of the soil prism with respect to the pile is bound to take place; this downward movement will increase the reaction R transmitted by the firm layer to the base of the soil prism, in such a way that the negative skin friction F_n will diminish, as demonstrated by Eq. 4. Whenever R becomes again equal to P, the negative skin friction will vanish, thus freeing the mechanism from the amount corresponding to frictional bearing capacity, as a result of which the pile will be able to carry the increase of dynamic load W_{sd}. The change undergone by the load-settlement curve due to the earthquake action is depicted schematically in Fig. 4. The swift settlement of the slab when acted upon by the <u>first</u> impact of the earthquake, is represented by the segment $\overline{ES}$; a

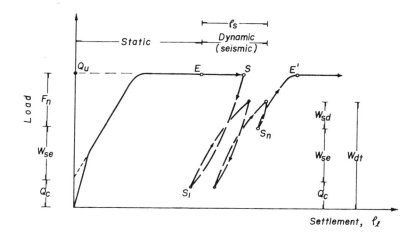

FIG. 4.- Evolution of the Load-Settlement Relationship During an Earthquake

relatively small settlement [1 to 3 cm (0.5 to 1.25 in.)]
will be sufficient to nullify the negative skin friction F_n,
and to make available the same amount of frictional bearing
capacity of the pile. When the load applied to the foundation system decreases due to rocking of the building, point
S will shift to the extreme position S_1, thus starting a
series of hysteresis loops that will end at point S_n when
the earthquake is over. At this point, the load on the pile
will resemble once more that corresponding to the static
initial condition, but with no negative friction whatsoever,
and the foundation will have undergone a cumulative settlement (ρ_s) with a magnitude compatible with the structural
performance. Upon reaching point S_n, the regional subsidence will induce once again the negative skin friction and
the initial condition of static limiting equilibrium represented by point E' will be re-established and therefore the
building will keep settling at the same rate than the adjacent soil.

Dynamic Safety Factor.- The total dynamic load, W_{dt}, applied
to the control system (cell-slab-soil-pile) during an earthquake, corresponds to the maximum value reached by the load
during the hysteresis loops, as observed in Fig. 4 from
which it can be shown that:

$$W_{dt} = Q_c + W_{se} + W_{sd} \tag{12}$$

where Q_c is the limiting bearing capacity of the deformable
cell, thus implying that in this element of the control
system the safety factor will be always equal to unity;
($W_{se} + W_{sd}$) represent the net component of the total load
applied to the soil prism by the slab; this load is transmitted to the pile by friction, and consequently the safety
factor should be expressed in terms of the frictional
bearing capacity of the pile (Q_f) according to the following
equation:

$$FS_d = \frac{Q_f}{W_{se} + W_{sd}} \tag{13}$$

Consequently:

$$W_{se} + W_{sd} = \frac{Q_f}{FS_d}$$

which entered into Eq. 12 will provide the allowable total
dynamic load W_{dta} used for design purposes:

$$W_{dta} = Q_c + \frac{Q_f}{FS_d} \tag{14}$$

As indicated in Eq. 8" the carrying capacity of the deformable cell can be written as:

$$Q_c = nQ_f$$

which entered into Eq. 14 gives:

$$W_{dta} = (n + \frac{1}{FS_d})Q_f \qquad (15)$$

The safety factor FS_d can be equal to 1.7 for conventional structures and to 2 for structures in which the settlement induced by the earthquake (ρ_s) has to be minimal.

The value of n is determined as explained before, from the shearing strength of the clays and the penetration resistance of the electric cone at the firm layer, as well as from the pile length. By means of Eq. 9 the diameter or side dimension is obtained by trial and error, which will satisfy the requirements for a balanced design of the pile for different values of n.

CONCLUSIONS

It can be concluded from what was established before, that a control pile will perform satisfactorily when subjected to both static and dynamic (seismic) loads provided the following basic assumptions are fulfilled:

1. The foundation slab should settle at the same rate than the surrounding ground surface. This condition is represented by Eq. 3' as follows: The static load transmitted by the slab to the soil plus the negative skin friction induced by the regional subsidence of the city, should be equal to the frictional bearing capacity of the pile.

2. The point bearing capacity of the pile should be large enough to prevent the tip from penetrating into the supporting firm layer. This condition is expressed by Eq. 8' which indicates that the point bearing capacity should be, at least, twice as large as the sum of the carrying capacity of the deformable cell and the lateral friction of the pile.

3. The capacity of the deformable cell is a fraction of the frictional bearing capacity of the pile given by Eq. 8", where the ratio n is a function of the shearing strength of the surrounding soil and of the firm layer, as well as of the length and diameter of the pile, as indicated by Eq. 9.

4. The allowable dynamic bearing capacity for each pile will be given by Eq. 14 where it can be observed that under the seismic action the deformable cell continues operating within its limit load, whereas the dynamic safety factor only affects the frictional bearing capacity of the pile.

APPENDIX I.- REFERENCES

1. Comisión de Vialidad y Transporte Urbano (COVITUR), "Manual de Estudios Geotécnicos", Mexico, 1985 (in press).

2. Peck, R.B., Hanson, W.E. and Thornburn, T.H., "Foundation Engineering", 2nd edition, John Wiley and Sons, New York, 1953

Performance Characteristics of Structures, 1985 Mexico City Earthquake

Charles Scawthorn, M.ASCE*,
Mehmet Celebi, M.ASCE** and Jorge Prince***

The 1985 Mexico City earthquake caused major damage to buildings, but not other structures, in the center of Mexico City, located approximately 400 km. from the epicenter. Due to soil conditions in this area, ground motions were especially amplified at a frequency of about 0.5 Hz. Due to this unusual amplification, damage was inordinately concentrated in buildings in the 6 to about 12 story range. Based on measurements in 1962 and 1986, average natural periods for buildings in that story range are estimated and, together with an existing mid-rise building seismic damage estimation methodology, are used to estimate building damage for the 1985 ground motions. These estimates are compared with data on observed damage and reasonable agreement is seen to result, within the limits of the available data on observed damage.

Introduction

The Mexico City earthquakes of September 19 (Ms 8.1, USGS) and September 21 (Ms 7.5, USGS) caused major damage in a limited portion of central Mexico City, located approximately 400 km from the earthquake epicenter. Other urban areas, much closer to the earthquake epicenter, experienced relatively little damage. In Mexico City, the damage was confined to the central portion of the City, built on a former lake. Outside of this area of only a few kilometers radius, little or no damage occurred in Mexico City. Further, damage in the central portion of Mexico City, where the building collapses were concentrated, was confined to buildings and, to some extent, underground water pipes. Building contents, bridges and overpasses, towers, tanks monuments and other structures were virtually undamaged.

In Mexico City, over 300 major buildings collapsed or were severely damaged. Unofficial estimates are that more than 10,000 persons died. Several thousand of these deaths occurred in only a handful of buildings, including the Edificio B. Juarez and Tlatelolco/N. Leon multistory apartment buildings. The pattern of deaths was closely related to the time of the main shock, at 7:17 AM. If the earthquake had occurred during business hours, the large number of office and school building collapses might have resulted in a much higher, perhaps order of magnitude higher, death toll.

----
* Dames & Moore, 500 Sansome St., San Francisco CA 94111
** U.S. Geological Survey, Menlo Park, CA 94025
*** Inst. Ingenieria, UNAM, Mexico 20 DF, Mexico

Mitigation of disasters such as the tragedy that occurred in Mexico City requires a clear understanding of complex, often inter-related, factors involving seismology, geology, the behavior of soils and structures under dynamic loading, emergency response, and the building codes, urban planning and recovery plans that existed prior to the disaster.

A clear, detailed, understanding of these complex matters must await several years of concerted effort by practitioners and researchers in Mexico and elsewhere. This paper discusses the pattern of damage experienced in Mexico City, indicating some trends and exploring the question to what extent could this damage have been predicted prior to the event. We rely on data kindly furnished by members of the faculty of the Inst. de Ingenieria at the Universite Nacional Autonomous de Mexico (UNAM), especially Prof. R. Meli and his co-workers. This data, hereafter referred to as the UNAM survey or data, concentrated on the damaged buildings in the central portion of Mexico City, an area of approximately 100 sq. km.

Building Damage

This section briefly presents and discusses the general pattern of damage occurring to buildings in Mexico City due to the earthquakes of September 19 and 20, 1985.

While steel framed buildings exist in Mexico City, the predominant construction material is reinforced concrete frame, often with brick infill. This method of construction typically resists lateral loads by moment connections between columns and girders (or slabs), shear being carried by the columns and sometimes by some shear walls. Concrete diagonal bracing is sometimes employed. The brick infill is not structural, and only serves as separation from the weather. Since brick panels are typically fairly large (3 by 5 or more meters), the panels are subdivided into smaller panels by secondary concrete beams and columns, termed "castillos", which are intended to resist out-of-plane loads. This brick infill is not otherwise reinforced, and is typically brittle under in-plane loads. When it fails at a particular floor, rotations tend to be concentrated in the columns.

Collapsed and partially collapsed buildings were located almost entirely in central Mexico City, on the geological formation known as the Lake Formation, a highly deformable silty clay approximately 30 m deep overlying other layers to several thousand meters. In the downtown area, the prevailing site period is approximately 2 seconds (Rosenblueth and Meli, 1986). This area of collapsed and severely damaged buildings is approximately 23 sq. km., while the area of significant damage is approximately 65 sq. km., a small fraction (less than 1%) of the total area of the Federal District.

Low- and mid-rise buildings were the greatest in number to sustain damage, Figure 1 and Table 1. This data is from the UNAM survey, which covered virtually all of central Mexico City. In Table 1, "Avg Dmg" in-

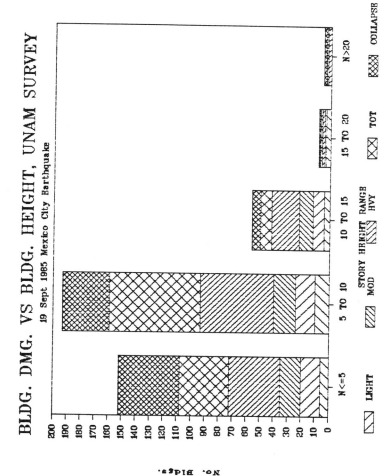

FIGURE 1:

BLDG. DMG. VS BLDG. HEIGHT, UNAM SURVEY

19 Sept 1985 Mexico City Earthquake

TABLE 1: MEXICO CITY BUILDING DAMAGE (after UNAM)

ZONES:	—5(=N—		—5(N(=10—		—10(N(=15—		—15(N(=20—		—20(N—	
	No.Bldgs	Avg Dmg	No.Bldgs	Avg Dmg	No.Bldgs	Avg Dmg	No.Bldgs	Avg Dmg	No.Bldgs	Avg Dmg
1	20	2.4	7	3.1	2	4.0				
2	11	4.0	10	4.1						
3	12	4.1	33	3.6	9	2.9	2	2.0		
4a	7	4.6	15	3.2	3	2.3	1	4.0	1	5.0
4b	2	3.0	11	3.5	7	3.4			3	4.0
4c	3	4.3	7	4.1	2	4.5				
5	23	4.7	37	3.5	7	3.0				
6	33	3.2	38	3.4	17	2.6	1	5.0		
7	1	4.0	6	4.3						
8	6	2.2	1	5.0						
9	4	3.0	3	3.7						
10	1	4.0	1	3.0						
11	5	4.6	6	3.2	3	1.7				
12	3	3.7	1	1.0						
13	1	3.0								
14	2	2.0	1	1.0						
15	2	5.0	3	1.7	1	1.0				
16	4	3.3								
17	8	2.1								
										SUM:
No.Bldgs:	148		180		51		4		4	387
Avg Dmg:	3.5		3.5		2.9		3.3		4.3	
StnDev D:	1.3		1.1		1.2		1.5		0.8	

NO. BLDGS WITH DAMAGE —>	NONE	LIGHT	MOD	HVY	TOTAL	COLLAPSE
ZONES:						
1	1	12	5	7	3	6
2				6	8	7
3		4	4	17	20	13
4a	6	1	7	5	8	11
4b		1	3	7	8	4
4c				1	7	4
5		2	6	16	19	27
6	6	7	12	35	32	8
7	1			1	3	3
8		2	1	3		1
9				6		3
10				1	1	
11	3	3	1	4		6
12	1	1	1	1	2	1
13	1			2		
14		2		1		
15	1	3		1		2
16				4	1	
17	3	1	1	2	2	
						SUM:
TOTAL (17 ZONES):	23	39	41	120	114	96	433

dicates observed damage averaged for each zone and each category of
building story height (also, "StnDev" is the standard deviation of
damage). Buildings were surveyed and observed damage reported using
terms such as "light", "heavy" etc. These terms were converted by the
present authors to a number on a scale of 0 to 5, where

Damage	DMG
None	0
Light	1
Medium	2
Heavy$_*$	3
Total	4
Collapse	5

* (Total, but no collapse)

When damage sustained is compared with total number of buildings exposed
to the ground motion, damage is seen to have been especially severe in
the 6 to about 12 story range, with low-rise buildings actually sustaining relatively little damage. This may be seen in Figure 2 (data from
UNAM, 1985), which shows Damaged Buildings (ie, Damaged Buildings/Total
Number of Buildings, expressed as a percentage) versus Number of Floors.
This relative lack of damage to low-rise buildings, and the above-noted
lack of damage in other types of structures, was due to the extreme
ground motions in Mexico City in this earthquake. The motions recorded
at the SCT on the south side of the central area are taken as typical
for the central area (Mena et al, 1985), Figure 3.

These motions are seen to be extremely strong in the neighborhood of a 2
second period, corresponding to the prevailing site period. Thus,
buildings with building periods of 1 to 2 seconds would be subjected to
increasingly severe forces as they were initially shaken, sustained
minor to moderate damage and increased in their fundamental period.
Buildings with periods of about 3 seconds and larger would be on the
"down-hill" side of the response spectra, and thus would be "shedding"
load as they were initially damaged.

Average Natural Period for Buildings in Mexico City

Relatively little data is available with regard to typical fundamental
periods of buildings in Mexico City. The most extensive set of data
available to this author are measurements conducted in 1962 by W. Cloud
of the USGS and J. Prince of UNAM (unpubl.), Table 2. These measurements
have been recently supplemented (Celebi et al, 1986) also shown in Table
2. A sample of these measurements (1962 and 1986) is also provided in
Table 2. Details of these tests and data are to be found in Celebi et al
(1986). The 1962 data set are plotted in Figure 3, where a typical
trend can be seen between building period and number of floors (in this

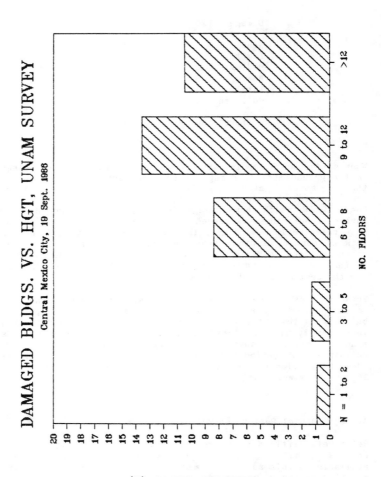

FIGURE 2:

DAMAGED BLDGS. VS. HGT, UNAM SURVEY

Central Mexico City, 19 Sept. 1988

FIGURE 3: SCT RESPONSE SPECTRA (after MENA et al, 1985)

(0, 2, 5, 10, 20% damping)

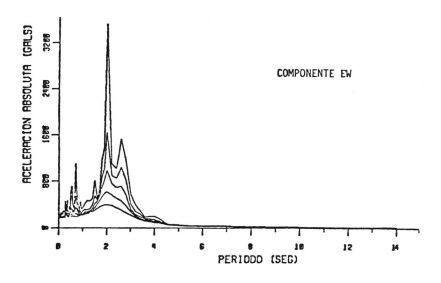

COMPONENTE EW

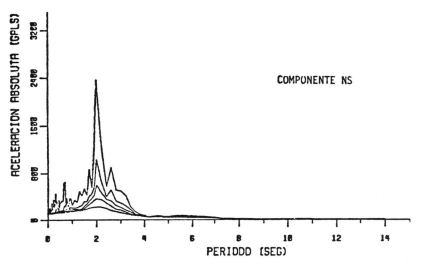

COMPONENTE NS

TABLE 2: MEXICO CITY BUILDING PERIOD DATA

Data Set	BLDG No.	BLDG NAME/ADDRESS	BLDG LENGTH (m)	WIDTH (m)	WIDTH (m)	NO. FLRS	MATL.*	SYSTEM** LONG	SYSTEM** TRANSV.	TL (sec)	TT (sec)	Avg T (sec)
1962	1	Science Bldg/UNAM	54.3	53	17	14	1	FR/core		1.12	1.11	1.12
(USGS, Cloud	2	Monterey				9				0.79	1.19	0.99
and Prince)	3	Viaducto 196	7.2	14	8	3				0.49	0.32	0.41
:	4	STIC/Plaza de Republica	34.8	32	18	10	1			0.62	1.24	0.93
:	5	Manchester y Reforma	49.15	25	14.3	10	1	FR	FR	1.08	1.38	1.23
:	6	Pachuca 75				8				0.7	0.83	0.77
:	7	Grad Studies Bldg/UNAM	9.68	49.5	7.05	3	1	FR	FR	0.2	0.24	0.22
:	8	Varsovia 9				12	1			1.18	1.05	1.12
:	9	Aristos/Insurgentes y Aguascalient	51	33	17.7	16	1	SW	SW	1.54	1.85	1.70
V	10	Tamaulipas y Montes de Oca	20.4	25	16	9	1	FR/SW		0.97	1.12	1.05
1986	6	PAC				8				1	1.1	1.05
(USGS, Celebi	9	ARI				16				2	1.85	1.93
and Prince)	4	REV (STIC)				10				0.8	1.42	1.11
:	5	MAN				10				1.72	1.6	1.66
:	0	CEL				10				1.69	2.04	1.87
V	0	LOT				28		FR	FR	3	3.3	3.15

NOTES:
* (RC=1, STL=2, MSNRY=3)
** FR=Frame; SW=Shear Wall
TL=Fund. Per., Longit. (sec.)
TT=Fund. Per., Transv. (sec.)
Avg. T=(TL+TT)/2

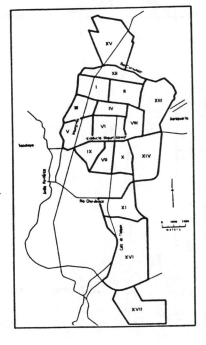

Zoning of Mexico City for survey of damage.

TABLE 2(cont): EXAMPLE 1962 AND 1986 DATA

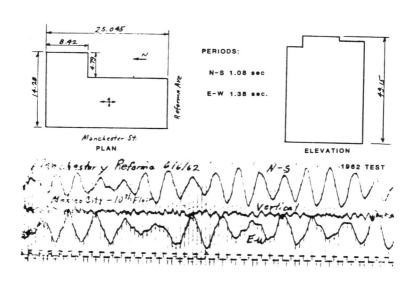

PERIODS:

N-S 1.08 sec

E-W 1.38 sec.

PLAN

ELEVATION

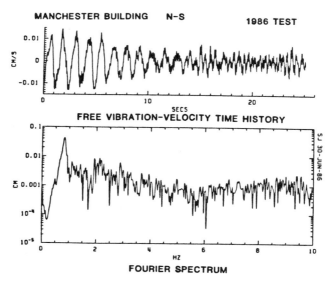

MANCHESTER BUILDING   N-S   1986 TEST

FREE VIBRATION-VELOCITY TIME HISTORY

FOURIER SPECTRUM

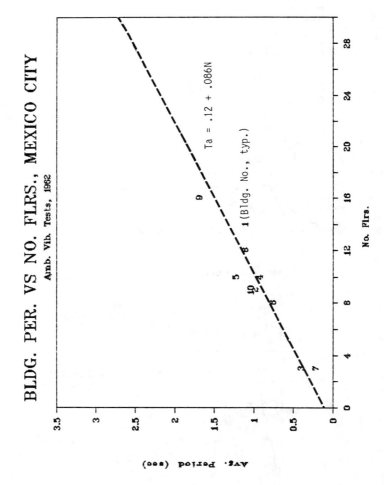

FIGURE 4:

BLDG. PER. VS NO. FLRS., MEXICO CITY

Amb. Vib. Tests, 1962

$Ta = .12 + .086N$

1 (Bldg. No., typ.)

No. Flrs.

Avg. Period (sec)

figure, the plotted numbers are the numbers assigned to the buildings in Table 2. The data have been regressed to determine the following rela- tionship between fundamental period (average of both directions) and number of floors, for buildings in Mexico City:

$$Ta = 0.12 + 0.086 \; N \quad \ldots (1)$$

where Ta = building fundamental period (average of both directions) and N = number of floors, (for this regression, no. observations=10, r=0.944). Using this relationship, estimated building periods are plotted against observed building periods, Figure 4 (in this figure, plotted numbers are the number of floors for individual buildings), where agreement can be seen to be satisfactory.

The 1986 data are compared with the above relationship in Figure 5 (plotted numbers here are building numbers in Table 2). Several of the buildings measured in 1962 were measured again in 1986 (nos. 4,5,6, and 9), and it can be seen that these buildings have softened, presumably due to the 1985 (and possibly 1979) earthquake. Two buildings measured only in 1986 are also plotted, and are seen to be considerably softer than the trend indicated by the 1962 data.

Upper and Lower Bounds on Average Damage

Detailed statistical analysis of damage in Mexico City is hampered at this time, due to several factors. Complete information regarding total building inventory and/or height distribution at risk in Mexico City is not yet available. Some building inventory information has been com- piled (UNAM, 1985), but for somewhat different zones of the city as com- pared with the damage survey zones, making detailed comparison dif- ficult. Further, the UNAM damage survey is not a random sample, but rather oriented toward more heavily damaged buildings, with little in- formation available for those buildings not surveyed. However, statisti- cal estimates of average damage can be bounded on the basis of two assumptions:

(a) from above (ie, upper bound, UB), by assuming that the UNAM survey data is random and representative of all buildings in the sample area, and

(b) from below (ie, lower bound, LB), by assuming that the UNAM survey data covered all damaged buildings, and all other buildings in the sample area had negligible damage.

These two assumptions are extreme however, and the resulting bounds are far apart.

Estimated vs. Observed Damage

It is of interest to briefly consider to what extent the damage sustained in central Mexico City could have been estimated, using

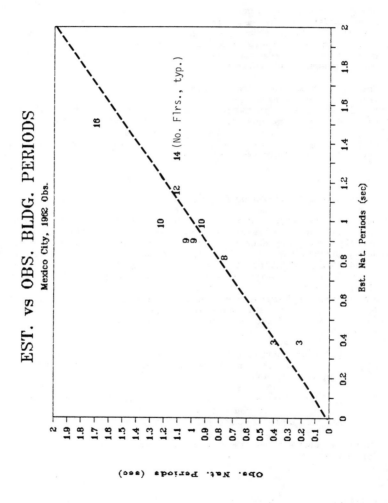

FIGURE 5:

EST. vs OBS. BLDG. PERIODS

Mexico City, 1962 Obs.

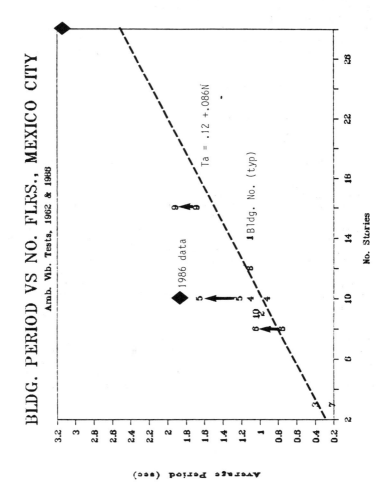

FIGURE 6

BLDG. PERIOD VS NO. FLRS., MEXICO CITY

Amb. Vib. Tests, 1962 & 1988

simplified models of mid-rise building seismic performance, derived from
previous earthquakes in other locations. This question is central to
seismic damage mitigation, in that identification of hazardous buildings
and estimation of their potential damage is fundamental to planning and
conducting seismic hazard reduction programs.

The present writer has previously developed a seismic damage estimation
algorithm for mid-rise concrete buildings, based on data from the 1978
Miyagiken-oki earthquake in Japan (Scawthorn et al, 1981). Data analyzed
from this earthquake was for buildings in the 5 to 10 story range. This
method determines damage (DMG) on a scale of 0 to 5 (0=No Damage,
1=Light, 2=Moderate, 3=Heavy, 4=Total, 5=Collapse) as a function of maximum interstory drift (Dr):

$$DMG = 1.95 \ (Dr \ - \ .14)^{.4} \qquad \qquad \ldots\ldots(2)$$

where Dr may be approximated as

$$Dr = 1.33 \ Sd^{-.5} \ N \qquad \qquad \ldots\ldots(3)$$

and N = number of floors, and Sd is response spectral displacement.

In order to explore whether this method could have been used to estimate
damage sustained in the Mexico City earthquake, this method together
with equation (1) has been employed to estimate damage as a function of
height, subjected to the SCT record of the 19 September motions (taken
herein as typical for the central area of Mexico City). Figure 6
presents the resulting estimate of average damage for the SCT record,
together with the upper and lower bounds on observed average damage. As
noted above, these bounds are very wide, so that firm conclusions are
precluded. We note however that the above methodology appears to provide
a reasonable estimate of damage (as much as can be inferred, given the
upper and lower bounds), in the range for which the methodology is applicable (ie, 5 to 10 stories, and perhaps somewhat more with
extrapolation).

It should be noted that the above methodology is based on several assumptions regarding overall structural behavior, and that a significant
portion of the damage in Mexico City was due to particular aspects of
structural behavior, such as pounding or torsional effects (eg, a corner
location) which are not explicity accounted for in the above
statistically-derived approach.

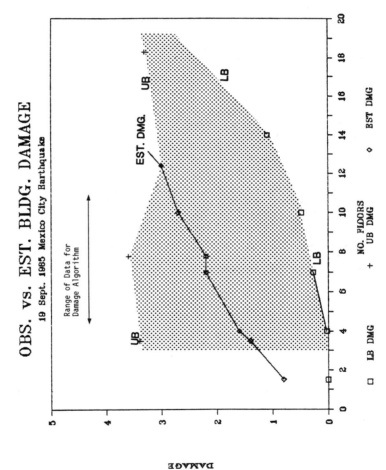

FIGURE 7:

OBS. vs. EST. BLDG. DAMAGE

19 Sept. 1985 Mexico City Earthquake

Acknowledgements

This writer wishes to express his appreciation to the faculty of Inst. de Ing. (UNAM), especially Prof. Roberto Meli, for their generosity in providing data regarding the 19 September earthquake.

REFERENCES

Celebi, M., and Prince, J., and Scawthorn, C. (1986) Vibrational Characteristic Change of Structures during the Mexico City Earthquake, Structures Congress '86, Am. Soc. Civil Engrs., New Orleans.

Celebi, M., et al (1986) U.S.G.S. Open-File Report (in preparation).

Mena, E. et al (1985) Acelerograma en el Centro de la Secretaria de Comunicaciones y Transportes. Sismo del 19 de Sept. de 1985, Informe IPS-10B, Inst. de Ing., UNAM

Rosenblueth, E. and Meli, R. (1986) The 1985 Earthquake: Causes and Effects in Mexico City, Concrete Intl., May.

Scawthorn, C., Iemura, H., and Yamada, Y. (1981) Seismic Damage Estimation for Low- and Mid-Buildings in Japan, Int. J. for Earthquake Engg. and Structural Dynamics, v. 9, n. 2.

UNAM (1985) Efectos de los sismos de Sept. de 1985 en las Constructtiones de la Ciudad de Mexico. Aspectos Estructurales, Segundo informe del Inst. de Ing. de la Univ. Nac. Auton. de Mexico., Nov.

Preliminary Dynamic Analyses of the Ministry of Agriculture Building

by

William C. Stone *
and
Ing. Neftali Rodriguez Cuevas **

Abstract

The Ministry of Agriculture building on Avenida San Antonio Abad was originally constructed as a 17 story reinforced concrete structure using a waffle slab system with interior reinforced concrete shear walls surrounding the elevator shafts and stairwells. The plan form was assymetrical and included an attached laterally braced annex which protruded from the south-west side of the building. During the 1985 earthquake it suffered significant damage but did not collapse. Rehabilitation plans for the structure and the results of free vibration tests conducted in the post-earthquake configuration are discussed. A structural model of the building was prepared as part of a preliminary study of its dynamic behavior during the 1985 earthquake. The model was developed using three dimensional finite elements as part of a benchmark study to determine the feasibility of this analytical approach. Observations on the computational requirements and difficulty of analyzing such detailed computer models are discussed.

Introduction

Frequency spectrum analysis of acceleration records from the lake bed region of Mexico City have indicated that the majority of the energy in the September 1985 earthquake was concentrated at approximately 0.5 hertz, which corresponds to a two second period of vibration. The implication of this data is well known. Buildings within the lake bed region which exhibited natural periods of vibration in the vicinity of two seconds were subjected to substantial lateral accelerations which in many cases were sufficient to induce complete structural failure. Typically, buildings between 6 and 17 stories were the ones which sustained the greatest damage.

Some buildings in this category, however, were able to survive by dissipating earthquake energy by means of inelastic deformation of shear walls and reinforced cross bracing. Retrofitting of several of

* Research Structural Engineer, National Bureau of Standards
** Professor of Engineering, Instituto de Ingenieria,
   Universidad Nacional Autonoma de Mexico

these structures has been deemed desirable, and, in many cases, free vibration tests have been conducted to determine the degree to which the height and plan form of these buildings should be changed in order to avoid resonance in a future earthquake.

One such structure is the Ministry of Agriculture building on Avenida San Antonio Abad (figure 1). Originally constructed in 1976 as a 17 story reinforced concrete structure (Fig. 2), it incorporates a waffle slab system with seven bays in the east-west direction and three bays in the north-south direction (figure 3). Lateral stiffness was increased by means of interior reinforced concrete shear walls surrounding the elevator shafts and stairwells. The plan form was assymetrical (figure 3) and included an attached laterally braced annex which protruded from the southwest side of the building. The X-bracing on the southwest annex (figure 4) was added later by the owner following damages sustained during the 1979 Petatlan earthquake.

During the 1985 earthquake, the building suffered several failures in the interior shear walls and in the X-braced annex. These failures served to lengthen the natural period of vibration for the building which undoubtedly contributed to its survival. Surprisingly, there were no signs of distress at the slab-column junctions (figure 5). Each column was exposed and inspected for cracks during the rehabilitation process. The overall good performance of these joints can be ascribed to the relatively large amounts of shear reinforcement and confining steel which were present in the vicinity of the slab-column junctions. In contrast, many older (pre-1976 code [1]) waffle slab structures of similar construction often exhibited punching shear failures or a "drop-out" phenomenon in which the cinder blocks used to form the waffle slab spalled away from the slab during the 1985 earthquake.

Free Vibration Testing

A few months after the earthquake, free vibration experiments were conducted on the Ministry of Agriculture Building. The building performed sufficiently well during these experiments to be considered for rehabilitation and the task facing consulting engineers was how to best reconfigure the structure to avoid the known soil resonance problem. The results of the free vibration tests were rather surprising and are shown in Table 1.

Table 1: Post-Earthquake Free Vibration Response of the Ministry of Agriculture Building

Mode	Period (seconds)	Mode-shape
1	3.13	Flexure: North-South
2	2.78	Flexure: East-West
3	1.14	Flexure: North-South
4	0.86	Flexure: East-West
5	0.64	Torsion

Figure 1: View of the Ministry of Agriculture
Building on Avenida San Antonio Abad
looking west, prior to removal of
upper floors in July 1986.

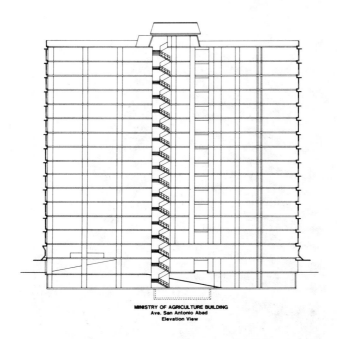

MINISTRY OF AGRICULTURE BUILDING
Ave. San Antonio Abad
Elevation View

Figure 2:   Elevation View Looking North,
Ministry of Agriculture Building

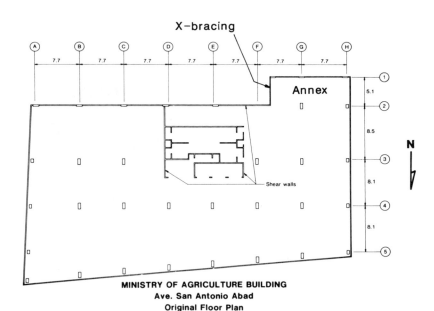

MINISTRY OF AGRICULTURE BUILDING
Ave. San Antonio Abad
Original Floor Plan

Figure 3: Plan View of Ministry of Agriculture
Building showing interior shear walls
and south-western annex.   Avenida San
Antonio Abad borders the building on the
right hand side.

Figure 4: Southwestern annex to the Ministry of
of Agriculture Building. X-bracing
originally extended the entire height
of the annex.

Figure 5: Interior slab-to-column junction
areas were exposed for inspection of
potential shear cracks. Despite failure
of the shear walls, no major cracking
was found near the columns.

The fundamental period of vibration in the north-south direction was more than three seconds. At first this might appear to be in conflict with the 0.12 second per story rule of thumb suggested by several researchers [2] following the earthquake for calculating the natural period of a building. Using that rule results in an estimated period for the Ministry of Agriculture building of about two seconds. Two factors appear to have been responsible for the increase in period: The failure of the interior shear walls transferred the lateral load resisting mechanism to the much more flexible column-slab system; Secondly, substantial amounts of archival records -- which equated to high live loads -- were observed in the upper floors of this structure during the conduct of the free vibration tests. Increasing the mass, particularly at a high elevation, and decreasing the system stiffness lead to longer periods of vibration.

The goal in the rehabilitation process is to achieve approximately a one second fundamental period by reducing high elevation mass, increasing lateral stiffness, and enforcing greater symmetry to prevent torsional coupling of the various modes of vibration. Current plans for achieving this objective call for reducing the height of the structure to ten stories and removal of the southwest annex. The interior shear walls will be reconstructed. Additionally, a substantial portion of the structure on the south side will be opened up to form a courtyard.

There are presently two architechtural options being considered for this mezzanine: in the first, exterior columns and girders from the original structure will be retained and stiffened in an effort to retain torsional symmetry (figure 6); and in the second, the courtyard is completely open (figure 7). The second option will require special consideration for the effects of the two re-entrant corners.

The removal of the upper floors of the building began in July, 1986 (figure 8) and was completed in early September, 1986. The final height is the level that can be seen on the right hand side of the building, shown in figure 8. Preliminary analysis of free vibration data taken from the building in the configuration shown in figure 8 indicates that the first mode period in the north-south direction is approximately 1.6 seconds in flexure. The east-west mode in flexure also appears to be about 1.6 seconds. It is anticipated that these figures will decrease further with the reconstruction of the shear walls so that the goal of a one-second fundamental period appears within reach.

The overall plan for the analysis project was divided into two phases. The first phase, which is just now getting underway, consists of preliminary static and modal analyses which will be used to determine what model parameters are necessary to achieve correlation with the free vibration test data. Phase II involves the selection of a suitable acceleration record for the site to be used in a non-linear stress analysis. The non-linear analysis will then be used to compare performance of the original 17 story structure with the rehabilitated 10 story design.

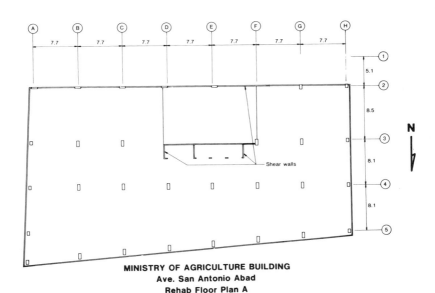

MINISTRY OF AGRICULTURE BUILDING
Ave. San Antonio Abad
Rehab Floor Plan A

Figure 6: Revised plan view of Ministry of
Agriculture Building following
rehabilitation Plan A; exterior
girders and columns are retained
to insure torsional symmetry.

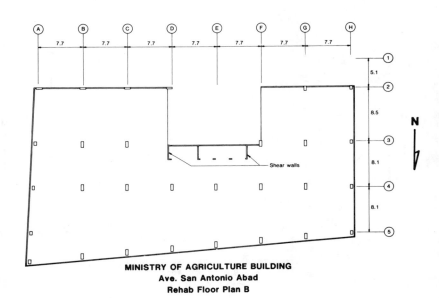

MINISTRY OF AGRICULTURE BUILDING
Ave. San Antonio Abad
Rehab Floor Plan B

Figure 7: Revised plan view of Ministry of
Agriculture Building following
rehabilitation Plan B; exterior
girders and columns are removed to
provide open courtyard.

Figure 8: View looking southward of the Ministry
of Agriculture Building during demolition
of the upper six floors.

An additional goal of the project was to use this structure as the
basis for a study on the feasibility of using a full three-dimensional
discretization model (solid finite elements), including the foundation
piles and the various soil layers, to conduct a non-linear soil-
structure interaction analysis. For obvious reasons, namely,
excessive computer time, such analyses have historically been deferred
in favor of simplified approximate methods such as those employed in
the well known programs ETABS and DRAIN [3 , 4]. In this study
approximate methods are being used in parallel with the 3D modelling
effort. However, most of the approximate analysis procedures do not
allow for the inclusion of the foundation system and soil, and they
cannot predict the effects of localized failures in the manner that
could be handled in a discrete solid model.

Finite Element Modelling

The advent of sophisticated computer aided design systems and recent
increased availability of supercomputers make it possible to conduct
a benchmark study in three dimensional modelling. A good question at
this point would be: "Why model a structure using 3D finite elements?"
There are two main reasons: simplicity of input data and perceptual
realism.   Given only three material properties -- modulus of
elasticity, density, and Poissons ratio, stiffness and inertial
parameters can be automatically generated by computer.   Manual entry
of structural element properties such as moments of inertia, cross-
sectional areas etc., which is required for frame elements, is not
necessary.

The real strength of the 3D approach, however, is visual realism.
Individual structural components and their performace in the context
of a complex system can be readily identified by viewing the model
directly, rather than by sifting through batch output, or at best with
existing CAD systems to pick out an individual member and look at its
shear and moment diagrams.   3D solid elements have surfaces onto
which can be mapped stresses, deformations, and other scalar
quantities of interest.   This capability cannot currently be
reproduced using one-dimensional beam elements.

Furthermore, useful data typically associated with frame elements,
such as end moments and shear forces   can be recovered from element
stresses by integration, so that no information is lost with this
approach.   Its forte is quick identification of "hot spots" and the
ability to visualize the effects of local structural systems, such as
shear walls, on the dynamic performance of the total system.

There are definite drawbacks to the finite element approach: a higher
density of elements is required to accurately recover local stresses
in long slender components such as columns. For example, a typical
frame member has 12 degrees of freedom associated with it, whereas an
8-node brick element has 24.   Depending on the number of brick
elements used to model a beam or column, the computational burden
could be as much as 10 to 20 times greater. Taking into consideration

the vast number of components in a building such as the Ministry of Agriculture, it is not unreasonable to expect models with 50,000 degrees of freedom or more. Execution of even a simple modal analysis of such a system would tax the limits of generally available engineering design computers. Solution of a full dynamic analysis for this system clearly requires a supercomputer.

The Ministry of Agriculture Building contains more than 6000 individual columns, beams, girders, and slab sections. Modelling all the individual structural elements one by one would have been extremely time consuming, even though concrete density and strength vary with floor elevation. To overcome this a uniform story geometry was employed. A precise plan was generated which consisted of surface representations of the column and shear wall sections (figure 9). This representation was then duplicated at each of the 17 story levels of the building. Columns and shear wall elements were then generated between these surfaces. By a similar procedure a second plan (figure 10) with beams, girders, block-outs, and interfaces with columns and shear walls was then developed and duplicated at each level. Three-dimensional finite elements were then generated corresponding to each of the slab levels. Appropriate material properties were then defined to achieve the desired stiffness and mass relationships that exist in the real structure.

At this point the modelling process does not appear to be much different from that used in a standard frame or planar stress analysis. However, one advantage of the 3D approach is that solid images can be generated based on the surface representations of the elements. This same feature also permits later mapping of stresses for results interpretation. Using this capability it is possible to examine the location of, for example, interior shear walls (figure 11) and to quickly identify what material properties have been assigned to them.

Vertical framing elements (figure 12), such as the X-braces on the south-west annex, were produced by forming a master set for the first floor level and copying it to the remaining floors. With these details complete the full structural model can now be generated. The 17 story stucture, viewed from the northwest, is shown in figure 13. A view from the southeast (figure 14), shows the location of the interior shear walls, the southwest annex, and the X-bracing of the annex. This model has 33,885 degrees of freedom and 6350 8-node brick solid elements.

To prepare models of the rehabilitated structure, the original 17-story model was reduced to 10 stories. The annex was also removed, as were floor sections in the proposed courtyard on the south side of the structure. Figure 15 shows Rehab Model A in which the columns and girders on the exterior side of the couryard have been retained.

Modal analyses for these structural models are currently underway and thus direct comparisons with free vibration test data were not available in time for this paper. However, in preparing the models

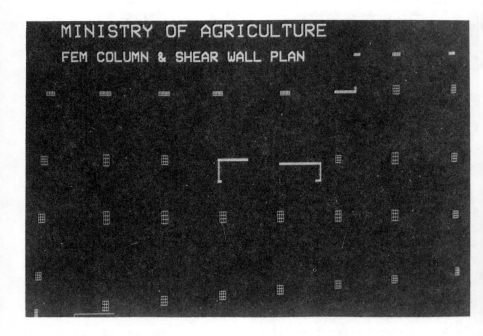

Figure 9: Finite element master mesh used to generate column and shear wall elements for remaining 17 floors.

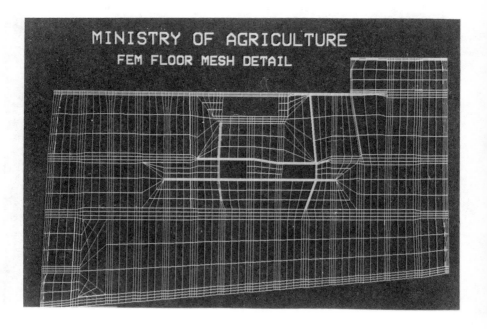

Figure 10: Finite element master mesh used
to generate beams, girders, and
floor slabs for the 17-story structure.

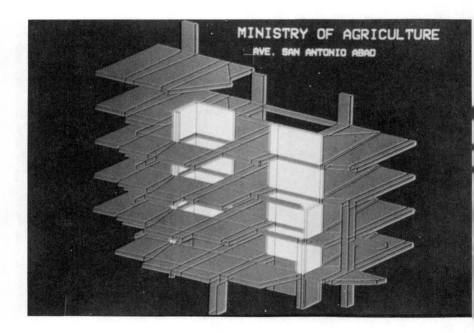

Figure 11: Color raster solid image of interior
shear wall elements

Figure 12: Color raster solid image of southwest annex elements, including
x-bracing

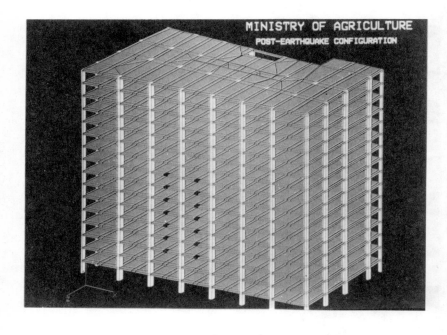

Figure 13:   Color raster solid image of
              finite element model of the
              Ministry of Agriculture Building
              looking towards the southeast
              in post-earthquake configuration
              (original 17-story height)

Figure 14: Color raster solid image of
finite element model of Ministry
of Agriculture Building looking
north-west. Note south-western
annex and x-bracing

Figure 15: Color raster solid image of
          finite element model of the Ministry
          of Agriculture Building in
          rehabilitation option A, in which
          southern exterior columns and girders
          have been retained around the courtyard
          to preserve torsional symmetry

for solution a number of interesting questions were raised.   For
example, how much computer run-time will be required?   The 17-story
structure model has a maximum stiffness matrix bandwidth of 408.   This
figure, combined with the previously mentioned 34,000 degrees of
freedom requires approximately six billion arithmetic operations for
solution of a static, linear equation problem. Keeping this number in
mind, and considering the speed for a number of well known engineering
computers (see Table 2),   it can be seen that solution time is
generally going to be measured in hours rather than minutes.   The
exception is a supercomputer that can execute arithmetic operations at
a rate varying between 200 to 800 million instructions per second
(MFLOPS) depending on the type of system, and the number of vector
pipelines employed.

Table 2: Comparison of Computer System Performance for the
         static analysis of the Ministry of Agriculture Building

Computer	MFLOPS	Max Memory (Megabytes)	Solution Time (seconds)	Performance Ratio
Vax 11/750	0.15	8	42880	1225
Micro VAX II	0.21	16	30628	875
Vax 11/785	0.4	64	16080	459
Vax 8600	0.85	68	7567	216
Vax 8550	1.35	80	4764	136
Supercomputer (Cray XMP,Cyber 205 etc) *	200–800	64	35	1

* Supercomputer solution time estimates assume 200 Mflop speed
     is presently achieveable; MFLOP = One Million Floating Point
     Operations per Second.

These speed figures are equivalent, in terms of the static analysis
problem, to about 12 hours for a VAX 11/750 or 35 seconds for a
supercomputer operating at 200 megaflops. Following extensive model
checking, the first modal analysis attempt was run for the 17 story
structure.   The Householder QR Method of eigenvalue extraction was
used for this analysis [5]. The job compiled successfully and ran for
four days (but only 19 CPU hours due to the presence of other
interactive users) on a VAX 8600 when it had to be dropped due to
excessive disk storage requirements. Based on the file dump it was
estimated that the problem was well into eigenvector recovery when the
job was terminated.   A VAX 11/750 has since been reconfigured as a
stand-alone system with a half giga-byte of disk storage and the
authors are confident that the model will run to completion.   Based
on the data from the modal analysis and the static calculations, it is
estimated that the static solution will require approximately 12 CPU
hours and the modal analysis will require approximately 129 CPU hours
for the 17 story problem.

Summary

Free vibration test data for the Ministry of Agriculture Building indicated that a substantial increase in building flexibility occurred during the 1985 earthquake due to localized failures in internal shear walls and lateral bracing. This led to a 3.13 second fundamental period for the 17-story structure in its post-earthquake configuration, whereas a natural period of approximately 2 seconds would have been calculated using the accepted 0.12 second/story rule-of-thumb for undamaged buildings. The feasiblility of modelling a complex structural system like the Ministry of Agriculture Building using three dimensional finite elements was demonstrated and estimates were presented for solution times the static and modal analyses. It is concluded that the use of a computer with a minimum computational speed of 200 megaflops will be required to execute such structural models.

References

1) "Reglamento de Construcciones para el Distrito Federal," Departamento del Distrito Federal, Mexico City, D.F., Mexico 1976

2) Rosenblueth, E., "The Mexican Earthquake: A Firsthand Report," CivilEngineering, January 1986 pp 38-40. American Society of Civil Engineers, New York, NY

3) Wilson, E.L., Hollings, J.P., and Dovey, H.H., "ETABS... Extended Three-Dimensional Analysis of Building Systems," University of California, Berkeley, CA. April 1975

4) Kanann, A.E., and Powell, G.H., "DRAIN-2D...Inelastic Dynamic Response of Plane Structures," University of California, Berkeley, CA, Aug. 1975

5) Bathe, K.J., and Wilson, E.J., "Numerical Methods in Finite Element Analysis, Prentice-Hall, Inc., Englewood Cliffs, N.J., 1976 pp 149-151; 460-473; 478-481; 378-379; 439-441.

IMPLICATIONS OF STRUCTURAL CHARACTERISTICS ON FAILURE.

Fernando Fossas R.*

SUMMARY

Performance of buildings with two common structural types, many of which suffered heavy structural damage or collapse, are analyzed. Conclusions are drawn that no structural type is inadequate, but that the flat plate type will usually require well designed shear walls to resist strong horizontal forces, and that structural steel frames must be carefully detailed in order to prevent faulty designs that may lead to failure.

Recommendations are made to promote reaserch on full scale testing of buildings subject to horizontal forces; it is pointed out that many buildings that suffered no damage in the past earthquake are liable to damage when a new earthquake comes.

* Director of Civil Engineering. Compañía Mexicana de Consultores en Ingeniería. Periférico Sur 3453 Mexico City.

255

Preface

It is a well known fact that most of the damages and the
collapses during this earthquake, occured in the central
part of the city, in buildings six to fifteen stories high,
and specially of the flat plate type. If we consider only
these statistics, the recommendations for future buildings
would be:

1. Avoid construction in the central part of the city.

2. Design buildings less than six or more than fifteen
   stories high.

3. Do not use the flat plate type of structure.

Those recommendations are not valid if we also consider:

1. That the main impulses of the quake in Mexico City had
   an average period of about two seconds (Reference 1).

2. That the period of vibration of the ground in the central part of the city is also about two seconds (References 2 and 3).

3. That the natural period of vibration of buildings six
   to fifteen stories high, either undamaged or after extensive damage has occured, is close to two seconds.
   And

4. That the most common structural type of buildings five
   to fifteen stories high in the central part of the city
   is (or was) the flat plate.

In a similar manner, if we analyze superficially the conse
quences of the Agadir and the 1976 Guatemala earthquakes,
where the most frequent and severe damages occured in one
story stone and adobe masonry wall buildings, (Reference
4) we would come to the conclusion of avoiding that height
and type of buildings, but here, again, the main impulses
of those quakes had an average period of less than a half
a second, the natural period of vibration of the ground is
less than a half a second, and the period of vibration of
the one and two story buildings is, usually, less than a
half a second.

The real conclusion is that, with earthquakes, the most
common danger of severe damages and of collapses is present

when the periods of vibration of the quakes, those of the
ground, and the ones of the buildings, are similar.   Of
course, the periods of vibration of the buildings and those
of the ground can be determined with modern techniques,
with-in a close approximation, but nobody can predict, so
far, what the average period of vibration of the coming
earthquakes will be.

Notwithstading, certain structural types are more vulnerable to earthquakes than others, and if those types are selected because of functional, economic, architectural or
aesthetic reasons, special care should be taken in the design and the construction of the buildings of those structural types.

For the sake of brevity, this paper will deal only with two
structural types: the reinforced concrete flat plate and
rigid structural steel frame.

Flat Plate Type

The concrete flat plate, either solid or ribed, has become
very popular in the last two or three decades because it is
economical, easy and quick to build, it has good aesthetic
and architectural characteristics, and the story height is
usualy less for this type than for other types, specially
the beam and slab. But details of design and structural
properties of this type have been frequently overlooked.

First of all, as has been shown elsewhere (References 5 and
6), unless adequately designed shear walls are provided,
most of the actual buildings of this type are not compatible with the resistance of horizontal forces, specially be
cause of the very high bond and anchorage stresses that are
developed at the intersection of the slabs with the columns.

If shear walls are included (which must be the usual case),
their strength, and their position in plan and in elevation,
should be carefully considered.

A shear wall that does not extend the full height from the
upper stories to the foundation (figures 1 and 2), as a
rule, will do more harm than good because it will cause severe weakness and discontinuity in the stories where the
shear wall is not present. This was a common cause of failures in many buildings where, for functional reasons, the
ground story had no adequate shear walls, in order to allow
the space for automobile parking and circulation in that
story. Figure 1 shows a wall many stories high, that stops
short of the ground story because, under that wall,is where
the main entrance door to the buildings is located.

In the case of corner lots, (figure 3) it is common to
build blind walls (that act as shear walls) adjacent to the

neighbouring lots, and not to build at all walls right at
the corner, where, if such walls would be built, they would
"balance" the wall at the opposite corner. The result is
that the "center of torsion" in plan is located at the intersection of the only two walls built, far away from the
center of gravity of the building; when the quake comes,
the building is subject to a considerable twist, which can
produce the failure of the columns oposite to the walls.

A very common failure was that of brick shear walls closing
the spaces within rigid frames. Most bricks in Mexico are
clay, hand made, poorly baked, 6 by 13 by 26 cm (2 1/2" by
5" by 10"), with an average compression resistance as low
as 10 kg/cm2 (150#/in2), and a tension resistance of only
about 1 kg/cm2 (15#/in2); furthermore, their resistance to
impact is nil.   Many buildings had blind walls made of the
se bricks in a single wythe; under the first waves, these
walls failed (sometimes they even exploded), and when the
succesive waves came, the building had either cracked walls,
or no walls at all, and therefore, the building was weaker
than when the quake started; moreso, the period of vibration was changed, sometimes for the worse.

The strength of columns was also an important factor that
contributed to the damages and collapses; building codes
in this country did not specify a minimum of area of the
stirrups in the columns, and the only requirement was a maximum spacing of such stirrups, indirect proportion to the
diameter of the longitudinal bars. For this reason, many
columns with sizes of 50x50 cm (20x20 in) and even larger,
were reinforced with only one or two sets of 6.3 mm (1/4")
stirrups spaced at 30 cm (12") (0.08 to 0.11% by volume).

The area of longitudinal bars, for many years, has been
specified in American Buildings Codes between 1 and 6% of
the cross section of the column (because of plastic flow);
as opossed to that, German Specifications have required a
minimum percentage of the stirrups or hoops in columns. No
theoretical considerations as to the minimum percentage of
stirrups can be fully demonstrated, but it is plain common
sense that, in order to have a ductile behaviour of the
columns, a minumum cross sectional area of the stirrups or
hoops should be specified; it is suggested that the volume
of the stirrups should be not less than 0.5% of the volume
of the columns for hard grade steel, and not less than 0.8%
for structural grade steel; furthermore, the stirrups
should extend all the way through the nodes, and should be
anchored adequately to the core of the concrete column.

The reinforcing steel that is active in the slabs should be
carefully considered in the flat plate type. All the reinforcing steel in the slab is effective in resisting vertical loads, but only that steel that runs through the columns,

Figure 1.

Shear wall in building
that stops short of
the ground floor.

Figure 2.

Building on a corner
lot with no wall at the
street corner

or that which is located close to the columns (say one
slab depth on each side), is fully effective for the frame
action under horizontal loads.

Column capitals at the top of the columns (under the slabs)
can be very effective in adding to the resistance of the
flat plate type (both in flexure and in shear), but such
capitals are not architecturally attractive, and are usualy
rejected in buildings for other than industrial use.

Finally, punching shear around the columns may be very severe in this structural type, specially for thin solid
slabs (Reference 7), and such shear increases greatly when
the slabs have perforations near the columns in order to
provide for plumbing, electric or air conditioning ducts
and instalations.

Structural Steel Frames

In Mexico, this type of structure has not been economically
competitive with reinforced concrete rigid frames in buildings less than fifteen stories high with pile foundations,
and less than twenty to thirty stories high if the buildings are located on firm ground.

For this reason, there were few buildings of this structural type within the critical height (six to fifteen stories),
in the central part of town; some of the buildings of this
type behaved well, but at least three (one on Pino Suárez
street and two on Lázaro Cárdenas street) collapsed. Other
buildings of this structural type suffered severe damage,
and will have to be torn down.

It is important to notice that the standard 12" and 14" wide flange sections, so popular in the United States for use
as columns in high rises, are not fabricated in this country. For this reason, it has been customary that the columns are fabricated with four plates welded longitudinally,
forming a holow box section. The size of the columns has
been such that no diaphragms or stiffeners can be installed
easily, so that local buckling at the floor levels can occur
because of the interaction of the beams and the columns.

Also for the sake of economy, regular rolled beams at the
floor levels have been substituted by trusses, formed by
small angles, plates or bars, and very vulnerable to local
buckling.

Figure 4 shows a common connection of a beam (rolled or
trussed) with a four plate column. It can be seen that the
flanges and the web of the beam will bend the column plates
locally, because there are no diaphragms to transmit the
tension and compression from the beam in one span to the
adjoining beam in the next span.

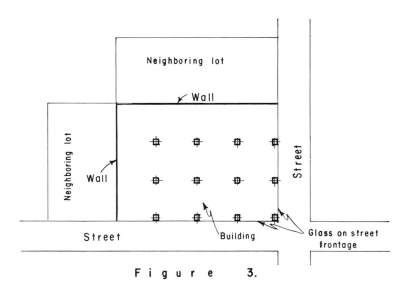

F i g u r e 3.

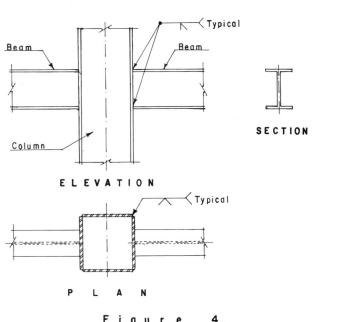

F i g u r e 4.

This problem can also occur in the diagonal bracing if such bracing is centrally located to the column, because the column plate bends when pulled by the bracing, and such system becomes ineffective.

On the other hand, it has been customary that, with structural steel frame buildings, the fabricator and erector will do all the calculations and the design of the structure; this practice has been standard because it allows the fabricator to use the materials available to him when the structure is fabricated, but it eliminates the control, and sometimes the supervision, of the engineer in charge of the building; consulting firms hardly ever are requested to check the design of the fabricator, and to supervise the erection and welding of the structural steel.

All the above points to defective design and workmanship as the cause of failures, and in many cases, such failures could have been avoided if a careful design and supervision would have been made.

CONCLUSIONS

It can not be said that a particular structural type was inadequate to resist earthquakes, but it must be born in mind that flat plate systems, unless reinforced by adequately designed shear walls, should not be recommended in zones of high earthquake potential.

Structural steel frames, more than other types, must be designed and built very carefully to avoid mistakes that lead to structural failures.

Structural engineers should work with, instead of for, architects, and engineers and architects together should reach sound and reasonable designs.

Full scale testing of buildings under horizontal forces should be encouraged, and research must be carried out in order to make such testing commercialy feasable and economical.

Many building that suffered no damage at all during the 1985 earthquakes are in danger of suffering heavy damage in a future earthquake with different period of vibration. They are, actually, "sitting ducks" waiting for disaster.

REFERENCES:

1. Prince A. Jorge, "Los tres acelerogramas de "campo libre" obtenidos el 19 de septiembre de 1985". Revista IMCYC # 176. México. Diciembre/Enero, 1986.

2. Herrera, I. and Rosenblueth E., "Response Spectra on Stratified Soil". Proceedings of the 3rd World Conferen ce on Earthquake Engineering. New Zealand. 1965.

3. Zeevaert L. "Foundation Engineering for Difficult Subsoil Conditions". Van Nostrand Reinhold Company. 1973.

4. Mc Dowel B., Earthquake in Guatemala. National Geographic. June 1976. Washington, D.C.

5. Fossas F., "Los sismos de México de los días 19 y 20 de septiembre de 1985. Pasado, Presente y Futuro". Revista IMCYC # 179. México, Abril de 1986. Also reprint in English. Structural Engineers Association of Southern California. Los Angeles, Calif.

6. Rosenblueth E. & Meli R., "El Sismo del 19 de Septiembre de 1985. Sus efectos en la Ciudad de México". Revista IMCYC # 180. México. Mayo de 1986.

7. Leyendecker E. and Fattal G., "Investigation of the Skyline Plaza Collapse". National Bureau of Standards. Washington, D.C. 1977.

OBSERVATIONS ON STRUCTURAL POUNDING

Vitelmo V. Bertero*, F. ASCE

ABSTRACT: In over 40% of the collapsed or severely damaged buildings in Mexico City, pounding of adjacent buildings occurred, and in at least 15% was the primary cause of collapse. The main objectives of this paper are to identify and discuss the primary causes of pounding of adjacent engineered buildings; and to assess their observed performance in regard to improving the earthquake-resistant design and construction of new adjacent buildings and retrofitting existing ones where separation appears to be inadequate. The primary cause for the severe pounding was the insufficient separation between these adjacent buildings and the main reasons for this insufficiency are identified as (1) the unexpected severity of the ground motions and the consequent insufficiency of the minimum seismic code requirements for the design of structures, particularly for lateral and torsional stiffnesses and strengths; (2) inadequate building configuration to resist torsional effects (lack of redundancy, particularly against inelastic torsional deformations); (3) cumulative deformation due to foundation movements; and (4) improper maintenance. Comparison of Mexico and U.S. earthquake regulations indicates that if buildings would be designed and constructed to satisfy just the minimum code requirements, and if ground motions like those recorded at SCT could occur in the U.S. cities, the problem of pounding between adjacent buildings located in soft soils could be even more serious in the U.S. than in Mexico City.

INTRODUCTION

Introductory Remarks. – The intensity, duration, and damage potential of the ground motions at the historic center of Mexico City during the 19 September 1985 Mexican earthquake substantially exceeded those previously recorded or anticipated for that site, thus significant structural damage could be expected. Damage statistics, a list of types of damage, and a discussion of possible causes of the observed damage have been presented in [4] and [6]. Analysis of this list reveals that in over 40% of the collapsed or severely damaged buildings, pounding between adjacent buildings occurred, and in at least 15% pounding was the primary cause for building collapse. Although pounding between adjacent structures which are not properly separated have been observed in most of previous severe earthquakes, the number of adjacent buildings severely damaged and dramatically partially collapsed in Mexico City in 1985 is very large and may in fact be the highest in the recorded history of earthquake damages. As a consequence of these dramatic failures and analyses of the statistical information cited above the following question have arisen: What are the main reasons for the observed damaging, and in many cases devastating, pounding of adjacent buildings? Considering that the historic center of Mexico City is crowded with adjacent buildings without any significant separation, why do only a relatively small number of these buildings suffer severe damage? An attempt to answer these questions motivated the preliminary studies reported herein which have the following objectives.

*Professor of Civ. Engrg., Univ. of California, Berkeley, CA, 94720.

Objectives. - The main objectives of this paper are to illustrate the performance of adjacent engineered buildings in Mexico City during the September 1985 earthquakes; to identify and to discuss the primary causes of severe pounding of these buildings; and to assess their observed performance and to identify research needs in regard to improving earthquake-resistant design and construction of new adjacent buildings and retrofitting existing ones where separation is inadequate.

OBSERVED PERFORMANCE OF ADJACENT BUILDINGS

General. - In discussing the performance of adjacent buildings it is convenient to group these buildings as follows: (1) Adjacent units of the same building separated through expansion (or construction) joints as illustrated in Fig. 1; (2) Units of the same building or adjacent different buildings which are far apart but connected byone or more bridges (Fig. 2); and (3) Adjacent different buildings, i.e. buildings having different structural and/or nonstructural characteristics (Fig. 3). It should be noted that there were several cases in which a building was severely damaged and in at least one case totally destroyed by the impact of a tall building some distance away (in some cases, across the street) that collapsed laterally (overturning) (Fig. 4). These cases will not be discussed herein and only a brief description of the observed performance of the above three different groups of adjacent buildings is presented.

Adjacent Units of the Same Building. - There are many large buildings in Mexico City, particularly in some very important housing developments, medical centers, and governmental buildings, which have been constructed of several identical units leaving between two adjacent units the so called expansion or construction joints. In most cases the clear separation (width of joint) between two adjacent units does not exceed 10 cm. Although in most cases there was clear evidence of permanent relative lateral deformation between two adjacent units (opening or closing of the expansion joints) and even of damage due to pounding (Fig. 1), no dramatic collapse was observed. Figure 1a shows a 14 story building consisting of three adjacent units. There were about 10 such buildings in one housing development in Mexico City. Although none collapsed due to pounding in most of them was clear evidence of relative lateral movement between two adjacent units as illustrated in Fig 1a. Part of these observed permanent relative movement was already observed before the 1985 earthquakes due to differential settlement of their foundation, and response to previous earthquakes. Figure 1b illustrates the significant separation between two 7-story units of a hospital building and Fig. 1c shows the significant nonstructural damage due to pounding of adjacent units which were separated by very narrow expansion joints as illustrated by the photo of **Fig. 1c** (ii).

Units of the Same Building or Adjacent Buildings which are Far Apart but Connected by Bridges. - There are in Mexico City several units or buildings which are connected by one or more bridges. Some of these bridges suffered significant damage due to the relative lateral movement of the connected buildings. Figure 2 illustrates one bridge connecting two different buildings: the bridge suffered severe nonstructural as well as structural damage due to the relative lateral deformation between the two adjacent buildings and the pounding of these two buildings (mainly the taller one) against the bridge. Note also that

a(i) Overall View

Fig. 1b Opening of Expansion Joint
in a 7-story Building

Opening   Closing
a(ii) Closeup Views of Expansions Joints
Fig.1a 14-story Building Composed of 3
Adjacent Units.

Fig. 1c Two Adjacent Units
with Severe Nonstructural
Damage

c(i) Overall View of Severely Damaged Units
FIG. 1 POUNDING EFFECTS ON ADJACENT UNITS OF
      BUILDINGS

Adjacent Units

c(iiii)
Closeup
View of
Expansion
Joint of
Building
1c(i)

FIG. 2 POUNDING EFFECTS ON TWO AD-
JACENT UNITS OF THE TALLER BUILDING
AND ON THE BRIDGE CONNECTING THE
TWO DIFFERENT BUILDINGS.

a(1) Overall View

Upper Stories of C   4th Story of A
a(ii) Closeup Views of Damages to A & C

Fig. 3a Collapse of two Intermediate Stories of Buildings (B) Located
Between a Shorter (A) and a Taller Building (C).

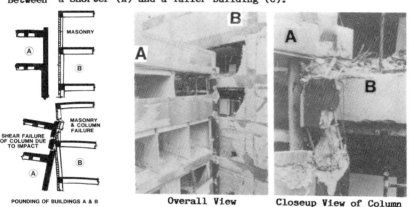

POUNDING OF BUILDINGS A & B

3b(i) Schematic of
Behavior

Overall View

3b(ii) Severe Nonstructural and Structural Damage

Closeup View of Column
and Masonry Failure

Collapse of
Several
Stories

Column
Failures

Overall
View of
Damage

Closeup
View of
Column
Failures
of
Building
B

Fig. 3b Damage to Buildings Having their Floor Systems at Different Levels

FIG. 3 POUNDING EFFECTS ON ADJACENT DIFFERENT BUILDINGS (continued on page 5)

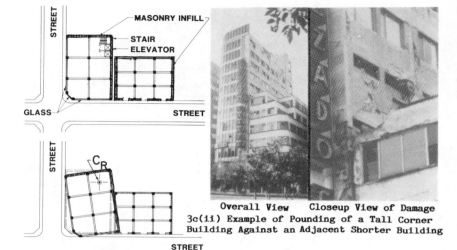

Overall View   Closeup View of Damage
3c(ii) Example of Pounding of a Tall Corner
Building Against an Adjacent Shorter Building

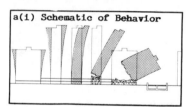

3c (i) Schematic of Behavior

Fig. 3c Pounding of Corner Building
due to Torsional Effects

a(i) Schematic of Behavior

a(ii) Overall View

Fig. 4a A 14-story Building Crushed by
the Collapse of a 21-story Tower

4b. A 3-Story Building Severely
Damaged by Collapsing Building
Across the Street

FIG.4   EFFECTS OF IMPACT OF LATERALLY COLLAPSING BUILDINGS ON BUILDINGS
SOME DISTANCE AWAY.

the taller building consisted of two adjacent units and that these units
suffered severe damage due to pounding.   The damage was so severe   that
these two units and the bridge were demolished.

Adjacent Different Buildings. - In the center of Mexico there is a heavy concentration of engineered buildings that were built one just besides the other, i.e. without practically any separation and having different height or different configuration or structural system, and/or different nonstructural components. This group of adjacent buildings suffered the most severe damage due to pounding and in some cases dramatic partial collapse resulted. In spite of the fact that the number of these buildings that suffered severe damage or partially collapsed due to pounding was greater than ever before witnessed in the aftermath of any earthquake, this number, relative to thé total number of adjacent buildings in Mexico City, is small. Figure 3a shows a 9-story building between a 4-story and a 10-story building. Due to pounding the 9-story buildings collapsed partially at its fifth and sixth stories and produced severe local damage on the fourth story of the shortest building and on the upper stories of the 10-story building. In Mexico City there are many cases in which the adjacent buildings have different story heights as illustrated schematically in Fig. 3b. The photos of Fig. 3b illustrate the severe damage (local failure of columns and even partial collapse of several stories) that were observed in several adjacent buildings of this type. Pounding was observed between tall modern corner buildings and adjacent buildings, induced by torsional effects resulting from the assymetry of stiffness caused by the use of infill masonry walls in the sides that were not along the streets (Fig. 3c).

Concluding Remarks. - (1) In the center of Mexico City there are a large number of adjacent buildings (units of the same building or different buildings) which are very close to each other (clear separation not exceeding 10 cm). (2) The percentage of these buildings that suffered severe damage due to pounding was very small. In spite of this the number of adjacent buildings that suffered severe nonstructural damages and structural local failures and dramatic partial collapse is large, and may in fact be the highest in the recorded history of earthquake damage. Now the question is what are the primary causes of the acceptable performance of most of the engineered adjacent buildings on the one hand and the dramatic failures of few others? An attempt to identify the primary causes and evaluate this paradox is presented below.

PRIMARY CAUSES FOR POUNDING OF ADJACENT BUILDINGS

General. - Obviously the primary reason for severe pounding of adjacent buildings was insufficient separation. The questions then are (1) What were the main causes for this insufficient separation?; (2) Was it the result of inadequate code regulations regarding minimum separation?; or (3) Was it due to violations of the minimum code requirements? Considering that for the large majority of adjacent buildings no serious damage occurred due to pounding, it could be concluded that in general the existing separation between these buildings was adequate and therefore the code regulations used in their design and construction were adequate. However, as it is discussed below, it appears that the minimum separation required by the different codes that were enforced since 1942 for the construction of adjacent buildings in the Federal District of Mexico were insufficient to avoid severe pounding between these buildings when responding to ground motions as those recorded at the SCT station during the 1985 earthquakes. What saved most adjacent buildings from pounding were other factors rather than adequacy of code requirements. These other factors are discussed later.

From preliminary analysis of the few data available it appears that the insufficient separation between the adjacent buildings that suffered severe damage due to pounding was the result of a combination of several factors and cannot be attributed to any factor alone. The author believes that among the primary causes for the apparently contradictory responses of adjacent buildings are (1) the unexpected severity of the ground motions and the consequent insufficiency of the minimum seismic code requirements for the design of structures, particularly for lateral and torsional stiffnesses and strengths; (2) inadequate building configuration and structural system to resist lateral shaking and particularly torsional effects (lack of redundancy of structural defense lines, particularly against inelastic torsional deformations); (3) cumulative tilting due to differential foundation settlement; and (4) improper maintenance.

Severity of the Ground Motions. - Analysis of the ground motions recorded at the SCT station reveals very severe dynamic characteristics, especially high intensity (about 0.20 g) and long duration of strong motions (greater than 30 seconds) with a predominant frequency of around 0.5 Hertz (T = 2 sec). Although the predominant frequency was expected according to data obtained during previous earthquakes (since 1954), the high intensity was not. According to records of the July 28, 1957 earthquake and damage observed in the aftermath, it was predicted that the peak acceleration at certain sites could have been as high as 0.10 g. In 1970 Esteva [3] evaluated the seismic risk for the entire country of Mexico considering all historical data, consisting primarily of subjective intensities rather than measured quantities. He generated curves of maximum expected velocities and accelerations assuming return periods of 50, 100, and 500 years. The maximum expected accelerations and velocities at the Federal District are indicated in Table 1.

TABLE 1	RETURN PERIOD (YEARS)	MAXIMUM	
		VELOCITY (CM/SEC)	ACCELERATION (CM/SEC^2)
	50	9-10	75-80
	100	14-15	100-110
	500	27-30	170-190

The curves were estimated for firm soil comparable to soft rock, and it is pointed out that except for the case of very compressible clays, or granular soils susceptible to liquefaction, the accelerations on soft soil can safely be assumed the same as those given for firm soil, but that the velocities should be multiplied by 1.5. Therefore, even if the 1985 earthquake is considered as a phenomenon of a 500-year recurrence, the predicted maximum velocity on soft soil (30 x 1.5 = 45 cm/sec) would have been significantly smaller than that recorded at the SCT station during the 1985 earthquake (61 cm/sec).

Insufficiency of Code Requirements. - Buildings severely damaged in the 1985 Mexican earthquakes were constructed at different times, and therefore were designed under different code regulations [4,5]. The first code designed to provide earthquake resistance to building structures in Mexico City was the Federal District Code of 1942. This code was modified in 1957, immediately after the July 28, 1957

earthquake, through an emergency code which was revised in 1959. This
revision, after being applied for many years, was officially approved,
with minor changes, in 1966. In 1976 a new moden seismic code was
approved. While previous codes were all based on the use of allowable
stresses, the 1976 code was oriented towards the use of strength and
limit design methods. In [1] and [2] the author has reviewed all the
seismic code regulations related to minimum required stiffnesses and
strengths that have been enforced for building construction in the
Federal District of Mexico since 1942 up to September 19, 1985 and
arrived at the following preliminary observations: (1) The strengths
required by the Federal District seismic code regulations in force since
their introduction in 1942 were insufficient to cope with the severity
of the response demanded by the dynamic characteristics (intensity,
frequency, duration of strong motion, severity of pulses) of ground
motions similar to those recorded at SCT. (2) A main cause for poor
performance of buildings was excessive deformations: lateral,
torsional, and in some cases, vertical. These excessive deformations
were a consequence of: inadequate initial stiffness; too low yielding
and maximum strengths; and inadequate deformation hardening. (3) The
stiffness inadequacy was a consequence of: insufficiency of seismic
code requirements; foundation movements; inadequate structural systems
(use of flat or waffle slabs and few structural defense lines, and poor
detailing--abuse of bundled bars); and significant deterioration of
stiffness and strength with the increasing number of cycles with
reversals of severe (yielding) deformations. (4) The overall good
performance (response) of nearly 98.6% of the buildings in the region of
greatest damage was due to the conservatism of Mexican designers in
proportioning, detailing, and constructing the structure, and
particularly to the overstrength of the buildings as constructed added
by the introduction of masonry infills, walls, and partitions, rather
than the use of adequate seismic codes.

It should be noted that until the 1957 emergency regulations there
were no seismic code requirements regarding stiffness, drift limits,
torsional eccentricity, and separation of buildings. The 1957 emergency
regulations limited the interstory drift index to 0.002. This limit was
kept in the 1959 code but it could increase to 0.003 when elements that
do not form an integral part of the structure (i.e. nonstructural
elements) were attached to the structure in a manner such that they
would not be damaged by its deformation. This code introduced more
severe requirements for torsional eccentricity. The 1966 code kept the
0.002 interstory drift limit. The 1976 code required that the maximum
lateral interstory drift should not exceed 0.008 save where
nonstructural elements were attached in such a manner that they would
not be damaged by deformations of the structure. In this case, the
limit was 0.016. It should be noted that these values were for the
ultimate limit state and therefore have to be divided by 4 for MRSF to
obtain the linear elastic interstory drift index limit.

The minimum code required strength vs. interstory drift index
diagrams of Fig. 5 have been prepared according to the strength and
drift requirements of the 1959 and 1976 Mexican codes. The question
that now has to be answered is "were the minimum lateral stiffness and
yielding strengths specified by these codes and illustrated in Fig. 5
adequate for controlling damage due to pounding to acceptable levels?"

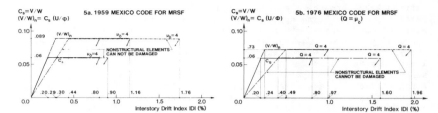

FIG. 5   DIAGRAMS OF EXPECTED LATERAL STRENGTH-INTERSTORY DRIFT INDEX
ACCORDING TO MEXICAN CODES MINIMUM REQUIREMENTS FOR RC-MRSF STRUCTURES
OF GROUP B OF BUILDINGS

This is a very difficult question to address because it depends on the
damage level, i.e. on the different limit states (serviceability,
damageability,   and   collapse).   Even   if   the   only   interest is in
controlling severe damage, finding a proper answer remains difficult
because this damage depends not only on the initial (elastic) lateral
stiffness but also on the yielding strength and on the ductility
required to absorb and dissipate the input energy to each of the two
adjacent buildings as well as on their relative values.   An attempt to
answer the above question is made below by reviewing the adequacy of the
Mexican code regulations regarding minimum required separation between
adjacent buildings.

Code Requirements Regarding Building Separation. - As already noted
above, until the 1957 emergency regulations there were no seismic code
requirements regarding drift limits and separation of buildings.   It is
therefore not surprising to see many old buildings in Mexico City
without any or very little separation.   **The 1959 code** introduced what
were considered severe drift limitations: 0.002H or 0.003H if
nonstructural elements were separated from structures such that they
would not be damaged by building deformation.   The 1959 code required
clear spacing at property lines and in construction joints of only 3 cm
(1.2 in.) or x + 0.006H* where x is maximum lateral displacement
computed at elevation H.   Assuming that the drift limitation minimum of
0.002H or 0.003H were just satisfied, the 1959 code-required separation
would have been 0.008H or 0.009H from the property lines, or 0.016H and
0.018H from the adjacent building assuming that the two buildings
complied with the code, i.e. were built after the 1959 code was in
force.   Assuming buildings of just 5 stories (H $\doteq$ 15 m), the clear
spacing should have been at least 24 cm or 27 cm.   This separation is
rarely seen in Mexico City for such five-story buildings.

Even if the designer had complied with the code, which at first
glance appears to be conservative, the required separation would not

_____
*Although not stated in the code, it is suspected that this increase in
the computed displacement x by 0.006H was mandated in order that the
inelastic deformations, as well as possible effects of foundation
movement   on   the lateral deformation of the superstructure,   be
considered.

have been sufficient to avoid pounding between buildings designed merely
to satisfy the minimum code-required lateral strength and stiffness, and
which were subjected to the September 19, 1985 recorded ground motion at
SCT. As illustrated in Fig. 5a for the nominal yielding strength and
stiffness resulting from the code minimum requirements, the maximum
lateral displacement could have been as great as 0.0116H (if
nonstructural elements were considered integral to the structure) or
0.0176H (if nonstructural components were properly separated from the
structure) if a ductility ratio of $\mu_\delta = 4$ was required during the
maximum response. These values, although they do not include possible
effects of foundation movement, are already significantly higher than
the mimimum code required values of 0.008H or 0.009H.

Similar results can be obtained when the 1976 code regulations are
considered. These regulations required that the maximum lateral
interstory drift index not exceed 0.008, save where elements that did
not form an integral part of the structure were attached in such a
manner that they would not be damaged by structural deformation. In
this case the limit of 0.008 was increased to 0.016. When these values
are compared with those of the 1959 (or 1966) code, it should be noted
that the 1976 values include the inelastic deformations, usually based
on a $Q \equiv \mu_\delta = 4$ and that the lateral yielding strength of buildings
designed by the 1959 (or 1966) code was higher than that of those
designed according to the 1976 code (0.089 vs. 0.073, see Fig. 5).
Thus, it appears that with regard to lateral stiffnesses the 1959
regulations were more stringent than those of the 1976 code,
particularly when nonstructural elements were properly separated from
the structure. The 1976 code required that every new building shall be
constructed away from the neighboring pieces of land a distance equal to
the accumulated displacement calculated at each level, being increased
by 0.001, 0.0015, and 0.0020 times its height in zones I, II, and III,
respectively. In cases where calculation was omitted, this separation
was to equal 0.006, 0.007, and 0.008 times the height of the structure
in zones I, II, and III, respectively. This separation should be larger
than 5 cm in every case. Analyses of these 1976 regulations indicate
that although the required spacing was similar to that of 1959 (0.008H
vs. 0.008H) for cases in which the nonstructural elements were integral
parts of the structure, because of the higher lateral yielding strength
required for buildings designed according to the 1959 code, it appears
that these buildings should have been less subject to pounding than
those designed according to the 1976 code.

The 1959 and 1976 codes clearly stated that at construction
(expansion) joints, the same criterion applies as for property lines,
unless special measures were taken to prevent damage from pounding.
Inspection of these joints after the 1985 earthquake revealed that in
many cases the widths were smaller than required by code (see Fig. 1).
Perhaps the code regulation is not sufficiently clear regarding what
should be the clear spacing between two units of a building, i.e. twice
the value specified by the code or just this value. If the two units
are identical, the probability of having them vibrating nonsynchronously
and reaching their maximum displacement, in the opposite sense
simultaneously, is low. It could, however, occur, particularly in the
inelastic range and therefore it would be prudent to require the

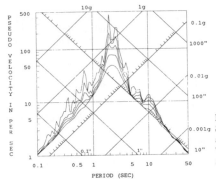

FIG. 6 LINEAR ELASTIC RESPONSE
SPECTRA FOR DAMPING VALUES OF 0,2,5,
and 10 PERCENT OF CRITICAL, OF
THE E-W COMPONENT RECORDED AT THE
SCT STATION DURING THE SEPTEMBER 19,
1985 MEXICAN EARTHQUAKE.

expansion joints to have a width equal to twice the distance from the
property line specified by the code.

An analysis of the 2% and 5% damped Linear Elastic Response Spectra
for the EW component of the ground motion recorded at SCT (Fig. 6)
reveals that for structures whose effective fundamental period of
vibration T is about 2 secs., the maximum displacement could be as large
as 165 cm (65 in.) for a damping coefficient of 2% and 102 cm (40 in.)
for 5% damping. Preliminary nonlinear (inelastic) analysis of the
response of a one-degree-of-freedom system to the ground motion recorded
at SCT indicates that for such a system having a lateral yielding
resistance of 0.10W (i.e. somewhat larger than the minimum required by
Mexican codes), and for values of T up to 1 sec., the lateral drift
index could be as large as 0.011. When these preliminary results are
compared with those specified by Mexican codes, it can be concluded that
if adjacent buildings would have just the stiffnesses and yielding
strengths required by the codes and they were built satisfying just the
minimum separation specified by these codes, the probability that these
buildings would have suffered damage due to pounding during the 1985
ground motions, which were similar to those recorded at the SCT station,
is high.

**Reasons for the Relatively Small Number of Buildings Damaged in Spite of
the Insufficiency of Code Minimum Requirements.** - As noted previously,
because of the insufficiency of Mexican code regulations regarding
lateral and torsional stiffnesses, lateral yielding strengths, and
separation between adjacent buildings, a large number of these buildings
in the center of Mexico City are not separated properly to respond
satisfactorily to ground motions like those recorded at SCT. Why then
were relatively few buildings severely damaged due to pounding?
Possibly, the main reasons are (1) that in most cases these adjacent
buildings vibrate almost synchronically, and even in cases where
significant nonsynchronous vibration occurred, in very few instances did
the maximum lateral displacement occur in opposite directions
simultaneously, and (2) the significantly greater strengths and
stiffnesses of buildings as constructed in comparison with the design

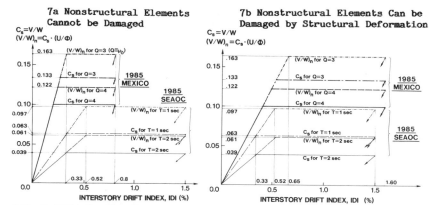

FIG. 7 COMPARISON OF EXPECTED LATERAL STRENGTH-INTERSTORY DRIFT INDEX DIAGRAMS ACORDING TO MINIMUM REQUIREMENTS OF THE 1985 MEXICAN EMERGENCY REGULATIONS AND THOSE OF THE 1985 SEAOC RECOMMENDATIONS.

stiffnesses and strengths of the bare structural systems which in turn may be due largely to the number of masonry infill walls and partitions observed in buildings in Mexico City. The addition of such masonry infills can significantly increase stiffness (lateral and torsional) and the yielding strength of the bare structural system.

1985 Emergency Regulations. – Although these regulations do not change the drift limits and clear spacing required by the 1976 code, due to the significant increase in the required lateral strength (see Fig. 7), new buildings should have significantly larger initial linear elastic lateral stiffness and smaller maximum lateral deformation under earthquake ground motions such as those recorded at SCT during the September 19, 1985 earthquake. Thus, the damage due to pounding of adjacent buildings designed and constructed according to these emergency regulations will be less than that for buildings designed according to previous codes.

IMPLICATIONS OF OBSERVED POUNDING OF ADJACENT BUILDINGS IN MEXICO CITY FOR U.S. EARTHQUAKE-RESISTANT DESIGN AND CONSTRUCTION PRACTICES

Comparison of Mexico and U.S. Code Requirements – UBC. – The UBC requires that the lateral interstory drift index not exceed 0.005 under the required lateral forces multiplied by K [8]. The UBC does not specify a value for clear spacing, but states that: "All portions of the structure shall be designed and constructed to act as an integral unit in resisting horizontal forces, unless separated structurally by a distance sufficient to avoid contact under deflection from seismic action." The problem is: **What is "a distance sufficient to avoid contact"? Is it twice the maximum interstory drift?** Although this is perhaps the most common interpretation of the code, such an interpretation is not in accord with the philosophy of the code, given that the code assumes that under extreme earthquakes the building will

deform 3/K times the distortion resulting from the code-required lateral
forces.   This would require separation of twice [0.005(K) x (3/K)]H,
i.e. 0.030H, which would be a rational separation.

The minimum lateral stiffnesses required by the Mexican codes are
generally significantly greater than those required by the UBC: compare
Figs. 5 and 8.   Furthermore, as the yielding strength required by the
UBC for buildings with fundamental periods T   1.38 secs is about the
same or smaller than that specified by the 1959 Mexican code, it appears
that if ground motions like those recorded at SCT could occur in U.S.
cities, the problem of pounding between adjacent buildings located on
soft soils could be even more serious in the U.S. than in Mexico City.

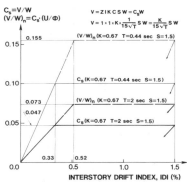

**FIG. 8 EXPECTED LATERAL STRENGTH-
INTERSTORY DRIFT INDEX RELATIONSHIPS
PER UBC REQUIREMENTS FOR RC-MRSF OF
APARTMENTS AND OFFICE BUILDINGS.**

9a 6-story Building (B) Located
Between a Shorter (A) and a
Taller Building (C)

Corner Building

9b(i)
Overall
View

9b(ii)
Closeup
View.

**FIG. 9 EXAMPLES OF ADJACENT BUILDINGS IN A U.S. CITY LOCATED IN ZONE
4 OF UBC SEISMIC RISK MAP (ZONE OF HIGHEST SEISMIC RISK)**

Figure 9 illustrates adjacent buildings in a U.S. city located in zone 4 of the UBC seismic risk map.

SEAOC 1985 Tentative Lateral Force Requirements. – The proposed SEAOC regulations [7] specify that: "Calculated story drift shall not exceed $0.04/R_w$ nor 0.005 times the story height unless . . . ." According to this regulation and the required design base shear $V = (ZIC/R_w)W$ (where $C = 1.25S/T^{2/3}$) for the case of RC-SMRSF (which is the only type of RC moment-resisting frame system allowed in seismic zones 3 and 4), the lateral stiffness for buildings with $T = 2$ secs and even with $T = 1$ sec required by SEAOC is significantly smaller than that required by the Mexican codes (see Fig. 7). For building separation SEAOC specifies that "separations shall allow for $(3/8)R_w$ times displacement due to design seismic forces." Considering that this displacement shall not exceed $(0.04R_w)H$, the total separation could be $2[(3/8)R_w \times 0.04/R_w)H]$. This separation is very large, considerably larger than that required by Mexican codes $[2(0.008)H]$ for the case that nonstructural components can be damaged by the deformation of the structure. For example, for two five-story buildings with an average story height of 10 ft (3 m), the clear spacing would be $2(0.015) \times 15$ m $= 45$ cm and for two ten-story buildings it would be 90 cm. Despite this apparently huge spacing, compliance with this code regulation may not guarantee that pounding will not occur because the required lateral yielding strength is relatively low (Fig. 7).

Concluding Remarks. – To avoid the effects of hammering of adjacent tall buildings, separation would be required that could lead to serious problems in the economical use of usually very expensive real estate. Thus, it appears that to avoid damage between adjacent buildings it is necessary to develop other regulations or requirements than just to specify adequate separation, such as including in the design and detailing of adjacent buildings the possibility of such hammering. One such regulation should be that for two adjacent buildings, with inadequate separation, the floor systems of the two buildings should be at the same level. The use of proper dampers between the adjacent buildings could also be effective. A simple solution has been suggested by Rosenblueth and Esteva in [5]. The problem of proper separation between adjacent buildings urgently requires consideration in our codes. Economical solutions for retrofitting existing adjacent buildings which do not have adequate separation should be researched immediately.

CONCLUSIONS AND RECOMMENDATIONS

Conclusions. – From the observed performance of adjacent buildings in Mexico City during the 1985 earthquakes and the results of the preliminary studies reported above, the following preliminary conclusions are drawn: (1) In over 40% of the collapsed or severely damaged buildings, pounding between adjacent buildings occurred and in at least 15% pounding was the primary cause of collapse. Relative to the total number of adjacent buildings with the very small separation that exists in the center of Mexico City, the number of buildings severely damaged by pounding is very small. (2) Although severe pounding was the result of insufficient separation between adjacent buildings, this insufficiency in general cannot be attributed to just one specific reason. It was the result of a combination of several of the following factors: (a) the unexpected severity of the ground motion and the consequent insufficiency of the minimum seismic code requirements for the design of structures, particularly for lateral and torsional stiffnesses and strengths; (b) inadequate building configuration and structural system to resist lateral shaking and particularly torsional effects (lack of redundancy of structural defense lines, particularly against inelastic torsional deformations); (c) cumulative tilting due to foundation movement; and (d) improper maintenance. (3) Comparison of Mexico and U.S. earthquake regulations indicates that if buildings were designed and constructed to satisfy just the minimum code requirements, and if ground motions like those recorded at the SCT station could occur in the U.S. cities, the problem of pounding between adjacent buildings located in soft soils could be even more serious in the U.S. than in Mexico City.

Recommendations. - (1) To conduct thorough studies of the performance (good and bad) of adjacent buildings in Mexico City in order to investigate the primary causes for such performance and to improve present code requirements by finding out proper separation between the different types of adjacent buildings. This will require integrated analytical and field experimental studies. (2) To investigate the probabilities of ground motions like those recorded at the SCT station occuring in U.S. cities so that a more thorough assessment can be made of the implications of the observed performance of adjacent buildings in Mexico City on U.S. earthquake-resistance design and construction practices. Furthermore, in order to conduct a thorough assessment, it would be necessary to study the differences between the building technology used in Mexico City and that used in U.S. regions of high seismic risk, particularly regarding the type of RC structural system and proportioning and detailing of its critical regions, foundation, nonstructural elements, workmanship, inspection, and maintenance, all important factors in the seismic response of the entire soil-foundation-building system. (3) Investigate economical solutions for retrofitting existing adjacent buildings which do not have adequate separation to avoid severe damage due to pounding.

REFERENCES

1. Bertero, V. V., The 19 September 1985 Mexico Earthquake: Building Behavior, UCB/EERC, Report No. 86-08, Earthquake Engineering Research Center, University of California, Berkeley, CA, July 1986.
2. Bertero, V. V., "The Mexico Earthquake of September 19, 1985: Performance of Building Structures," Proceedings of the Second International Conference on Engineering and Technology, August 20-22, 1986, Society of Hispanic Professional Engineers, Los Angeles, CA, 12 pp.
3. Esteva, L., Regionalizacion Sismica de Mexico Para Fines de Ingenieria, Universidad Nacional Autonoma de Mexico, Report No. 246, April 1970, 17 pp.
4. Instituto de Ingenieria, UNAM, "Effectos de los Sismos de Septiembre de 1985 en las Construcciones de la Ciudad de Mexico, Aspectos Estructurales," Segundo Informe del Instituto de Ingenieria de la Universidad Nacional Autonoma de Mexico, Mexico, November 1985, 48 pp.
5. Newmark/Rosenblueth, Fundamentals of Earthquake Engineering, Prentice-Hall, Inc., Englewood Cliffs, NJ (1971).
6. Rosenblueth, E. and Meli, R., "The 1985 Earthquake: Causes and Effects in Mexico City," ACI, Concrete International Design and Construction, Vol. 8, No. 5, May 1986, pp. 23-36.
7. SEAOC Seismology Committee, "Tentative Lateral Force Requirements," Structural Engineering Association of California, San Francisco, CA, October 1985.
8. Uniform Building Code, International Conference of Building Officials, Whittier, CA, 1982, 1985.

R/C FRAME DRIFT FOR 1985 MEXICO EARTHQUAKE

by

Mete A. Sozen[1] and Ricardo R. Lopez[2]

ABSTRACT

This paper contains the results of a parametric study of the displacement response of multi-story reinforced concrete frames. Nonlinear lateral displacement responses were calculated for 8-, 12- and 16-story frames having different combinations of strength and stiffness. Two ground motions were considered: (1) an acceleration record with a peak value of 0.16g obtained in the soft-soil region of Mexico City during the 19 September 1985 earthquake and (2) an acceleration record with a peak value of 0.5g representing ground motion on stiff soil. Results of the analyses were compared to study trends of drift response with changes in nature of base motion, frame strength, and frame stiffness.

Introduction

The total direct damage caused by the 19 and 20 September Michoacan earthquakes in Mexico City is estimated to approach four billion dollars (U.S.). Compared with the wealth and size of the entire city, the reported loss appears as a serious but not catastrophic. But the intensity of the damage is brought into better perspective when it is considered that almost all of the loss occurred in a small part of the city with an area of approximately 5000 acres. In that context the economic loss, mostly related to building damage, approached $800,000 per acre. The earthquake had a devastating effect on construction.

Represented by the index value of an effective peak acceleration, the event measured in Mexico City on 19 September 1985 would be classified as an earthquake of moderate intensity. Currently, a design-basis earthquake indexed by an effective peak (ground) acceleration of 0.5G is not considered to be extreme for ordinary construction in a region of high seismicity. Against that background, a maximum measured ground acceleration of 0.1G (Reference 1) does not appear to be consistent with the devastation observed. The apparent contradiction arises from the drastically different frequency-content characteristics of

---

[1]Professor of Civil Engineering, University of Illinois, Urbana, IL.
[2]Research Assistant in Civil Engineering, University of Illinois, Urbana, IL.

the ground motion in that part of Mexico City founded on
Lake Texcoco from those attributed to soft ground in other
parts of the world.

   This paper presents a comparative study of the effects
of ground motion on reinforced concrete frames having
different strength and stiffness characteristics. The focus
of the paper is on lateral displacement or drift response.
It is concerned with the question: what combinations of
stiffness and strength result in acceptable displacement
response on soft soil and on stiff soil for multi-story
reinforced concrete frames? In the studies, toughness of
the frame was taken for granted. To produce reinforced
concrete frames that will remain integral within acceptable
limits of drift is well within current technology. The
central question is how to limit the frame to acceptable
drifts given the intensity and nature of the ground motion.

   Despite the references to building types and components
in the paper, it should be emphasized that the studies are
limited to the theoretical plane. The frames studies are
planar and rest on rigid foundations. The material is
represented by a particular statement of hysteretic response
for reinforced concrete. The frame elements are free to
move in the vertical plane without hindrance from
nonstructural elements. The numerical models differ from
actual building frames in many respects. Nevertheless, the
comparative effects of ground motion and structural
parameters are instructive and, likely to be,
representative.

Ground Motions

   Acceleration records used to calculate frame response
are shown in Fig. 1. they were selected to enable
comparisons of the effects of the ground motion experienced
in Mexico City during the 19 September 1985 earthquake and
those of one on stiff ground that would be considered to
represent a reasonable upper bound fro design in regions of
high seismicity.

   For the motion in Mexico City, the East-West component
of the record obtained at the Secretaria de Comunicaciones y
Transportes (near the intersection of Xola and Universidad
Avenues) location was adopted. The component chosen has a
peak acceleration of 0.16G. The version used is the one
conditioned by the Instituto de Sismologia (UNAM). The
maximum horizontal acceleration inferred by Prince et al (1)
by considering both E-W and N-S components measured at that
site was 0.2 G (in the direction S60E). The inferred
maximum was not used in the calculations for this paper
primarily because the intent was to use a representative
motion for Mexico City on 19 September and not necessarily
the maximum motion. There is strong evidence that the

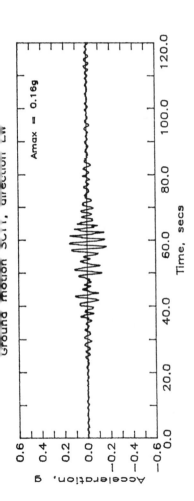

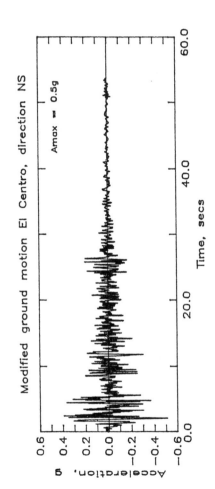

Fig. 1 Acceleration Histories

ground motion varied perceptibly even within the lake-bed
region of the city (1) and it is beyond the scope of this
study to establish a bound to the ground motion. However,
the motion shown in Fig. 1a is considered to provide a good
representation for the motion experienced in the heavily
damaged parts of the city. To avoid the implication that it
represent the maximum motion in Mexico City on 19
September, it will be deliberately referred to as the SCT1
record in the paper.

The record shown in Fig. 1b is the N-S component of
that measured during the Imperial County Earthquake of 1940
in El Centro, California, Although it may not be claimed
that this motion represents a universally applicable ground
motion for stiff sites, it has been generally found to be
acceptable as a vehicle to determine earthquake effects on
such sites. The record in Fig. 1b, digitized and
conditioned at the California Institute of Technology (3),
has been normalized to a peak acceleration of 0.5 G in order
to provide a reasonably pessimistic estimate of what may be
expected on stiff soil in a region of high seismicity.

Linear acceleration and displacement response spectra
calculated for the two motions are compared in Fig. 2 and 3
at damping factors of 2 and 10% of the critical. These two
values of the damping factor are of interest because 2%
represents a plausible estimate for the equivalent viscous
damping in an undamaged reinforced concrete frame while 10%
represents a credible estimate, in terms of equivalent
viscous damping, of the energy-dissipation ability of a
reinforced concrete frame that has experienced system
yielding.

The difference in frequency content of the two ground
motions, as reflected in response spectra, has been well
known (4, 5). It is, nevertheless, instructive to pause to
reconsider the comparison.

Judged on the basis of maximum effects, the two motions
might be considered to be of comparable intensity. That
observation underlines the greater amplification of the SCT1
motion but the extremely high demands set up by that motion
are not likely to be appreciated unless it is emphasized
that the response maxima occur at widely different periods
for the two motions. To put it simply in practical terms,
it may be said that the El Centro motion puts its demands to
low-rise buildings while the SCT1 motion had its maximum
effect on buildings of moderate height. From the
acceleration spectra with a damping factor of 10%, it may be
concluded that the maximum response acceleration for El
Centro is approximately 1 G while for SCT1 it is only 0.6 G.
But in terms of structural design forces, the maximum effect
for SCT1 is considerably more because the maximum demand
occurs for a building, say, 20 stories high rather than a

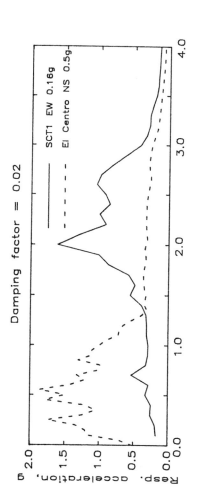

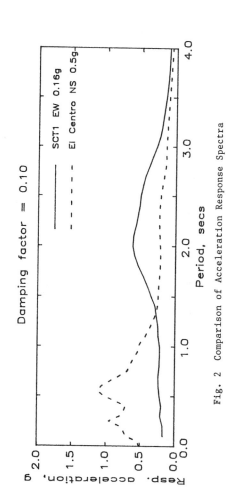

Fig. 2 Comparison of Acceleration Response Spectra

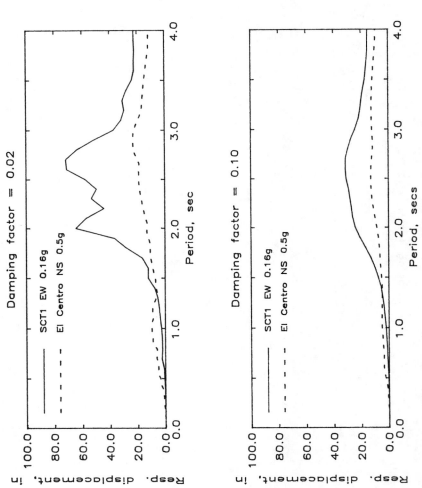

Fig. 3 Comparison of Displacement Response Spectra

building 5 stories high. Furthermore, if the structural
system softens, as structures typically do under strong
motion, the tendency for the El Centro motion is an
unloading or a reduction in demand while for SCT1 the
response curve is essentially flat around two seconds. An
increase in effective period does not lead to a significant
reduction in response to the SCT1 record.

Frame Properties

        In order to study the relative effects of the two
ground motions on structures, the dynamic response of a
series of planar reinforced concrete frame were analyzed.
elevations of the frames are shown in Fig. 4. Number of
stories varied from 8 to 16. Height of the first story
above the base, assumed to be fixed, was 14 ft. The height
for all other stories was 12 ft. Columns were on 24-ft
centers. It was assumed that the transverse span was 18 ft.
and that the unit weight of the building was 175 psf
resulting in a story weight of 252,000 lb. Concrete was
assumed to have a Young's modulus of 3,500,000 psi.

        Girder depths were assumed to be 2 ft. including the
8-in. slab at all levels. Cross-sectional dimensions of the
columns varied as listed in Table 1.

        Combinations of the strength properties of the girders
and the columns divide the frames into two groups. The
first group comprises the eight-story frames. These were
assigned strength properties to investigate the effect of
column size (stiffness) and frame strength. Column depth
varied from 5 to 3 ft. resulting in the calculated initial
periods listed in Table 1. These periods were calculated on
the basis of plain gross sections. Column and girder yield
capacities varied for each column depth, resulting in the
listed base shear strength coefficients of 0.2 and 0.3.
Base shear strength was defined as the base shear for the
mechanism with yield hinges in the columns at the base of
the structure and all girders at girder-column connections.
The lateral story forces were assumed to vary linearly with
height above base. Assumed yield moments for the columns
and girders are listed in Table 1 along with the cracking
moments.

        Group 2 includes the frames with 16 and 12 stories as
well as the two 8-story frames with 5-ft. deep columns. The
base shear strength coefficient for these frames varied in
inverse proportion to the square root of the number of
stories. For each frame height, there were two frames with
different base shear strength coefficients.

        It should be repeated that the "frames" do not
represent actual buildings. They are numerical constructs
with multiple degrees of freedom and strength and stiffness

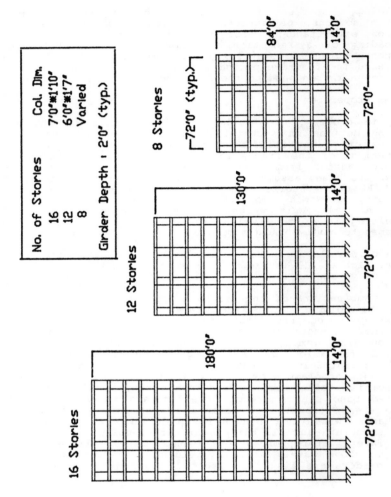

Fig. 4   Frame Elevations

TABLE 1

FRAME PROPERTIES

Mark	No. of Stories	Base Shear Strength Coeff	Column Depth	Column Width	Initial Period sec	Column Crack M, M_{cr} kip-ft	Column Yield M, M_y kip-ft
S16.7	16	0.24	7'-0"	1'-10"	1.3	3500	11000
W16.7	16	0.16	7'-0"	1'-10"		3000	8000
S12.6	12	0.21	6'-0"	1'-7"	0.97	2200	6500
W12.6	12	0.14	6'-0"	1'-7"		2000	4250
S8.5	8	0.3	5'-0"	1'-4"	0.72	1250	3000
W8.5	8	0.2	5'-0"	1'-4"		1000	2000
S8.4	8	0.3	4'-0"	1'-4"	0.82	1250	3000
W8.4	8	0.2	4'-0"	1'-4"		1000	2000
S8.3	8	0.3	3'-0"	1'-4"	0.96	1250	3000
W8.3	8	0.2	3'-0"	1'-4"		1000	2000

Girder Yield Moment

    500 kip-ft for Series S
    325 kip-ft for Series W

Girder Cracking Moment

    250 kip-ft for Series S
    100 kip-ft for Series W

properties representing as-built frames. They were not
proportioned according to a building code but were assigned
strengths that were considered to be within practical range.
Member strength and stiffness were not varied over the
height of the structure.

Response Calculation

    Dynamic response calculations were made using the
computer program LARZ (6) with the Takeda hysteresis (7).
The hysteresis was implemented for the "cracking" and yield
moments listed in Table 1. The curvature at cracking was
determined as the ratio of the cracking moment to EI, the
product of the moment of inertia for gross section and the
assumed Young's modulus. The curvature at yield was
determined by assuming that the effective value of the EI
was reduced to half as a result of partial cracking. For
the girders, the curvature at cracking was based on the
gross section stiffness while that at yield was taken as
0.015 related to a fully cracked section.

    LARZ was used with an integration interval of 0.012
sec. for SCT1 and 0.004 sec. for El Centro. The only source
of energy dissipation was material hysteresis as represented
by the Takeda hysteresis (7) for reinforced concrete.
Fluctuations of axial load on the columns were not
considered in determining hysteretic response.

Calculated Displacement Response

    Calculated displacement histories for the top story of
each frame analyzed are shown in Fig. 5 through 9. Figures
5 and 6 contain the responses of the eight-story frames to
the ground motion SCT1. The variables were the stiffness,
or column size, and the base shear strength. Figure 7 shows
the top-story displacement histories for two selected
eight-story frames with five-ft. columns responding to the
ground motion El Centro. The displacement histories in Fig.
8 and 9 are grouped to permit comparison of the effect of
base shear strength and the ground motion.

    For the ground motion SCT1, the calculated response
waveform was dominated by by oscillations at a period of
approximately two seconds, the dominant period of the ground
motion. For the ground motion El Centro, calculated
displacement-history waveforms were dominated by
oscillations corresponding to the lowest effective
translational periods of the frames.

    In general, response calculated for SCT1 reached a
maximum at 50 to 70 seconds after "start" of earthquake, at
approximately the same time as the maximum ground
accelerations were attained (Fig. 1). It is interesting to
note that the weaker frames started moderately high response

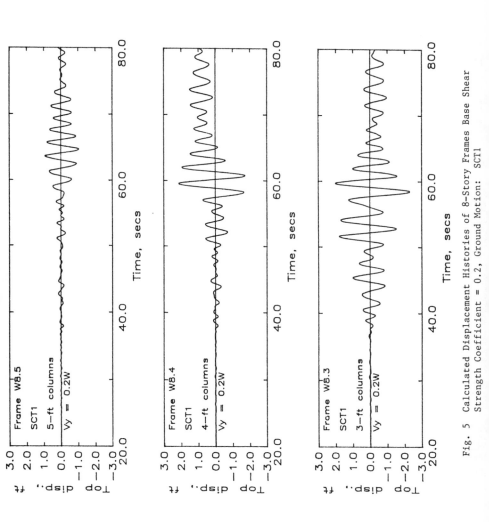

Fig. 5 Calculated Displacement Histories of 8-Story Frames Base Shear
Strength Coefficient = 0.2, Ground Motion: SCT1

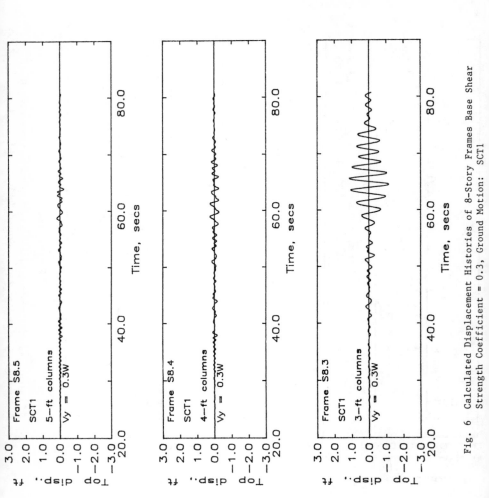

Fig. 6   Calculated Displacement Histories of 8-Story Frames Base Shear
Strength Coefficient = 0.3, Ground Motion: SCT1

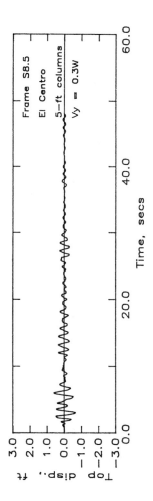
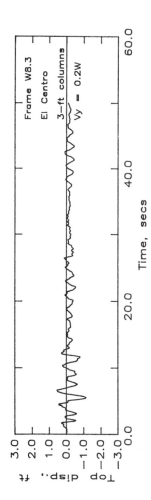

Fig. 7   Calculated Displacement Histories of 8-Story Frames Base Shear
         Strength Coefficient – 0.3, Ground Motion: El Centro

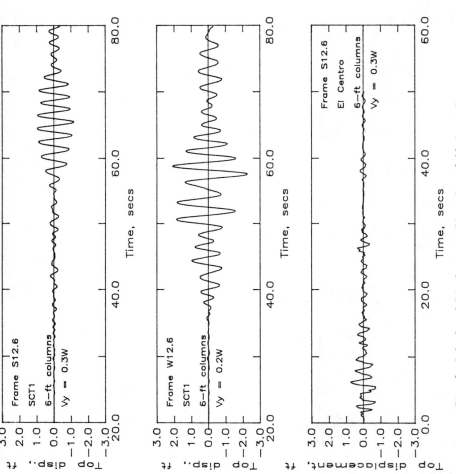

Fig. 8 Calculated Displacement Histories of 12-Story Frames

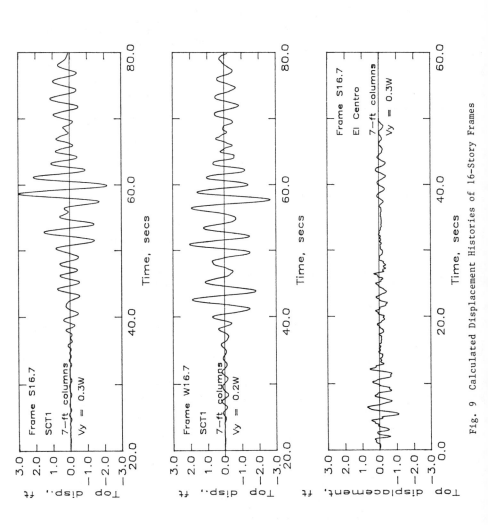

Fig. 9 Calculated Displacement Histories of 16-Story Frames

at approximately 40 sec. (Fig. 5) while the stronger ones
were virtually dormant till after 50 sec. (Fig. 6). Also,
the smaller the column size, the earlier was the initiation
of moderately high response. Maximum response to El Centro
occurred typically within the first ten seconds of strong
motion (fig. 7).

In certain cases (Fig. 5), a tendency is observed for
the frame to develop a permanent drift, immediately after a
large excursion. Although this is a plausible event and may
be rationalized in terms of the force-displacement
characteristics, it is important to recognize that the
permanent drift can be sensitive to the assumed unloading
stiffness in the hysteresis relationship and does not merit
as much confidence as the maximum displacement and frequency
content calculated.

While the total response history of the structural
system is of interest from the viewpoint of behavior, design
criteria by necessity tend to be single valued. The
calculated response of the frames will be judged in terms of
single criterion: maximum lateral displacement. Granted
adequate toughness or ductility, lateral displacement of the
frame is its most important characteristic because it
determines the level of damage to structural elements and,
more importantly, to building components attached to the
frame.

Consider the results presented in Fig. 5 and 6. Top
displacement maxima are summarized in Table 2. The values
listed are overall drift ratios, or ratios of lateral
displacement (drift) at top to the height of the frame. The
results demonstrate that, for these eight-story frames,
strength made a decisive difference. Stiffness was also a
factor. As the column dimension increased, response
displacement decreased. It is also evident that, for the
8-story frames, there was a quid-pro-quo relationship
between strength and stiffness. To control drift, low
stiffness could be compensated by high strength and vice
versa.

It is also interesting to note the effects of the
extreme strength-stiffness combinations for SCT1. The change
in calculated drift ratio from the case for base shear
strength coefficient equal to 0.2 and column depth equal to
3 ft. to the case for base shear strength coefficient equal
to 0.3 and column depth equal to 5 ft. was tenfold. As
would be concluded from the displacement response spectrum
(Fig. 3), to start with a building of relatively low period
and to maintain it there (by providing strength to avoid
softening) was very important for response to the ground
motion experienced in Mexico City on 19 September 1985. On
the other hand, the overall drift ratios listed for response
to El Centro indicate that calculated drift ratios are
relatively insensitive to changes in stiffness and strength

TABLE 2

MAXIMUM TOP-STORY (OVERALL) DRIFT RATIOS FOR EIGHT-STORY
FRAMES (in % of Frame Height)

Base Shear Strength Coeff. c^*	Ground Motion	Column Depth		
		3 ft	4 ft	5 ft
0.2	SCT1	2.3	2.1	1.1
0.2	El Centro	1.2	-	-
0.3	SCT1	1.2	0.28	0.23
0.3	El Centro	-	-	0.67

$^*c = V_y/W$, ratio of base shear corresponding to structural yield to

total weight

in the range covered. In neither of the two cases
considered was El Centro found to be demanding.

To judge whether a response is acceptable depends on
the nature of the building and its contents as well as the
risk that the owner is willing to take or local authorities
are willing to tolerate. In general, 1.5% represents a good
target value for the drift ratio but must not be considered
as a sharp dividing line between success and failure.

Overall drift, ratio of top-story displacement to
height, provides a first-cut evaluation measure. However,
it may give false indications about the nature of total
response. Consider the values in Table 2. It would appear
that the drift-response results for two strength/stiffness
combinations (c = 0.2/column depth = 5 ft. and c =
0.3/column depth = 3 ft.) are comparable. (c = V_y/W, base
shear strength coefficient corresponding to structural
yield.) Figure 10 shows the distributions of drift over the
height of the frames for the six cases of eight-story frames
responding to SCT1. The broken line in each plot indicates
lateral displacement for a constant drift ratio or slope of
1.5%. Because of the difference in the deflected shapes
related to column stiffness, it would be concluded from Fig.
10 that the case for 5-ft. columns is preferable.

A measure of overall drift that is less objectionable
than top-story drift is the characteristic drift, X_c,
obtained from Eq. 1.

$$X_c = X_{top} * (\textstyle\sum m_i \phi_i^2 / \sum m_i \phi_i) \qquad (1)$$

X_{top} = calculated drift at top level

m_i = mass at level i

ϕ_i = lateral displacement at level i for the
displaced shape at maximum, normalized
to a top-level displacement of unity.

Expressed as a ratio of total height of frame, it
provides an index for comparison of one result by another,
but it does not by itself lead to a criterion of
acceptability. Table 3 lists the characteristic drift
ratios for the six cases calculated for SCT1. It is seen
that the "distance" between the two extreme cases considered
has widened. The solution for the 5-ft. columns appears
decisively better.

From the viewpoint of simple and direct engineering
decision making, the story-drift ratio provides a more
convenient criterion. It is explicitly related to damage at
a given story even if it ignores behavior at other stories.
Maximum story-drift ratios are listed in Table 4 and shown in

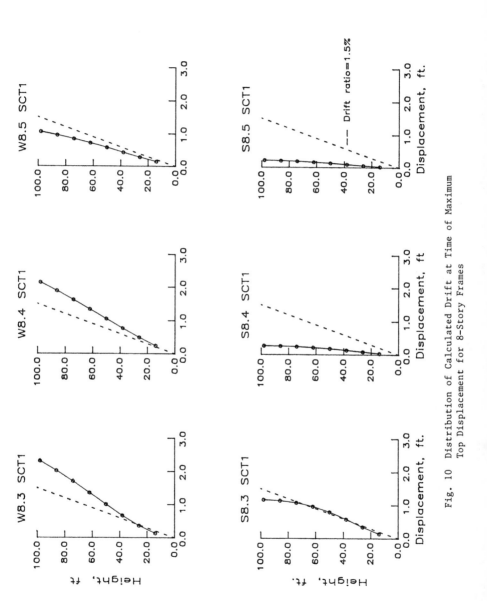

Fig. 10 Distribution of Calculated Drift at Time of Maximum Top Displacement for 8-Story Frames

TABLE 3

MAXIMUM CHARACTERISTIC DRIFT RATIOS FOR EIGHT-STORY FRAMES
(in % of Frame Height)

Base Shear Strength Coeff. c	Ground Motion	Column Depth		
		3 ft	4 ft	5 ft
0.2	SCT1	1.6	1.5	0.79
0.3	El Centro	0.87	-	-
0.2	SCT1	0.96	0.21	0.18
0.3	El Centro	-	-	0.51

TABLE 4

MAXIMUM STORY DRIFT RATIOS FOR EIGHT-STORY FRAMES
(in % of Frame Height)

Base Shear Strength Coeff. c	Ground Motion	Column Depth		
		3 ft	4 ft	5 ft
0.2	SCT1	2.9	2.4	1.2
0.2	El Centro	1.6	-	-
0.3	SCT1	2.0	0.42	0.33
0.3	El Centro	-	-	0.92

Fig. 11. Using 1.5% as an inflexible criterion, it is found
that three of the 8-story frames considered for SCT1 do not
qualify. For a base shear strength coefficient to 0.2, only
the stiffest frame is found acceptable. For a base shear
strength coefficient of 0.3, frames with 4 and 5-ft. columns
rate very well but the one with 3-ft. columns is decisively
inadequate. From Fig. 11, it appears that both strength and
stiffness were important issues for low-rise frames subjected
to the type of motion represented by SCT1.

Maximum story-drift ratios for the 12- and 16-story
frames are summarized in Table 6 and illustrated in Figs. 12
and 13. The results from the two heights of frames are not
to be compared directly because the column size varies
(Table 1). Considering cases with c = 0.3, it is observed
that the demands for El Centro are less than those for SCT1.
It is also of interest to note that the calculate
displacement response of the 16-story frame is relatively
insensitive to strength. For that frame, increasing the
strength by 50% did not produce a like decrease in drift in
terms of top-story drift, characteristic drift, and story
drift. Given a frame of that type, the main option for
controlling drift appears to be changing the stiffness..

Figures 14 and 15 show calculated drift response of
single-degree-of-freedom   oscillators   with   varying
stiffnesses (initial periods) and base shear strength
coefficients. For a given initial period, the stiffness
and mass of the oscillators were kept essentially the same
while the strength was increased to the desired base shear
coefficient. In Fig. 14 the displacement is shown
normalized with respect to the assumed yield displacement
(displacement ductility). The data in Fig. 14 exhibit the
expected trend. As the base shear strength coefficient
increases, the calculated displacement ductility tends to
decrease. The displacement data in Fig. 15, which are not
normalized, indicate that while the displacement ductility
may be insensitive to increase in the base shear strength
coefficient for the oscillator with T = 1.6 sec., the
displacement is not. For that oscillator, calculated
displacement increased with increase in base shear strength.
This result confirms the trends indicated by the calculated
response of the frames.

Summary and Conclusions

The structural strength and stiffness requirements
imposed by two different ground motions were compared from
the viewpoint of drift control in moderate-rise reinforced
concrete frames. One of the ground motions (SCT1)
represented the one experienced in Mexico City during the 19
and 20 September 1985 earthquakes. Maximum acceleration for
SCT1 was 0.16 G. The other (El Centro) represented a
reasonable upper bound for the motion that might be expected

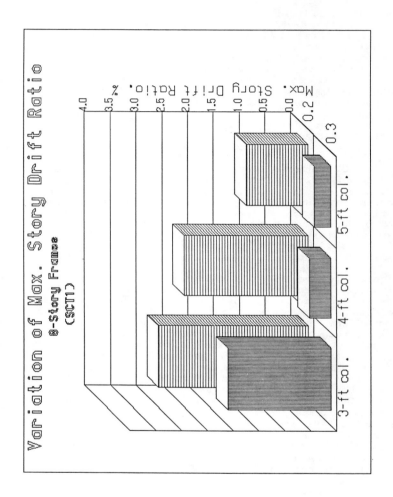

Fig. 11 Maximum Story Drift Ratios for
8-Story Frames. Ground Motion
= SCT1

TABLE 5

MAXIMUM CHARACTERISTIC DRIFT RATIOS FOR 12- AND 16-
STORY FRAMES (in % of Frame Height)

Number of Stories	Ground Motion	Base Shear Strength Coeff. c	Characteristic Drift Ratio %
12	SCT1	0.16	1.1
12	SCT1	0.24	0.79
12	El Centro	0.24	0.34
16	SCT1	0.14	0.93
16	SCT1	0.21	1.1
16	El Centro	0.21	0.29

TABLE 6

MAXIMUM STORY DRIFT RATIOS FOR 12- AND 16-STORY
FRAMES (in % of Frame Height)

Number of Stories	Ground Motion	Base Shear Strength Coeff. c	Story Drift Ratio %
12	SCT1	0.16	1.8
12	SCT1	0.24	1.1
12	El Centro	0.24	0.8
16	SCT1	0.14	1.4
16	SCT1	0.21	1.6
16	El Centro	0.21	0.8

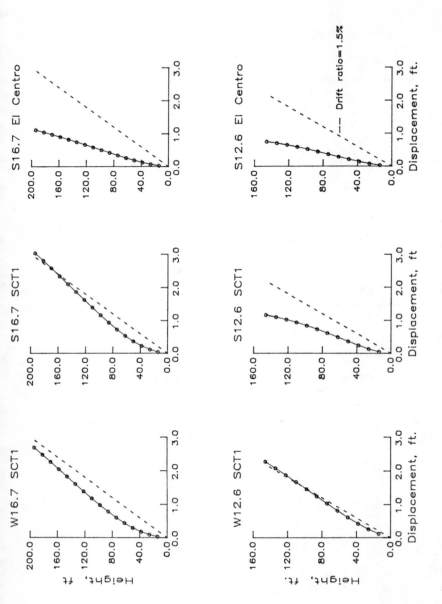

Fig. 12   Distribution of Calculated Drift at Time of Maximum Top
Displacement for 12- and 16-Story Frames

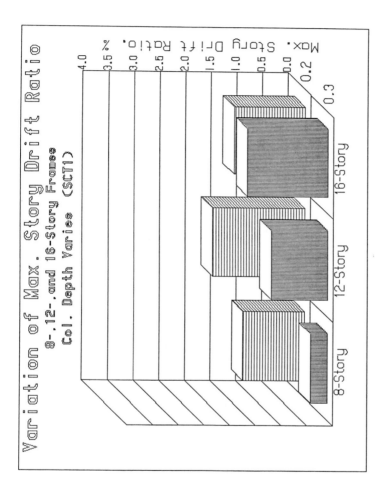

Fig. 13 Maximum Story Drift Ratios for 8-, 12-, and 16-Story Frames. Ground Motion = SCT1

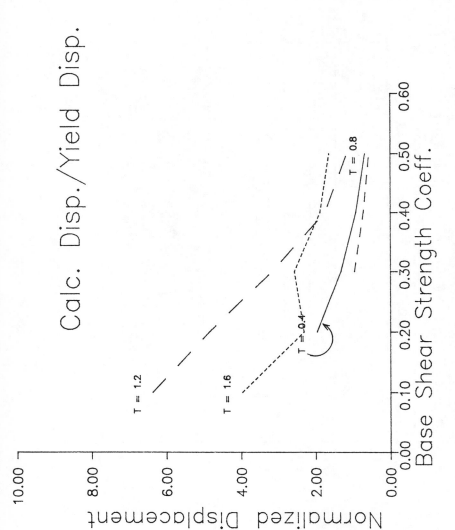

Fig. 14   Normalized Calculated Drift Response of Nonlinear SDOF Oscillators for SCT1 Ground Motion

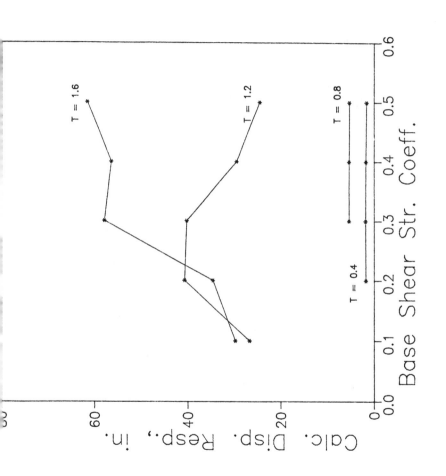

Fig. 15   Calculated Drift Response of Nonlinear SDOF
          Oscillators for SCT1 Ground Motion

on stiff soil. Its maximum acceleration was taken as 0.5 G (Fig. 1).

Planar frames of 8-, 12-, and 16-story height (Fig. 4) with different combinations of strength and stiffness properties were considered. Base shear strength coefficient (ratio of base shear strength at yield to weight) was either 0.2 or 0.3. Initial periods for the frames are listed in Table 1.

Response displacements of the frames were calculated using a nonlinear hysteresis (7) with the computer routine LARZ (6). Frame base was assumed to be fixed. There was one horizontal degree of freedom for each story. Frame joints were free to rotate within the vertical plane.

Direct comparisons of the requirements imposed by the SCT1 and El Centro motions confirmed the inferences that may be made from a simple comparison of the displacement response spectra for a damping factor of 10% (Fig. 4):

(1) For the 8-story frames, calculated story drift response to SCT1 was decisively more sensitive to frame strength and stiffness than that calculated for El Centro.

(2) For the 12- and 16-story frames, story drift response to SCT1 was approximately twice that calculated for El Centro.

Calculated story-drift responses for SCT1 indicated that drift control for the eight-story frames could be improved more efficiently by increasing stiffness than by increasing strength although increases in both tended to reduce drift. For the sixteen story frames, it was found that drift control depended almost exclusively on stiffness, given a threshold strength.

Caution must be exercised in transferring conclusions that appear well defined in the mirror of analysis to the many-dimensioned reality of construction. Considering the conformance of the results described with conclusions derived from simpler response spectra and with some of the observations of building behavior in Mexico City, it is proper to conclude that:

(a) Many buildings in Mexico City experienced a loading well beyond that explicitly anticipated by building codes and relevant literature. it is now more important for the sake of future construction to understand why those that survived did rather than explain the failures.

(b) Buildings in the low-to-medium-rise range that experienced motion similar to that described by the SCT1 record are likely to have had strength and stiffness resources above and beyond those explicitly considered in structural models.

(c) It would be appropriate to consider the observed insensitivity of drift response to strength in the design criteria for moderate-rise buildings in parts of Mexico City likely to experience ground motions similar to SCT1.

Acknowledgments

The work leading to this paper was supported by the National Science Foundation.

The writers acknowledge their debt to the staff of the Instituto de Sismologia of UNAM who extended the writers their unstinting cooperation.

The helpful advice of Professor S. L. Wood, Department of Civil Engineering at the University of Illinois (Urbana), for data processing and analyses is gratefully acknowledged.

References

1. J. Prince et al, "Accelerogramas del Sismo del 19 Septiemere de 1986, "Reports IPS-10A through D, Instrumentacion Sismica, Instituto de Ingeniaria, UNAM, Mexico City, 1985.

2. E. Rosenblueth and R. Meli, "The 1985 Earthquake: Causes and Effects in Mexico City," Concrete International, American Concrete Institute, Volume 8, No. 5, 1986, pp. 23-34.

3. "Strong Motion Earthquake Accelerograms, Digitized and Plotted Data," Volume ii, Part A, Report EERL 71-50, California Institute of Technology, Pasadena, CA, September 1971.

4. L. Zeevaert, "Strong Gound Motions Recorded During Earthquakes of May 11th and 19th in Mexico City," Bulletin of the Seismological Society of America, Vol. 51, No. 1, February 1964, pp. 209-231.

5. E. Rosenblueth and J. Elorduy, "Characteristics of Earthquakes on Mexico City Clay," UNAM, 1971.

6. M. Saiidi, "User's Manual for the LARZ Family" Computer Programs for Nonlinear Seismic Analysis of Reinforced Concrete Planar Structures" SRS 466, University of Illinois, Urbana, November 1979.

7. T. Takeda et al, "Reinforced Concrete Response to Simulate Earthquakes," Journal of the Structural Division, ASCE, Vol. 96, No. ST12, December 1970, pp. 2557-2573.

Evaluation of Performance of Concrete Buildings Damaged
by the September 19, 1985 Mexico Earthquake

Roberto Meli*

As a part of a general evaluation of the structural behavior of
buildings during the 1985 earthquake in Mexico City, a detailed study
of 8 damaged concrete buildings has been performed. The paper contains
a general description of the buildings, of their damage and of its
possible causes. An approximate method of evaluation of seismic strength is proposed and applied to the eight buildings. General conclusions
about the causes of damage and about changes needed in the design practice are proposed .

Introduction

An outlook of the characteristics of earthquake in Mexico City and
of the structural aspects of the damage produced in buildings has been
published recentely (ref 1). Detailed reports containing statistics of
damages and descriptions of the behavior of particular buildings have
also been prepared (ref 2) .

Briefly, damaged buildings concentrated in a limited zone settled on
the bed of an old lake where the subsoil is constituted by deep deposits
of very deformable silty clay whose natural period of vibration are such
that the incoming seismic waves were greatly amplified, giving rise to
a quasi-harmonic ground motion with a dominant period of about 2 sec.
Peak ground accelerations reached about 0.2g in this area and accelerations response spectra for 5% damping showed peaks of nearly 1g for a -
2 sec period. Damaged buildings were mostly flexible structures in -
the range of 5 to 15 storeys. The vast majority of cases of collapse or
of severe damage were in concrete buildings either with beams and monolithic slab floor systems or with waffle slabs. A small number of steel

* Head of the Structural Dept, Institute of Engineering, National Univer
  sity of México .

buildings existed; a couple of dramatic failures occurred among them.
Load bearing masonry buildings fared extremely well; their good performace can be attributed to their low number of storeys and to the common
high density of shear resisting members in both directions, giving rise
to safety factors under lateral loads that are significantly larger than
those corresponding to frame buildings.

Dominant modes of failure were due to shear or eccentric compression of
columns, causing progressive deterioration of concrete strength under the
large number of repetitions of loads and giving rise in several cases to
the loss of the capacity of the columns to sustain the gravity loads and
to the collapse of the entire buildings. Evidence of flexural hinging
at beam ends was surprisingly scarse, whereas shear cracking of beams
and of ribs of waffle slabs was not uncommon; yield lines in waffle slab
systems were clear in several buildings and about half a dozen of cases
of complete punching failure of badly detailed waffle slabs were found.
Cracking and spalling of concrete at beam-column joints occurred in some
cases where no transverse reinforcement existed in this zone. Widespread
evidence of large foundation rotations and settlements during the earth_
quake was found. Pounding of adjacent buildings was rather frequent,
causing in some cases the collapse of the upper part of the building.
Table 1 shows some statistics about the prevailing modes of failure and
table 2 the characteristics that were most common among damaged buildings.
Percentages are related to 331 buildings representing a large majority
of those severely damaged or collapsed .

As a part of the general evaluation of the effects of the earthquake in
structures, a detailed study of a set of typical buildings was performed.
Information collected for each building included structural drawings, a
survey of damage and the in situ determination of some structural properties. Qualitative assessments of structural behavior and of causes
of damage were made, along with approximate evaluations of building sa_
fety and with some refined analysis of structural behavior. A summary
of the evaluation of the first eight buildings being studied is presented
in this paper .

Methodology of Evaluation

Building selection was based primarily on the availability of comple
te and reliable information on structural characteristics and on the
feasibility of having free access to the building, in order to obtain a
detailed damage survey. Buildings that were typical of structural sys_
tems and of construction quality used in Mexico City, that were regular
and whose structural behavior was easier to understand and to analyze
were preferred. The eigth buildings included in this report are concrete
structures, located in the lake bed zone and built after 1960; six of
them have waffle slab and the remaining two have slab and beam floors;
there are concrete shear walls in only three of them, but all have some
masonry infills at least in one direction. All have a partially compen
sated foundation, with friction piles except in two cases where the
foundation is totally compensated without piles. They suffered different
degrees of structural damage, but all of them are feasible to repair .

A summary of the main features of the 8 buildings and of their damage
is given in the next chapter. The detailed report of each building can
be found in Part II of ref 2 .

For each building crack patterns in all structural members were ob_
tained; differential settlements were measured and the natural period
of vibration in two directions was determined by measuring ambient vi_
brations. Concrete cores were extracted in some cases .

The main lateral load resisting system was identified and qualitati_
ve explanation of the mode of failure and of the general seismic beha_
vior was advanced. With the purpose of setting a procedure for a less
detailed evaluation of a large number of buildings, an attempt was made
to assess indexes of damage and of seismic strength; methods used in
Japan and China to evaluate the seismic damage and safety of existing
buildings were adapted to local practice. The index of damage was based
on the level of damage of each particular member and on the percentage
of members affected in each story. A scale from 1 to 5 was used for
the damage to individual members and from 1 to 10 for story damage.
A different index was determined for each story in each direction.
Table 3 indicates the damage index for the most affected story in each
direction of all buildings, with a indication of the story that governed
the index .

With the same purpose of establishing a quick procedure to evaluate the seismic safety of large numbers of buildings, an index of seismic strength was proposed, based on approximate estimations of the lateral load needed to produce a story failure mechanism. Again the procedure was adapted from criteria proposed in Japan (ref 3). The index is de_ fined in terms of the seismic coefficient (ratio of base shear to total weight) for which the shear imposed to each storey equates the resisting shear of this story .

The shear force applied to each storey is obtained by a static equi_ valent method, assuming a triangular distribution of lateral forces. Resisting interstory shear is calculated as the sum of the capacities of all vertical members (columns, concrete walls and masonry infills). Capacity of vertical members may be governed by their shear or eccentric compression failure or may be limited by the shear or bending capacity of the floor members connecting them (beams   or flat plates) .

When reinforcement and material properties are known, as in the 8 buildings being studied, resisting shear forces can be calculated by approximate formulae for the resistance to different limit states of the members   involved in the failure mechanism and by calculating the shear force corresponding to such strength. When detailed structural drawings are not available, only a rough estimation of the shear capa_ city of the story is feasible by assigning a shear resisting stress to each type of vertical element and multiplying it by the cross sectional area of the different members. From approximate evaluations for typical construcion in Mexico City, assumed shear strength varied from 5 to 10 kg /cm2 for concrete columns according to their height to depth ratio, from 12 to 20kg/cm2 for concrete shear walls according to their aspect ratio and to the confining members. For masonry walls resisting shear stress varied from 1 to 2kg/cm2 depending on the material and on the type of reinforcement or confinememt. Strength can be grossly overesti_ mated in this fashion if storey capacity is governed by the failure of floor members.

Story resistant shear is calculated by the sum of   the contri_ butions of individual members affected by a participation factor that takes into account that capacity of different members is not reached simultaneously; these factors varied from 0.7 to 1.0 .

Final result of the procedures is the seismic coefficient for which
the applied story shear equates the resisting shear of the story. This
resistant seismic coefficient can be compared to that specified by the
code, affected by the appropiate ductility reduction factor according
to the dominant failure mechanism and to the characteristics of the
structure.

To take into account different effects that produce concentrations
on seismic forces in some part of the strcuture or that reduce the
seismic strength of some story or member, a correction factor for
structural irregularity can be applied to the calculated seismic coeffi
cient. The correction factor is obtained as the product of partial
factors related to in plan asynmetry, to stiffness and strength discontinuity
of different storeys and to building slenderness .

The above described evaluation procedure is being applied to a large
sample of buildings that suffered different levels of damage in Mexico
City. The resistant seismic coefficient will be correlated with the
damage index. Conclusions about the intensity reached by the earthquake
in different parts of the city and about the degree of seismic strength
needed to maintain the level of damage sufficiently low, can be drawn
by this comparison .

To calibrate the procedure and to assess its ability to predict
observed behavior, the 8 buildings under study were evaluated. As an
example, in fig 1 the variation of the resistant seismic coefficient
and of the damage index between the different storeys of one of the buil
dings is shown for both directions. Results correspond to the first and
less sophisticated method of evaluation that does not explicitly take
into account the reinforcement and the possibility of failure being
governed by the horizontal members (beams or waffle slabs). For the
type of buildings being studied the procedure is very crude, but it is
the only one that can be applied at a large scale due to the lack of
more detailed information for most buildings.

As can be appreciated from fig 1 the degree of damage varies inversely
with the resistent seismic coefficient, and an acceptable correlation
exists between the two variables. In table 3 the indexes corresponding

to the most damaged story in each direction are given for the 8 buildings
studied. The most affected story is not always the ground floor; it is
more frequently found in the middle third of the height and it is not
the same for one direction than for the other. A plot of the index of
damage versus the resistant seismic coefficient is found in fig 2.
Despite the large dispersion and the scarcity of data for some regions,
a clear reduction of the index of damage takes place when the resistant
seismic coefficient increases. For instance, if the acceptable level of
damage for an earthquake of this intensity is considered as that corres
ponding to a damage index of 2.5, it can be considered that buildings
should have a minimum seismic resistant coefficient, calculated by this
criterion, equal to 0.2. It must be remembered that this coefficients
overestimates the lateral strength of the structure as could be verified
by the cases when the same coefficient was calculated with the more
refined procedure.

Short Description of Specific Buildings

    A brief description of the 8 buildings, of their damage and of their
behavior is made in this chapter. Some properties and indexes related
to the approximate evaluation of the seismic safety are given in table 3.
    LR12-01. A 12 story corner building with a trapezoidal plan.
Floors are rather thin waffle slabs with low longitudinal reinforcement
in the ribs. Columns are rectangular with a small width in the transver
se direction. There are masonry infills in two corner sides and an eccentric
concrete core. Parking ramps in the basement and in the first two
floors give additional eccentricity and produce short columns. Damage
pattern reveals a combination of three impending modes of failure: ne
gative and positive yield lines in the waffle slabs in the transverse
direction; settlement of the concrete core producing flexural cracks of
the slab and generalized shear cracking of the columns; damage is highest
in storeys 2 to 5. It can be speculated that initially the concrete
core absorbed an important portion of the lateral loads, that gave rise
to large overturning moments in the foundation producing settlements of
the friction piles and rotations of the core base; thus lateral forces
absorbed by the frame action of the columns and waffle slab increased

significantly,giving rise to large damage in these members and in the
infills. The high flexibility of the structure is confirmed by the 2.3
sec period measured in the transverse direction and by the practically
total destruction of masonry infills and partitions.

MM09-02. A 9 story regular building with strong concrete end walls
in the transverse (N-S) direction and only frames in the longitudinal
one. Design was conservative according to the 1976 code, especially
regarding column strength. Careful detailing and execution could be
appreciated; columns and joints have large amounts of transverse reinfor
cement. Damage is concentrated in the lower 5 stories. There is a
clear evidence of plastic hinging at beam ends and of some shear cracking
of the columns, both for the longitudinal (E-W) direction. Some signs
of hinging of column bases appear at ground floors. There is no damage
due to the seismic action in the transverse direction, where the lateral
strength and stiffness were significantly larger, even if the safety
factor for the overturning moment at the wall bases was exactly what
required by the 1976 code. On the other hand the safety factors for
hinging of beam ends were about 50% larger and those for shear of columns
in the longitudinal direction were about twice what required by the code.
Natural period in the transverse direction is 61% that in the longitudi
nal one, reflectling not only the higher flexibility but also the
extent of damage in the E-W direction. Because of its regularity and
of the different structural systems and level of performance in the two
orthogonal directions the building gives bases for the decisions about
the seismic strength that must be provided for frame and shear wall
systems.

MM05-03. A five story rectangular building with deep basement, fully
compensated foundation and very slender columns in the first floor of
double height. Floors are monolithic slabs with haunched beams of rather
low depth for the 7.5 m span in both directions. One concrete shear
wall in the short (N-S) direction showed poor concrete quality and
inadequate anchorage to the frame structure. In the same direction
there is a brick masonry shear wall with a thick mortar covering rein_
forced with wire mesh in both faces. Masonry walls in the long direction
were supposedly isolated from the main structure, but their reinforcement
was actually anchored to the columns and beams and their separation from

the concrete elements was less than 1cm. The main damage was the shear failure of the concrete shear wall and of the columns at its ends. Damage was concentrated in the second and third floors. Some shear cracking of interior columns also appreeared in the same storey. Some flexural and shear cracking of beams is apparentley due to gravity doads. The high flexibility of the ground floor is probably responsible for large amplifications of lateral forces in the following story where the damage was maximun. The period measured in the transverse direction is shorter than the period in the longitudinal direction, revealing that the infill walls in the facade and in the back side have a larger contribution to the stiffnes than the two shear walls in the transverse direction. The period in the transverse direction is exceptionally long for a 5 story building and is due to the flexibility of the ground floor .

LR07-04. An almost square 7 story building used for garment factory and probably subjected to large live loads during the earthquake. Lateral load resisting system is constituted only by the frame action between the waffle slab and the rectangular columns with low amount of transverse reinforcement. The large height of the first floor gave rise to a large slenderness ratio of the columns in the ground storey. Masonry walls in the transversedirection are braced by slender concrete struts poorly anchored to the main structure.

Damage is widespread from the first to the fifth story and mainly consists of large shear and compression cracks of columns with buckling of longitudinal reinforcement in some cases. Some signs of yield lines appear in the waffle slabs, but much more important and widespread is the shear cracking in the ribs outside the solid zone .

Crushing of concrete in the area of contact between the slab and the column indicates large inelastic rotations of the connections. The staircase with a low strength masonry core shows an almost complete destruction. The building is leaning about 20cm toward the street. The mechanism of failure by bending in the waffle slab and at columns ends is more clear in the longitudinal direction, whereas shear of the columns dominates in the transverse direction. Fundamental period in the longitudinal (N-S) direction is extraordinarily large indicationg both the flexibility of the original strcuture enhanced by the double height of the first story and the reduction of stiffness due to the

the large damage. In the transverse direction the fundamental period
is much lower due to the stiffening effect that the masonry infills can
provide, despite of the extent of their damage .

LR11-05. A 11 story rectangular building with a very short width in
the direction of the street. It has robust circular columns (1 m diame
ter up to the 2nd floor) and a 40 cm thick waffle slab whose solid zone
around the columns is very small in the short direction. Poor brick
masonry infill walls existed in the long direction. It was used for
garment manufacturing and storage,and probably subjected to high live
loads .

Damage is concentrated between the second and sixth floor and is mainly
due to seismic action in the short direction; it is constituted by shear
cracking especially in interior columns, by local crushing of concrete
at column slab interface and by large shear cracks in the ribs of the
short direction, inmediately outside the solid zone. Some signs of ne
gative moment yield line formation in the short direction and of buckling of longitudinal reinforcement in the lower bed of the waffle slab
appear .

The masonry infills in the transverse direction were almost destroyed by
the earthquake and had been demolished before the survey and the measure
ments of periods   that were exceptionally large in both directions .

LR08-06. An 8 story housing building with a high density of bric walls
in both directions except in the short direction of the ground floor.
The size of the columns in the short direction is very small giving ri
se to a weak ground floor in this direction. Main structural damage is
constituted by shear cracking of columns in the short direction and also
by vertical cracks due to eccentric compression. Damage is greater in
ground floor but is also distributed in upper storeys. No major damage
is observed in the waffle slab. Masonry partitions suffered large
cracking and partial destruction, especially those in the short direction, whereas the infills at both ends of the transverse (E-W) direction were in good conditions and maintained a large lateral stiffness of
the structure as revealed by the short fundamental period measured.

LR10-07. A 10 storey almost square building with large spans, a 45 cm thick waffle slab and square columns. It suffered significant non struc tural damage in the 1979 earthquake, with cracking of columns of the rear facade in the basement. Masonry walls of the service core and of the N-S sides were replaced and reinforced with concrete bond beam and columns. New masonry walls, strengthened in the same fashion were added in the back facade. In some cases the walls did not cover the entire story height but left a 50 cm window opening in the upper part. The damage in the recent earthquake was mainly by shear cracking of columns especially in the upper floors and in the E-W direction. A column in the S-E corner was completely sheared off. Widespread flexu ral and shear cracking of the waffle slab is evident mainly from 5 th to 7 th floors. Masonry walls show major diagonal cracking especially those of the service core. The building showed a general settlement and an inclination of about 50 cm toward the N-E corner. The service core area settled with respect to the rest of the building giving rise to some flexural yield lines in the slab. It could not be ascertained which part of the settlement was due to the present earthquake and which already existed. The mechanism of failure of the central core is similar than in the LR12-01 and LR15-08 buildings. The long measured periods reveal that despite of the addition of reinforced infills the building in extraordinarily flexible .

LR15-08. A 15 story building, part of a complex of three large office buildings. Its plan is square and is enlarged in the first two stories. It has rather robust concrete columns with two shear walls only in the transverse direction and a waffle slab floor system, 45cm thick. It is reinforced with high strength cold twisted bars (60 kg/mm^2, nominal yield stress).

In the first 4 stories only minor damage appear. From the fourth to the eleventh there is widespread shear cracking of columns, especially near the service core. In this same area there is severe shear cracking of the waffle slab around the column. Some of the ribs around the solid zone also show severe diagonal cracking. Non structural damage was very severe and signs of very large interstory drifts are evident. The cen tral service core has a pronounced differential settlement with respect

to the rest of the structure.Differences of level between the core and
the end frames were of more than 25cm.

These settlements produced only minor cracking of the floor slabs; the
foundation beams could not be inspected. The measured period in the
longitudinal direction (without shear walls) is 25% larger than in the
transverse direction. A twin building of the same compelx has been al_
ready strengthened with additional shear walls placed mainly in the lon
gitudinal direction. The fundamental period of the repaired building was
reduced to 1.5 sec in both directions, against the 2.6 sec period of the
unrepaired building in the E-W direction .

Zacatecas building. The building was not subjected to the general procedure of evaluation of performance, because its collapse was due to overturning and not to weakness of storey   shear capacity. The building
had 9 typical storeys used for housing,plus one service storey in a part
of the roof and two service storeys in some other parts. The structure
of the 9 typical storeys was constituted by rectangular columns and by
beams with nonolithic concrete slabs .

The two service floors at the top had load bearing masonry walls. The
plan was irregular and had a high density of masonry partitions and
infills in all the storeys. The foundation was a 2.65m deep box plus 23
friction piles. The ratio of maximun height to minimum width of the
building is 4.75, but the value is misleading due to the irregular form
of the building; the same ratio valued for a section at the center of
the plan is 2.4.

According to eyewitnesses the building oscillated mainly in the E-W direction producing large amplitude displacements and the settlement of
the foundation in the west side. The leaning of the building rised progressively, finally producing its complete overturning when the ground
motion had already stopped. The first story on the west side almost
completely sank into the ground, whereas the piles in the east side were
extracted from the soil. There was no sign of major damage produced in
the structure before it fell on the ground .

Detailed studies of the foundation failure are being performed by other
groups. Some general data about the loads on the foundation are as
following. The total weight of the building was 2345 ton. From an

equivalent static analysis for a seismic coefficient of 0.06, a base shear of 141 ton and an overturning moment of 2820 ton were obtained. The deterioration of the cohesion between the pile and the soil due the repetition of dynamic loads was probably the main cause of the progressi ve failure of the piles on the compression side, in the direction of minimum moment of inertia of the foundation plan.

Conclusions

All the buildings included in the evaluation had been subjected to a seismic design and, even if a thorough comprobation has not been made, it can be said that they all complied with the code requirements, at least in what is concerned to lateral load capacity; quality of materials and of execution was generally within the standards and some defects found in several buildings are not considered to be decisive in their performance. All of them were excessively flesible, at least in one di rection, not fullfilling in many cases code limitations about allowable drifts, that were probably calculated in the design process with non conservative assumptions about lateral stiffness. Measured fundamental periods were extraordinarily long: in the average the ratio between the period (in sec) and the number of stories was 0.18. The great flexibi lity indicated by such long periods can only partially be atributed to the structural damage suffered by the building. Features that contributed to the high flexibillity were the use of waffle slab floor systems, the double height of ground storeys, and in general the excessive slenderness of columns, produced by the practice or using very narrow columns in one direction, for architectural reasons.

Basically the damage can be related the lack of lateral load capacity. The story shear that should be resisted in order to avoid damage by an earthquake of this intensity was significantly greater than what requi red by the code. In some cases the energy introduced by the ground motion could be dissipated with inelastic rotations of the beams or of the waffle slabs without major damage to the vertical resisting members. Nevertheless in most buildings story shear capacity was governed by the strength of columns (in shear or eccentric compression), revealing that the bending strength of floor systems is underestimated in common design practice and that much larger safety factors should be adopted in the design capacity of columns if a ductile mode of failure governed by the bending strength of beams is sought .

It is noteworthy that in most buildings the maximum damage did not occur in the lower storeys but mainly in the middle third of the height. The evaluation of the lateral load capacity confirms that the weaker storeys are located in this zone because of the practice of sharply re_ ducing column size in upper storeys .

The contribution of masonry walls to the lateral strength and stiffness was significant especially when all the bays in two parallel peripheral sides had masonry infills. From the inspection of table 3 it can be derived that the level of damage and the measured periods in the trans_ verse direction where this type of wall existed, were always lower than in the other direction. The settlement of a central stiff core with respect to the rest of the structure was observed in three buildings and indicates that the concentration of lateral strength and stiffness in a reduced area should be avoided because overturning moments produce large compression forces that can give rise to compression failure of the vertical structural members or of their connection to the floor sys_ tems or of the foundation beams and the piles .

The evaluation method that has been proposed is considered to be useful as a screening procedure of the seismic capacity of similar buildings. A clear reduction of the level of damage is observed as the seismic resistant coefficent increases. When this coefficient exceeded 0.20 the damage was minor.

This index of seismic strength cannot be directly transferred to a design seismic coefficient because it generally overstimates the story capacity.

AKNOWLEDGEMENTS

The detailed information about the structural design of the evaluated buildings was provided by different design offices. Particularly signi_ ficant at this regard was the collaboration of Dirac, S. A. Carlos López has been in charge of the survey and the evaluation of the eight buildings; Jorge Avila and Mario Rodríguez also participated in this task. Eduardo Miranda provided significant information and made a careful review of the manuscript.

REFERENCES

1. "The 1985 earthquake: causes and effects en Mexico City"
   prepared by E. Rosenblueth an R. Meli for the subcommitte on Norms
   and Construction Procedures. Concrete International, Vol 8, No. 5
   may 1986, pp 23-24

2. R. Meli et al "Evaluación de los efectos de los sismos de septiembre
   en las estructuras de la Ciudad de México", Institute of Engineering,
   Internal report, sep 1986 .

3. Aoyama, H., "A Method for the evaluation of the seismic capacity of
   existing reinforced concrete buildings in Japan" Bull N Zealand Nat
   Soc for Earthq Eng, vol 14, No. 3, sep 1981, pp 105-103

TABLE 1. PREVAILING MODES OF FAILURE IN COLLAPSED OR SEVERELY DAMAGED BUILDINGS

Mode of Failure Observed	Percent of cases
Shear in columns	16
Eccentric compression in columns	11
Unidentified type of failure of columns	16
Shear in beams	9
Shear in waffle slab	9
Bending in beams	2
Beam-Column joint	8
Shear and bending in concrete shear walls	1.5
Other sources	7
Not possible to identify	25

TABLE 2. CHARACTERISTICS OBSERVED IN COLLAPSED OR SEVERELY DAMAGED BUILDINGS

Characteristic observed	Percent of cases
Pronounced asymmetry in stiffness	15
Corner building	42
Weak first story	8
Short columns	3
Excessive mass	9
Previous differential settlements	2
Unsatisfactory foundation performance	13
Pounding	15
Previous earthquake damage	5
Punching in waffle slabs	4
Upper story failure	38
Intermediate story failure	40

Table 3. SOME PROPERTIES OF THE EVALUATED BUILDINGS

Building Identification	Number of Storeys	Year of Construction	N-S Direction			E-V Direction		
			Index of Damage *	Resistant Coefficient	Measured Period (sec)	Index of Damage *	Resistant Coefficient	Measured Period (sec)
LR 12-01	12 + Basement	1980-82	5.7 (3)	0.11	1.7	4.7 (7)	0.12	2.3
MM 10-01	10 + Basement	1970-71	0.5 (6)	0.30	1.3	6.9 (4)	0.11	2.1
MM 05-03	5 + Basement	1964-65	4.5 (2)	0.18	1.1	7.1 (2)	0.13	0.7
LR 07-04	7 + Basement	1968-69	7.0 (2)	0.11	2.1	7.0 (2)	0.16	1.3
LR 11-05	11 + Basement	1971	2.5 (3)	0.21	2.5	3.5 (5)	0.19	2.6
LR 08-06	8	1979	5.0 (1)	0.08	0.7	5.0 (1)	0.13	0.4
LR 09-07	9	1975	6.7 (7)	0.12	2.2	7.7 (7)	0.11	1.9
LR 15-08	15 + Basement	1980-81	3.8 (4)	0.13	2.1	4.3 (5)	0.12	2.6

* Number in parentheses indicates the storey with maximum damage

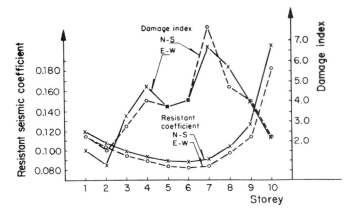

Fig 1 Variation of damage index and seismic resistant coefficient for LR 10-07 Building

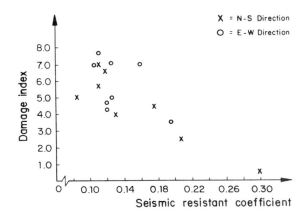

Fig 2 Results of the approximate evaluation of
the 8 buildings

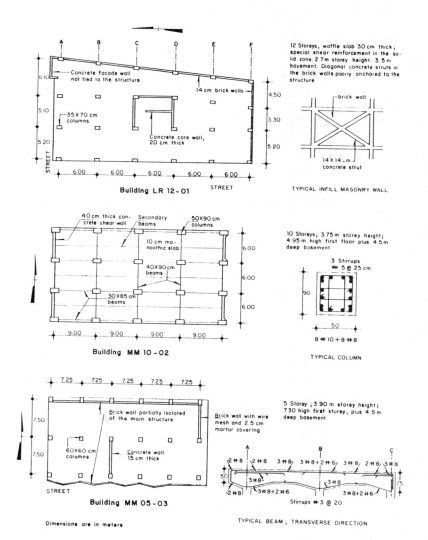

12 Storeys, waffle slab 30 cm thick;
special shear reinforcement in the solid zone. 2.7m storey height. 3.5 m
basement. Diagonal concrete struts in
the brick walls poorly anchored to the
structure

Building LR 12-01

TYPICAL INFILL MASONRY WALL

10 Storeys; 3.75 m storey height;
4.95 m high first floor plus 4.5 m
deep basement

Building MM 10-02

TYPICAL COLUMN

5 Storey ; 3.90 m storey height;
7.30 high first storey, plus 4.5 m
deep basement

Building MM 05-03

Dimensions are in meters

TYPICAL BEAM ; TRANSVERSE DIRECTION

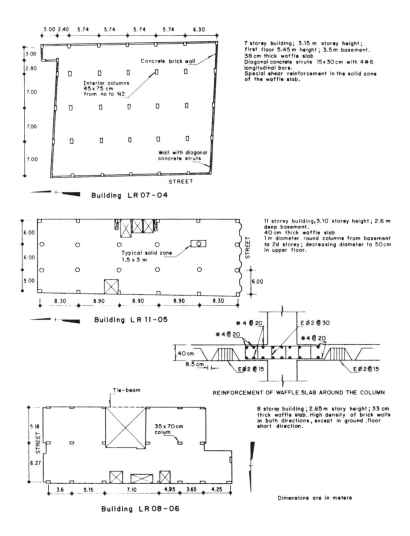

Building LR 07-04

7 storey building; 3.15 m storey height;
first floor 5.45 m height; 3.5 m basement.
38 cm thick waffle slab
Diagonal concrete struts 15x30 cm with 4#6
longitudinal bars.
Special shear reinforcement in the solid zone
of the waffle slab.

Building LR 11-05

11 storey building; 3.10 storey height; 2.6 m
deep basement.
40 cm thick waffle slab
1 m diameter round columns from basement
to 2d storey; decreasing diameter to 50 cm
in upper floor.

REINFORCEMENT OF WAFFLE SLAB AROUND THE COLUMN

Building LR 08-06

8 storey building; 2.65 m story height; 33 cm
thick waffle slab. High density of brick walls
in both directions, except in ground, floor
short direction.

Dimensions are in meters

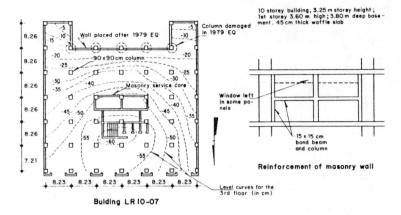

10 storey building, 3.25 m storey height;
1st storey 3.60 m high; 3.80 m deep basement. 45 cm thick waffle slab

Building LR 10-07

Reinforcement of masonry wall

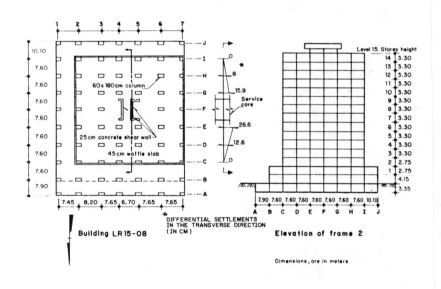

Building LR 15-08

DIFFERENTIAL SETTLEMENTS
IN THE TRANSVERSE DIRECTION
(IN CM)

Elevation of frame 2

Dimensions, are in meters

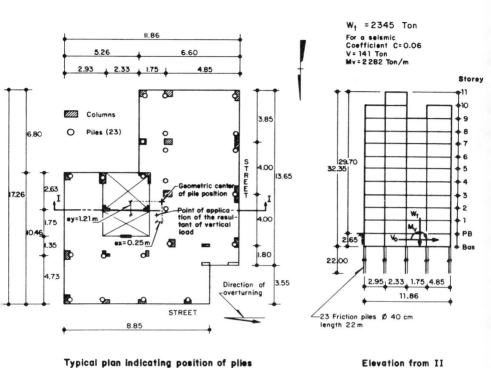

Typical plan indicating position of piles

Elevation from II

Dimensions are in meters

Zacatecas Building

BEHAVIOR OF REINFORCED CONCRETE FRAMING SYSTEMS

by

S. K. Ghosh and W. G. Corley*

ABSTRACT

On September 19, 1985, Mexico City was hit by what is believed to have been the most damaging earthquake in its recorded history. More than 200 engineered buildings were either destroyed or severely damaged.

In this report, a ground motion recorded in the severely damaged portion of the city was used to calculate the responses of hypothetical buildings including those having periods of about two seconds, the predominant period of the ground motion. Calculated drift considering inelastic behavior was compared with drift capacities of concrete specimens tested in the laboratory.

Results of the comparisons suggest that structures designed by North American specifications and having details similar to those of the 1983 ACI Building Code, Appendix A, could have survived the earthquake.

*S. K. Ghosh, Member, ASCE, Associate Professor of Civil Engineering, University of Illinois at Chicago; W. G. Corley, Fellow, ASCE, Executive Director, Engineering and Resource Development, Construction Technology Laboratories, a Division of the Portland Cement Association, Skokie, Ill.

INTRODUCTION

As described elsewhere,[1] the Mexican earthquake of September 19, 1985, consisted essentially of two subevents, the first one occurring 26 seconds before the second slip, making references to focal coordinates open to discrepancy. Roughly speaking, the focus lay in the Pacific 400 km to the southwest of Mexico City at a depth of about 18 km. The Richter surface wave magnitude (M_s) of the compound event was 8.1. Measured peak accelerations in the epicentral region were 0.15g and the duration of shaking with acceleration not less than 0.10g exceeded ten seconds.

Records from about a dozen accelerographs installed in the Valley of Mexico indicated that the macroseismic waves arrived with an exceptionally high energy content around a period of 2 seconds. Those areas in the city where the prevailing ground period was approximately 2 seconds resonated, reaching very high amplitudes of oscillation.[2] Harder or softer ground, or ground where the very deformable clay formations were appreciably thinner or thicker, attained smaller amplitudes. Within the Valley of Mexico, the peak ground accelerations recorded were about 0.01g on rock, 0.04g on University City grounds, 0.20g in the region of high intensity, and almost certainly greater at some spots.[2] Considerably smaller accelerations developed in the transition zone, between hard and soft ground.

Another important characteristic of the ground motion was its steady pace. Figure 1 shows the record from the accelerograph at the Secretariat of Communication and Transportation.[3] At this site, the ground moved a total distance of about 400 mm peak-to-peak, completing each cycle in about 2 seconds. Figure 2 indicates the frequency content of this recorded motion.[4] The velocity response spectrum for the motion is compared with the response spectrum for the El Centro, 1940, N-S component. While the spectral velocity for the El Centro record exceeds that of SCT 1985 for periods up to 1.5 sec, the motion at SCT had an impressively higher velocity response for higher ground motion periods.

According to Rosenblueth,[2] "there is no record anywhere in the world with a horizontal peak ground acceleration of 0.20g associated with a two-second period. The ground motion's regularity in the hardest hit area of Mexico City is manifest in the spectra for the records at the site mentioned. They are almost like those for a harmonic motion of 2.0 second period although they do have significant ordinates at periods approaching one second. The motion lasted

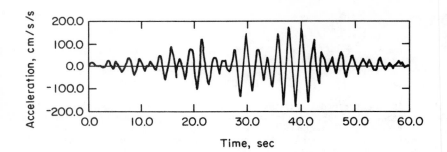

Fig. 1 S60E Component of Ground Accelerations
Determined from N and E Components Measured
at SCT in Mexico City.

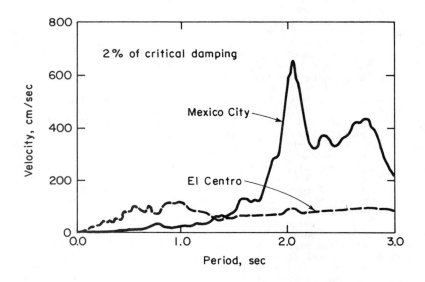

Fig. 2 Comparison of Velocity Responses, El Centro
1940, N-S and SCT, Mexico City, 1985, S60E
Component.

perceptibly over three minutes. Records show a very large number of significant cycles."

The foregoing indicates quite clearly that the ground motions experienced in Mexico City in the earthquake of 1985 were unique with respect to intensity, regularity, frequency, and duration, making the earthquake "selectively devastating."[2] This uniqueness can be attributed to the well-known soil condition of the valley of Mexico described in Ref. 5.

Object and scope

As a result of the severity of the ground motions, more than two hundred major buildings collapsed or were badly damaged in the valley of Mexico. To better understand the devastation caused by the ground motion, this paper describes observed damage to selected reinforced concrete frame components and compares the observations with responses calculated for hypothetical buildings designed to meet proposed new North American specifications. Results of laboratory tests on large components are used to interpret observed and calculated performance.

RESPONSE OF BUILDINGS

According to observers[1-8] of damage caused by the 1985 earthquake in Mexico City, in the localized area of the highest ground motion intensity, most of the buildings that collapsed or suffered the greatest damage were 7-15 stories tall. According to Ref. 2, a double resonance phenomenon between earthquake-ground and ground-building accounts for most of what happened. "We had measured the fundamental periods of many buildings under small oscillations, and so did Professor Kobayashi and his team, on undamaged buildings after the earthquake. Results of both sets of measurements give the fundamental periods in sway for office buildings 5 to 25 stories tall as 0.12 times the number of stories, with a rather small spread. So buildings with small-amplitude fundamental periods in the range of about 0.75 to somewhat less than 2.0 seconds oscillated violently. The oscillations caused cracking and damage that lengthened building period causing the buildings to enter the range of resonance with the ground.[3]

Figure 3 shows the response of elastic single-degree-of-freedom systems,[6] having varying periods but a fixed 2% of critical damping, to the S60E component of the SCT, Mexico City, 1985, ground motion. As the period of a single-degree-of-freedom system approaches the predominant two-second period of the ground motion, the response is dramatically high, confirming the phenomenon of resonance. For both shorter and longer periods, the response is much more subdued, although it remains quite strong even for periods approaching 3 seconds.

An analysis similar to the one depicted in Fig. 3 can be applied to realistic reinforced concrete buildings. The basic structure selected for the analysis is a six-story building,[9] rectangular in shape, with five 13-ft (4 m) stories, a bottom story of 16 ft (4.9 m),

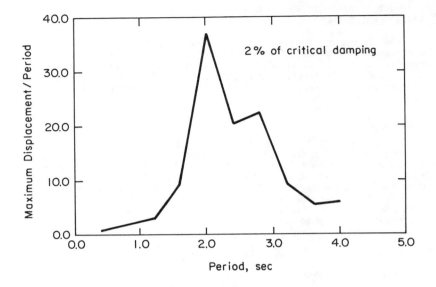

Fig. 3   Variation of Maximum Response Displacement/Period
with Period for the SCT Motion, S60E Component (2%
of critical damping).

and a penthouse. Floors consist of 9-in.-thick (230 mm) flat plates
with 32-ft (9.75 m) square bays.

Four bracing schemes are investigated, as might be done during a
preliminary design. Scheme 1 combines ductile or special moment
frames in one direction with load-bearing shearwalls in the orthogonal
direction. Schemes 2 through 4 also utilize ductile or special moment
frames in the E-W direction. The lateral load-resisting system in the
N-S direction consists of a Building Frame System (an essentially complete space frame provides support for gravity loads; resistance to
lateral load is provided by shearwalls or braced frames) in Scheme 2,
a Dual System* in Scheme 3, and ductile or special moment frames in
Scheme 4. Figure 4 shows the framing system for Scheme 4. Details of
the others are reported in Ref. 9.

---

*An essentially complete space frame provides support for gravity
loads. Resistance to lateral load is provided by (a) A specially
detailed moment resisting space frame which is capable of resisting
at least 25% of the base shear, (b) shearwall or braced frames. The
two systems are designed to resist lateral load in proportion to
their relative rigidities.

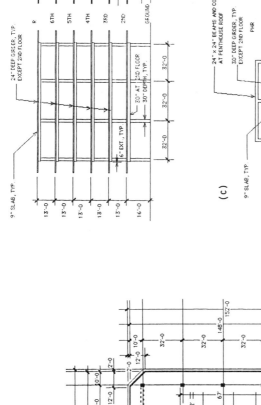

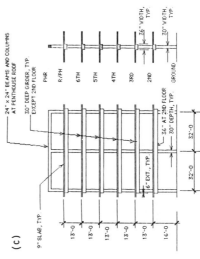

Fig. 4   (a) Plan (b) E-W Frame Member Sizes
(c) N-S Frame Member Sizes.

Structural members comprising the four schemes were sized in conformance with the "Tentative Lateral Force Requirements" (October 1985) issued by the Seismology Committee of the Structural Engineers Association of California[10] for gravity loads and Uniform Building Code[11] Zone 4 seismic forces. An importance factor "I" of 1.0 (standard occupancy structure) was assumed. Note that the ductile or special moment frames in the E-W direction are differently sized in Scheme 1, Scheme 2, and in Schemes 3 and 4 because of a specific SEAOC requirement[10] concerning the combination of different lateral load resisting systems in orthogonal directions of the same building.

Periods of all six natural modes of vibration were determined for each structural scheme in each principal direction by eigenvalue analyses of two-dimensional models described in Ref. 9. Similar periods were also determined from eigenvalue analyses of three-dimensional models, also described in Ref. 9, by constraining them to move along one or the other of the principal directions. Results are listed in Table 1. In general, two-dimensional and three-dimensional analyses yielded periods that were in reasonable agreement.

Dynamic elastic response history analyses were performed on the seven lateral load resisting systems of the four structural schemes described above (the systems in the E-W direction of Schemes 3 and 4 are identical) under the first 44 seconds of the S60E component of the SCT, Mexico City, 1985, ground motion shown in Fig. 1. The systems analyzed had fundamental periods of vibration ranging from 0.549 to 2.139 seconds, using values in Table 1 obtained from two-dimensional analysis. The analyses were carried out using the computer program DRAIN-2D.[12]

DRAIN-2D is a general purpose program for the dynamic analysis of plane elastic or inelastic structures. The dynamic response is determined using step-by-step integration, assuming a constant response acceleration during each time step.

Viscous damping in the form of a linear combination of mass-proportional and stiffness-proportional components was used in the dynamic analyses using DRAIN-2D. Five percent of critical damping in the fundamental and second modes was assumed. The three schemes with the longest periods were also analyzed assuming 10% and 20% of critical damping.

Figure 5 shows a plot of the computed top deflections against fundamental periods. As expected, as the fundamental period of the structure approaches the predominant two-second period of the ground motion, the elastic response increases dramatically in magnitude. While higher damping reduces response, even at a very high damping of 20% of critical, the response of the buildings having fundamental periods close to two seconds shows drift in the range of 1.5%.

Table 1   Periods from Eigenvalue Analysis, seconds

	Scheme 1		Scheme 2		Scheme 3		Scheme 4		
	3-D	2-D	3-D	2-D	3-D	2-D	3-D	2-D	
T_1	1.30	1.42	1.41	1.68	1.64	2.14	1.94	2.14	
T_2	0.40	0.43	0.43	0.54	0.35	0.68	0.58	0.68	East-West
T_3	0.19	0.23	0.21	0.30	0.14	0.37	0.30	0.37	
T_4	0.11	0.14	0.13	0.20	0.08	0.24	0.19	0.24	
T_5	0.08	0.10	0.08	0.15	0.05	0.17	0.13	0.17	
T_6	0.06	0.07	0.06	0.12	0.04	0.13	0.10	0.13	
T_1	0.59	0.59	0.57	0.64	0.60	0.55	1.75	2.07	
T_2	0.11	0.10	0.11	0.11	0.13	0.12	0.54	0.66	
T_3	0.05	0.04	0.05	0.04	0.06	0.05	0.29	0.37	North-South
T_4	0.03	0.02	0.03	0.02	0.04	0.02	0.19	0.26	
T_5	0.02	0.01	0.03	0.01	0.03	0.01	0.14	0.21	
T_6	0.02	0.01	0.02	0.10	0.03	0.01	0.11	0.17	

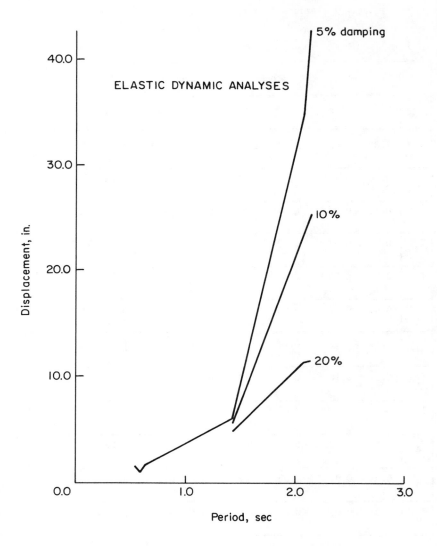

Fig. 5 Calculated Elastic Displacement of Multi-Degree-of-Freedom Systems Subjected to Ground Motion of Fig. 1.

Although the above investigation confirms resonance of ground motion and structure and also demonstrates the role played by viscous damping in such resonance, it does not account for inelastic structural response. Most structures are of course designed to respond inelastically to moderate and major earthquakes.

There are two aspects of inelastic response that are of concern to the present investigation. Firstly, the period of a reinforced concrete structure progressively lengthens as it suffers inelastic deformations in certain locations while responding to an earthquake.[13] Secondly, inelastic hysteresis has an effect similar to damping on structural response to an earthquake.[14] Since both aspects are important as far as ground motion-structure resonance is concerned, an investigation of the phenomenon, to be practical, must be carried out through inelastic rather than elastic response history analysis of structures having varying initial (elastic) fundamental periods.

BEHAVIOR OF REINFORCED CONCRETE FRAMES

Dynamic inelastic response history analyses were performed on the orthogonal lateral load resisting systems of the buildings considered under the first 44 seconds of the S60E component of the SCT, Mexico City, 1985, ground motion. The program DRAIN-2D was used for these analyses also.

Program DRAIN-2D accounts for inelastic effects by allowing the formation of concentrated "point hinges" at the ends of elements where the moments equal or exceed the specified yield moments. The moment versus end rotation characteristics of elements are defined in terms of a basic bilinear relationship which develops into a hysteretic loop with unloading and reloading stiffnesses decreasing in loading cycles subsequent to yielding. The modified Takeda Model,[14] developed for reinforced concrete, was utilized in the program to represent the above characteristics.

The strength levels (yield moments) assigned to the ends of beams and columns were in accordance with factored bending moments at these locations caused by Zone 4 seismic forces calculated using Ref. 10. The strength of each column stack was kept uniform at the value chosen for the base of that particular column stack. The strength of all the beams at a particular floor level were also made equal to the largest factored bending moment anywhere along that line of beams. The assigned positive and negative flexural capacities were equal at every critical section. Figure 6 shows a plot of the computed top deflections against fundamental periods.

The overall elastic and inelastic responses of the lateral load resisting systems of the building in Fig. 4 to the S60E component of the SCT, Mexico City, 1985, ground motion are presented in Table 2. The table lists the lateral deflections at various floor levels for two different amounts of viscous damping. It is evident from the table that yielding at certain locations decreases the response of the building considered to the SCT ground motion in both orthogonal

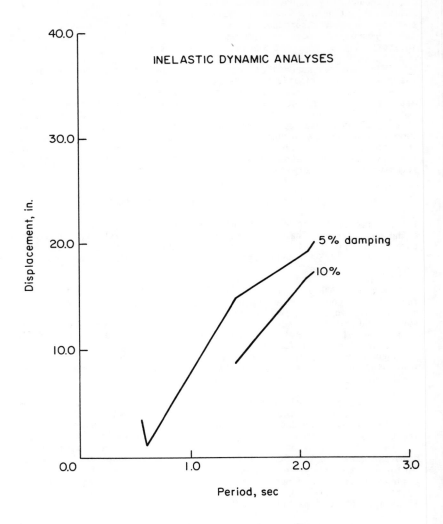

Fig. 6 Calculated Inelastic Displacement of Multi-Degree-of-
        Freedom Systems Subjected to Ground Motion of Fig. 1.

Table 2 Comparative Elastic and Inelastic Responses of Concrete Building Subject to the S60E Component of the SCT, Mexico City, 1985 Ground Motion.

(a) Elastic Response, inches

Scheme	4 N-S		4 E-W	
Damping Level	5% of Cr.	10% of Cr.	5% of Cr.	10% of Cr.
1	6.10	4.19	6.87	4.11
2	13.71	9.41	15.67	9.33
3	21.28	14.57	25.18	14.95
4	27.59	18.86	33.30	19.73
5	32.19	21.97	39.26	23.23
R	34.95	23.84	42.83	25.33

(b) Inelastic Response, inches

Scheme	4 N-S		4 E-W	
Damping Level	5% of Cr.	10% of Cr.	5% of Cr.	10% of Cr.
1	4.23	3.71	4.05	3.41
2	8.42	7.43	8.08	6.88
3	12.44	10.95	12.14	10.39
4	15.50	13.67	15.60	13.36
5	17.72	15.61	18.26	15.68
R	19.24	16.91	20.16	17.31

Note: Fundamental periods of Schemes 4N-S and 4E-W are 2.07 and 2.14 sec., respectively.

directions. The response remains strong, however, even for 10% damping. The calculated roof level drifts in the N-S and E-W directions are 2.0% and 2.1%, respectively, for 5% damping. The corresponding values for 10% damping are 1.7% and 1.8%, respectively.

As indicated, frame buildings having periods that approach two seconds would be severely excited by ground motions recorded in the vicinity of the SCT building during the 1985 Mexico City earthquake. Drift in the range of 1.8% would be anticipated for the structure analyzed.

In an attempt to evaluate the serviceability of buildings, the drift capacities of reinforced concrete frame components can be compared with the calculated demands.

Inelastic Behavior of Columns

It was widely noted that column damage was more prevalent than beam damage in the 1985 Mexican earthquake. Figure 7 shows examples of severe column damage. The usual examples of columns made short by attaching "nonstructural" elements are shown in Fig. 7(a). In Fig. 7(b), loss of capacity caused by inelasticity in the column rather than the beam is shown. Both columns in Fig. 7 have only light tie reinforcement. Prior to 1976, the Mexico City Building Code required only column ties. After 1976, the code required closer spacing of ties above and below joints but less than confinement reinforcement called for in ACI 318-83.[15]

Tests of components with inelastic behavior forced into the column are described in Ref. 16. In Fig. 8, load versus drift capacity measured for a specimen with column ties similar to those prevalent in post-1976 Mexico City buildings with column damage is shown. As can be seen, maximum drift limits of as little as 2.0% can be expected for buildings with light confinement. Substantially less inelasticity would be available in columns with light tie reinforcement. Consequently, buildings with less than one-half the column confinement required by ACI 318-83 could be expected to have severe column damage.

Figure 8(b) shows measured drift capacity for a column with confinement meeting requirements of ACI 318-83. This specimen reached a drift of nearly 4%, enough to meet the calculated demands for the 1985 Mexican earthquake.

Inelastic Behavior of Beams

The corollary to the observation that column damage led to collapse of many buildings during the 1985 Mexico City Earthquake is that few buildings exhibited hinging in the beams. Figure 9 shows one example of a structure where hinging did occur at beam level in the joints. Although damage occurred, the building remained standing.

Tests of specimens where hinging was confined primarily to beams are reported in Ref. 17.

(a) Column Attached to "Nonstructural" Element.

(b) Loss of Column Capacity.

Fig. 7   Columns Damaged in September 1985 Mexico City
         Earthquake.

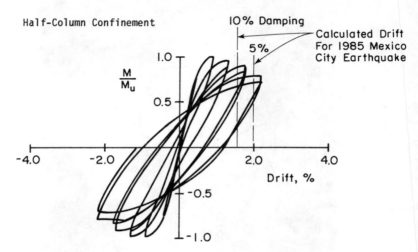

(a) Loss of Capacity at 2.0% Drift for Hinging in Column
    with about Half of Confinement Required by ACI 318-83.

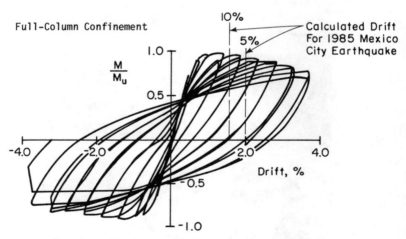

(b) Capacity Maintained for Hinging in Column with
    Confinement Required by ACI 318-83.

Fig. 8 Load Versus Drift for Test Specimens with Column Highing
        from Reference 16.

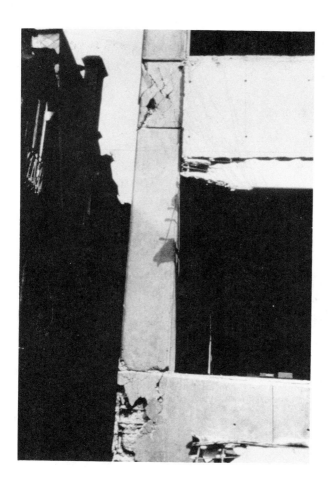

Fig. 9 Beam-Joint Hinging.

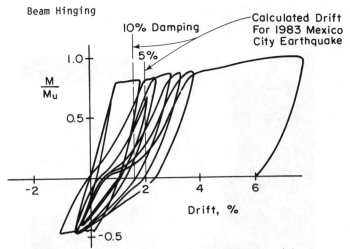

Fig. 10 Load Versus Drift for Test Specimen with Beam Hinging from Reference 18.

Load versus drift measured for test specimens from Ref. 18 are shown in Fig. 10. As can be seen, drifts greater than 7% were realized with details similar to those found in buildings in Mexico. Consequently, drift limits should not have been exceeded in buildings where hinging was primarily in beams.

Beam-Columns Joint Behavior

Many examples of beam-column joint failure were seen in Mexico City. Figure 11 shows a joint with severe damage in a building that was still standing. As can be seen in the photograph, no hoop or confinement reinforcement was provided in the joint.

Tests of beam column joints without hoop reinforcement are reported in References 17 and 18.

Figure 12 shows load versus drift measurements for beam column joint specimens tested in laboratories. As can be seen in Fig. 12(a), drift capacity of beam column joints without hoop reinforcement can be as little as 1.0%. With hoop reinforcement equivalent to that required in ACI 318-83 Appendix A,[15] drift in excess of 6.0% has been measured.

The comparisons of Fig. 12 suggest joints without hoop reinforcement could be expected to have a high failure rate if hinging did not occur elsewhere in the frame. However, joints with hoop reinforcement could survive the deformation demands with a large reserve deformation capacity.

Fig. 11   Failure of Beam-Column Joint With
No Hoop Reinforcment.

(a) Joint Without Hoops.

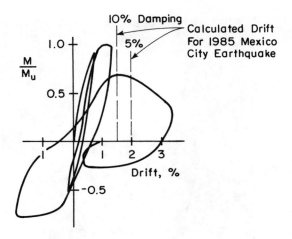

(b) Joint With Hoops.

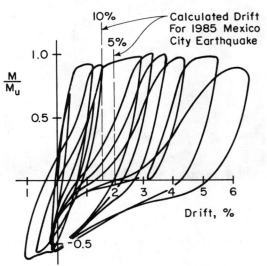

Fig. 12   Comparison of Moment Versus Drift Capacities
from Reference 17.

COMPARISON OF ANALYTICAL AND EXPERIMENTAL RESULTS

Figures 8, 10, and 12 show experimental data giving measured drift capacities of frame elements reinforced similarly to those in Mexico City and others reinforced similarly to those required by ACI 318-83 Appendix A. In addition, calculated drift requirements for a fictitious building subjected to the 1985 Mexico City earthquake are indicated on each figure.

Although column hinging is generally not desired in a structure, Fig. 8 suggests that buildings with suitably reinforced hinging regions in columns could have survived the ground motions. However, columns without confinement reinforcement at potential hinging regions would have been expected to drift beyond the capacity provided.

Figure 10 suggests that drift capacities of beams should not have been exceeded in this earthquake. This assumption is only valid if there is no failure in the beam-to-column joints.

As shown in Fig. 12, beam-column joints without hoop reinforcement have little chance for survival. However, properly detailed joints containing hoop reinforcement can produce elements likely to survive the severe drift requirements of the earthquake.

CONCLUDING REMARKS

The September 19, 1985, Mexico City Earthquake caused significantly more excitation of buildings than had previously been assumed could occur. As a result, more than 200 engineered buildings collapsed or were severely damaged.

In this paper, calculated drift requirements for a well-proportioned building subjected to ground motions similar to those in Mexico City were compared with capacities of building elements tested in the laboratory. These comparisons suggest that a well detailed building could have survived this earthquake.

REFERENCES

1. Committee on Natural Disasters, Commission on Engineering and Technical Systems, National Research Council, "Impressions of the Guerrero-Michoacan, Mexico, Earthquake," Earthquake Engineering Research Institute, California, October 1985.

2. Rosenblueth, E., "The Mexican Earthquake: A Firsthand Report," Civil Engineering, Vol. 56, No. 1, American Society of Civil Engineers, New York, January 1986, pp. 38-40.

3. Mena, E., et al., "Acelerograma en el Centro SCOP de la Secretaria De Comunicaciones y Transportes. Sismo del 19 de Septiembre de 1985," Institute of Engineering, National University of Mexico, September 21, 1985.

4. "In the Wake of the Quake," Concrete International, Vol. 8, No. 1, American Concrete Institute, Detroit, January 1986, pp. 9-12.

5. "Effects of the September 19, 1985, Earthquake in the Buildings of Mexico City," Preliminary Report of the Institute of Engineering, National University of Mexico, October 1985 (translated from a Spanish Version Issued September 30, 1985).

6. Sozen, M. A., "A Preliminary View of the 19 September 1985 Mexico Earthquake and Its Implications for Research Related to Public Safety," Statement Filed with the Senate Subcommittee on Science, Technology, and Space, October 30, 1985.

7. Cluff, L. S., "Firsthand Experience of the M_S 8.1 Earthquake that Struck Mexico City on 19 September 1985," Bulletin of the Seismological Society of America, Vol. 75, No. 6, December 1985, pp. 1843-1846.

8. Ghosh, S. K., and Kluver, M., "The Mexico City Earthquake: Impressions and Tentative Conclusions," Building Standards, Vol. LV, No. 1, International Conference of Building Officials, Whittier, California, January-February 1986, pp. 4-8.

9. Forbes, M. A.; Ghosh, S. K.; and Corley, W. G., "Applications of the 1985 Blue Book to a Reinforced Concrete Building," Proceedings Structural Engineers Association of California Convention, Coronado, California, October 1985, 264 pp.

10. Seismology Committee, Structural Engineers Association of California, "Tentative Lateral Force Requirements," Sacramento, California, October 1985.

11. International Conference of Building Officials, Uniform Building Code, 1985 edition, Whittier, California, 1985.

12. Kanaan, A. E., and Powell, G. H., "A General Purpose Computer Program for Inelastic Dynamic Response of Plane Structures," Report No. EERC 73-22, University of California, Berkeley, August 1975.

13. Takeda, T.; Sozen, M. A.; and Nielsen, N. N, "Reinforced Concrete Response to Simulated Earthquake," Journal of the Structural Division, ASCE, Proceedings Vol. 96, No. ST12, December 1970, pp. 2557-2573.

14. Derecho, A. T.; Ghosh, S. K.; Iqbal, M.; Freskakis, G. N.; and Fintel, M., "Structural Walls in Earthquake-Resistant Buildings-- Dynamic Analysis of Isolated Structural Walls--Parametric Studies," Final Report to the National Science Foundation under Grant No. ENV 74-1476, Portland Cement Association, Skokie, Illinois, March 1978.

15. ACI Committee 318, "Building Code Requirements for Reinforced Concrete (ACI 318-83)," American Concrete Institute, Detroit, 1983, 111 pp.

16. Johal, L. S.; Musser, D. W.; and Corley, W. G., "Influence of Transverse Reinforcement on Seismic Performance of Columns," Third U.S. National Conference on Earthquake Engineering, Charleston, August 1986.

17. Hanson, N. W., and Conner, H. W., Tests of Reinforced Concrete Beam-Column Joints Under Simulated Seismic Loading (RD012.01D), Portland Cement Association, 1972, 11 pp.

18. Hanson, N. W., and Conner, H. W., "Seismic Resistance of Reinforced Concrete Beam-Column Joints," Journal of the Structural Division, Proceedings of the American Society of Civil Engineers, Vol. 93, No. ST 5, October 1967, pp. 533-560; also PCA Development Department Bulletin D121.

PERFORMANCE OF STEEL STRUCTURES

Robert Hanson, M.ASCE*

Abstract

A description of the various types of steel structures built in Mexico City is made, including comparisons of the older types of steel construction with more modern buildings. Performance of steel buildings in the September 1985 earthquake are discussed and related to the local geotechnical conditions including foundation behavior. The Edificio 21 Atlas and Conjunto Pino Suarez buildings are discussed in more detail.

Introduction

Shortly after the devastating earthquake struck Mexico City on September 19, 1985, reports indicated that some steel buildings had been severely damaged and/or collapsed. In October, 1985 an investigation team organized by the American Iron and Steel Institute visited Mexico City to investigate the effects of the earthquake on steel buildings. Investigators included Hank Martin, AISI Western Regional Director; James Marsh, AISC Western Regional Manager; Mark Saunders, Vice President, Rutherford and Chekene, Structural Engineers, San Francisco; and the writer.

The effects of the Ms=8.1 earthquake on September 19 and the Ms=7.5 earthquake 36 hours later were manifest in Mexico City which has a population of 18 million plus and an inventory of approximately 1 million buildings. Although Mexico City is over 250 miles from the earthquake's epicenter its unique soil conditions, including deep saturated lake bed deposits, created a condition where the surface ground motions in Mexico City exceeded those in the epicentral region.

Other papers in these Proceedings provide information on the earthquake ground motion, local geotechnical, conditions and damage to structures. Only the performance of steel buildings in Mexico City will be discussed herein. Buildings in the epicentral region were not visited by the writer and therefore are not discussed.

---

* Professor of Civil Engineering, University of Michigan, Ann Arbor, Michigan, 48109-2125.

Of the 330 buildings in Mexico City that suffered
severe damage or collapse twelve were steel frame
buildings. Of the ten collapsed buildings three were built
between 1957 and 1976 (Conjunto Pino Suavez) and the others
were built in the 1940's. No badly damaged or collapsed
steel buildings were constructed after 1976. Four of these
collapsed or damaged structures will be discussed in
detail. From these observations and preliminary studies it
is possible to raise important questions regarding the
design of earthquake resistant of steel framed buildings.

Performance of Steel Buildings

Steel buildings in Mexico City date back over sixty
years. As a construction system steel is more expensive
than concrete in Mexico so it was surprising to find so
many structures in which steel members form the building
frame. Many of the old colonial landmarks were constructed
with a steel frame surrounded by unreinforced concrete or
masonry. Examples include the Palace of Fine Arts (Figure
1), the Monument of the Revolution and the Department of
Federal District headquarters which survived the earthquake
undamaged.

Steel construction began in the late 1920's when the
main railroad station, the Museum of Natural History, banks
and department stores were constructed using imported

Figure 1.   Palace of Fine Arts - An Example of Older
              Steel Frame Composite Construction

rolled shapes in riveted simple-framed Type 2 construction.
Lateral resistance was provided either by masonry infill
walls or by steel kneebrace frames. In the next two
decades, many steel buildings were built with similar types
of construction. Pipe columns are found in construction of
this time period. The same can be said for rails, which in
some instances were used as secondary floor beams in
vault-types of flooring.

Multi-story construction formally started in the 1950s
with the Roble Building (24-story), the Latino Americana
Tower (43-story), the Miguel E. Abed Building (35-story),
the Seguros Anahuac (27 story), the Seguros La Comercial
buildings (25 and 28-story), the Banco Internacional
building (32-story) and others. Some of these buildings
were finished in the beginning of the 1960's. The common
type of construction was Type 1 moment-resisting framing
with imported wide-flanged columns and beams or
three-welded-plate sections. Column construction usually
consisted of two channels with riveted cover plates. Most
joints were field riveted.

For the last three decades almost no structural steel
has been imported. The relatively high cost of steel
relative to labor costs combined with size of member
limitations of the Mexican steel mills has resulted in
light weight framing systems using trussed beams and
girders and box columns. The joints provide moment
resistance and cross or vee bracing systems are sometimes
used to provide increased lateral stiffness. Composite
concrete floor slabs help to interconnect these highly
redundant buildings.

With the exeption of Conjunto Pino Suarez, which will
be discussed in detail later, the performance of steel
structures built in the last 30 years was exemplary, even
those buildings with a period near the two second critical
excitation period which were subjected to forces far in
excess of those contemplated in their design. As an
example, the new National Lottery Building, a triangular
building with built-up box columns and truss girders
(Figure 2), suffered no damage. The building was exposed
to significant ground motion as witnessed by the severe
cracking and settlement of the sidewalk around the
building.

Dozens of modern steel buildings have been constructed
in the lake bed zone and received no damage. Examples of
two such buildings include the 27 story Seguros Anahuac
(Figure 3) and the 19 story Banco Mexicano (Figure 4).

Figure 2. National Lottery Building - Undamaged
Notice Latino Americana building in the background and the
undamaged reinforced concrete building in the foreground.

Figure 3. Edificio Anahuac-
A 27 story steel framed
building constructed in
the 1950's.

Figure 4. Banco Mexicano
Modern 19 story steel
framed building with
Glass Curtain Walls

Figure 5.   Latino Americana
Tower - 43 story steel frame

Unfortunately, not all steel buildings survived the earthquake as well as the Latino Americana Tower (Figure 5) and the others mentioned. Two of the older steel buildings identified in the UNAM survey were the Edificio 21 Atlas (Figure 6) and an unnamed structure (Figure 7) located between Edificio Atlas and Latino Americana Tower. Edificio 21 Atlas will be discussed later. As shown in Figure 7, the unnamed structure was constructed with steel columns fabricated from two channels with riveted cover plates and what appears to be rolled floor beams. The structure, typical of many structures built during the same time period, received its limited lateral resistance from unreinforced masonry. It should be noted that the photo in Figure 7 was taken in February 1986 while the structure was undergoing demolition. Earthquake design regulations had not been adopted at the time these buildings were constructed.

    The number of damaged buildings in Mexico City was significant and therefore provides an excellent opportunity to extend our knowledge of the behavior of buildings subjected to severe earthquakes. Though the number of buildings damaged was significant, the percentage was very small considering the intensity of the ground motion as compared with the code design levels. The following description will concentrate on damage to one older building which had been damaged during an earlier earthquake and subsequently strengthened and to a complex of five newer buildings of which two collapsed.

Figure 6.   Edificio 21 Atlas - Only the lower
            six stories of this building remain

Figure 7.   Unnamed Steel Building - Photo taken during
demolition.   Notice the slender built-up columns and
unreinforced infill masonry.

Edificio 21 Atlas

Originally a 14 story building constructed in the 1940's, Edificio 21 Atlas was damaged in the 1957 earthquake, repaired and strengthened, and damaged again in 1985. This building can be considered representative of similar buildings built in the 1940's in USA Midwest cities such as St. Louis and Memphis except for the strengthening. The original steel moment frame system had steel angle knee joints to provide lateral stiffness. The strengthening techniques consisted of adding nine bays of X bracing in the longitudinal direction and nine bays of X bracing in the transverse direction of the building (Figure 8).

The upper seven stories of the building collapsed (Figure 9) causing the collapse of the front half of the neighboring seven story reinforced concrete building. The remaining portion can be seen on the right side of Figure 9. It is conjectured that pounding of the neighboring concrete building and the Atlas building caused the collapse. The supplemental braces performed as expected from laboratory tests at the University of Michigan (References 1, 2, 3). A major consideration when adding bracing to existing structures is their connection to the existing elements and the new loads to be carried by these elements.

Conjunto Pino Suarez

The Conjunto Pino Suarez was a five building complex built in the early 1970s with three identical 21 story buildings (two bays wide (23 meters) and 4 bays long (28 meters)) and two identical 14 story buildings founded on a common deep stiff foundation mat (a subway station). Figure 10 shows all five buildings during the framing construction stage and Figure 11 shows the subway foundation plan and the building complex layout. The 21 story building "D" (column lines 16-18) collapsed to the right falling upon the adjacent 14 story building "E" (column lines 21-25) causing its collapse. The 21 story building "C" (column lines 12-14) was approaching collapse.

The structural framing system had trussed beams constructed from steel angles and angles welded together to make tube sections. The columns were hollow box sections made of four plates fillet welded at the edges. These members had internal stiffeners which were welded to three sides on the interior length and to all four sides at the member ends.

Figure 8. Edificio 21 Atlas - Both the X bracing and the knee bracing are visible. Photo is taken over site of the collapsed reinforced concrete building.

Figure 9. Edificio 21 Atlas - Collapsed upper stories fallen over adjacent reinforced concrete building whose remaining rear section can be seen on the right.

Figure 10. Conjunto Pino Suarez during construction.

The trussed beam to column connections were moment resisting connections (Figure 12). The longitudinal direction had one line of V bracing in the exterior wall in the bay of the stairway, elevators, and toilet rooms, and two lines of X bracing, one on either side of the elevator/stairway bay. The connection of the floor truss, exterior V brace and interior X brace at the column is shown in Figure 13.

The most spectacular member failures are the local buckling and tearing of the columns (Figures 14 & 15). The trussed beam to column connection had local buckling, yielding and fracture. Damage to the bracing and bracing connections were relatively minor except following the local collapse of the columns to which they framed. Assuming that the three 21 story buildings were nearly identical with identifiable live loads, they will provide the opportunity to study the progressive damage of a steel building leading to collapse. The large rigid common foundation and closeness of this site to the location of the SCT recorded ground motion provide a good estimate of input motion. It should be noted that the measured period of the 21 story buildings prior to the earthquake was 2.0 seconds and the peak spectral response of the SCT record was also at 2 seconds. It is premature to speculate on the behavioral sequences leading to this collapse. Further research is needed to accomplish this goal.

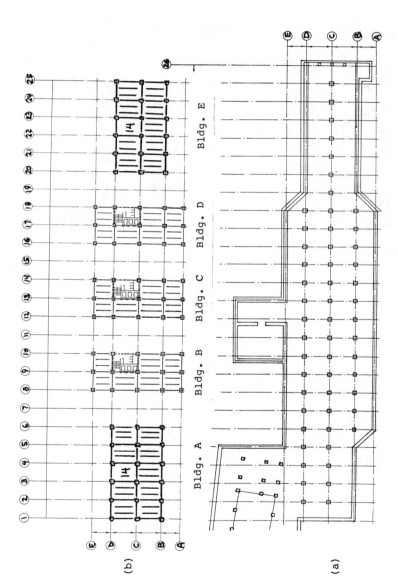

Figure 11. Conjunto Pino Suarez – (a) Subway Level Plan and (b) Superstructure Level Plan

Figure 12. Pino Suarez - Interior beam to column
moment connections in both framing directions.

Figure 13. Pino Suarez - Vee brace to column
connection on the exterior wall. X brace on lower left.

Figure 14. Pino Suarez - Buckling of Columns on Column Line 1'. The "C" clamps provide stability across the local column buckling.

Figure 15. Pino Suarez - Detail of Local Column Buckling. Note the welds at the edges of the plates.

Conclusions

        The September 1985 Mexico earthquake has provided the
opportunity to expand our understanding of the response of
steel buildings to severe earthquake excitation. The
research necessary to extract this information in a
reliable, useful forme for application world wide is just
beginning. Therefore, the conclusions are presented as
questions to be answered rather than answers themselves.

        1. The long period, long duration, large amplitude
ground motions experienced in Mexico City (250 miles from
the epicenter) provides a dynamic input much larger than
previously anticipated by building codes for tall
buildings. Are the attenuation and ground motion
characteristics for a large magnitude earthquake in the
Eastern USA (east of the Rocky Mountains) likely to cause
similar dynamic input motions? Should mechanical damping
devices be utilized to limit dynamic response amplitudes?

        2. Box columns are popular in Mexico and in the USA
because they can be designed to provide economical flexural
resistance about both principal axes. Are current AISC
Specifications satisfactory for members subjected to
inelastic moment reversal when subjected to large axial
compression loads? What ductility levels can these primary
structural members tolerate?

        3. Effective, economical details for providing ductile
connections of beams and girders to box columns must be
demonstrated. How much ductile capacity is needed? Are
the requirements for additional detailing of special moment
steel frames going to reduce system ductility?

        4. Simple structural systems, easy to analyze and easy
to construct, are gaining popularity. Does the absence of
significant alternative load paths (redundancy) require
substantially more ductility from the only load path
available? Do current seismic requirements ensure adequate
ductility for these simple systems? Should highly
redundant load path systems permit lower requirements on
individual ductile connections for some of the paths?

        5. Compact section requirements for rolled sections
are specified for special moment resisting frames (ductile
moment frames). Should similar requirements be established
for trussed girders and beams as commonly used in Mexico
City?

6. Most of the modern steel buildings in Mexico City,
located on severe excitation sites and with building
characteristics for which significant dynamic response was
experienced, performed well. Should this give us
confidence that buildings designed in accordance with
current codes will perform well? What is the current
margin between building damage and building failure
(collapse)? What should the margin be?

Acknowledgements

    The writer thanks the Committee of Structural Steel
Producers of the American Iron and Steel Institute for its
financial support for the field investigation in Mexico
City. Special thanks to Hank Martin who provided many of
the photos used as figures in this paper and to Hank Martin
and Enrique Martinez-Romero for allowing me to extract and
condense sections of Reference 4 for this paper.

References

    1. Astaneh, Abdul and Subhash C. Goel, "Cyclic
In-Plane Buckling of Double Angle Bracing", Journal of the
Structural Division, ASCE, Vol. 110, No. 9, Sept., 1984.

    2. Astaneh, A., S.C. Goel, and R.D. Hanson, "Cyclic
Out-of-Plane Buckling of Double Angle Bracing", Journal of
the Structural Division, ASCE, Vol. 111, No. 5, May, 1985.

    3. El-Tayem, Adel and Subash C. Goel, "Effective
Length Factor for the Design of X Bracing Systems", AISC
Engineering Journal, Vol. 23, No. 1, 1986, pp. 41-45.

    4. Hanson, R.D., H. Martin and E. Martinez-Romero,
"Performance of Steel Structures in the September 19 and
20, 1985 Mexico Earthquake", Proceedings of the AISC
National Earthquake Conference, Nashville, TN, June, 1986.

The 1985 Mexico Earthquakes: Effects on Water Supply Systems

Gary M. Lee, A. M. ASCE[1]

Introduction

The earthquakes which Mexico City experienced on the morning of September 19, 1985 caused damage below ground level which was just as devastating as the structural damage at the surface, and posed a serious threat to the health of millions of the City's inhabitants. Beneath the streets of Mexico City, the systems of pipes which brought potable water to the City were seriously damaged. An analysis of that damage, and of the City's response to the crisis, offers important lessons to other localities which face the threat of severe seismic activity.

The Water Supply Systems Before the Earthquake

To serve its ever-growing population, the Departamento del Distrito Federal (Department of the Federal District, hereafter D.D.F.) operates and maintains 72,000 kilometers (45,000 miles) of water lines. Actual administration of the water supply and distribution systems is entrusted to the Direccion General de Construccion y Operacion Hidraulica (General Directorate of Hydraulic Construction and Operation, hereafter D.D.F. Utility), which employs a professional staff of 1,000 engineers and technicians. Until the 1985 earthquakes, the D.D.F. Utility was housed in a modern, centrally-located office building.   This headquarters was equipped with advanced computer systems and sophisticated communications facilities.

Eighty percent of Mexico City's raw water supply comes from an underlying aquifer and, after treatment, is fed to the City through aqueducts from the north, west and south. The water lines themselves range in size from 5 centimeters (2 inches) to 305 centimeters (120 inches). The newest of the large-diameter pipes were constructed in the 1950's and 60's. Despite the phenomenal growth the City has experienced, the D.D.F. Utility has managed to provide water service to approximately 94% of the population.   The water service is unmetered, and the City's intensely urban population has always enjoyed a high rate of usage.

----
[1]Managing Partner, E. T. Archer & Company, 1310 East 104th Street, Kansas City, MO 64131.

Damage to the Water Supply System

One of the most striking aspects of the earthquake damage to the water supply system is that the area of underground damage to water lines was much larger in size than the area of above-ground structural damage. This fact suggests that underground utility pipes are even more vulnerable to earthquake damage than buildings. The inter-dependency of pipelines, of course, increases their overall vulnerability considerably.

The initial damage assessment following the earthquakes found that 80 to 100 pipe failures had occurred in the primary water distribution system, i.e. in those pipes over 50 centimeters (20 inches) in diameter. Damage in the primary system was primarily to those aqueducts coming from the south and mostly to older, clay pipe. In the secondary system, those pipes 20 centimeters (8 inches) to 50 centimeters (20 inches) in diameter, the damage assessment teams estimated that 1,000 leaks required repair. The tertiary distribution system, those pipes smaller than 20 centimeters (8 inches), was estimated to contain thousands of leaks.

The damage assessment teams discovered strong similarities in the nature of the water line failures. In the large diameter pipes, most breaks were sheer failures. These failures occurred at rigid connections in the system, such as tee connections, cross connections, gate valve vaults and at water line entrances to buildings. The sheer failures in larger pipes were in contrast to smaller diameter pipe failures, which were mostly telescopic in nature.

The process of damage assessment and pipeline repair extended over many weeks and, in fact, goes on to this day. The prime objective of the emergency effort which followed the earthquakes was to bring the water supply system under control, and to restore some service of potable water to the estimated 3 to 3.5 million people to whom service was broken. In order to understand this effort, it is necessary to examine the effects of the earthquakes on the operational system of the D.D.F. Utility.

Effects to the Operational System

One of the most serious losses to the D.D.F. Utility was above-ground: the Utility central office was demolished by the earthquakes. Lost with the headquarters were all user-service records, as-builts, personnel records, computers, data base and communications equipment.

Loss of the technical infrastructure placed a severe strain on the D.D.F. Utility at a time when its human resources were stretched to the limit. In the process of reorganization which followed the loss of the central office, the utility laboratory building was designated the new headquarters. Telephone service was re-established as quickly as possible, and a phone bank was created to handle reports of breaks in service. Computers were salvaged from the central office debris,

and other computers were borrowed. The result of this herculean
effort was that within one week of the disaster all initial damage
reports were handled and a preliminary damage assessment was possible.

Efforts to repair the major breaks in the water lines did not wait
for a complete damage assessment, however. It was clear that repair
efforts must begin immediately, and that the Utility's resources must
be concentrated on the areas of most critical need. The D.D.F.
Utility's leadership decided that repair of water lines took
precedence over sewer line repair, that water line repair should begin
before assessment was complete or even begun, and that a system of
emergency potable water supply had to be immediately established.

These efforts were organized on a round-the-clock basis, and
continued for weeks. Perhaps the most difficult disaster effort was
the emergency water supply system. For days after the earthquakes,
most people in the stricken areas could find water only at the broken
valve boxes, which had collected water from the breaks and thereafter
functioned as cisterns. The danger of disease was great, particularly
in light of the then-unknown number of sewer line breaks which were
undoubtedly a source of contamination of the water supply. As a
critical first step, the Utility advised the public, through radio
announcements, flyers and newspapers, how to disinfect water through
boiling.

The emergency water supply system devised by the Utility was to
use portable reservoirs served by tank trucks bringing water from
available wells. In this effort, the Utility received assistance from
neighboring Mexican states in the form of tank trucks. Other
governments provided portable water reservoirs.

The emergency water supply system of tank trucks and portable
tanks was supplemented by a parallel program which distributed
one-liter plastic bags of disinfected water. The distribution of
plastic bags occurred in areas which the portable tank system could
not reach, or in areas where its output was too restricted to meet the
minimum needs of the residents. Together, these emergency systems
managed to provide enough safe drinking water to meet the needs of the
stricken areas, although the output was, of course, far below the
pre-earthquake average of 150 liters _per_ person _per_ day.

Lessons and Conclusion

The physical damage to water lines which occurred in the 1985
Mexico earthquakes consisted, as described, of both sheer and
telescopic failures. These failures suggest that water systems in
areas prone to severe seismic activity should anticipate these types
of failures in their pipe designs. In particular, large diameter
pipes should be designed for some flexibility at what would normally
be rigid connections. In the same vein, telescopic failures point out
the need for pipe design which allows greater lateral movement within
joints.

Lessons learned from the effects of the earthquakes on the operational system of the D.D.F. Utility are no less important. The primary lesson is that no entity responsible for utility operation can count upon the technical infrastructure surviving a given disaster, whether natural or man-made. A worst-case scenario can assume only that some of the normal personnel contingent will be available, and that those who are available will possess some of the technical skills which are vital in emergency management. The D.D.F. Utility did an extraordinary job in extremely difficult circumstances; its challenges and efforts should serve as an example to others of the exceptional difficulties a disaster can impose.

EFFECTS ON INFRASTRUCTURE

Froylán Vargas-Gómez*

Abstract

Effects on the transportation and communications infrastructure due to the earthquakes of September 19 and 20 are described and analyzed.

It can be concluded that these effects were actually moderate, and this can be explained through the earthquakes characteristics, but damages could be more severe in future events with different characteristics; for this reason some research trends are proposed.

Effects on infrastructure

A 200 km long rupture in the subduction fault between the Cocos and the Northamerican Plate, just in front of the Michoacán and Guerrero States Coast, produced on September 19, 1985 an earthquake with magnitude Richter 8.1, which may be classified as the most destructive in the Mexican History. Only 36 hours later, that earthquake was followed by another similar one of magnitude 7.5, which made even worse the damages caused by the first movement.

In spite of the important magnitude of these events and of the intensity of the damages caused to urban buildings, their effects on the transportarion and communication infrastructure were relatively low and were concentrated in the surroundings of the Lázaro Cárdenas industrial port in Michoacán, in Ciudad Guzmán in the State of Jalisco and in the metropolitan area of Mexico City.

The damages caused in Lázaro Cárdenas, Mich. may be explained due to the proximity of this port to the epicenters of the earthquakes. On the other hand, the damages caused in Ciudad Guzmán, Jal., and in Mexico City were determined basically by the subsoil characteristics; in the particular case of Mexico City, they were even worse as a result of the high density of buildings and public services in reduced areas. Follows a description of the most important damages observed in the communication and transportation infrastructure in

* Subsecretario de Infraestructura.- Secretaría de Comunicaciones y Transportes.- Xola y Av. Universidad.- 03028 México, D. F.

each of the above mentioned regions.

Damages caused in Lazaro Cardenas, Michoacan

The Lazaro Cardenas port infrastructure, which was still under construction at the time of the earthquake, registered some damages at several installations which may be attributed to the unexpected intensity of the earthquake. Among the affected constructions, we can mention the following cases.

Multiple-use Warehouses

These warehouses are constituted by single-cell steel frames, with peak roofs. The foundation is supported by footings and in each frame the footings are joined by a tie bar. The warehouses are located near a pier, constituted by a concrete platform supported by piles driven through fill material. As a consequence of the earthquake, the floor inside the warehouses and at the outside experienced important deformations, probably due to the dynamic compaction of the fill-material which was loose.

This deformation caused the rupture of the longitudinal walls and bulkheads in the periphery of the warehouses, though the steel frames did not experience any damage. This phenomenon can be explained by the great flexibility of the steel structures. After the earthquake, inspection trenches were made to confirm that the ties between the footings did not suffer any damage.

In the surroundings of the warehouses some evidences of sand liquefaction could be observed, which was evidenced by the formation of small volcanoes, through which the water was expelled, as well as by track warping in the access railway to the pier and by a 40 cm settlement of a control tower, whose structure did not register any damage due to the evenness of this settlement.

Marine and Port Training Center

This training center is constituted by a group of two-story buildings, except a dormitory building with three levels. All buildings had flat slabs over reinforced concrete columns, with brick walls in only one direction.

The center was built on a granular material fill zone where liquefaction evidences could be observed. The yards developed 50 cm wide x 3 m deep cracks, as well as small craters through which water mixed with sand and mud was expelled. Due to the liquefaction of some parts of the foundation soil, the buildings underwent differential settlements up to 15 cm, causing the fracture of some columns and walls at the first level of the dormitory building.

Grains Terminal

The main building of this terminal is constituted by a battery of bins, cast continuously with a framed building, which projected from the upper part of the bins five stories, where the system control was located.

As a consequence of the earthquake, the columns of the first level failed and the projected building reduced its height to just four levels; this collapse was almost uniform.

Research is being carried out in concern with the probable causes ot this failure, and among others we can mention:

a)   Sudden lateral stiffness change at the level of the collapsed floor.

b)   Transmissibility problems at construction joints between struc- tures of different nature.

c)   Problems related to the use and handling of construction materials.

At this terminal there was a structure constituted by frames with beams and concrete columns, filled with brick walls. This building suffered severe damages and almost collapsed; the walls presented fractures and partially came down and the beam-column joints developed plastic hinges.

From the battery of bins, a duct bridge with descending height, on which a belt conveyor was supported to transport the grain to the shipping dock, came out. This duct-bridge was constituted by two branches at straight angles. The piers of the first branch, which were the highest, presented considerable damages without collapsing, but those of the lowest branch overturned and collapsed completely. These last piers were anchored to the dock platform. The damaged structures were inspected and some dificient constructive details were found. Nevertheless, in spite of the deficiencies observed, the main cause ot those collapses was the unexpected intensity of the earthquake at the epicenter zone (Grade IX in the modified Mer- calli Scale) , which was greater than the assumed in the structural projects (Grade VIII, according to the building code).

Lazaro Cardenas Bridge

The "Lazaro Cardenas Bridge" was built to give access to the industrial port located at the Cayacal Island, over the right arm of the Balsas River near its outlet.

The bridge is constituted by two twin structures, each with two traffic lanes. Each superestructure has six single 30 m spans with reinforced concrete decks on five precast prestressed 1 girders.

Each substructure has seven reinforced concrete supports, five piers and two framed bents on foundation caissons. Each pier consists in a central column with circular section which supports a double-cantilever beam with variable depth.

As a consequence of the earthquake, the bridge underwent important damages, the approach embankments on both sides failed with longitudinal cracking produced by the shear failure of the slopes and the settlement at the base of the section. This failure produced a settlement of some 25 cm at the access slabs on the extreme bents.

Some spans of the superestructure displaced transversely about 5 cm; these displacements, normal to the road axis, apparently did not produce any damage to the superestructure nor to its neoprene bearings, but on the other hand, they did produce the rupture of the lateral support butts at the crowns of the substructure. At the expansion joints between different sections, there were evidences of beating at adjacent spans, which indicates that the longitudinal displacements were also important, but limited by the extreme bents diaphragms.

The greates damage occurred at the upper section of the pier columns, at the root of the cap beam. Almost all of these joints showed cracks and spalling of the concrete cover. In some cases, spalling of the concrete discovered the main vertical reinforcement of the column, which yielded at some sections due to buckling. At least in one of the piers, this failure apperently produced rotation of the cap beam and a consequent twisting of the superestructure.

It was necessary to shore these structures in order to insure its stability; this was done by steel pipes abutted around the damaged columns. Besides, the traffic was limited to one single lane in one of the bridges and this traffic had to observe low driving speed.

The damages experienced by the embankment approaches may be attributed to a deficient load capacity of the soft soil at the base under the actions imposed by the earthquake. The definite reconstruction of these embankments, taking into consideration the effects of an earthquake of the same intensity as the past one, would probably imply the adoption of sections with wider bases, by lower ing the slopes or by introducing stepping berms.

The pier damages may be explained by the lack of ductility of the beam column joint, where the stirrups were apparently too separ ate. Besides, the effects of the rotational inertia of the super-structure mass probably contributed to these damages, since it was applied to long cantilevered arms. However, once more, the unexpected intensity of the earthquake can be considered as the main cause; this intensity was above that of design, since the earthquake epicenter was just a few kilometers away.

The bridge is being repaired at present, increasing the diameter of the columns.

Effects on the surrounding highway and railways system

Immediately after the earthquake, working brigades from the Maintenance General Directorate and patrols from the Federal High-way Police, both belonging to SCT, Ministry of Communications and Transportation, made an exhaustive reconnaissance of the transpor-tation system in the affected states, in order to determine damages which could represent dangerous situations for the users or interrup-tions of communications in some towns.

Fortunately, as before mentioned, in general the roads system damages were minimum and only some bridges presented some important problems, but only in a few cases it was necessary to close them to the traffic and build a detour.

At the Zihuatanejo-Lazaro Cardenas road, a part of the Pacific Coast highway, some land slides occurred which partly blocked a small length near Zacatula, Gro., close to the Balsas River left margin.

Thirty-three bridges in this roads were inspected, and only minor damages such as the following were observed:

-    Transverse relative displacements between adjacent superstruc-ture spans.

-    Yielding of some lead bearing plates, as revealed by a vertical step at the expansion joints and railings.

-    Signs of beating between adjacent spans of the superstructure, caused by longitudinal displacements and revealed by the spalling of parapet beams, curbs and expansion joints.

It has to be mentioned that some ot these bridges, important because of their length and height, showed a satisfactory behaviour, such as the bridge over the River La Union, Gro.

At the Acapulco-Zihuatanejo road, part of the same coastal high way, the bridge "Cuajilote" experienced important damages consisting in lateral displacements of the superstructure in more than 20 cm and excessive opening of the joints. Repair works started immediately, using hydraulic jacks acting horizontally in order to replace the slabs to their original position. During the repairs, the traffic was limited to one lane.

At this same road, the bridge "Arroyo Seco" was damaged, the masonry bodies cracked directly below the superstructure bearing. At one of the piers, one end of the concrete crown was spalled and the superstructure beams lost support.

The Ciudad Altamirano-Zihuatanejo road was a relatively new road with many curves due to the abrupt mountainous area. Low design specifications were observed and many landslides occurred, mainly at high cuts. These landslides closed the road between kilometer 95 and 125. In order to put it in service again, it was necessary to remove 305,000 m^3 of material, using SCT and rented equipment. Only one lane could be opened to traffic at the middle of November, two months after the earthquake, and the whole of the repair works were finished at the middle of January, that is 4 months later.

Somewhere near km 74 of this road, an important failure was observed at a cut slope at the right side of the road, where the natural material was an altered rhyolite with a great soil content. The failure occurred along some 100 m length, with a height of 75 m, displacing important earth volumes to the road. The repairs were realized cutting, at equal spaces, 4 m wide berms provided with adequate drainage.

At km 99 of the same road, a balcony-embankment failure was produced, consisting in the embankment material run-off, fracture and displacement of a retaining wall and important cracking and vertical deformations of the road. Reconstruction of the wall was made, lowering its foundation and increasing its cross section.

The damages produced at this road may be attributed to the earthquake's intensity and to the low specificacions used in the design. These specifications considered a high risk level because low traffic volumes were expected.

At the railway <u>Apatzingan-Infiernillo-Lazaro Cardenas</u>, near the epicenter zone, some tracks experienced warping due to transverse deflections and twisting of the rails. This is one more evidence of the intensity and violence of the earthquakes.

At the road <u>Lazaro Cardenas-Coahuayana</u>, another part of the Pacific Coast highway, near 60 bridges were inspected, and many of them showed minor damages, similar to those above mentioned, but only a few ones were more seriously affected.

Among them is the bridge "NEXPA", in which the superstructure is constituted by simple spans with prestressed girders; at the joints there were signs of beating due to the longitudinal movement and there were transversal displacements, which produced the rupture of the lateral butts. These problems were observed at the piers founded on soft soil, not so at those in the right margin which are supported by firm rock.

At the "MEXIQUILLO" bridge, the earthquake produced the fracture of the masonry body at one of the piers. Shoring of the structure was made and it was necessary to detour traffic.

At the "COLORADA" bridge, the superstructure formed by three freely supported slabs, underwent rotation around a vertical axis which caused transverse displacements between adjacent spans of sone 20 cm.

At one branch of this road, an access to the TICUIZ town, there is a bridge with the same name, which experienced severe damages due to the earthquake:

- Lateral displacement of the structure, some 20 cm at one end and 30 cm at the other.

- Failure of the bent beam in the right abutment with diagonal tension cracks and crushing under the bearing plates. Fracture of a pier plain concrete body at its base.

- Fracture and overturning of the approach walls.

We can here mention that this same bridge had already been affected by an earthquake in January, 1973. Structural members which had been repaired thereafter did not experience any damage during the 1985 earthquakes.

In concern with the earth road structure, from <u>Playa Azul</u> to <u>Coahuayana</u>, detached rocks over the road and obstructions of ditches could be observed almost all along the way; besides, most bridges approaches also registered settlements.

Of special concern after the earthquake was the bridge called "BARRANCA HONDA", a concrete arch bridge with a 90 m span, on the road from Carapan to Playa Azul, since this bridge was being extensively rehabilitated. At the time of the earthquake, numerous elements in the floor system of this bridge were fractured due to excessive live loads. At that moment, only half of a new deck slab had been cast, and the mass distribution was asymmetrical. A care ful inspection, a few hours after the movement, revealed the absence of damages in the structure.

The same result was obtained after the inspection of the continu ous bridge "EL MARQUES", on a sharp grade horizontal curve, located at this same road, whose structure was also seriously damaged due to overload effects.

At the last part of this road, between Playa Azul and La Mira, some embankment cracks up to 1 m wide were produced; it was necessary to scarify here the pavement and rebuild it along a 1.5 km length.

At the railway under construction between Ajuno and Calzontzin stations in the Michoacan State, minor damages were observed under the superstructure bearings of an underpass at Tingambato.

The viaduct at km 35 in this same railway was built by the cast-in-place segmental system, with a central span about 80 m long and 60 m side spans. The piers are about 60 m high. The cross-section of the superstructure is a single cell prestressed-concrete caisson. The structure is located at a sharp grade horizontal curve.

Through the evidences found, it could be inferred that at one of the ends of the superstructure, there was a transverse displacement of some 35 cm, but afterwards that end came back to its original position. At the opposite end, there were no evidences of displace ment, and the body of the corresponding abutment split in two halves due to a vertical fracture along the whole height. The piers and the superstructure were not affected.

Damages caused in Ciudad Guzman, Jalisco.

This was one of the cities which most resulted affected by the earthquakes. Effects concentrated at colonial buildings, particularly at the Cathedral were vaults and towers were fractured. Also numer ous traditional adobe houses with earth and wood roofs were se ,-

verely damaged, as well as some buildings built with a system widely
used in the region, consisting of brick floors supported by steel
beams; the earthquales revealed the low strength of this system to
lateral forces.

Effects were not much felt in the city inner roads system, ex-
cluding the temporary obstruction of some streets due to the debris
of collapsed constructions; likely, the roads and railways network
connecting this city did not show important damages, except at the
Guadalajara-Colima expressway under construction, where a 200 m
long crack appeared at a high embankment at km 23 from Acatlan,
Jalisco.

Damages caused in the Mexico City Metropolitan Area

As well known, the Mexico City Metropolitan Area was seriously
damaged by the September 1985 earthquakes. About 1000 buildings
resulted seriously affected. In some cases it was necessary to
evacuate buildings in order to realize major repair and strengthening
works and in other cases, the buildings collapsed or were so severely damaged that their unstable condition requested for demolition
to avoid further public danger.

The extension of the effects, specially at the central zones of
the city, founded on highly compressible soft soils of a former lake
bed, can be explained by the unexpected characteristics of the September 19 earthquake; its long duration, its oscillation predominant
period which was basically about 2.0 sec. and its high amplitudes.

At the zones of the city with soft subsoil depths up to 30 m
until the first hard layer, where the clayey mass has its own oscillation period near 2.0 sec. The seismic excitation must have been
considerably amplified due to an effect similar to resonance. The
most affected buildings, besides of being founded on these zones,
had fundamental oscillation periods near 2.0 sec. With the materials
and constructive systems commonly used in the valley, these buildings are those with a concrete structure with a height between 7
and 14 floors. On the contrary, old buildings with less floors or
very high buildings resulted almost undamaged.

Works in the transportation infrastructure are, in general, at
grade constructions (roads, streets, railways) or bridges and underpasses of little height (6 to 8 m), with very stiff structural members.
Therefore, their own vibration periods are short, less that 0.5 sec.,
so the effects on these works were minimum.

As a direct consequence of the earthquake, at some streets of
the city pavement splits could be observed, due to emersion of aban

donned rails which had been left embedded in the pavement (Av. Alvaro Obregon and 5 de Febrero street); this fact may establish the intensity at these sites as grade IX modified Mercalli; or due to sudden settlements of loose fills used as base materials. Also, many curbs and sidewalks were severly fractured. At some sites important cracks could be observed, but these cracks were formerly produced by ground shrinkage due to excessive drying, which were only reacti-vated by the earthquakes.

Also, as a direct consequence of the earthquake, some underpasses underwent localized damages at the superstructure bearings; on the other hand, the fall of some cables temporarily interrupted some trolley-bus lines.

Nevertheless, the main effects on the transportation infrastructure were produced by indirect consequences of the movements. First, many streets were completely blocked by the debris of collapsed buildings, and others had to be closed to motor traffic and even to pedestrians because of severely damaged buildings which constituted dangerous situations and could collapse because of simple vibrations induced by traffic. We can mention several streets and avenues which were obstructed at long portions, such as Calzada de Tlalpan, Cuauhtemoc Avenue, Eje Central and 20 de Noviembre-Pino Suarez, from North to South. In the East-West direction, some parts of Fray Servando, Izazaga, Paseo de la Reforma, Juárez, Xola, and Chapultepec Avenue. The total length of the blocked streets was about 20 km; besides, the breakout of traffic lights due to electricity interruptions immediately after the earthquake completely disturbed traffic, making rescue and help labors really difficult. Thousands of citizens spontaneously helped at the first few critical hours to restore traffic. The Federal District authorities set out an emergency traffic plan, closing access to zones where damages were concentrated, as the business center of the City and using only the available free streets. This plan was diffused through the different communications media.

Once the emergency was left behind, during the cleaning operations to take away the debris, many streets resulted even more damaged. More than 2 000 000 m^3 of debris had to be removed from the center of the city and taken to outside dumpsites. Many pavements were damaged by the heavy equipment used for clearance. Other streets were damaged by the weight of the debris temporarily stowed on them. For such reasons, the Federal District General Direction of Public Works had to modify the normal pavement reconstruction program projected for the period October-December 1985 and apply an emergency repavement program from November 11 till December 31, which required an investment of more than two billion pesos at about 20 streets. These works were made at night turns in order to minimize traffic disturbances.

Other aspects of the transportation infrastructure observed a very good behaviour during the earthquakes and were able to continue operating without interruptions, except at the necessary time to real_ ize inspections. Among them we can mention the metropolitan sub - way (metro), which did not suffer any damage at underground or at elevated structures; only a few stations had to be temporarily closed to protect people from nearby severely damaged and dangerous con- structions.

Likewise, the Mexico City International Airport only interrupted operations during a couple of hours after the first earthquake, during which careful inspection was made of the runways, terminal building and auxiliary devices.

The control tower of this airport is a very slender and flexible structure; its oscillations due to the vibrations transmitted through the soil and originated by the impact of airplanes during landing and take-off operations are easily perceived by people. Nevertheless, in spite of the above mentioned characteristics, it suffered no struc- tural damage by the earthquake. Thanks to the airport adequate be- haviour, it was possible to maintain aereal communications between the city and the rest of the world and so receive opportunely all kind of assistance as medicines, food, equipment and experts which arrived from many friend countries by airplane.

The road and railway communications were also operating at all times, since the network connecting Mexico City did not experience damages, as well as the passenger and freight terminals. This en- abled a free traffic of people and supplies, which become so import ant in emergency cases.

In concern with communications, the only unfortunate interruption occurred in the telephone system, since more than half of the city telephones went out of order and the long distance service broke down for a long time. This failure, which unfortunately had negative results to attend emergencies, was due to an excessive concentra- tion of the system which failed when just one downtown building collapsed.

Insofar as telecommunications is concerned, the privately owned TV broadcasting system was interrupted during a few hours immedi- ately after the earthquake as a consequence of a partial collapse of its central installations; the same happened to some radio stations, which interrupted their broadcasting from Mexico City due to damages in their buildings. Communication through the official TV system and most radio stations was maintained because no telecommunication station inside the country was damaged and the main installations of the system at the telecommunications central tower operated con ‑ tinuously. This building 18 stories high, with eaoh story higher than usual, is a reinforced concrete structure with waffle flat slabs on columns, stiffened with shear walls along its whole height. In the past, some problems of inadequate behaviour had been observed at its foundations getting it out of plumb. This situation is now under control and the structure behaved satisfactorily during the earth quake, since only very local damages were produced, as was the cracking of a few columns at the higher levels and the spalling at the edges of a shear wall. These damages could be attributed to construction details more than to an inadequate general behaviour. Nevertheless, the displacements of the upper part of the building originated the overturning of batteries which were ready in case of emergency supply of energy; these overturned batteries produced a sort of fire which could rapidly be controlled.

Conclusions

The effects on the transportation and communications infrastructure caused by the 1985 earthquales may be considered moderated.

Nevertheless, the behaviour of this infrastructure in future probable earthquakes with different characteristics, could be quite different.

Therefore, it is considered necessary to review the design and construction practices used at present for this kind of works, at the light of their behaviour during the last earthquakes, and taking into account that they constitute an important part of the "life lines".

The transportation and communication infrastructure must be designed under the criterion that, even after a large earthquake, it must continue operating in order to guarantee the supplies and assistance entry to the damaged area.

According to this, the following research trends are proposed:

In concern with bridges, it seems that the design strength criteria of critical sections in structural elements followed up to date area satisfactory and probably provide conservative results. Nevertheless, it also seems that the displacement estimates have been inadequate and that they are actually higher than those provided by the computations. Consequently , it is necessary to provide improvements for the expansion joints and bearing plates designs. It is specially considered desirable to review the design criteria for the side butts and for the longitudinal connections between successive superstructure spans.

- Some of the observed failures indicate possible ductility deficiencies at the critical sections rather than strength deficiencies,
  and it will be necessary therefore to improve the design details
  of these sections in order to increase their ductility.

- Referring to earth structures, the embankments of soft soils and
  high sharp slopes in cut sections should be reviewed, considering their stability under the effects of an earthquake, with inten
  sity according to the site seismic risk.

Finally, it's observed that communication networks must have
several centers, in order to prevent the failure of the whole system
produced by the failure of just one center, and it is recommended
that emergency urban traffic plans be foreseen by using specially
built avenues which would give service even after a big disaster.

Summary of the Effects of the 1985 Mexico Earthquake
to Power and Industrial Facilities

S. J. Eder[I] and S. W. Swan[II]

Abstract

A major industrial area and two power plants are near the epicenter
of the Magnitude 8.1 Mexico Earthquake of September 19, 1985. All
investigated facilities are modern, generally well constructed, and
included some seismic considerations in their designs. The power
plants are founded on rock and firm soils and performed exceptionally
well. Much of the industrial area is situated on river deposit
sediments, and higher ground motion and certain foundation failures
led to various significant earthquake effects. The observations of
the performance of facilities and available ground motion records
provide insight to the expected performance of modern power and
industrial facilities.

Introduction

This paper summarizes the findings from two post-earthquake
investigations of the Lazaro Cardenas industrial area (see
Reference 1) and a later return investigation (May 1986). Facilities
investigated in the high intensity region of the epicentral area of
the September 19, 1985, Mexico Earthquake include La Villita
Hydroelectric Plant, El Infiernillo Hydroelectric Plant, Lazaro
Cardenas Substation, the SICARTSA Steel Mill, the Fertimex Plant,
Lazaro Cardenas Industrial Port, and the COPSA Cement Plant.

Ground Motion Data

The locations of the earthquake epicenter, available ground motion
recording instruments, and investigated facilities are shown in Figure
1. The recording instruments at La Union, La Villita, and Caleta de
Campos were founded on rock. The ground motion response spectra for
these instruments are shown in Figures 2 to 4 (Reference 2), and are
representative of the motion at the two hydroelectric plants. Peak
horizontal ground acceleration (PGA) was 0.14g.

The Zacatula instrument was founded on Rio Balsas deposit
sediments, similar to the soil conditions in the Lazaro Cardenas
industrial area. Ground motion response spectra from the Zacatula
recording are the best available estimates for the industrial area and
the substation (Figure 5, Reference 3). The duration of strong ground
motion was about 50 seconds, with a PGA of 0.28g. The Zacatula
recording is shown in Figure 6 (Reference 3).

I. Project Engineer, EQE, Inc., San Francisco, California
II. Associate, EQE, Inc., San Francisco, California

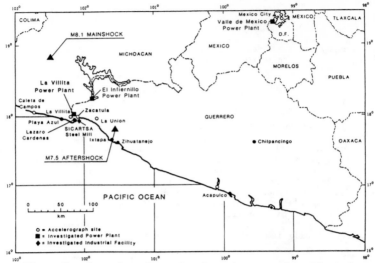

Figure 1: Location of earthquake epicenter, investigated
facilities and ground motion recording instruments

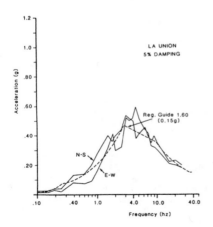

Figure 2: La Union, horizontal
ground motion response spectra,
5% damping

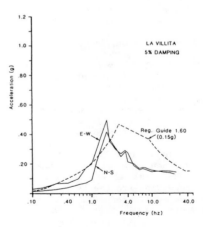

Figure 3: La Villita,
horizontal ground motion
response spectra, 5% damping

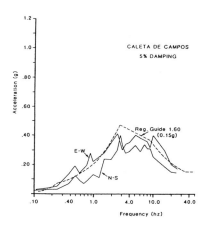

Figure 4: Caleta de Campos, horizontal ground motion response spectra, 5% damping

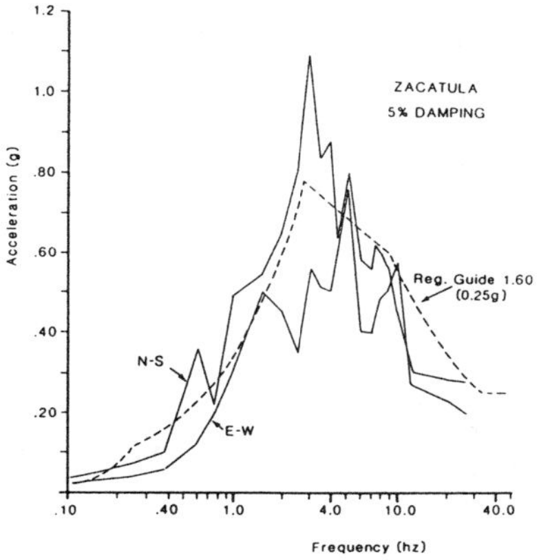

Figure 5: Zacatula, horizontal ground motion response spectra, 5% damping

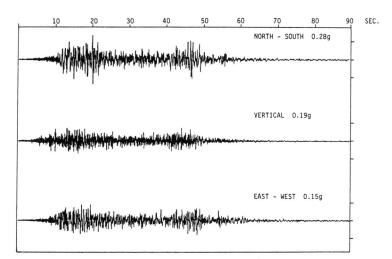

Figure 6: Zacatula, strong ground motion recording

Ground Motion Intensities

The town of Lazaro Cardenas was assigned a Modified Mercalli Intensity (MMI) of IX (Reference 4). Earthquake effects in Lazaro Cardenas are shown in Figures 7 and 8. The industrial area is within a ten mile radius of town, and MMI's were similar or greater. The Fertimex Plant, constructed on an island at the mouth of the Rio Balsas, may have had higher MMI due to the observed large sand boils, severe ground settlement, displaced railroad tracks, and reported tsunami (see Figures 9 and 10). An estimate of MMI for the two hydroelectric plants is difficult to obtain due to their remote locations. Minor rock slides occurred near both plants; these may have been a result of the heavy seasonal rains.

Power Facilities

El Infiernillo Hydroelectric Plant is located on the Rio Balsas about 40 miles from the epicenter of the main shock. El Infiernillo earth dam is about 500 feet tall and 1000 feet wide. The plant was constructed in the 1960's, and includes four units at 160 megawatts (mW) and two units at 180 mW. The plant is on a rock site, and the power station is built into a tunnel.

Three units were in operation at the time of the earthquake. Two units disconnected from the power grid by actuation of a high voltage circuit breaker in the station switchyard, tripped by faults in the Mexico City distribution network. The third unit disconnected by actuation of a ground fault relay, possibly caused by spurious vibration during the earthquake. Other reports indicated that a relay was triggered by water sloshing up through a vent line and onto the generator. All units were put back into service once alternate distribution paths were established.

Seismic loading was considered in design of the plant, and most equipment items are well anchored. Electrical and mechanical equipment performed well; the only known equipment damage was an oil leak in a high voltage transformer in the station switchyard. With the exception of the ground fault relay, there were no malfunctions, false indications, system resets, or abnormal occurrences in the plant control systems. Other earthquake effects include superficial damage at the crest of the dam.

La Villita Hydroelectric Plant is located downstream of El Infiernillo dam, about 25 miles from the epicenter, at the Jose Maria Morelos dam. The earth dam is about 150 feet tall and 1000 feet wide. The plant was constructed in 1973, and includes four units at 76 mW each. The plant design included seismic considerations (Reference 5). It is on a rock site. The power station building is a high bay braced steel frame structure with 3-story mezzanine. The switchyard control building is a 1-story concrete frame structure.

There were two units in operation at the time of the earthquake; both disconnected from the power grid, one by proper actuation of a protective relay (associated with switchyard problems at the SICARTSA

Figure 7:   Fallen sections of masonry walls along main streets of
Lazaro Cardenas

Figure 8:   Severely damaged wing of 2-story school building in Lazaro
Cardenas

Figure 9:   Large sand boil at Fertimex Plant

Figure 10:   Effects of tsunami at Fertimex Plant

Figure 11:   Damage at crest of Jose Maria Morelos dam

Figure 12:   Slid transformer
at Lazaro Cardenas substation
switchyard

steel mill), and another by a Bucholtz relay actuated by sloshing of oil in a switchyard transformer.

Earthquake effects at the plant were minimal. There was superficial damage at the dam crest (see Figure 11). A few ceiling panels in the control room of the power station were dislodged, and a water cooler overturned. Piping, cable trays, equipment, tanks, and structures performed well.

Lazaro Cardenas Substation is a new, nearly complete main 400 kV switching station for El Infiernillo and La Villita power plants. It will be the substation for the new 1000 mW thermoelectric plant that is under construction there. The substation is on a compacted soil site, about 25 miles from the epicenter. The control building and diesel generator building are 1-story reinforced concrete frame structures.

The substation was not in operation at the time of the earthquake. Damage to the substation was limited to the switchyard: three ceramic insulator poles for disconnector switches failed, and a large high voltage transformer slid about 1 inch, bending attached conduit (see Figure 12). There was no damage to the well anchored, modern electrical cabinets, nor to the emergency diesel generator. Cables hung directly on support brackets, without trays, were undamaged.

SICARTSA Steel Mill

The SICARTSA Steel Mill is adjacent to Lazaro Cardenas, about 25 miles from the epicenter. The plant was constructed in the 1970's, and a new unit is under construction. The very large and modern complex encompasses about 10 square miles. The plant is at the mouth of the Rio Balsas; site conditions are soft alluvium and sand.

There were some severe earthquake effects to the steel mill. Ground slumping alongside channels damaged pipe and cable tray support racks and a tall stack. Loss of site power due to switchyard and power plant damage, control system problems due to many protective relay actuations, and panic evacuation of personnel resulted in significant production losses. Failure of a large pressurized gas storage tank was the costliest earthquake effect (see Figure 13); purchase of gas from other sources is still required. The earthquake performance of various sections of the plant are summarized below.

The Auxiliary Power Plant includes three coal fired boilers that feed two 11 mW turbine generators and two turbine driven compressors. The power station is housed within a high bay braced steel frame structure, which is adjacent to the steel frame boiler support structure. Earthquake damage to the power station included a buckled crane rail, cracked masonry panels, broken windows, and fallen ceiling panels, partitions, emergency lighting, and book shelves. Problems in the control room of the power plant included fallen control cabinet components (recorders and circuit boards) and relay chatter. The power plant shut down due to proper and some spurious actuation of protective relays. Damage within the boiler structure was mainly attributed to impact from a boiler due to anchorage failure. Large

Figure 13: Failure of pressurized
gas storage tank at SICARTSA

Figure 14: Failed switchyard components at SICARTSA substation

Figure 15: Damaged outdoor racks at SICARTSA from ground settlement

bore piping expansion joints, small bore piping and instrument tubing, conduit, HVAC ducts, and large fans were damaged due to reasons associated with the boiler movement. The power plant equipment installations are generally well anchored and performed well.

The Main Substation and Switchyard for the SICARTSA Plant suffered significant earthquake damage. The main substation control building, a 1-story concrete frame structure with infill masonry panels, was severely damaged. Concrete spalled at many structural joints, and the roof was near collapse. Equipment installations of the control building are well anchored, and performed well. Switchyard damage included broken ceramic insulators (as shown in Figure 14) and failed anchorage and oil leaks on a large high voltage transformer.

Outdoor Racks are used at SICARTSA to route piping, cable trays, and conduit between various sections of the plant. Many racks extend for more than 1 mile in length. The racks consist of braced steel frames supported on steel columns. Ground slumping during the earthquake caused significant damage to some racks, including undermined foundations, buckled bracing, and uneven settlement. No pipes or conduit on the racks were observed to be damaged. Much of the piping simply rest in cradles on the racks. Two instances of cable tray damage were observed: A large conveyor belt structure settled about 10 inches onto a rack, causing buckling of cable trays spanning the two structures (Figure 15); a cable tray slid on its bracket support at a connection of a riser and an overhead bridge section, distorting the run. No loss of electrical function of cables was reported to occur in either instance.

The Pumping Station is housed within a smaller high bay steel/concrete frame structure with masonry infill panels. The structure had light architectural damage including cracked stucco facing and minor masonry cracks. The pumping station has three large horizontal pumps that handle circulating/cooling water for much of the plant. The pumps and all related equipment are well anchored and were undamaged. A major concern immediately after the earthquake was regain of power to these pumps to resume flow of critical cooling water.

The SICARTSA Laminating Plant is housed within a large hybrid steel/concrete frame industrial building with corrugated sheet metal siding and infill masonry panels. The building is several hundred yards long, 2- to 4-stores tall, and includes a large amount of heavy industrial, mechanical, and electrical equipment. The building structure performed well; only minor differential settlement was observed at building expansion joints. Earthquake damage at the facility included sliding of unanchored equipment, damaged equipment anchorages, a damaged transformer, and several cases of fallen ceiling panels. The many equipment installations performed well in general. There was no significant damage observed to piping, cable trays, and conduit.

The Main Smeltery at SICARTSA is a large steel frame industrial building with corrugated sheet metal siding and roofing. The structure is about 100 feet tall. Interior reinforced masonry walls are used through the 6-story mezzanine of the building. There was no significant structural damage to the smeltery. The major earthquake damage was due to loss of power and evacuation of the labor staff, which resulted in cooling and hardening of molten steel in many of the vats. The control room of the facility is located about 50 feet above grade in the building mezzanine. Control room earthquake damage included shifted ceiling panels, fallen lights, and partially collapsed raised computer flooring. The computer room on the floor above the control room suffered overturned and shifted equipment, and damaged computer equipment components. The was no damage observed to conduit, cable tray, and piping installations at the facility.

The Blast Furnace at SICARTSA is contained within a tall steel/concrete frame building with corrugated sheet metal and masonry infill siding. There was no significant earthquake damage to the building structure. Earthquake effects were evident in the main control room of the facility. The light steel framing on the control panel was slightly distorted due to apparent twisting action. The distortion of the panel framing caused minor damage to conduit tied to the support frame. Other effects in the control room (about 60 feet above grade) included fallen emergency lighting, distorted ceiling panels, and deformed computer flooring.

The Administration Building is a large 2-story reinforced concrete frame building with masonry and concrete infill walls. The structure was severely damaged in the earthquake. Exterior masonry panels cracked and fell, an entrance way partially collapsed, interior masonry walls fell, and concrete spalled at many building joints. Earthquake damage inside of the building (see Figure 16) included fallen ceiling panels and lights, fallen partitions, overturned unanchored bookcases and storage racks, fallen items from storage racks, and fallen batteries from a battery rack. Many unanchored computer equipment slid or overturned.

Unit 2 of SICARTSA is about 80% completed. Many of the equipment items are completely installed. Only a cursory review of Unit 2 was made; it appeared in general to perform very well. The only observed significant earthquake damage was anchorage failure and overturning of two large transformers in the substation switchyard (Figure 17). Cable trays partially installed on overhead racks (aligned, but not bolted and without cables) were thrown about.

Fertimex Plant

The Fertimex Plant is a large fertilizer plant adjacent to the SICARTSA steel mill. The plant is a modern industrial complex, currently under construction. Construction began in the late 1970's, and the plant was about 90% complete at the time of the earthquake. The plant is constructed on an island composed mainly of sand. Major portions of the site settled up to about 1 foot, and there were many foundation related damages to various structures and equipment installations. The intensity of ground motion at the plant was obviously high (see above). The Fertimex Plant lost about 9 months time towards scheduled start-up date due to the earthquake related

Figure 16: Damage inside of SICARTSA administration building

Figure 17: Overturned transformers at SICARTSA Unit 2

Figure 18: Settlement at Fertimex water treatment plant

damage. Earthquake effects to various portions of the Fertimex Plant
are summarized below.

The Auxiliary Power Plant at Fertimex is a one unit gas fired plant
with a capacity of 50 mW. It is housed within a steel and concrete
frame building with reinforced brick siding. The most significant
earthquake damage at the power plant was due to differential
settlement of the turbine pedestal foundation. This caused severe
binding damage to the turbine generator. Other damage to the facility
included minor concrete spalling, dislodged ceiling panels, and fallen
light fixtures in the plant control room. There was no significant
damage to conduit, cable tray, and piping installations. Rod hung
large and small bore piping appeared undamaged. The majority of
equipment components are well anchored and performed well.

The Main Substation control building is a 1-story reinforced
concrete frame structure with infill brick panels. The building was
moderately damaged by the earthquake, due to differential foundation
settlement. Many electrical control cabinets within the facility
suffered anchorage failure, and were leaning slightly. The cabinets
were still operable. Conduit and cable tray installations had no
significant damage.

Outdoor Racks at Fertimex are used to route piping, cable trays,
and conduit between various sections of the plant. Both steel and
concrete frame support galleries are used, and range from 15 to 30
feet tall. Earthquake damage to the racks included differential
settlement and displacement, shifted bridge sections, and some minor
concrete spalling at concrete frame joints. None of the piping or
conduit supported on the racks were observed to be damaged. There was
some cable tray damage due to differential displacement of the
overhead racks. There were no reported cable function failures.

The Water Treatment Plant at Fertimex includes a series of outdoor
horizontal pumps that service nearby above ground storage tanks.
There was severe differential ground settlement in the area (see
Figure 18). Many pump pipe flanges and attached piping were damaged
due to the settlement. In a few instances, horizontal pumps were
damaged due to the imposed loads from the attached piping that were
subjected to severe settlement of supports. Above ground liquid
storage tanks performed well; many were empty, and are constructed on
engineered deep-pile foundations. Some conduit sections sheared in
areas of excessive settlement; no electrical cable damage was
reported. Cable trays performed well.

The Solids Handling Plant is a very large facility composed of a
switchgear building, solids handling building, freight car loading
docks, and sophisticated conveyor belt systems that route materials to
other areas of the plant for processing. The switchgear building is a
2-story concrete frame building with brick infill panels. The solids
handling building is a large steel/concrete frame industrial structure
with brick infill panels and corrugated sheet metal siding. The
building is several hundred feet long, and reaches a maximum height of
about 150 feet.

There was extensive damage to the switchgear building (Figure 19), including cracked and fallen masonry panels, severely spalled concrete at many structural joints, and partial roof collapse. Damage to equipment within the building includes anchorage failure and overturned electrical cabinets, fallen HVAC ducts, fallen overhead lights, and damaged electrical cabinets. The rod hung fire protection system was undamaged. Conduit and cable tray systems at the facility performed exceptionally well. A few cable trays supported on steel frames between the control building and the adjacent solids handling building had minor damage due to differential displacement of the two structures. The large solids handling building and equipment installations performed well. Conduit routed through steel frame portions of the solids handling building that were under construction at the time of the earthquake suffered some damage. The structural bracing had not yet been completely installed, and excessive building deflections strained attached conduit, fracturing many couplings. No electrical cable function failures were reported.

The Centrifuge Plant at Fertimex is housed within a large steel frame industrial building with infill brick panels. The building contains massive industrial equipment, supported independently on interior steel framing. Earthquake damage to the building included buckled ground floor steel columns and failed bracing, and cracked infill panels. Ceiling panels fell in the plant control room, about 60 feet above grade in the building mezzanine. Equipment outside of the plant were damaged due to differential foundation settlement. There was one instance of damage to conduit. Conduit spanning between the inner framing and exterior core of the building cracked at right angle couplings due to more than 5 inches of relative motion between supports. Most equipment inside of the building are anchored and performed well. Rod hung piping and cable trays performed well.

Other Industry

The COPSA Cement Plant is a relatively small facility adjacent to the SICARTSA Steel Mill. The plant includes a small concrete frame control building, two large steel silos, and a 4-story steel frame control building. One large steel silo, completely full of cement, collapsed onto and destroyed the control building (see Figure 20). An identical silo, only partially full, suffered pulled up anchor bolts and a slightly deformed base plate. A railroad track at the plant buckled. No ground failures were observed in the immediate vicinity and other nearby tracks appeared undamaged. The 1-story control building was not investigated in any detail, but did not appear to have sustained any damage.

The Lazaro Cardenas Industrial Port area includes a wharf area, a container handling facility, a large grain handling facility, a bottling plant, a large equipment manufacturing plant, and other (non-investigated) industry. The port area is about 25 miles from the epicenter of the main shock. This area was not investigated in any detail, so only brief observations of earthquake effects follow.

Ground settled at the wharf, causing minor damage to the dock and to the wheels of loading cranes. A concrete frame structure (housing

Figure 19: Damage to switchgear building at Fertimex solids handling plant

Figure 20: Buckled rails and collapsed silo at COPSA cement plant

Figure 21: Damaged bridge pier at Lazaro Cardenas industrial port

a control facility) atop a large silo assembly suffered partial collapse. Large steel and concrete frame warehouse buildings appeared undamaged. One of three identical silos overturned. A large sign in front of the bottling facility was leaning considerably, but the building appeared undamaged. One of two parallel 2 lane 8-span highway bridges across the Rio Balsas in the port area was severely damaged (see Figure 21).

Acknowledgements

The authors thank the Electric Power research Institute (EPRI) and the Seismic Qualification Utilities Group (SQUG) for their sponsorships of the investigations. The authors also extend thanks to Commission Federal de Electricidad (CFE) representatives Ing. Arturo Hernandez, Ing. Eduardo Gangoiti, Ing. Francisco Feregrino, Ing. Fidel Robles, and Ing. Antonio Uribe, SICARTSA representative Ing. Enrique Perez Acosta, and Fertimex representatives Arq. Jesus A. Garcia de la Cadena and Ing. Alejandro Beristain Flores. Also, the authors acknowledge the cooperation and help of engineers at the Instituto de Ingenieria, Universidad Autonoma de Mexico (UNAM) in Mexico City and at the Institute of Geophysics and Planetary Physics, University of California at San Diego (UCSD).

Conclusions

Findings from investigations of the 1985 Mexico earthquake reinforce previous conclusions of the SQUG: equipment installations and control systems generally perform well. A key observation is that typical power plant commodities are not particularly sensitive to long duration motion at levels comparable to eastern U.S. nuclear plant safe shutdown earthquakes. Further analyses are being conducted of significant earthquake effects.

References

1. Eder, S.J., *Performance of Industrial Facilities in the Mexican Earthquake of September 19, 1985*, EPRI NP-4605, Project 1707-30, Final Report, June 1986.

2. Prince, J. et al, *Preliminary Response Spectra from Accelerograms Recorded at Close Range, at the Guerrero Accelerogram Array for the September 1985 Events*, Instituto de Ingenieria, UNAM, and Institute of Geophysics and Planetary Physics, UCSD, Preliminary Report No. GAA-1C, October 1985.

3. Mena, S. et al, *Analisis del Acelerograma "Zacatula" del Sismo del 19 de septiembre de 1985*, Instituto de Ingenieria, UNAM, Informe IPS-10A, September 1985.

4. Rosenblueth, E., *The Mexican Earthquake: A Firsthand Report*, Civil Engineering, ASCE, January 1986, Vol. 56, No. 1.

5. Comision Federal de Electricidad, *Manual de Diseno de Obras Civiles, Mexico*, Vol. 1, 1969, pp. 224-287.

SEISMIC REHABILITATION:
WHY, WHEN AND HOW

By: Ignacio Martín[1]

ABSTRACT

Existing buildings must be rehabilitated for seismic loads because of strength deficiencies or upgrading of the seismic provisions in building codes. After an earthquake strikes repairing and stiffening damaged buildings may be economically feasible. Common methods of seismic rehabilitation are: repair of cracks, reconstruction of structural elements, addition of stiffening elements, and addition of dampers.

A major consideration is the eccentricity that may be introduced by adding stiffening elements. Strengthening an existing building for seismic loads usually requires a more extensive structural analysis than the design of a new building. The use of a tridimensional analysis is recommended to discover where the potential weakness of the repaired building are.

A case history is presented. The seismic strength of the buildings of a housing project was upgraded. Several possible methods of rehabilitation were considered using dynamic analysis. Reinforced concrete shear walls were added and connected to each floor by post-tensioned strands. The shear walls were supported on concrete caissons, which were post-tensioned to prevent uplifting of the foundation.

WHY?

Traditionally society accepts risks and in some cases it calls them "acts of God" or "force majeure." The level of acceptance depends on the degree of advancement of a particular society, a death by appendicitis would be acceptable to a tribal society or to the western society at the beginning of last century, but is not acceptable to our society today. It also depends on special circumstances, at war times the acceptance of risks is higher than during peace times.

The acceptance of risks depends to a large degree on the probability of occurrence. Rüsch and Rackwitz, 1972, have suggested the following levels of acceptance of risk:

Avoidable risks connected with
daring people 10^{-3} per year

[1]Partner, Capacete, Martín & Associates, San Juan, Puerto Rico.

Avoidable risks connected with
careful people 10^{-4} per year

Unavoidable risks 5×10^{-5} per year

Society is concerned, but accepts the risk of automobile travel which has a yearly death rate per person per year of 3.6×10^{-4}.

MacGregor, 1976, has suggested a probability of failure of structures of not less than 10^{-5} per year, which for a 50-year life of a building corresponds to 5×10^{-4}.

The question is then, should society upgrade its structures in a seismic region to meet this safety criteria? This question cannot be answered without considering the financial capacity of society to pay for the cost of the required upgrading. Unfortunately, society lacks this financial capacity and continues to accept the seismic risks as it accepts the risk of death in automobile travel

In a city in a seismic region, people are not concerned with the structural strength of the theaters, stadiums, office buildings they visit or the bridges they use, until a tragedy like the Mexico City earthquake of September 19, 1985 strikes.

Insurance companies should be deeply concerned with the probability of occurrence of seismic risks. An engineering evaluation of the risk accepted at the time a building is insured should be made. The potential risk involved in the portfolio of insured buildings should be evaluated by a thorough engineering study.

There are examples of community action on this matter. In 1968 New Zealand gave local authorities the power to require owners to demolish or upgrade buildings which may be earthquake risks. In 1972 buildings in the commercial center of the city of Wellington were required to be strengthened by 1982 and elsewhere by the year 2000. This target has been reported to be attainable. (Smith, 1985).

Why rehabilitate a building? This answer lies with establishing an acceptable probability of risk and a model code to conform to. Then, society must look for the financial means to rehabilitate the building. The next question is when to rehabilitate.

WHEN?

It is evident that a weak building should be repaired before an earthquake strikes, but what makes a building weak? The following cases should be considered:

a) Old buildings designed before seismic codes were in force. Usually these buildings have been strong enough to resist several earthquakes and may have been strengthened during their lifetime.

b) Buildings designed for a seismic code, but the code has been upgraded in later years.

c)   Buildings   designed   to   meet   modern   seismic   codes,   but
deficiencies in design and/or construction have been found.

d)   Essential buildings which should be strengthened.

e)   Buildings in which the use has change through the years.
There were several cases in the Mexico City earthquake.

f)   Buildings that are expanded or rebuilt.

To upgrade existing buildings before an earthquake strikes,   it is
advantageous to have:

a)   An inventory of buildings with sufficient   records   such   as
plans, specifications, and structural computations.

b)   Records   of   measured   natural   periods   of   the   existing
buildings.

c)   Enforcement of present building codes for the expansion or
reconstruction of an existing building.

d)   Adequate financing for buildings requiring upgrading.

The limitations on financing and availability of inventory records
permit limited upgrading of existing buildings before an earthquake
strikes.

After an earthquake strikes the need for repair and rehabilitation is evident, but it requires an immediate assessment of damage. The
Mexico City earthquake assessment of damage is a credit to Mexican
engineering. Very rapidly an inventory of damage was secured with the
cooperation of the public and private sectors and engineering
institutions.

Two levels of expertise are required: a preliminary assessment
should be made first and then experts should pass judgment on marginal
cases. The criteria to be followed should be concerned with: safety
repairability and economics.

If the natural period of a building has been measured before an
earthquake strikes, and it is measured again after the earthquake, the
degree of stiffness degradation may be evaluated, which can shed some
light on the need and level of repair required. A program of measurement of the natural period of buildings in a city may prove to be
valuable when assessing damages after an earthquake strikes.

Government agencies should initiate surveys to evaluate the
condition of buildings and the need for rehabilitation. After the San
Fernando earthquake in 1981, the United States Veterans Administration
has implemented a program (McConnell, 1985) to rehabilitate their
existing hospitals, which is a fine example of a rehabilitation
program. The Applied Technology Council, 1978, has published emergency
earthquake inspection and reinspection forms.

HOW?

Whether the rehabilitation of a building takes place before or after an earthquake, members are usually strengthened to a load capacity higher than the original design. This changes the dynamic characeteristics of the building and requires a careful structural analysis of the structure as a whole.

Another major consideration is the reinforcement of an area that has been found weak. A careful review of the structure must be made to determine the existence of other weak elements of the structure that may fail. Buildings with a first floor soft story may be reinforced with shear walls to avoid failure in that story, but the result may be to transfer the failure to the upper stories, which may have been stronger than the first story, but not strong enough to resist an earthquake.

Common methods to rehabilitate a building are:

a)   Crack repair

b)   Rebuilding structural elements

c)   Addition of stiffening elements

d)   Addition of dampers

Epoxies have provide an effective method of repairing cracks which is much more effective than the doubtful methods of repairs with mortar and reinforcement stitching. The fire resistance of an epoxy repair usually does not meet fire code requirements, but the probability of a fire coinciding with the few seconds of duration of an earthquake is remote.

Members can be stiffened by providing concrete jackets to existing concrete columns and beams. The resulting structure must be carefully analyzed, because it should have a lower natural period and create higher dynamics effects. Steel members can be strengthened by welding plates, which also changes the dynamic properties of the structure.

Concrete shear walls can be strengthened by adding reinforcement and shotcreting. Anchors should be installed to insure the bonding of the added material to the existing concrete.

Additional stiffening elements can be new shear walls, steel bracing or the addition of ductile moment resistant frames. The addition of new shear walls usually has the problem of providing for the uplift forces that may develop, as an added shear wall usually does not support gravity loads. Another problem is the possible interference with existing foundations. An added shear wall must be properly attached to the existing structure, therefore, the adequacy of floors as diaphragms must be ascertained.

Steel bracing can be a relatively simple solution to strengthen an existing building. Architectural problems, such as interference of bracing elements with openings must be solved. As with shear walls, the uplift forces that will be developed must be provided for, which may require a heavy foundation or the installation of uplift piles.

A major consideration when reinforcing a concrete or masonry building with steel bracing is the relative stiffness of the existing building and the new steel bracing. The existing building may be considerably stiffer that the added steel bracing system, therefore, initially the existing building will carry a larger percentage of the dynamic loads than the steel bracing system, which will not come into full play until the existing building has cracked and its stiffness has been degraded. In fact, the steel bracing system may become a secondary line of defense, which will not be activated until substantial damage has occurred in the building.

As in the case of epoxy crack repairs, it may not be possible to fireproof a steel bracing system, but if this system is provided for seismic strength only this requirement may be waived.

Seldom can the addition of an effective ductile moment frame be made to a building, mainly due to space considerations. The relative stiffnesses of the existing building and the added frame must be evaluated, because as in the case of a steel bracing system, the added ductile moment frame may become a secondary line of defense that will come into full play only after substantial damage has occurred in the building.

Dampers are beginning to be commercially available in the market and in some cases dampers may be added to an existing building by substituting structural elements with dampers for the existing structural element. Once the dampers are installed the dynamic effects on the structure are reduced, and in this way the chances of surviving an earthquake are increased. The use of dampers requires a word of caution: during the life of the building periodic inspections should be made to assure the operability of dampers.

When reinforcing an existing building, a major consideration is assuring that the connection of the added elements to the existing building will be able to transmit the dynamic effects. In some cases post-tensioning has been used to tie the new construction to the old.

Another problem that requires major consideration is the eccentricities that may be introduced in a building when adding stiffening elements, which may cause more harm than good. Strengthening an existing building requires substantially more structural analysis than designing a new one. In most cases it is recommendable to use tridimensional analysis to discover where new weaknesses are, once the evident ones may have been corrected by the stiffening elements. Good engineering judgment must be used to assess the stiffness of an existing structure--especially when it has been subjected to an earthquake--when compared to the stiffness of the added structural elements. The cost of the structural analysis and engineering should not be overlooked in the determination of the cost of rehabilitating a damaged building: it may be more than 20 percent of the cost of repair.

HOW GOOD ARE THE REPAIRS?

It is difficult to assess how good a repair may be, but data is beginning to be gathered on the behavior of buildings damaged in a previous earthquake, repaired and then subjected again to another severe earthquake. Mexico City was subjected to a major earthquake in 1957, when modern buildings had already been built. Some of these buildings were repaired and subjected to the 1985 earthquake. A thorough study of the performance in 1985 of the buildings repaired after 1957 is in order.

Research is needed to assess the efficiency of repair methods. Bertero and Popov, 1977, have repaired beam-column subassemblages by injecting epoxy into the cracks of tested models and retested the model. While the epoxy repair was effective in restoring stiffness at service limit states, it could not redevelop bond and premature bar slippage within an epoxy repaired interior joint was observed. Research is urgently needed in the field of repair of cracks with epoxy in members subjected to cyclic load reversals.

The effectiveness of jackets to reinforce concrete columns has been studied by Ramírez and Bárcena, 1975, but this research was limited to monotonic loading, which does not shed light on the behavior under cyclic loading. Concrete jackets should be tested under dynamic loading to ascertain the effectiveness of bonding between the new and the old concrete.

The mathematical modeling of a strengthen building requires close scrutiny by researchers and designers, especially in the assessment of the stiffness of a damaged building and the effectiveness of the connections of added stiffening elements to the existing structure.

In summary, the rehabilitation of buildings for earthquake loading requires the immediate attention of not only the engineering profession, but of the insurance industry and the financial community as well.

A CASE HISTORY

A housing project consisting of nine buildings with a total of 490 apartments was strengthened to upgrade the seismic resistance of the buildings.

The buildings are rectangular in plan view and have different dimensions and heights ranging from 4 to 13 floors. Some of the buildings have stepped down floors. Each story is formed by precast lightweight concrete box units arranged in a checkerboard pattern. The columns were vertically prestressed.

Tests performed on similar units showed appreciable lateral drift under cyclic loading and early stiffness degradation.

In the long direction these buildings have a two-stage behavior under seismic loads: the elevator core of the buildings contributes to the lateral strength of the structure, but a few seconds after severe ground excitation, the only lateral resisting elements are the precast lightweight concrete frames. A dynamic modal analysis of the structures was performed considering the second stage behavior.

The modal analysis was made using a design spectra based on the smoothed pseudo acceleration curves corresponding to the two horizontal components of the 1952 Tehachapi earthquake magnified by 1.5, shown in Figure 1, assuming a viscous damping of 5 percent of critical damping. The buildings were assumed to be uncoupled in the two main perpendicular directions.

The fundamental period of the buildings in the long direction determined in the modal analysis can be approximated by the equation 0.15N, where N is the number of floors. The step-down buildings had smaller fundamental periods, as could be expected.

The results of the dynamic analysis showed that the structures could not meet the ductility demands. In addition to the actual tests of the box units, the following deficiencies in strength were found:

a)   Top reinforcement bars had insufficient anchorage lengths.

b)   The frame beam positive reinforcement did not have sufficient number of bars extending into the connections.

c)   Shear stresses at the beam-column connections were excessive.

d)   There were insufficient column ties.

e)   As determined by Bresler, 1971, the combination of lightweight concrete and grade 60 reinforcement is not conducive to the development of high ductility.

The following strengthening procedures were considered:

a)   Removal of the upper stories. As the number of stories is decreased the structures become stiffer, and the total lateral force would not have changed, therefore, this procedure was discarded.

b)   Addition of steel bracing elements to create lateral resisting trusses within the building. Four alternate solutions were dynamically analyzed. The resulting structures still depended on the strength of the existing members, which lacked the demanded ductility, therefore, this alternate was discarded.

c)   Addition of knee brackets at the beam-column connections of the box units. The dynamic analysis of this alternate increased the dynamic seismic stresses by about 10 percent due to the additional stiffness provided by the brackets. Although this alternate could have been implemented without modifying the building foundations, the difficulties of installing shear connectors through the steel of the columns and beams and the displacement of the cut-off points of the top bars prevented the implementation of this alternate.

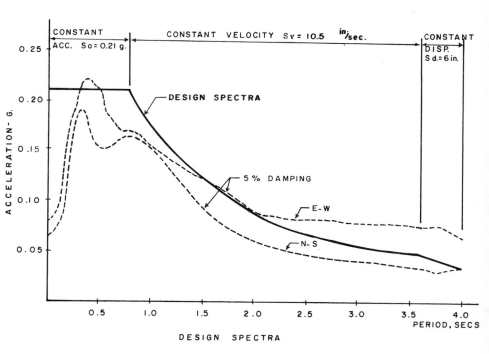

FIG. I

d)   Addition of shear walls to about two-thirds of the building height. The sudden loss of stiffness at the top of the added shear wall substantially increases the shear forces at the top floors, which is the reason for discarding this alternate.

e)   Addition of full height shear walls connected every third floor to the existing structure. The high concentration of shear stresses at the interaction points was an undesirable condition which was the reason for discarding this alternate.

f)   Addition of full height variable section shear walls. This was a seismically acceptable alternate, but was discarded because of construction difficulties.

g)   Addition of full height constant section shear walls tied to the existing building at all floors. The distribution of shear forces between the shear walls and the four frames in the existing building is shown in Figure 2. This alternate was finally selected and implemented.

A typical shear wall consisted of a C-shaped concrete structural wall with an opening, which added a large closet to the abutting apartment. The structural wall carries little gravity loads, therefore, it was anchored to the ground by post-tensioned caissons that carry the seismic induced uplift forces. Figure 3 shows the plan view of the shear wall which is 8-inch thick and is 8-foot wide, and the concrete strength is 3500 psi.

The caissons were post-tensioned with 48, 1/4 inch, 240-ksi wires, through a foundation slab 3.5-foot thick. Figure 4 shows a typical vertical section of the wall.

The structural walls were tied to the existing slabs at each floor by shear keys cut in the existing slabs and by two post-tensioned 0.5-inch 270-ksi strands.

The existing elevator cores were post-tensioned to improve their flexural strength and their stability. The joints between the elevator cores and the buildings were modified to eliminate the hammering effect that may occur between the buildings and the elevator cores.

The cost of the seismic rehabilitation of this group buildings in 1986 dollars is 4 million and the engineering costs to cover analysis, design of the strengthen and inspection of construction exceeded 10 percent of the construction cost.

CONCLUSIONS

1.   The seismic rehabilitation of an existing building requires considerable more structural analysis than the analysis required to design a new building.

2.   The use of a tridimensional analysis is recommended to discover where the potential weaknesses of a building to be repaired are.

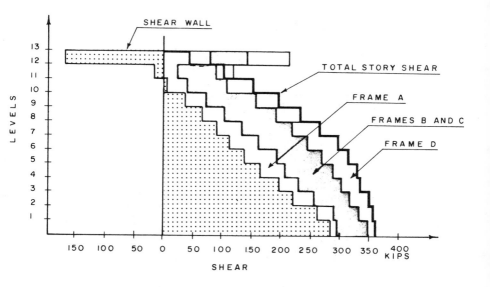

FIG. 2

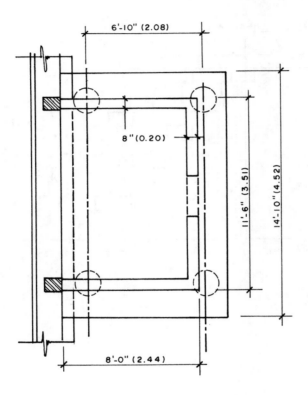

FIG. 3

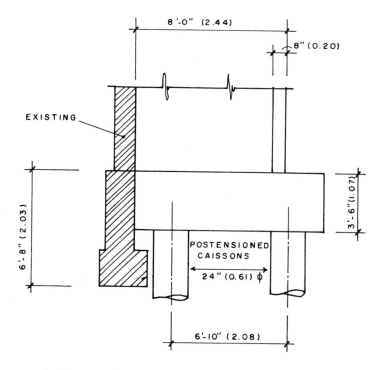

8'-0" (2.44)

8" (0.20)

EXISTING

6'-8" (2.03)

3'-6" (1.07)

POSTENSIONED
CAISSONS

24" (0.61) φ

6'-10" (2.08)

FIG. 4

3. The mathematical model to analyze a structure to be repaired requires a careful assessment of the stiffness of the damaged building as compared to the stiffness of any added structural elements.

4. A program of stiffening existing structures with deficiencies in seismic strength should be established by any community in a seismic area. Such program should reflect not only the need to upgrade the seismic strength of existing structures, but also the financial capacity of the community to implement it.

APPENDIX - REFERENCES

Applied Technology Council. "Tentative Provisions for the Development of Seismic Regulations for Buildings," ATC 3-06, National Science Foundation, 1978.

1. Bertero, Vitelmo V., and Popov, E.P., "Seismic Behavior of Ductile Moment-Resisting Reinforced Concrete Frames," American Concrete Institute Publication SP-53, 1977, pp. 247-291.

2. Bresler, Boris "Lightweight Aggregate Reinforced Concrete Columns," American Concrete Institute Publication SP-29, 1971, pp. 81-130.

3. MacGregor, James G., "Safety and Limit Design for Reinforced Concrete," The 1975-76 Visiting Lectureship Canadian Society of Civil Engineers.

4. McConnell, Richard D., "Evaluation and Modernization of Veterans Administration Facilities," Proceedings of a Workshop on Rehabilitation Renovation, and Reconstruction of Buildings, February 14-15, 1985, American Society of Civil Engineers, pp. 20-23.

5. Ramírez, J.L. and Bárcena, J.M., "Eficacia Resistente de Pilares de Hormigón Armado de Baja Calidad Reforzados por Dos Procedimientos Diferentes," Informes de la Construcción No. 272, July 1975, Madrid.

6. Rüsch, H. and Rackwitz, R., "The Significance of the Concept of Probability of Failure as Applied to the Theory of Structural Safety," Development-Design-Construction, Commemorative publication on the occasion of the 100th Anniversary of Held und Francke Banaktiengesillschaft, Munich, 1972.

7. Smith, Ian C., "Renovation of a New Zealand City: Lessons from Refurbishment and Replacement in Wellington City Business District," Proceedings of a Workshop on Rehabilitation, Renovation, and Reconstruction of Buildings, February 14-15, 1985, American Society of Civil Engineering, p. 35.

DAMAGE ASSESSMENT AND SEISMIC BEHAVIOUR OF
STEEL BUILDINGS IN MEXICO CITY

By: Enrique Martínez-Romero *,**   F. ASCE

Abstract: Preliminary reports on the September 1985 earth
quakes indicated 10 steel buildings collapsed and 2 more --
severely damaged. The total number of buildings found either
collapsed or severely affected was 330.

Further investigations under way have detected numerous steel
framed buildings in the most affected area of Mexico City -
which survived the earthquake, either with some damage or without
it. A progress report of such investigation is provided in
this paper, together with a brief description of the type -
of the structural systems and its observed damage on the af
fected ones.

Some ideas of retrofit of existing steel buildings are --
given to enhance its seismic behaviour and upgrade to the -
new 1985 Emergency Regulations, in particular that which --
uses supplemental damping.

Introduction:

This paper is intended to complement and enhance the pre
liminary surveys made on the buildings damaged by the Sep
tember 1985 earthquakes, (Refs. 1, 2 and 3), as regard to
those steel framed buildings located in the most affected
area or Mexico City. It also pretends to discuss its collap
se of damage characteristics in order to derive some useful
lessons.

This paper provides also a progress report of a project -
currently under way (4), addressed to identify those engine
ered steel buildings located in the same area of the City, -
which were not included in previous reports, either for hav
ing received medium to minor general damage, or no damage -
at all.

Some of the buildings surveyed reported non structural dam
age in first instance, and after removal of the material --
covering the steel skeleton, structural damage appeared occasionally.

This matter is discussed and its possible repair and - -
strengthening for its subsequent use and occupancy is analized.

 * Consulting Structural Engineer. Av. Nuevo León 54-2o.
   piso Col. Condesa   06140   México, D.F.
** Professor Facultad de Ingeniería, U.N.A.M.

Among these possibilities, supplemental damping is pro--
posed as an alternative for upgrading existing structures
to meet the seismic requirements of the current Emergency
Regulations (5), without incurring significantly into inelastic response. (6).

Overview of Damage to Steel Buildings:

The American Iron and Steel Institute, signed an agreement with the author to sponsor incentives to a team of
qualified engineering students to perform a preliminary
survey on the steel buildings located in the soft clayed
area of Mexico City.

The author has interacted both with the Mexican Institute
of Steel Construction (IMCA) and the Facultad de Ingeniería
of the National Autonomous University of Mexico (FI-UNAM),
to select the students and to coordinate the project on a
personal voluntary basis. Thus, the working team was
integrated by the students Joaquín Sánchez-Hernández and
Luis Enrique Váldez-López, from FI-UNAM; Héctor Soto-
Rodríguez, from IMCA, and the author himself. The AISI
contact coordinator is Mr. Harry W. Martin, P.E., Regional
Director.

The following information is presented as a non-official
progress report of this working team, and is subjected to
preliminary indication of the damage assesment on steel
buildings. A final report of this project will soon be
issued by AISI, accompanied by proper documentation.

102 engineered steel buildings have been identified so
far in the most affected area of Mexico City. Its
identification was sometimes possible thru information
recopiled from Architects, Consulting Engineers and Steel
Fabrications, particularly in cases of undamaged buildings.
Phisical inspection of the structural framing system was
not permitted in some cases, and therefore there exists
some uncertainties on this matter. However, we are rely-
ing on the information obtained by third parties, such as
building's maintenance crews and users. It is expected to
have access to the files kept by the Federal District
Department's Building Licenses Office in order to
corroborate this information.

Table 1 shows the current status of different types of
engineered steel buildings, after the september 1985 earth
quakes. Buildings were divided according its main framing
system, the type of damage, the year of construction and
the number of stories, for uniformity purposes with
previous damage reports (1,2.3).

TABLE 1   SUMMARY OF ENGINNERED STEEL BUILDINGS LOCATED IN THE MOST SEVERELY AFFECTED AREA OF MEXICO CITY

Type of Struct. System	Type of Damage	Year of Construction			Number of Stories				Total
		<1957	57-76	≥1976	≤6	7-11	12-16	≥16	
M R F O (Moment Resistant Frame in both directions only) 41 buildings	TC	-	-	-	-	-	-	-	0
	PC	-	-	-	-	-	-	-	0
	SSD	1	-	-	-	-	-	1	1
	SD	1	-	-	-	-	-	1	1
	MSD	-	1	2	-	-	3	-	3
	NSD	-	-	-	-	-	-	-	0
	U	11	16	9	4	13	12	7	36
M R F D (Moment Resistant Frames with Diagonal Bracing) 25 buildings	TC	-	2	-	-	-	1	1	2
	PC	-	1	-	-	-	-	1	1
	SSD	-	1	-	-	-	-	1	1
	SD	1	1	-	-	-	1	1	2
	MSD	3	1	1	-	3	2	-	5
	NSD	2	-	-	-	-	1	1	2
	U	2	5	5	4	-	5	3	12
M R F W (Moment Resistant Frames with Concrete Shear Walls) 6 buildings	TC	-	-	-	-	-	-	-	0
	PC	-	-	-	-	-	-	-	0
	SSD	-	-	-	-	-	-	-	0
	SD	-	-	1	-	-	-	1	1
	MSD	-	1	-	-	-	1	-	1
	NSD	-	-	-	-	-	-	-	0
	U	-	1	3	-	-	2	2	4
S C S W (Simple Construction whith Concrete Shear Walls) 4 buildings	TC	-	-	-	-	-	-	-	0
	PC	-	-	-	-	-	-	-	0
	SSD	-	-	-	-	-	-	-	0
	SD	-	-	-	-	-	-	-	0
	MSD	-	-	-	-	-	-	-	0
	NSD	-	-	-	-	-	-	-	0
	U	4	-	-	2	2	-	-	4
S C K B (Simple Construction with Knee braces and diagonal Vertical Bracing) 3 buildings	TC	-	-	-	-	-	-	-	0
	PC	1	-	-	-	-	1	-	1
	SSD	-	-	-	-	-	-	-	0
	SD	1	-	-	-	1	-	-	1
	MSD	-	-	-	-	-	-	-	0
	NSD	-	-	-	-	-	-	-	0
	U	1	-	-	-	-	-	1	1
S C K W (Simple Construction with Knee braces and Masonry Filler Walls) 15 buildings	TC	3	-	-	3	-	-	-	3
	PC	3	-	-	2	1	-	-	3
	SSD	-	-	-	-	-	-	-	0
	SD	3	-	-	1	2	-	-	3
	MSD	-	-	-	-	-	-	-	0
	NSD	1	-	-	-	1	-	-	1
	U	5	-	-	4	1	-	-	5
O S C S * (Other Steel-Concrete Structural Systems) 8 buildings	TC	-	-	-	-	-	-	-	0
	PC	-	-	-	-	-	-	-	0
	SSD	-	-	-	-	-	-	-	0
	SD	-	-	-	-	-	-	-	0
	MSD	-	-	-	-	-	-	-	2
	NSD	-	-	-	-	-	-	2	2
	U	-	4	4	-	4	2	-	6
T o t a l		43	34	25	20	28	31	23	102

TC=   Total Collapse
PC=   Partial Collapse (Demolition Required)
SSD=   Severe Structural Damage (Partial Demolition)
SD=   Structural Damage (Repairable)
MSD=   Minor Structural Damage
NSD=   Non-Structural Damage
U=   Undamaged

* Includes: Concrete-Cored suspended-Slabs (CCSS), Concrete Columns/Shear walls and Steel Trussed Beams ** (CWTB) and Boxed-Columns -Lifted-Concrete Slabs. (BCLS)

** One-way, Two-way or Space-truss floor systems

Seven different basic framing systems were selected and seven different basic types of damage from "total collapse" (TC) to "undamaged" (U), were identified. It can be observed, for example, that since the number of buildings surveyed was 102 (near 100), both the individual figures tabulated and those indicated as totals, very closely represents the "percentages" themselves.

Thus, at a glance we notice that about 43% of the identified buildings were built prior to 1957 and that about 31% of them are between 12 and 16 stories. By the same talking, about 41% of the buildings have moment-resistant framing in both directions, and 25% have the same structural system plus diagonal bracing.

The undamaged buildings reported 68% and the collapsed and severely affected ones were no more than 12% of the total.

Table 2 shows the damage pattern divided by the year of construction and by the number of stories. From it we learn that about 75% of the collapsed or severely damaged steel buildings were built prior to 1957, whereas the 25% remaining were built between 1957 and 1976. It is interesting to note that buildings built after 1976 experienced a remarkably low 1% of repairable structural damage and 3% of minor structural damage only.

Considering the number of buildings built prior to 1957, we may be able to see that 26 out of 43 behaved satisfactorily, that is, about 60% of them. A higher percentage of good seismic performance is seen for the period of construction between 1957 and 1976, that is, 26 out of 34, or 76%. An even better performance was displayed by buildings built after 1976, since 21 out 25, behaved well.

Table 3 indicates the causes of damage identified in most of the affected buildings. It is convenient to note that more than one possible cause of damage may be related with the same building, and therefore the sum of the number of buildings from this table, has no relation with the number of damaged buildings.

Excessive lateral and torsional deflections was the main cause of damage. Thus it is clear that most buildings were demanded high values of ductility and energy dissipation to save them from collapse.

In the case of short buildings, with natural periods around 0.5 sec., the frame ductility was not very effective and the required strength was furnished by the infill walls or by diagonal bracing.

In such buildings perhaps the infill walls and diagonal

TABLE 2   SUMMARY OF DAMAGE TO STEEL BUILDINGS

TYPE OF DAMAGE	Year of Construction			Number of Stories				TOTAL
	< 1957	57-76	>1976	< 6	7-11	12-16	>16	
Total Collapse(TC)	3	2	0	3	0	1	1	5
Partial Collpse * (PC)	4	1	0	2	1	1	1	5
Severe Structural Damage *,** (SSD)	1	1	0	0	0	0	2	2
Structural Damage (Repairable) (SD)	6	1	1	1	3	1	3	8
Minor Structural Damage (MSD)	3	3	3	0	3	6	0	9
Non-Structural Damage (NSD)	3	0	0	0	1	1	3	5
Undamaged (U)	23	26	21	14	20	21	13	68
	43	34	25	20	28	31	23	102

    *   Demolition Required
    ** Partial Demolition Required

TABLE 3   SUMMARY OF CAUSES OF DAMAGE

POSSIBLE DAMAGE CAUSE	NUMBER OF BUILDINGS
A) Adjacent Building collapsing upon it	3
B) Adjacent Building impacting upon it	7
C) Excessive Lateral deflections	26
D) Excessive Torsional deflections	11
E) Unsatisfactory Foundation Behaviour	9
F) Overloaded (excessive mass)	5
G) Previous Earthquake Damage	2
H) Loss of infill walls or diagonal bracing	5
I) Undetermined yet.	7

Note: More tham one possible cause of damage was identified in some buildings.

bracings absorved the initial lateral thrusts until they cracked or failed either by buckling or by tension, repetively, leaving the bare steel frame alone to carry the successive thrusts, displaying large joint rotations and intrastory sways. This was particularly true for the SCKW, the SCKB and the MRFD structural systems (Table 1), which collapsed after several thrusts.

The second and third causes of damage in importance were the unsatisfactory foundation behavior and overloading, both of them independent from the sutructural system. As it has been explained in previous reports, the tilting of some foundations on controlled-friction piles, induced by the high overturning moments produced by the earthquake loading magnified the lateral deflections of the steel superstructure. In the same way, excesive masses found on some buildings, produced larger lateral loading when accelerated by the earthquake, causing severe overstressing and lateral and torsional deflections of the structure, which in turn incremented the actions on it (P-Δ effect) to accelerate the collapsing mechanisms. That, we think, was one of the main causes of the collapse of the Pino-Suarez complex tower No. 2, together with a poor ductile behavior of the trussed beam ends and top and bottom portions of the outer boxed columns.

Table 4 presents the seven structural systems indentified in the surveyed buildings and how they are related to the year of its construction and to its height. It is apparent that the most extensively used structural system in steel construction is the MRFO, and that it performed exceptionally well during the earthquake, since only one of the 41 buildings identified with this system, experienced several structure damage (Pino-Suarez). Most of them fell into the range of 7 to 16 stories with natural periods ranging from 0.8 to 1.8 seconds, and therefore the high demands of strength by the earthquake ground motion, which exceeded that required by the code in use, was supplied by considerable incursions of the structure into the inelastic range developing ductile behavior. These were exceptions, of course. Some structural systems using trussed beams, identified as HCTB or BCTB in Table 5, were not capable of experiencing adequate joint rotations and therefore buckling or failure in tension at the end diagonal web members occurred prior to formation of plastic hinges and inelastic joint behavior, as exhibited by the Pino-Suarez complex buildings. (6).

This ductile behavior of the MRFO steel structural system was not quite the case of some moment-resistant concrete-framed buildings in which the successive degradation of the beam-to-column joints hasten its collapse after just a few seismic shocks, as disscussed elsewhere (7).

TABLE 4   SUMMARY OF STRUCTURAL SYSTEM OF STEEL BUILDINGS

Type of Struct. System (No.)	No. of Collapses*	Year of Construction			Number of Stories			
		<1957	57-76	>1976	≤6	7-11	12-16	>16
M R F O (41)	1	13	17	11	4	13	15	9
M R F D (25)	4	8	11	6	4	3	10	8
M R F W (6)	0	0	2	4	0	0	3	3
S C S W (4)	0	4	0	0	2	2	0	0
S C K B (3)	1	3	0	0	0	1	1	1
S C K W (15)	6	15	0	0	10	5	0	0
O S C S (8)	0	0	4	4	0	4	2	2
T o t a l (102)	12	43	34	25	20	28	31	23

    * Includes, total and Partial Collapses and Those Severely Damaged (TC+PC+SSD)

TABLE 5   SUMMARY OF TYPE OF STEEL CONSTRUCTION

Type of Steel Construction	Year of Construction			Number of Stories				Total
	<1957	57-76	>1976	≤ 6	7-11	12-16	>16	
H C S B	13	2	2	3	6	3	5	17
H C T B	4	5	9	6	4	5	3	18
C C S B	23	5	0	9	8	7	4	28
B C S B	2	4	1	1	2	4	0	7
B C T B	1	14	9	1	4	10	9	24
B C L S*	0	1	2	0	3	0	0	3
C W T B*	0	2	2	0	0	2	2	4
C C S S*	0	1	0	0	1	0	0	1
T o t a l s	43	34	25	20	28	31	23	102

HCSB=   H-Shaped Columns and Solid-Web Beams
HCTB=   H-Shaped Columns and Trussed Beams
CCSB=   Built-up Columns and Solid-Web Beams
BCSB=   Boxed Columns and Solid-Web Beams
BCTB=   Boxed Columns and Trussed Beams
BCLS=   Boxed Columns Lifted-Concrete Slab
CWTB=   Concrete Columns/or Walls, Trussed Beams**
CCSS=   Concrete-Cored Suspended Slabs

    * Types grouped as OSCS (Other Steel-Concrete Structural System)
** One-way. two-way or Space Trussed floor System

However, it is the author's opinion that it is not quite
reliable to depend on the ductile inelastic behavior of
some steel building systems in areas where long duration
high-intensity earthquakes ocurr relatively often, as hap-
pens in México City, particularly on short buildings whose
natural period lies under 0.8 sec. Ductility in such cases
should perhaps be considered more as a "second defense
line" or as an additional factor of safety against
catastrophic collapse of the building, as it will be discus
sed later on this paper.

The second more popular building system found in the
survey was a combination of moment resistant frames and
diagonal bracing MRFD. About 48% of this buildings were un
damaged by the earthquake whereas the remaining 57% suffered from minor structural damages to collapses. Apparent
ly poor detailing in the bracing connections and unproper
location of the braced frames were detrimental in the overall building strength and induced considerable accidental
torsional loading for which the structure was not designed.

Here is convenient to emphazise that a premature failure
of some diagonal bracing may have left the frame not only
carrying considerably higher loads but also changing its
original torsional center, undergoing larger lateral deflections and rotations, and in some cases impacting
against adjacent buildings, producing thus further structural damage. The design of such diagonal braces and its
proper detailing should be carefully revised and its overall behaviour thoroughly understood.

The third most used structural framing was found to be
the SCKW, that is, the simple-construction framing with
knee braces and infill masonry walls. This type of
construction was popular in the 1920's - 1930's decade
and consisted of rolled sections of ASTM A-7 steel in
riveted construction. Columns were normally made out of
two-rolled channels either with tie plates or full cover
plates. Beams connect to columns open sides with seat
angles, stiffened or unstiffened, and to the channeled
sides with normal clip angles to the web. Knee braces
made of two-angles back to back provides limited lateral
resistance, and the infill walls give the frame the
required lateral strength. The skeleton itself looked always very slender as compared to more recent constructions.

Considering the unexpectedly severe earthquake ground
motion, the heavy masses that normally this type of
constructions were carrying, the fact that they were mostly designed for vertical loading, and the materials employ
ed, the performance of this type of construction can only
be regarded as impressive, in spite of having suffered
some collapses.

There were some facts that propiciated some of these constructions to collapse. Among others the fact that, in many cases, during its life they suffered substantial alterations which may have added two or three floors with little or no structural reinforcement, removed some of the numerous original masonry infill walls and partitions, loosing its overall stiffness (lateral and torsional) and its original damping. The replacement of thick infill walls by slender single-angled diagonal braces, as found in some cases like the Atlas building, dramatically weakened the overall strength at the original structure. (6).

Table 5 displays the eight types of constructions found in the survey. They are classified also by its year of construction and its number of stories, in order to get a better overview of the development of steel construction techniques in Mexico City. It illustrates the fact that the more common type of construction employed in the recent years is the BCTB (Boxed Columns and Trussed Beams) in the MRFD or MRFO (Moment Resistant Frames with or without Diagonal Bracing).

As explained earlier, this type of frames exhibited local problems at the beam-to-column connections as well as some local inestabilities on the columns ends caused by the slenderness of the unestiffened plates forming the box column, as well as by the poor weldments joining such plates. The new seismic design provisions which will appear next october 1986 are to contemplate more restrictive connection details to improve the performance of this type of construction which apparently has demonstrated to be practical and economical in Mexico. However, it is proper to thinkover the fact that the apparent economy of these construction practice might not justify its limited ductile behavior, which as mentioned before, should be taken as the last resource of structural strength to avoid collapse.

GENERAL COMMENTS AND OBSERVATIONS.

This earthquake has left valuable information to learn from. It provides therefore, an unmatched opportunity to utilize the inventory of damaged and undamaged buildings to calibrate our current seismic design practices for its validation or change. It is also giving us the opportunity to discuss and confront our opinions to adopt a more conservative conceptual seismic design approach based on the lessons given by the full-scale models which either survived the earthquakes with little or no damage at all, or suffered severe damage, for the sake of higher safety in building construction and reduction of the life loss risk.

It is therefore mandatory first, to identify the problems existing in the thorough stablishment of the minimum requir

ed demands for serviceability, damageability and collapse
limit states of building construction, and second, to fully
understand the structural response and collapse mechanism
for a reliable evaluation of the strength supply. These two
steps should be correlated to the realistic evaluation of
the earthquake forces and seismic demands, so that we may
guarantee that the supply is always larger than the
demand.

From this earthquake it was found that in general, tall
steel structures performed well and displayed a good ductile behaviour. Ductility therefore, was quite effective
in reducing the response of those structures whose natural
period was above 2.0 sec. (8).

On the other side, shart steel buildings with fundamental period under 0.5 sec. accounted with a larger supply
of strength as required by the building code. Such an
extra-strength was due to the infill walls which added
significant stiffness and strength to the bare frame (up
to 180%) because in most cases they were "packed" into
the frames (9). Consequently, the natural period was decreased reducing the seismic demands. This explains why so
many old steel buildings with the SCKW structure system
survived the earthquake.

Buildings with intermediate height and fundamental
period between 0.5 and 2.0 sec., suffered considerable
damage in general, since neither accounted with the extra-
strength and stiffness nor with the ductile inelastic behavior of the structure, particularly when built with
trussed beams and slender boxed-columns.

From all of the above mentioned we may recall in the fact
that the increases in the actual supplies of strength
should maintain a proper balance between stiffness,
strength and energy dissipation, such that the desired per
formance criteria may be attained. On the other side, we
must direct our efforts to control and, if possible, to
decrease the seismic forces acting on the structures, for
instance, by increasing the damping.

In this manner, it may be possible to predetermine and
control all limit state responses at the structure as well
as to ensure the timely activation of different defense
mechanisms, particularly those related to energy dissipation, endurance and toughness characteristics at the collapse limit state responses (10).

Comments on Retrofit of Existing Buildings.

The Emergency Regulations issued on October 1985 state
that those buildings which were unaffected by the earthquake, or which received non-structural damage or even

minor structural damage should not necessarily conform the
higher demands of seismic design that they stablish, since
buildings have given sound proofs of its endurance and
strength to withstand such an intense ground motion. On
the other side, only those buildings which were damaged,
are to be retroffited and upgraded according to the E.R.

However, when considering this matter engineers are faced
with several doubts and question themselves, for instance:

1. How confident are we that the apparently undamaged build
   ing did not suffer degradation of its original strength,
   and that it will perform again in the same manner at the
   next major earthquake?

2. Why some buildings performed well while others almost
   identical suffered damage? If the second is to be reinforced and upgraded to meet the E.R., shouldn't the
   unaffected structure be retrofitted in the same manner,
   as well?

3. Could building users afford to vacate unexpectedly
   their buildings for several months, until it is repaired after an eventual earthquake damage? If so, at what
   cost?, or ...

4. Will it be worthwhile to condition an unaffected
   important structure, designed according to late codes,
   to meet the E.R., for the sake of higher reliability
   and safety?... if so,...

5. How could we improve the building's seismic performance
   and response (undamaged or damaged) at low costs, in
   a short time and with the minimum of inconveniences
   to users? ... and/or finally...

6. How could we effectively provide a second-line defense
   to building systems to enhance its response to extreme
   earthquake loading and increase its overall safety?

Let us try to comment these questions and to consider
some answers:

1. It is logical that, considering the intensity and long
   direction of the September 1985 ground motions, building systems have undergone substantial overloading and
   inelastic deformations during several cycles, and suffered degradation of its strength, particularly those
   made out of reinforeced concrete which with minimum
   tracking reduce considerably their stiffness and load
   carrying capacity. Steel structures as well are not
   quite saved from this degradation either, even though in
   a lesser degree, since some undetected cracks on weldments or strain-hardened materials might have built-up
   stress concentrations and permanent deformations in

members and connections, reducing thus its carrying
capacity and ductile behaviour when overstressed again
in the same pattern.

Therefore, yes! it is possible that the overall load-
carrying capacity of the structures which survived the
earthquake had been reduced in some degree and will probably sustain some damage if eventually subjected to
other extreme earthquakes. This in fact actually hap-
pens to some building structures which didn't show
damage in the September 19 eartquake, but after the
September 20 aftershock, which was less strong.

2. There were several examples in México City of identical
buildings which received different damage in spite of
being in the same area. Even though there are not yet
quite convincing arguments to explain such an odd
situation, and probably there will never be..., some
explanations dealing with "extrange paths of the
seismic 5 waves like deviations or reflections", or
"local irregularities of the soil..." or ... "slight
differences in the quality of building materials..."
or... "local deffects appeared in the damaged structure
..." , etc.   The fact is that we don't really know
what happened and why it happened! ...   Therefore, under
the evidences, the answer will probably be: let's retrofit the undamaged building as well...

3. Some building's owners and users are neither able not
willing to vacate their properties temporarily to allow
its repair. Even more, some others are not allowing
inspection crews to remove ceilings and plaster to detect some probable structural damage (cracks in
concrete members or cracks in weldments, yielding
and local buckling on steel members). This of course
is understandable, but occassionally... unreasonable.
In the case of some Government offices renting space
in private buildings, or even using their own buildings, the cost and consequences of vacating temporarily
their headquarters have been extremely high and even
disastrous for their logistics and operation, and therefore they will definetely just can not allow the same
thing happen again, ...period!

Under these circumstances, the most likely answer to
question number 4 will be... Yes! And then... question
5 and 6 will arise immediately.

Well, let's consider some viable alternatives to
such general questions. For instance... How about sup-
plementary damping?...

The author has been considering very seriously provid
ing supplemental damping as an alternative for upgrading structural strength improving building's seismic

performance. This is nothing new, of course. Increasing damping in structures has long been recognized as a means for reducing earthquake response. Prior to this time de design engineer has been faced with the need to improve the expected earthquake performance at an existing building with a variety of structural system options from which to choose.

Past earthquake retrofit designs have primarily involved increasing strength to achieve the desired perormance. Typically these include adding shear walls, adding or increasing the size of diagonals in concentric-braced-frame structures, adding excentric braces or strengthening columns and beams indiscriminally. All of them involve major construction operations for which buildings are norm ally to be temporarily evacuated. In many cases, these conventional retrofit procedures are adequate, but induce larger overturning moments, shears and gravity loads to the building's foundation, since larger masses are generated, and eventually the foundations themselves are to be carefully revised and reinforced (by adding piles most of the times), at even higher costs.

Last earthquake's experiences have indicated that it is not quite reliable to depend on inelastic energy absorption as the mechanism to attain increasing damping and resist severe ground motions. While inelastic deformation has been demonstrated to be a viable means for increasing damping in structures, the amount of damping is generally not very great. Inelastic deformation large enough to signific antly increase damping results in damage to the structure.

Therefore it is the author's opinion that the addition of supplemented damping should be investigated as a proced ure for improving expected earthquake performance. On one side, the original structural system might need not be strengthened, but rather locally repaired. On the other side, the phisical addition of dampers do not necessarily involve major construction operations, but rather simple ones, provided that the architect or the user allows its convenient location.

Specifically, the author suggests the use of structural dampers which include viscoelastic material as the primary emergency absorption medium, since significant shear force, both displacement-and-velocity-proportional, can be developed. These types of materials have been used for nearly two decades for reducing the response of buildings to wind-induced vibrations.

An early example of this is the dampers instaled in the world Trade Center Buildings in New York (II). More re--

cently, viscoelastic dampers have been installed in The
Columbia Center Building in Seattle (12).

The engineering properties of energy absorption and stif
fness of viscoelastic materials have been investigated
in connection with earthquake response (13) and recently in
connection with earthquake response (14-15). Based on the
nearly two decades of monitoring the dampers in The World
Trade Center buildings, and other experiments, it appears
that the engineering characteristics of viscoelastic
materials are stable in connection with aging.

The Direct Shear Seismic Damper (DSSD) can be used to
achieve two objectives: (1) to increase damping in
structures, thereby reducing or minimizing the cyclic
earthquake energy demand on the building (considerably
reduced acceleration ordinate in the response spectra),
and (2) to provide controlled deformation and stiffness
in the building. Both of these features contribute to
reducing the potential for earthquake-caused damage to the
building. Importantly, viscoelastic material can undergo
large deformations without failing, that is, a linear
stiffness characteristic is maintained at large strains.

The author has experienced the use of direct shear
structural dampers in the redesign of a steel building in
Mexico City which was under fabrication at the time that
the new Emergency Regulations were made mandatory and consequently had to be upgraded to such requirements. The addition of supplemental damping to this building avoided
a heavy reinforcing of both the superstructure and the
foundation. A second convenient use of DSSD was found in
the retrofit of a 12 story steel building in Mexico City,
which suffered structural damage with the september 1985
earthquakes (16).

In both cases it was found that supplemental damping increased structural damping from 5% (normal) to 25%, with
an increase of stiffness. This fact reduced the story shear
and overturning moments in about 51% and thereby the necessary reinforcing steel required for upgrading the buildings
to the new E.R. was less than 10% of its original tonnage.
The lateral deflections of the building were also considerably reduced about 42% of the original values.

CONCLUSSIONS.

Preliminary results of a survey of 102 Engineered Steel
Buildings located in the most affected area of Mexico City
corroborate the excellences of this construction material
for buildings in highly seismic zones. Considering the extreme loading conditions to which buildings were exposed
during the September 1985 earthquakes, the behavior of

engineered steel buildings in Mexico City was outstanding. About 68% of the surveyed buildings were enterely unaffect ed. The small number of collapsed buildings was related with overloading and possible construction mistakes.

Several types of steel constructions were identified in the survey; some of them, built in the 1920's decade, withstood the earthquakes without significat damage; some others of the same age which collapsed, were found inadequately reinforced from previous earthquake damage and several building's expansions.

Continuous structural systems which included boxed columns and trussed girders are popular in Mexico. Some tall buildings using this system performed well. However some others with the same systems either collapsed or suffered severe structural damage. They did not displayed adequate ductile behaviour.

There are questions on how reliable is it to depend on the inelastic structural behaviour of steel buildings systems and more conservative design approaches are suggested. Among them, the one which includes supplemental damping is disscussed and found as a valuable alternative to economically and safely retrofit and upgrade damaged and undamaged buildings, respectively.

References:

1) Meli, R. et al. "Efectos de los sismos de septiembre de 1985 en las construcciones de la Ciudad de México. Aspec tos estructurales" Primer Informe del Instituto de Inge niería, UNAM, México (Oct. 1985)

2) Meli, R. et al. "Efectos de los sismos de septiembre de 1985 en las construcciones de la Ciudad de México. Aspec tos estructurales" Segundo Informe del Instituto de Inge niería, UNAM, México (Nov. 1985)

3) Borja, G. et al. "Estadística del daño en las edificacio nes de la Ciudad de México, producido por los sismos de septiembre de 1985." ICA Group. (Jan. 1986)

4) Martínez-Romero E. et al. "Evaluación de daños en las - edificaciones metálicas producidos por los sismos de sep tiembre de 1985 en la Ciudad de México." Investigación patrocinada por el AISI y el IMCA.; en preparación.

5) Departamento del Distrito Federal, "Normas de Emergencia al Reglamento de Construcciones para el Distrito Fede--- ral." Diario Oficial de la Federación, México (Oct. 1985)

6) Hamson, Martín and Martínez-Romero' "Performance of Ste el Structures in the september 19-20, 1985 México Earth-quakes". Proceedings. AISC'S National Engineering Confe-rence. Nashville, Tenn. (June 1986).

7) Fossas, F., "Los sismos de México en los días 19 y 20 de septiembre de 1985. Pasado, Presente y Futuro". Revista IMCTC NO. 179. México. (Abril 1986)

8) Avila, J. Meli, R. "Respuesta inelástica ante el acelo grama de SCT del Sismo del 19 de septiembre de 1985". Procedings. IV Conferencia Nacional de Ingeniería Estruc tural. Veracrúz, Ver. (Mayo 1986).

9) Bertero, V.V., "The Mexico Earthquake of September 19, 1985. Performance of building structures". Proc. of the 2nd International Engineering and Technology Conference AMIME/SHPE. Mexico City, Mexico (Aug. 1986)

10) Aktan, A.E., and Bertero, V.V., "States of the Art and Practice in the Optimun Seismic Design and Analytical Response Prediction of R/C Frame wall Structures". Re-- port No. UCB/EERC-82/06. Earthquake Engineering Research Center, Univ. of California, Berkeley, CA. (July 1982)

11) Feld, L.S., "Superstructure for 1,350-ft. World Trade Center", Civil Engineering. A.S.C.E., New York, (June 1971) p. 66.

12) Wiesner, K.B.," Taming Lively Buildings"., Civil Engine
    ering, A.S.C.E. New York (June 1986) p. S4

13) Mahmoodi, P., "Structural Dampers", Journal of the Struc
    tural Division, Proceedings of the A.S.C.E., New York,
    (Aug. 1969)

14) Bergman, D.M., and Hamson, R.D., "Characteristics of Vis
    coelastic Mechanical Damping Devices." Proceedings of -
    the Applied Technology Council Seminar on Base Isolation
    and Passive Energy Dissipation (ATC-17), San Francisco,
    (March 1986).

15) Scholl, R.E., "Brace Dampers: An Alternative Structural
    System for Improving the Earthquake Rerformance of Buil
    dings", Proceedings of The Eight World Conference on --
    Earthquake Engineering, San Francisco, (July 1984)

16) Scholl, R. and Martínez-Romero, E. "Earthquake Retrofit
    Design of a 12-Story Building using Structural Dampers".
    Proc. of the 2nd International Engineering and Techno--
    logy Conference, AMIME/SHPE. Mexico City, Mexico (Aug.
    1986).

Repairing and Strengthening of Reinforced Concrete
Buildings Damaged in the 1985 Mexico City Earthquake

Jesus Iglesias *

This paper describes briefly the criteria and techniques used for the repairing and strengthening of reinforced concrete buildings damaged in Mexico City during the 1985 earthquakes. It is based on the review of more than 60 buildings being repaired and strengthened, which is being carried out by the Metropolitan Autonomous University with the support of the Public Works Department of the Federal District and the National Council of Science and Technology. Damage assessment, strengthening schemes and the most commonly used techniques for shoring, bracing and repairing of buildings are discussed.

Damage Assessment

In accordance with the Emergency Regulations of October 18, 1985 (ref 1), the owners of buildings damaged by the earthquakes are required to submit to the authorities for review a technical report showing whether the damage affects the stability of the building. If this is the case, major repairing and strengthening of the structure according to a design performed under the new regulations are necessary. The authorities have prepared special format for the abovementioned technical report (ref 2), which includes a classification of the types of damage suffered by the structure and the foundation. This report must be prepared by a specialist in structural design approved by authorities.

Based on the importance of the reported damage, the structural specialist indicates whether major repairing and strengthening are needed. In this case, he must also submit drawings, calculations and a construction program. Often, the authorities have requested a second opinion on the report and the proposed repairing and strengthening scheme before a license is granted.

* Professor, Universidad Autónoma Metropolitana, Departamento de Mate-
riales, Av. San Pablo 180, México 02200 D.F.

The demolition of a building also requires the submittal of the report, indicating the reasons why it is necessary and a description of the proposed method. In general, the decisions to demolish a building have been based mainly on economic and social factors.

In some cases, when the damage in the lower stories of the structure are minor, the solution has consisted in demolishing only the upper stories and repairing the remaining ones.

Temporary Shoring and Bracing

The Emergency Regulations require damaged structures to be shored for vertical loads and braced for 25% of the lateral loads estimated according to the abovementioned rules and taking into account the live loads that will exist during construction.

Figure 1. Shoring with timber elements

Figure 3. Shoring with tubular scaffolding

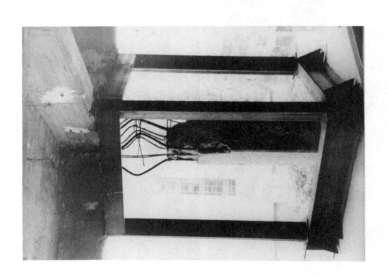

Figure 2. Shoring with steel elements

The most commonly used elements have been timber elements (fig 1) steel elements (fig 2) and tubular scaffolding (fig 3).

In severely damaged buildings, bracing for the specified lateral loads has proved so expensive that the bracing actually used is only nominal (figs 1, 3).

Design Procedures

One of the most common difficulties encountered in designing the repairing and strengthening schemes has been the fact that the original drawings and calculations are not available. Very often only the architectural drawings exist. This lack of adequate information sometimes made it necessary to determine the characteristics of the building from measurements and observations at the job site.

The properties of concrete are usually obtained with the aid of cores and the Schmidt hammer. The position and number of reinforcement bars may be determined by locally removing concrete cover and in some cases with the aid of the Pachometer, but when it is not possible to get reliable information, the existing reinforcement is usually ignored in the design.

Soil-exploration is carried out, specially if settlement or tilting of the building have occurred.

The design strategy is based in general on an interpretation of the observed damage, and an attempt is made to correct the causes producing it and to adapt the design to the requirements of the function of the building. The most common objectives are:

Stiffening and strengthening the structure.

Eliminating discontinuities and irregularities in plan and elevation

Repairing and strengthening of structural elements.

Repairing of foundation when severe settlement and tilting exist.

Seismic loads, specially in tall buildings, have been usually determined by modal analysis and the design spectra of the Emergency Regulations. However, in many cases a static analysis has been considered adequate.

With regard to detailing of the steel reinforcement, it has been very difficult to comply with the requirements of the Emergency Regulations, a fact which has compelled designers to apply them with considerable looseness. This is also the case with friction pile foundations, specially if there has not been settlement or tilting after the earthquakes.

Repairing of Structural Elements

The most commonly used methods for repairng damaged structural

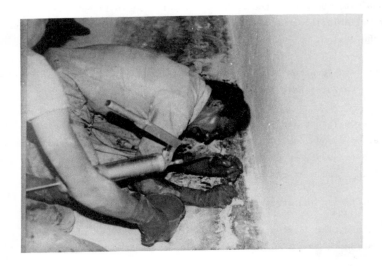

Figure 4. Crack injection of a damaged slab

elements are:

Resin Injections. Very frequently, epoxy resins have been injected in cracks of damaged elements. The equipment used varies from grease guns (fig 4) to high pressure injection machines.

Replacement of Damaged Parts. When the longitudinal reinforcement has buckled, the ties are ruptured and the concrete has been crushed, the removal and replacement of the damaged parts is often carried out. Sometimes, hydraulic jacks have been used to recover the original geometry of columns (fig 5).

Figure 5.   Replacement process of damaged
parts in columns.

Strengthening of Structural Elements

The most commonly used techniques for strengthening structural elements are:

Reinforced Concrete Jacketing. This technique has been extensively used for the strengthening of beams and columns. In some cases it has

been applied only within the story as a local strengthening, but in
general continuity is achieved by passing the new longitudinal bars
through holes drilled in the slab (fig 6).

Figure 6.   Reinforced concrete jacketing of beams
and columns

Steel Jacketing. Local strengthening of columns has been frequently
accomplished by jacketing with steel elements (angles and straps)
(fig 7).

External vertical clamps (fig 8) or steel straps attached with epoxy
resins (fig 9), have been often used for local strengthening of beams.

Steel profiles have also found application for the strengthening of
column capitals in waffle slab systems (fig 10).

Figure 7. Jacketing of column with angles
and straps

Figure 8. Strengthening of beam with steel clamps

Figure 9.   Strengthening of beam with steel
            straps attached with epoxy resins

Figure 10.   Strengthening og column capital

Introduction of New Structural Elements

Incorporation of new structural components in damaged buildings has been the most common solution for stiffening and strengthening the structure and eliminating descontinuities and irregularities in plan and elevation. The types of structural elements used are:

Concrete Walls. The addition of new reinforced concrete shear walls (fig 11) has been the most common practice. Usually, the main longitudinal reinforcement situated at the wall ends is forming part of the jacketing of the existing columns and passes continuously along the entire height of the wall.

Figure 11. Reinforcement of added shear wall

Reinforced concrete infilled walls with local strengthening of existing columns (fig 12) has also been used in several cases.

Figure 12. Reinforcement of infilled wall

Frames and Trusses. If the function of the building or the
concentration of loads on the foundation caused by the addition of new
walls limits their use, then the incorporation of frames and trusses,
either of reinforced concrete (fig 13) or steel elements (fig 14), has
been the alternative.

Foundations

Repair and strengthening of foundations is mainly due to two types of
problems: the change of loads on the foundation by strengthening the
structure and the failure of the foundation itself.

In the first case, the most common practice has been the reinforced
concrete jacketing of basement beams and the addition of new piles.
Generally, segmented concrete piles have been used driven by hydraulic
jacks (fig. 15).

If the building has suffered excessive and non uniform settlement,

Figure 13. Addition of a reinforced concrete frame

Figure 14. Addition of steel elements bracing

Figure 15. Driving of a concrete pile segment

Figure 16. Control pile

the addition of new piles in combination with ballast and excavation has been used to control the movement of the structure. In this case, control piles have often been employed (fig 16).

Conclusions

The 1985 Mexico earthquakes, damaged hundreds of buildings at Mexico City. The great number of structures that are now being repaired and strengthened are subject to many different criteria and techniques, which in several cases lack the appropriate analytical and experimental support. The success of all this work will finally be tested by the next earthquakes.

Aknowledgement

The author gratefully acknowledges the assistance of professor Francisco Robles in the elaboration of this paper.

References

1.   "Normas de emergencia en materia de construcción para el Distrito Federal", Diario Oficial, vol 392, No. 34, October 18, 1985.

2.   "Dictamen técnico para evaluación de edificios". Secretaría General de Obras, Departamento del Distrito Federal, México. D.F., 1985.

EMERGENCY REGULATIONS AND THE NEW BUILDING CODE

By **Emilio Rosenblueth,*** Hon. M. ASCE

Abstract. The 1942 Federal District Building Code was crude and overoptimistic. The 1957 earthquake prompted the drafting of emergency regulations, modern and more realistic. They evolved into the 1966 and 1976 Codes. The latter had an ultimate strength format with explicit recognition of ductility, specified dynamic and static analyses and contained many innovations. Effects of the 19 September 1985 earthquake indicated that the code was insufficiently explicit in some respects and insufficiently conservative in others. The ensuing emergency regulations corrected conspicuous deficiencies, particularly concerning the high amplification on soft ground and the reduction in effective ductility in some failure modes, due to the motion's exceptional duration. A new code is due in October 1986. Research in progress is described which will serve as basis for the new code. Of special interest is knowledge acquired about tectonics, seismicity, local soil effects, soil-structure interaction and nonlinear structural behavior.

Introduction

The first earthquake resistant provisions in the country date from the 1942 Federal District Building Code (1). They responded to the severe earthquake of 1941 (M_S = 7.7). They were timid and rudimentary. Buildings under 16 m (52 ft) in height were exempted. Ordinary taller structures were to be designed for a uniform 0.025 g, and hospitals and the like for twice as much, with a 33% increase in assigned stresses. Masonry walls and partitions were not allowed credit in resisting lateral forces.

The sobering event of 28 July 1957 (M_S = 7.7) gave rise to the first modern provisions, even if still in a working stress format and permitting only static analysis. They were prepared in four weeks, extensively discussed with engineers and architects, and became law as a set of emergency regulations in December of that year (2). They microzoned the Federal District into areas according to the soil conditions; raised the base shear coefficients considerably on the softer ground, specified horizontal acceleration proportional to elevation above ground, and required a double analysis for frames with filler walls: one with full, lateral forces, recognizing the filler wall contributions and the other with half those forces neglecting these contributions.

---

*Professor, Intituto de Ingeniería, Universidad Nacional Autónoma de México, 04510 DF, Mexico. National Researcher, Mexico.

The regulations were revised. A new code was essentially ready in 1962 and legally approved in 1966 (3). A more thorough revision was practically complete in 1972 and became law in 1976 (4). It was in force when the September 1985 earthquake occurred. It contained rather advanced earthquake resistant provisions. September 1985 seems to have proved that they were not sufficiently conservative. A new set of emergency regulations were issued a month after the main shock (5), with the commitment of producing a fully revised code by October this year.

After reviewing the 1976 Building Code, the present paper describes the 1985 Emergency Regulations and current research intended to serve as basis for the new building code.

The 1976 Code

This is an ultimate-strength code.

Structures are classified into groups according to their intended use: A, very important such as hospitals; B, most ordinary structures; C, low fences and temporary warehouses. Design seismic forces are specified for those in group B; for A they should be multiplied by 1.3. Earthquake resistant design is not required for group C.

Structures are classified according to type, and a table of nominal ductility factors Q is included. Among other requirements to allow assuming the higher Qs, the ratio of the smallest to the average story-shear load factor (resisting divided by acting story-shear) has to exceed certain limits. The purpose is to prevent the weak-story structural solution when adopting high values of Q. The range of specified Qs covers from 1 to 6. As far is known no one ever designed with Q in excess of 4, as it would have demanded compliance with quite strict limitations.

The Federal District is divided into zones according to the Code, in rough agreement with the zonation of 1957 Emergency Regulations (Fig. 1). The soil in zone I ("hilly"), mostly in the west of Federal District, is hard and consists essentially of volcanic tuff and dense cohesionless material with no more than 3 m (10 ft) of clay. In the transition zone, -- zone II -- the clay layers do not exceed 20 m (66 ft) in total thickness. This thickness is exceeded in the lake bed zone (zone III). A fourth zone embraces areas where there is not enough information to allow classification into one of the first three. The zoning was chosen because it was closely correlated with the distribution of damage to buildings in 1957, most of it having occurred to structures within zone III, and because evidence of the importance of local soil effects on damage distribution was incontestable. Such evidence was reinforced by results of analyses that predicted the spectra of moderate earthquakes with good accuracy (6, 7).

For each of the first three zones the Code specifies an acceleration spectrum. The one for zone I appears in Fig. 2. Spectral ordinates are to be divided by the reduction factor Q', which is equal to Q when the period of vibration T exceeds T_1, and is interpolated between 1 and Q for shorter periods, producing the design spectra shown in the figure.

The spectral shapes are intended to cover uncertainties in computed natural periods and variations in the site prevailing periods.

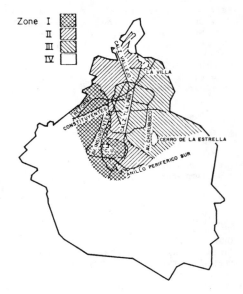

FIG. 1.- The 1976 Building Code Microzoning

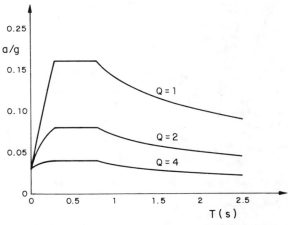

FIG. 2.- Design Acceleration Spectra for Zone I, 1976 Code

The Code allows use of four methods of analysis. The simplified method is applicable to regular structures with bearing walls provided their height does not exceed 13 m (43 ft). It calls for a set of base shear coefficients and horizontal accelerations proportional to elevation above ground and does not require computation of story torsions, of overturning moments, of drifts nor of combined action of ground motions in perpendicular directions.

The static method admits two variants and is restricted to structures up to 60 m (197 ft) tall. The first variant does not require estimating periods of vibration. The base shear coefficient is made equal to the maximum design spectral acceleration divided by Q. Horizontal accelerations are taken proportional to elevation above ground. The second variant allows reducing the base shear coefficient in proportion to the design spectral ordinate as a function of the fundamental period of vibration computed from Rayleigh's quotient. When $T > T_2$ horizontal accelerations are then taken as a combination of a quantity proportional to h and one proportional to h^2, where h is elevation above ground and the fraction of the first quantity is proportional to T/T_2. This is intended to take higher modes into account. In both variants the overturning moments are reduced as a function of elevation, the statically computed story torsions are amplified dynamically and an accidental torsion is added. There are provisions for appendages and the like.

The Code goes into some detail concerning modal analysis. It also allows step-by-step dynamic analysis using representative accelerograms.

Since the 1957 Emergency Regulations a presumably generous separation was required between adjacent structures to prevent pounding. This provision was rarely respected in practice. The other two provisions that one wishes had been followed more often concern the separations between filler walls and frames when design called for such separations, and the bound on the ratio of minimum to average shear story load factors so as to prevent weak-story conditions.

In retrospect we recognize that the 1976' Building Code was not sufficiently strict in requiring confinement of concrete, chiefly through use of lateral reinforcement, in specifying development lengths of longitudinal bars at intersections, in detailing design criteria for flat plates and in limiting the use of open-web steel members. The 1985 Emergency Regulations correct these and other shortcomings, at the same time calling for more conservative design, specially on zones II and III of the Federal District.

The 1985 Emergency Regulations

On the 3rd of October the President officially set up the National Reconstruction Commission. The Commission embraces several committees. The Committee for the Metropolitan Area of Mexico City is chaired by the Mayor of the Federal District and has a number of subcommittees. The Subcommittee on Norms and Construction Procedures was entrusted with producing a set of emergency regulations and commentary to these regulations, guiding the production of a manual for reinforcing existing structures, guiding a number of exploration and research projects that would give basis to the 1986 and succeeding versions of the Federal District Code and proposing the 1986 version with its commentary.

The Emergency Regulations were officially issued a month after the main shock. The Commentary (8) took two months longer. And the Subcommittee is to propose a new code in October this year.

The Emergency Regulations integrate the observations and interpretations of earthquake effects by experienced engineers, analysis of earthquake records obtained at various sites within and outside the Valley of Mexico and of their response spectra (9 - 14), descriptions of damage and their statistical analysis (15, 16) and the revision of the 1976 Code, which at the time of the main shock was under way at the Institute of Engineering of the National University of Mexico.

It was decided that the Emergency Regulations consist in no more than the changes that were deemed indispensable to the 1976 Code, both because there was no time to draft an entirely new code and so as not to tax engineers with a long list of new provisions and new concepts. Aside from administrative provisions the main changes were:

Load factors and strength reduction factors.- The format of the 1976 Code in design against collapse includes a set of load factors, one of strength reduction factors and one of reductions in nominal sections of reinforced concrete members. The design compressive strength of concrete, before applying the strength reduction factors, is taken as 0.8 times the specified f_c'. The load factors are 1.4 for unfavorable dead and live loads in structures of groups B and C and 1.5 in those of group A, 0.9 and zero for favorable dead and live loads respectively in all structures and 1.1 for combined ordinary and accidental loads. These factors were preserved. Some strength reduction factors, on the other hand, were lowered as depicted in Table 1. These modifications are mostly intended to reflect the effects of strength deterioration of unconfined concrete and of the adhesion between clay and friction piles.

Ratio of design seismic forces from group A to those for group B structures. This ratio was raised from 1.3 to 1.5. The large number of hospitals, clinics, and government office buildings that underwent collapse or severe damage prompted this increase. It is true that there were reasons to explain what happened: the hospitals and clinics affected had mostly been built before 1957 in accordance with inadequate criteria; the government office buildings affected were located in the area of maximum damage, their heights were in the most vulnerable range (7 to 15 stories), many were rented or bought from private owners and hence had been designed as belonging to group B and in several instances there was an unforseen overload of files in the upper stories. But because of the enormous dispersion in the severity of damage to nominally identical structures it was felt that a 30% increase in seismic design forces gave insufficient additional protection.

TABLE 1.— Some strength reduction factors

Material	Stress	Condition	1976 Code	1985 Regulations
Steel	Tension or shear		0.9	0.9
	Flexure		0.85-0.9	0.85-0.9
	Compression	In open-web members if $Q<3$ and in compact sections	0.75-0.85	0.75-0.85
	Compression	In open-web members if $Q \geq 3$	0.75-0.85	0.7
Reinforced concrete	Flexure		0.9	0.9
	Eccentric compression	Confined core if $Q<3$	0.85	0.85
	Eccentric compression	Confined core if $Q \geq 3$	0.85	0.6
	Eccentric compression	Unconfined core if $Q<3$	0.75	0.75
	Eccentric compression	Unconfined core if $Q \geq 3$	0.75	0.6
	Shear or torsion in beams and walls		0.8	0.8
	Shear or torsion in columns	If $Q<3$	0.8	0.8
	Shear or torsion in columns	If $Q \geq 3$	0.7	0.5
Soil	Bearing capacity		0.35	0.35
	Adhesion	Against friction piles	0.7	0.35

Design spectral ordinates. All design spectral ordinates for group B were raised 35% in zone II and 67% in zone III. They were left untouched in zone I. Elastic response spectra obtained at various sites within the Federal District apparently justified increasing spectral ordinates considerably more in zone III and reducing them in zone I (see Fig. 2). The fact, though, that the vast majority of structures in zone

III survived with little or no damage, even in the hardest hit area, despite their being designed for the 1957, 1966 or 1976 standards or for less, indicated that strength reserves, internal and radiation damping and inelastic behavior -- especially ductility -- would drastically reduce design requirements in zone III relative to elastic spectra. Later studies (17) partly confirmed this thesis. In zone I, on the other hand, the possibility of moderate earthquakes originating under the valley or its surroundings made it at least premature to lower the design requirements, as such earthquakes excite lower periods of vibration, especially on hard ground.

Live load on office floors.- A substantial increase was introduced in these loads. The clause in the Code calling for recognition of exceptional loads is preserved and a very explicit prohibition of modifying the use of a building, save with authorization of a recognized structural engineer, is spelled out.

Ductility factors.- Use of $Q = 6$ was suppressed. More stringent requirements were imposed in association with $Q = 4$ in what concerns regularity of story shear load factors, percentage of lateral forces resisted by frames and confinement of concrete; this ductility factor does not apply to frames with open-web steel members. Such steel frames, structures with flat plates (including waffle slabs) and those in which frames resisted a smaller share of lateral forces were assigned $Q = 3$. A ductility factor of 2 applied to most ordinary buildings without special transverse reinforcement in concrete members; and $Q = 1$, as in 1976, applied to tanks and other special structures.

Flat plates.- Requirements for the percentage of slab steel going through columns, for the width of column strips and for reducing effective column stiffnesses for analysis under lateral forces were spelled out and made considerably more conservative than in the 1966 and 1976 Codes. Together with the limitation on Q the new provisions reflect the high vulnerability of these structures when they were designed as was the practice in Mexico City.

Torsion.- Story eccentricities were limited to 20% of the plan dimension in the direction in which eccentricity is measured. The reason is that linear analysis does not detect torsions due to sources of eccentricity outside the linear range.

Simplified method.- The maximum height of structures whose design may be based on the simplified method of analysis was reduced from 13 to 8.5 m. Because of the increase in design accelerations all structures should now be designed for higher overturning moments. These could become significant.

Reinforcing details.- Drawings of member intersections to scale were now required. The maximum number of bars in a bundle was reduced from four to three and the maximum tie spacing in columns was lowered. The 1985 earthquake caused concrete spalling in columns, especially at corners where there was concentration of longitudinal reinforcement. There were also many instances of failure associated with insufficiency of transverse reinforcement and others with steel congestion.

Connection of filler walls to structures.- Requirements for tying or for isolating filler walls from the structure were made very explicit.

Separation between adjacent structures.- These code requirements too are made very explicit. Further, the Emergency Regulations specify that structures that were under construction in September 1985 must be made to comply with the separations required for new structures although the requirements are somewhat more liberal and less explicit for existing structures.

1986 Code

General.- It would be premature to say what changes the new building code will contain. It will no doubt incorporate conclusions derived from empirical evidence gained in 1985 but will also be guided by results of research. The following paragraphs describe the research that is in progress to provide bases for those changes. Preliminary conclusions derived from this research will be examined and interpreted in August. The research will continue and will be combined with results of other projects, to provide input to later code editions.

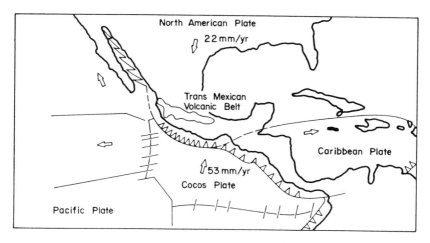

FIG. 3.- Subduction of Cocos Plate

Tectonics (18).- As a consequence of horizontal compression at ocean ridges and of the action of gravity and drag forces due to convection currents in the mantle, the Cocos plate subducts under the North American Plate (Fig. 3). It apparently breaks into several blocks having dip angles of between 10° and 15°. Earthquakes caused by slip between the Caribbean and North American Plates and between the latter and the Pacific Plate reach Mexico City with intensities too low to affect design.

As each segment of the Cocos Plate reaches a depth at which it melts it emerges as magma. The surface manifestation of this is the Trans-Mexican Volcanic Belt, which is subjected to negative bending moments. Other stresses operate on the North American Plate in the rest of the country.

Over long periods of time the average slip between Cocos and the North American Plate is in the NNE-SSW direction. Temporarily superimposed on this there are alternating, small displacements parallel to the Pacific Trench, probably responsible for the systems of faults marked A and B in Fig. 4, which underlay the volcanic belt, while system C is associated with tensions induced by upward flowing magma.

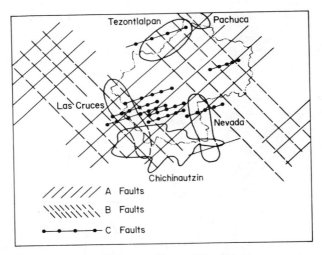

FIG. 4.- Valley of Mexico

Geology of the Valley of Mexico (18).- The Chichinautzin Range (Fig.5) is 600 000 yr old. Its rise closed the Valley of Mexico to the south, making of it an enclosed basin. Much older ranges come from rising magma due to melting of the lower portion of the North American Plate as it is heated by the surging molten Cocos Plate, while the younger ranges have been formed directly by the magma from this plate.

The basin determined the formation of an extensive lake during glacial periods. Present remnants are Lakes Texcoco, Xochimilco and Chalco.

Mostly clay and some silt were deposited during the glacial periods, and mostly sand, gravel and boulders during the interglacial ones. Fig. 5 is a typical boring log in the center of the city. We find an archeologic fill usually 1-3 m (3-10 ft) thick followed by soft clay with water contents of up to 400 percent with sand lenses; the "first hard layer" of silty sand at depths of about 30 m (98 ft) with a thickness of 1-3 m (3-10 ft); a second more compact clay layer having water contents up to 200 percent; the "second hard layer," again silty sand, followed by fairly compact deposits of variable grain size; occasionally in this formation one finds compact clay: remnants of old glacial age lakes. The hard layers dip toward Lake Texcoco, the first such layer becoming thinner and disappearing, while the water content of the clay increases, exceptionally exceeding 600 percent. At the center of Lake Texcoco, rock (the Balsas Upper Cretaceous formation) was met at a depth of 2065 m (6675 ft). Exploration of the valley's subsoil is in process, with determination of mechanical properties in the field and in the laboratory, including wave velocities.

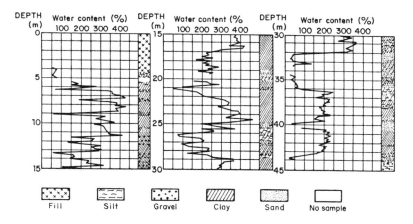

FIG. 5.- Log in Center of the City, After Ref. 19

Earthquake generation.- From the viewpoint of the seismicity of the Federal District we must consider several areas as earthquake sources. First, the fault systems under the Valley of Mexico and in its vicinity. Earthquakes are specially frequent at intersections of the main faults, where they have reached magnitude (M_b) 5 during the present century. In the rest of the valley and surroundings M_b has not exceeded 4.

The maximum magnitude (M_S) of events originating during the last century in the rest of the North American Plate has been 7.1. The potentially most active faults have been identified. Then there are the earthquakes caused directly by subduction, near the Pacific coast, with a maximum M_S of 8.2. Finally we must consider those originating in tension fractures in the Cocos plate after it has subducted, with a maximum known magnitude M_S of 8.

The non-Poisson nature of the generating process of high-magnitude events originating near the Pacific coast must be taken into account. There is a high probability of a major earthquake with focus in the Acapulco (Guerrero) Gap (just WNW of Acapulco) during the next several years. As a first approximation it is assumed that this earthquake will certainly occur in the immediate future, although its magnitude is being treated as a random quantity, while all others are regarded as generated by a Poisson process.

Local effects.- Local soil effects on earthquake characteristics in the Valley of Mexico are dramatic. For low-intensity motions they have been, in general, satisfactorily predicted using linear one-dimensional analysis (20). For the earthquake of 19 September 1985 there is need to recognize nonlinear soil behavior. This can be done approximately by resorting to equivalent linearization. There are doubts, however, as to the method's accuracy and as to the relevance of two- and three-dimensional effects, especially surface waves at sites where records have not been obtained. The following projects are under way; more accurate nonlinear one-dimensional analyses; rigorous analysis of two-dimensional stratified domains with irregular boundaries and oblique incidence of body waves (21); approximate analyses of more realistic two-dimensional models using a very rapid scheme, with practically no upper frequency limit (22), and rigorous analysis of axially symmetric stratified domains with arbitrary boundaries (23).

Methods are being developed for more accurate three-dimensional models of the Valley of Mexico, allowing for incoming surface waves and oblique incidence of body waves. (Three-dimensional analyses using conventional finite elements are out of the question.)

Existing networks of seismographs and strong-motion instruments in and outside the Valley of Mexico are being substantially increased. Some instruments will be installed underground.

One purpose of the analytical studies is to allow a finer microzonation of the valley than the one produced in 1957. Its need is evident from the facts that the recorded peak ground acceleration varies by a factor of about 2.0 in each of the three zones and that the prevailing ground period of vibration goes from about 0.5 to 1.5 s in the transition zone and from 1.5 to 5.0 s in the lake bed zone.

These studies are being supplemented with analyses of microtremor spectra obtained by Kobayashi et al. (24, 25) at 95 sites within the valley. Additional microtremor spectra will be obtained by the Institute of Engineering.

Soil—structure interaction.- Different foundation types are being analyzed for soil conditions and earthquake spectra typical of various sites within the Federal District. Finite element analyses are being used. Field and laboratory tests are being performed to study the behavior of piles under earthquake excitation.

Nonlinear structural behavior.- Projects in progress include analyses of the effects of the vertical variation of mass and stiffness in buildings and of story torsions in the linear and nonlinear ranges.

Local materials.- Local sources of good aggregates for concrete were depleted many years prior to 1985. Even the "good" aggregates of decades ago had smaller unit weight and modulus of elasticity than those acceptable by world standards; these features became more pronounced in recent years. Unit weights over 10% below world standards and moduli of elasticity as low as 57% of those standards were common. There are doubts about the behavior of such concrete in some modes of failure when subjected to seismic loads. A research project is being carried out to aid in intepreting earthquake effects on existing structures and the Federal District Department has issued provisions permitting only the better aggregates in structures. Such aggregates can be brought in from nearby locations or obtained by washing local materials.

Dynamic structural properties.- Natural periods and modes of vibration of several buildings are being measured under ambient vibrations (26). Measurements are throwing light on such matters as soil-structure interaction. A few forced-vibration tests are also contemplated. Some buildings will be provided with strong-motion instruments to elucidate their behavior when subjected to earthquakes.

Behavior of actual structures.- Analysis of the performance of damaged and undamaged structures, including those strengthened after previous earthquakes, is expected to throw much light on the influence of various structural characteristics.

Concluding Remarks

The evolution of earthquake resistant provisions in the building codes for Mexico's Federal District has closely followed the experience gained in Mexico City with every major earthquake since 1941. It has incorporated as well the experience accumulated in other cities of the world and, increasingly, the results of research. Because conditions in the Federal District differ much from those in other major cities, the codes must rely heavily on local experience and on research that takes into account local conditions.

The following salient lessons learned in 1985 have determined most clauses in the ensuing emergency regulations and most research projects that will guide the drafting of the 1986 Building Code.

1 Earthquake magnitude and focal distance contain only part of the information required for characterizing ground motion, even on firm ground. Given the magnitude, focal distance and local soil properties, the peak ground acceleration, spectral shape and earthquake duration can easily vary over wide ranges.

2 Large-magnitude earthquake generation occurs according to processes that can differ significantly from Poisson processes.

3 Local effects are very significant and justify a detailed microzonation. One-dimensional analyses of stratified media give

a first approximation to earthquake characteristics on the ground surface. Efficient methods are being developed to incorporate two- and three-dimensional effects.

4   Soil-structure interaction can significantly alter structural response.

5   Structural response to narrow-band disturbances can be much more reduced through nonlinear behavior -- especially through ductile behavior -- than response to wide-band disturbances. These benefits decrease appreciably for very rigid structures.

6   Strength deterioration is sensitive to the duration of motion. In some modes of failure under long-lasting excitation it more than counterbalances the benefits of ductility. This is particularly true of unconfined reinforced concrete and of adhesion between sensitive clay and friction piles.

7   Structural safety is much dependent on the vertical distribution of strength as compared with acting forces.

8   Story torsion can be induced by asymmetry in the nonlinear range, undetected in linear analysis.

9   The safety of reinforced concrete structures subjected to major earthquakes depends much on the quality of aggregates.

Acknowledgments

Writing of the present paper was partly supported by the Consejo Nacional de Ciencia y Tecnología. I am grateful to Roberto Meli, Mario Ordaz and Francisco J. Sánchez-Sesma for their input to the paper, critical revision of the manuscript and valuable suggestions.

Appendix I.- References

1   Departamento del Distrito Federal, "Reglamento de Construcciones para el Distrito Federal," *Diario Oficial de la Federación*, México (Jul. 1942).

2   Departamento del Distrito Federal, "Normas de Emergencia al Reglamento de Construcciones para el Distrito Federal," *Diario Oficial de la Federación*, México (Dec. 1957).

3   Departamento del Distrito Federal, "Reglamento de Construcciones para el Distrito Federal," *Diario Oficial de la Federación*, México (Feb. 1966).

4   Departamento del Distrito Federal, "Reglamento de Construcciones para el Distrito Federal," *Diario Oficial de la Federación*, México (Dic. 1976). Also "Normas Técnicas Complementarias del Reglamento de las Construcciones para el Distrito Federal" (15 Apr. 1977).

5   Departamento del Distrito Federal, "Normas de Emergencia al Reglamento de Construcciones para el Distrito Federal," *Diario Oficial de la Federación*, México (Oct. 1985).

6   Rosenblueth, E., "Teoría del diseño sísmico sobre mantos blandos," *Ediciones ICA*, Serie B, 14, Mexico (Aug. 1953).

7   Rosenblueth, E., Herrera, I. and Rascón, O.A., "Earthquake spectrum prediction for the Valley of Mexico", *Proc. 3rd World Conference on Earthquake Engineering*, New Zealand, Vol I (Jan. 1965), pp 61-74.

8   Subcomité de Normas y Procedimientos de Construcción, Comité de Reconstrucción del Area Metropolitana de la Ciudad de México, "Comentarios a las Normas de Emergencia al Reglamento de Construcciones del D F," *Instituto de Ingeniería*, UNAM (Jan. 1986).

9   Prince, *et al.*, "Acelerogramas en Ciudad Universitaria del sismo del 19 de septiembre de 1985," *Instituto de Ingeniería*, UNAM, México, Informe IPS-10A (20 Sep. 1985).

10 Mena, R. *et al.*, "Acelerogramas en el Centro SCOP de la Secretaría de Comunicaciones y Transportes, sismo del 19 de septiembre de 1985," *Instituto de Ingeniería*, UNAM, México, Informe IPS-10B (21 Sep. 1985).

11 Quaas, R. *et al.*, "Los dos acelerogramas del sismo de septiembre 19 de 1985, obtenidos en la Central de Abastos de México, D.F.," *Instituto de Ingeniería*, UNAM, México, Informe IPS-10C (23 Sep. 1985).

12 Prince, J. *et al.*, "Espectros de las componentes horizontales registradas por los acelerogramas digitales de México, D.F., sismo del 19 de septiembre de 1985. Acelerogramas en Viveros y en Tacubaya," *Instituto de Ingeniería*, UNAM, México, Informe IPS-10D (1 Oct. 1985).

13 Mena, E. *et al.*,"Análisis del acelerograma 'Zacatula' del sismo del 19 de septiembre de 1985," *Instituto de Ingeniería*, UNAM, México, Informe IPS-10E (Oct. 1985).

14 Mena, E. *et al.*, "Respuesta sísmica observada en el Lago de Xochimilco-Chalco durante el sismo de septiembre 19 de 1985," *Instituto de Ingeniería*, UNAM, Mexico, Informe IPS-10F (Apr. 1985).

15 Meli, R. *et al.*, "Efectos de los sismos de septiembre de 1985 en las construcciones de la Ciudad de México. Aspectos estructurales," Segundo Informe del Instituto de Ingeniería, UNAM, México (Nov. 1985).

16 Rosenblueth, E. and Meli, R. "The earthquake of 19 September 1985 Effects in Mexico City," written for the Subcommittee on Norms and Procedures, Committee for Mexico City's Metropolitan Area, National Reconstruction Commission, Mexico, *Concrete International*, 8, 4 (May 1986), pp 23-34.

17 Meli, R. and Avila, J. "Respuesta inálastica ante el acelerograma
    del 19 de septiembre de 1985," *Memorias V Congreso Nacional de
    Ingeniería Estructural*, Veracruz, Ver. (May. 1986), pp A5-01—A5-11.

18 Mooser, F., "Tectonics of the Valley of Mexico," to be published by
    Instituto de Ingeniería, UNAM (1986).

19 Marsal, R. and Mazari, M., *El Subsuelo de la Ciudad de México*, 2nd
    ed., UNAM, México, 1969, 3 Vols.

20 Romo, M.A. and Jaime, A., "Características dinámicas de las arcillas
    del Subsuelo del Valle de México y respuesta del análisis sísmico
    Primera etapa," *Instituto de Ingeniería*, UNAM, Internal Report,
    Proy 6504 (1986).

21 Bravo, M.A., Sánchez-Sesma, F.J., and Chávez-García, F.J., "Ground
    motion on stratified alluvial deposits for incident SH waves," *Bull.
    Seism. Soc. Am.*, submitted (May. 1986).

22 Sánchez-Sesma, F.J., Chávez-García, F.J. and Bravo, M.A., "Seismic
    response of a class of alluvial valleys for incident SH waves,"
    Bull. Seism. Soc. Am., submitted (May. 1986).

23 Sánchez-Sesma, F.J., "Diffraction of elastic waves by three-
    dimensional surface irregularities," *Bull. Seism. Soc. Am.*, *73*, 6
    (1983), pp 1621-16-36.

24 Kobayashi, H., Seo, K., Midorikawa, S. and Kataoka, S.,"Measurement
    of microtremors in an around Mexico, D.F.", Report on Seismic
    Microzoning Studies of the Mexico Earthquake of September 19, 1985,
    Part I, *The Graduate School of Nagatsuto*, Tokyo Institute of
    Technology, Yokohama, Japan (Jan. 1986).

25 Kobayashi, H., Seo, K. and Midorikawa, S., "Estimated strong ground
    motions in the Mexico City due to the Michoacan, Mexico earthquake
    of Sept. 19, 1985 based on characteristics of microtremor", Report
    on Seismic Microzoning Studies of the Mexico Earthquake of
    September 19, 1985, Part II, *The Graduate School of Nagatsuto*, Tokyo
    Institute of Technology, Yokohama, Japan (Feb. 1986).

26 Rodríguez, N., "Análisis experimental de vibraciones en edificios",
    Memorias V Congreso Nacional de Ingeniería Estructural, Veracruz,
    Ver. (May. 1986), pp. B8-01—B8-11.

Appendix II.- Notation

a_0 = ordinate at $T = 0$ in design acceleration spectra
h = height above ground
Q = ductility factor assumed in design
Q' = force reduction factor for $T < T_1$
T = natural period of vibration
T_1, T_2 = characteristic periods in design spectra

THOUGHTS ON A DIFFERENT APPROACH TO SEISMIC DESIGN CODES

Oscar de Buen[1] , M. ASCE

ABSTRACT.

The aim of this paper is to show that some of the principles on --
which conventional structural design is based are not directly applicable to seismic design. Seismic design, and the corresponding design co
des, have to incorporate new indexes of comparison based on structural
behavior under real earthquakes. Specifically, lessons about structu--
ral behavior learned as a consequence of 1985 Mexico earthquakes must -
be incorporated in our seismic design codes.

INTRODUCTION.

As most human activities, structural design is full of uncertain--
ties. The uncertainties in engineering problems arise from the inhe- -
rent variability of natural phenomena, the lack of understanding of many causes and effects involving physical phenomena and the scarcity of
information about many of them. The future can never be exactly predic
ted, but the possibility of occurrence of certain events must be considered and the corresponding probabilities investigated.

The goal of structural design is to obtain structures that have an
acceptable probability, uniform for all structures of the same type, of
not becoming unserviceable during the building's life. The designer has to
consider, simultaneously, aspects related to the building's operation,
aesthetics and economy involving its total final cost, including design,
construction, maintenance, reparation and, eventually, replacement. - -
Structural design must, then, be based on a concept of security which -
takes into account the probability of failure.

Today's knowledge makes it impossible to determine, from a probabi
lity point of view, what an acceptable risk is, and it is also impossible to determine the life span of a given type of construction. Mechanical properties of materials, dimensions of structural members and - -
quality of construction are also random variables, and the importance -
of errors in the mathematical modeling of structures and the lack of --
precision of analysis and design methods is, and will always be, highly
uncertain.

The profession has not enough information on topics as basic as --
the variation of parameters which govern the strength of materials and
structural members or the design values of dead and live loads, and - -
there are uncertainties due to the idealizations and simplifications --
needed to obtain the analytical model of the very complex real construc
tions, to the construction process, to residual stresses in steel struc
tures and shrinkage or plastic flow in concrete structures, to unknown
differential settlements of supports, and to structural degradation; --

---

[1] Prof. Emeritus of Civil Engineering, Universidad Nacional Autonoma de
Mexico. Consulting Structural Engineer.

these uncertainties will always exist, notwithstanding future develop--
ments in structural engineering.

Dead and live loads can be evaluated fairly accurately, but uncertainties related to accidental loads, like wind and earthquake, are con
siderable, as natural phenomena are not under man's control. Nevertheless, strong winds are common, and our knowledge of their main characte
ristics is sufficient enough to evaluate their design values reliably.-
However, the situation changes completely with respect to earthquakes,_
given the present (and probably future) inability to describe the - -
strongest ground shaking that might possibly occur at any specified location.

We have enough information on material and member response under -
static loads, but we lack the equivalent knowledge for dynamic loads, -
although this has been a field of great activity during the last couple
of decades.

The design of structures to be built in earthquake active areas is,
then, a problem with no apparent solution: we have to choose structu--
ral systems and to design their component elements to resist unknown --
loads employing response mechanisms whose behavior is far from unders--
tood.

CONVENTIONAL METHODS FOR ANALYSIS AND DESIGN OF STRUCTURES.

The aim of the analysis and design methods currently employed in -
structural engineering is to compare the foreseeable behavior of new --
constructions, not yet built, with previously erected similar structu--
res, whose behavior is known to have been satisfactory. Since the be--
ginning of the nineteenth century, Navier proposed to apply formulas ba
sed on the theory of elasticity to existing structures, whose behavior_
had been adequate, to evaluate working stresses for different materials,
and then to use them in new designs to obtain safety factors similar to
those of the existing buildings.

Nowadays we know that stresses or deformations computed by methods
based on elastic linear response of materials and structures have no --
relation whatsoever with the behavior of actual constructions; neverthe
less, most of our modern structures are still being designed by follo--
wing the method pioneered by Navier 160 years ago, so that computed - -
stresses are nothing more than a comparison index between new and old -
structures.

Stresses are not the only comparison index; in plastic design - --
strengths are compared; in other cases, the comparison index is the - -
strength of critical members or sections, maximum deformations, or dyna
mic characteristics; we always use parameters that can be easily evalua
ted and which provide the opportunity to predict the behavior of future
structures by comparison with similar structures built in the past.

Design methods based on load and resistant factors have been incor
porated in most recent building codes. Their goal is to obtain structu
res whose design strength has a sufficiently low probability of being -
exceeded by the actions corresponding to each significant limit state.-
To reach that goal, resistance factors, generally smaller than one, and
load factors, greater than one in most cases, are used to take into - -
account the possibility that actual actions exceed design actions, and_
that actual strengths turn out to be smaller than nominal. Statistical
and probabilistic analyses are then used to determine load and resis- -
tance factors in order to arrive to an adequately low probability of --

failure. Nevertheless, a calibration process has to be used to evaluate the more important parameters that are needed to obtain, through the new design method, structures not significantly different from those -- built until now. That probability and structural reliability theories are not capable to solve the problem of structural safety by themselves is then acknowledged. Design of new structures is still based on comparison with already built structures.

SEISMIC DESIGN.

The design of structures to be built in seismic areas is accomplished by following methods similar to those used for any type of structure, regardless of their environment. Dynamic actions due to soil motion are generally translated into "equivalent" static lateral loads, - whose magnitude depends on the structure's weight and on the design - - seismic acceleration; horizontal loads are applied at the floors of - - high-rise buildings. Total base shear is made equal to the building's weight times an adimensional factor, the seismic coefficient. Analysis and design are made using the methods employed for structures under static load.

Uncertainties. There are many uncertainties in the method just -- described.

The most significant uncertainty is related to the selection of -- the design seismic coefficient; it depends on the unknown characteristics of the strongest earthquake that might occur during the unknown -- useful life of the building and also, to a very important degree, on -- the structure's characteristics. For example, the responses of two - - structures subject to the same earthquake can be completely different - if their height, slenderness and stiffness are different; if one of them is able to respond plastically with no loss of strength and the other - one is not; if their foundations are different.

There are many more uncertainties. How are the equivalent lateral forces distributed ? Is it enough to evaluate them by multiplying each floor weight times the seismic coefficient ? How should lateral forces be computed at different building levels ? Is it convenient to apply - a significant percentage of the total horizontal load at the top floor?. Should a dynamic analysis be made ? How do the horizontal forces dis-- tribute themselves between different lateral load resistant elements, - structural or non-structural ? Does this distribution change during an earthquake ? How do we consider dynamic eccentricities ?.

Another very important source of uncertainties arises from our -- - lack of knowledge about the dynamic response of structural elements. - Under low intensity actions their response is elastic, but under stronger loads their behavior changes. Would the structure be able to re- - sist several cycles of severe loading, in the inelastic range, without loss of strength ? Should it deteriorate gradually until, perhaps, co-llapse ? How can we evaluate the changes on stiffness due to the structure's degradation, and their effect on its behavior ?.

Choosing the design earthquake. Since engineers first started - - approaching seismic design problems rationally, it was realized that -- structures designed to support relatively low horizontal loads were - - able to resist, with no serious damage, strong earthquakes which produced lateral forces far exceeding the design loads. This was explained by assuming that a significant proportion of the seismic effects was -- resisted by the brick masonry walls used extensively in those buildings.

In the last few decades masonry walls have almost completely disappeared, and in many modern buildings they do not exist any more. Seismic coefficients have not been significantly increased, and the concept of ductility, of paramount importance in modern earthquake design, has been introduced to justify, again, small design lateral loads: structures are designed to resist a small percentage of the seismic loads corresponding to an unlimited elastic behavior on the grounds that if - - they respond adequately in the inelastic range, their own properties -- put an upper bound to the loads they have to resist. For this assumption to be true, structural members must be able to develop important - plastic deformations in localized areas, with no previous failure of -- any type and no loss of strength, under several cycles of dynamic loading.

According to the 1942 Mexico City building code - the city's first building code - it was mandatory to design office and apartment buildings that were sixteen or more meters tall (52 feet or more) to resist horizontal lateral loads corresponding to a 0.025 seismic coefficient;- accelerations were assumed constant in every floor. Schools, hospitals and other important buildings were designed for a 0.10 seismic coefficient. Constructions less than 16 m tall did not require aseismic design. Stresses were increased 33% for load combinations including seismic effects.

The basic seismic coefficient was increased to 0.06 after the July 1957 earthquake; the new value was based on displacements of the Latinoamericana Tower measured during that earthquake. According to seismicity - studies and to the behavior of structures since 1957 to 1985, that coefficient was conservative....

The 16 m limit was dropped after the 1957 earthquake, since most - of the collapsed buildings were less tall than that. They did not have, obviously, the high density of brick walls common to the 1942 buildings.

Since 1976, the seismic coefficient for office and apartment buildings built in the area of the ancient lake has been 0.24, but design was - made with loads corresponding to that coefficient divided by a ductility factor, equal to 4.0 in ordinary steel or concrete structures; as a consequence, most buildings were designed to resist loads corresponding to a 0.06 net coefficient. Accelerations were considered linearly variable, with zero intensity at street level and a maximum at the top of the - - building. Design was made assuming a 100% seismic load in one direction and 30% of the loads in an orthogonal direction. Stresses were increased 33%, or load factors decreased in an equal proportion. Schools, hospitals, and the like, were designed for loads 30% higher than ordinary buildings. The 1976 building code was in force in September 1985.

The 1976 code divides the city in three zones, according to soil - characteristics and, recognizing their influence on the propagation of earthquake waves, gives different seismic coefficients for each zone -- (0.06 is the largest, and it corresponds to the ancient lake area). - The influence of the type of foundation is not considered by any means.

The greatest uncertainty in seismic design arises from the lack of knowledge about the maximum forces that the structure will be called to resist. This makes seismic design differ completely from any other - - structural design problem. The evaluation of moments and shears on a - bridge due to traffic is difficult, due to the mobility of loads and - their dynamic effects, but all the vehicles' characteristics are known, and if their weight is increased the bridge is reinforced, another stronger bridge is built, or heavy vehicle traffic is prohibited.

We are not as fortunate in seismic design. Design is based, --
not on the strongest earthquake the buildings will have to resist, - --
which is unknown, but on the past earthquakes registered in the area. -
However, our information on past earthquakes is very limited; the first
strong motion was recorded less than 50 years ago, an instant in our --
planet's life.

Lack of rationality in modern methods of seismic design. Modern
seismic design methods, based on the traditional comparison indexes, -
are completely irrational. We cannot compare allowable stresses with
stresses produced by unknown forces, or resistances with actions we
know almost nothing about. This was shown, in a frightful way, by --
the September 19, 1985, earthquake: in some structures built on soil
corresponding to the ancient lake, accelerations were five times - - -
larger than code accelerations. Nevertheless, seismic design must be
based, even more than design under static loads, on the observed behavior, adequate or not, of real structures under real earthquakes. But
comparison indexes must be changed.

In the morning of Thursday, September 19, 1985, Mexico City - --
experienced, during two never-ending minutes, the most violent forces -
nature can unleash. Several hundred buildings were destroyed, many - -
more were severely damaged, and several thousand human lives were lost.
In spite of that tragic balance, structural engineering's most impor- -
tant conclusion derived from the events of that day is that the real --
strength of structures is much higher than the strength we try to give
them during the analysis, design and construction stages. If that were
not the case, given the earthquake intensity, duration and frequency --
content, destruction would have been much worse.

Our city was an enormous laboratory. Thousands of real buil- --
dings of every type, material and height were subjected to a violent
earthquake; some of them collapsed, some suffered different levels of -
damage and the remainder, by far the greatest percentage, resisted the
earthquake with minimum or no damage. As structural engineers, we have
to understand why some buildings collapsed and some remained undamaged;
we must learn as much as possible from that catastrophe, in order to --
plan, design and construct new buildings which will be safer and will -
decrease drastically the loss of live and property in future earthquakes.

Structures designed and built under the same building code, sub--
mitted to theoretically equal actions, had every conceivable behavior,-
from no damage to complete collapse. All of them fulfilled the code --
comparison indexes: those were, no doubt, incorrect.

The September 19 earthquake was extraordinary and unexpected. Until then the Mexico City Building Code seismic coefficients were appa--
rently correct and, even, conservative. In the several earthquakes - -
that ocurred during the almost thirty year period since 1957, structu--
res behaved well, from a strength point of view, with very few excep--
tions. There were some doubts about the convenience of increasing the
structures lateral stiffness because damages in windows and nonstruc- -
tural walls and partitions were frequent.

TOWARD A NEW APPROACH TO SEISMIC DESIGN.

No large city in the world had been struck before by an eartquake
having all the characteristics that make earthquakes specially destructive: high intensity, very long duration and almost constant periodi--
city through an important number of cycles.

Seismology researchers ask themselves if the earthquake was really unusual; they are concerned about the period of recurrence of - - - earthquakes of this type, and if they can be exceeded or not; they are_ also worried about the possibility of occurrence of earthquakes with -- different characteristics, capable to produce more severe damages in - other zones or in structures different from those more punished now. -- All those peculiarities have to be known to define design seismic for-- ces for structures to be built in the future.

These researchers are theoretically right, but the necessary - - studies on seismicity and structural reliability will take time, and - we can not stop construction. In addition to that, there is no - - reason to assume that those studies' results will be much more reliable than the research that produced the design rules in force in Sep- -- tember 1985. We do not know what will happen in ten, fifty or one -- hundred years from now, but we do know that we lack the knowledge and information required to establish seismic design intensities which -- will permit the design of safe and economically feasible structures.

As we said before, the September 19 earthquake showed that the - actual resistance of structures well conceived, designed and built, - is much higher than their intended resistance. But it also showed that that extra resistance can be easily lost because of excessive tor- -- sion, abrupt changes in stiffnes from floor to floor, shear or buck- ling failures, or connections and details wrongly planned or executed.- This is specially true for long duration earthquakes, which demand high ductility and energy absorption capacity without appreciable damage.

New building codes must, no doubt, require that structures be - designed with reasonably high seismic coefficients, and specify analysis and design procedures commensurate to the construction's importance. But those are not the only, or even the more important, aspects they must cover. Building codes must pay special attention to the -- aspects which provide buildings with that additional strength which - - makes them able to resist earthquakes stronger than the design - - - earthquake without collapse, and even with no important damage. The_ se aspects receive very scant attention in our building codes.

I believe that we have followed an excessively theoretical - - - approach in seismic design. We have depended too much on results - of theoretical research, supported on bases not too reliable, and we have forgotten that structural engineering is an art, with strong - scientific basis, but not an exact science. Given basic parameters, the solution of a problem is not unique, and structural behavior - - strongly depends upon many aspects, of difficult evaluation, not inclu_ ded in our traditional building codes.

In the design of new buildings, special attention has to be - - paid to their configuration; geometric and structural irregularities, horizontal or vertical, have to be eliminated in order to avoid excessi_ ve torsion and concentration of high ductility demand in localized - - areas, which will probably be unable to provide it. Structural and - nonstructural elements have to be carefully designed, with special care_ in their interaction, to avoid local failures which decrease the struc- ture's lateral stiffness, increase torsions and trigger progressive da-- mage. Materials and structural systems have to be carefully choosen, - analitycal models as precise as possible must be conceived ant the most_ convenient analysis and design methods utilized. The design of connec- tions and the revision of all possible causes of instability failures - must be carefully done in steel structures, and special attention has -

to be paid to reinforcement distribution, bar anchorage and shear reinforcement in concrete structures, to avoid nonductile failures. The --
construction process requires thorough supervision to detect and co- --
rrect inadequate practice and errors.

A much closer collaboration between architects, soil mechanics - -
specialists, structural engineers, builders and supervisors is needed,-
in every step of the construction process, from the planning and architectural project stages to construction and supervision.

The relationship between strength and ductility must also be carefully reviewed. In recent years, a great deal of emphasis, perhaps more than adequate, has been put on ductility. It is true that ductility
affords, generally, an economical way to resist severe seismic actions,
and provides an extra mesure of energy absortion capacity which can be
needed under very strong earthquakes. However, it is also true that it
is not, theoretically, an essential property, as it is possible to - ---
build nonductile structures if they have adequate strength. In the - -
last few decades, every strong earthquake has shown the superior perfor
mance of structures provided with vertical bracings and/or shear walls,
less ductile but stronger, and with ductility demands much smaller than
in rigid frames. Nevertheless, building codes penalize these more ri--
gid structural systems.

Another change to the approach followed until now consist of requi
ring building codes to be addresed to all the specialists who partici--
pate in the building design and construction process, and not only to -
structural engineers, who always are held responsible for the project,-
notwithstanding the fact that they have to work in a context frequently
defined by arquitects and other specialists.

Responsibilities have to be shared between code writers, city offi
cials, architects, structural engineers and builders, since all of them
contribute to the final characteristics of any completed building.

CONCLUSIONS.

We have shown that structural design, as generally used, cannot be
applied to seismic engineering, as intensity and characteristics of future earthquakes are unknown. Besides, behavior of future construc- --
tions will depend on their own properties, including their foundation,-
and the relationship between foundation, structure and seismic response
is not yet well understood. It is then clear that the most important -
phase of analysis and design is the design, as the most sophisticated -
dynamic analysis is worthless, given the enormous uncertainties in - --
earthquake actions and the impossibility of adequate modelling of - .- -
complicated real constructions. On the other hand, actual structural -
behavior has dramatically shown the importance of good design and construction practices.

It is clear that the approach followed until now in seismic engi--
neering must be changed. After many years of research to define design
earthquakes we have not yet obtained the desired results in terms of --
structural reliability and we are far from reaching them, as each new -
earthquake changes significantly our previous knowledge. On the other
hand, we have acquired important knowledge on seismic behavior of struc
tures by studying how real constructions behave under strong ground - -
motions. Given that we have to design to resist unknown actions, compa
rison indexes must be changed, switching emphasis from stresses and - -
strengths to materials, structural systems and construction details. -

I am not suggesting to drop stress and strength analysis and evaluation, but not to lose perspective that the results of computations are just - comparison indexes, useful only if they are applied to comparable situa tions.   The aim of building codes in areas subject to severe earthqua-- kes mut be to ensure that new structures are similar to previous cons-- tructions whose seismic behavior has been adequate; otherwise, very - - conservative measures have to be taken.   To reach that end, we have to establish all the necessary comparison indexes, related to materials, - structural systems, construction details, soil-foundation-structure - - interaction, relationship between structural and soil dynamic characte- ristics, importance of non-structural elements, and every other signifi cant factor.

I firmly believe that in the near future, research must concentra- te on defining those indexes, and to reach that goal it is absolutely - neccesary to understand how buildings behave under strong soil motions and, specifically, how they behaved during the September 19 earthquake. Results of the research must be evaluated by multidisciplinary groups, in which the participation of structural engineers and builders has to be much more important than in the past.

The Impact of the Construction of Public Works by the Earthquakes of September 1985

Francisco Norena Casado[1] and Carlos E. Castaneda Narvaes[2]

Abstract

The earthquake of September 19th and 20th, 1985, is discussed with emphasis on general damage. The works of the Head Office of Urban Services is described in relation to emergency response. Cooperation among government agencies is described, including the works of the Department of Construction and Hydraulic Operations, works of the Department of Public Works and Housing and its Emergency Planning Commission, and the works of the Building Control Commission.

The Earthquakes of September 19th and 20th, 1985.

The earthquakes of September 19th and 20th, 1985, which gravely affected different cities of the country, caused disastrous effects in Mexico City.

The magnitude, intensity and characteristics of such earthquakes, especially the first, exceeded the foresights of our prevailing code of November 19th, 1976. This means that although a code may not specify its provisions in terms of intensity, it does specify coefficients, minimum dimensions, properties of construction materials, methods of analyses, preliminary design, and form of quality control during construction.

The prevailing November 1976 code incorporated the emergency guidelines established after the strong earthquake of July 28th, 1957, when the Angel fell from the top of the Independence Monument. This earthquake made evident the deficiencies of the 1942 regulation which reflected the established practices of other countries and the experience from the 1941 earthquake in the state of Jalisco. The 1942 regulation exempted construction of less than five stories from seismic design. For taller construction it required the assumption of the action of static horizontal acceleration as if applied very slowly and uniformly, equal to one fortieth of the force of gravity. This was justified since the buildings designed in Japan by Tachu Naito in Tokyo for a uniform acceleration of one tenth of the force of gravity resisted exceptionally well the earthquake of 1923 which was directly responsible for 40,000 lives and through the subsequent fires for another 140,000 lives.

---

[1] Secretary General of Construction of the Federal District of Mexico.

[2] Construction Control Coordinator

Since Mexico City is less exposed to earthquakes than Tokyo, it seemed justifiable for the 1942 regulation to consider a fortieth also taking into account the use in Mexico of brick walls with scaffolding and chains (rebars) to resistant lateral forces. The 1943 earthquake, which was moderate, inspired confidence.

The severity of the 1957 earthquake generated the new regulation with more requirements than before. Nevertheless, with the earthquakes of 1962 and 1964 and their effects on construction in Mexico City and Acapulco, as well as the experience with modern buildings in other cities of the world, and the results of national and foreign research, resulted in a new regulation in 1966. This was later replaced by the 1976 code which incorporated the last known experience and was considered so advanced that it influenced the regulations of New Zealand, Canada, the United States, El Salvador, Nicaragua and Venezuela. Nevertheless, it was not possible to foresee a powerful earthquake like that of September 1985.

Basically, the 1985 earthquake differs from the others for its intensity, regularity and duration. The significant fissures in the ground, the warping of train rails, ruptured aqueducts and destruction of buildings gives this earthquake, in the zone of maximum damage in Mexico City, the intensity of nine on the modified mercalli scale, the most widely used scale in our country. In the larger part of the moderate zone the quake reached eight and even five in the area of the National University of Mexico. In Lazaro Cardenas Avenue, it also reached nine. Using the same criteria, a maximum intensity of seven can be assigned to the capital city during the 1957 earthquake.

At present we work with emergency guidelines that were issued by the Ministry of the Federal District and decreed in force by the President of the Republic, Miguel de la Madrid Hurtado as of October 18, 1985. At the present time, a new regulation is being prepared.

General Damage

The damages suffered in Mexico City were of all kinds: The loss of lives is the most lamentable even when the early hour of 7:19 a.m. spared the death of hundreds of thousands of students and workers. The drinking water system, the sewage system, the electrical and telecommunications systems were damaged. Apartment buildings, hospitals, theaters, hotels, schools, television and radio studios fell to the ground or were partially destroyed. Streets, roads, highways, and sidewalks suffered strong damages. Immediately after the earthquake, the Ministry of the Federal District with the participation of national citizens and the collaboration of foreigners, began the task of reconstruction.

The Works of the Head Office of Urban Services (DGSU)

a) Debris removal

	Trips	Cubic Meters
1985	68,363	478,599
1986	26,709	186,905
Total	96,072	1,100,169

Final disposal of debris

	Trips	Cubic Meters
1985	93,763	656,341
1986	63,404	443,828
Total	157,167	1,100,169

b) Public lighting

Total	582	services
Temporary lighting	119	
Restoration of light	246	
Light pole rehabilitation	137	

c) Solid waste collection

Total	9,324	services
From hospitals	4,576	
From shelters	4,748	

Equivalent to 18,235 cubic meters
At present, 1,600 cubic meters per week

d) Road related work

Pothole patching for 103 streets	260,836	sq. meters
Removal of dangerous facades from	1,471	buildings
Sidewalk reconstruction	43,300	sq. meters
Reconstruction of curbs	18,202	meters

e) Rescue of victims

Total	594	
Living	237	(96 rescued directly; 141 with the aid of other areas)
Dead	357	(220 rescued directly; 137 coordinated with other areas)

f) Other support efforts

Signs:

Total	130
For collapsed areas	50
For detours	80

In the neighborhood of Tepito:

Debris removal
Containers for solid waste deposit
Installation of toilets
Installation of portable showers
Surveys of needs
Coordination of voluntary workers
Water supplied by trucks
Fumigation
Support to demolition operations

Works of the Department of Construction and Hydraulic Operations

At present, Mexico City has the following water and sewage systems:

Potable water system of the Federal District:
35.8 cubic meters per second are administered via:
--Water from the basins of the Cerma and Cutzamala rivers.
--Extraction of groundwater from 784 wells from the valley
   of Mexico.
--For conducting the water there are 443 kilometers of
   aqueducts, 555 kilometers of primary lines, and 12,060
   kilometers of secondary networks.
--In storage there are 200 tanks with a total capacity of
   1.5 million cubic meters.

With this infrastructure, services are provided to 95% of the 10 million inhabitants of the Federal District, the 3% that do not have installed services are provided water by tank trucks.

Sewage System:

For the disposal of residual and stormwater there is available:
--12,184 kilometers of secondary networks
--1,208 kilometers of primary networks
--64 pumping plants with an installed capacity totalling 500 cubic meters per second.
--400 kilometers of main drains for conducting and with-drawing the water from the Valley of Mexico.

This system covers 74% of the population. The 26% that lack service are located on the perimeters of the city.

The system for treating residual water and its distribution is complementary for uses that do not require the quality of drinking water such as for filling lakes for recreational uses and for irrigation.

These systems are very extensive and complex with installations and elements which are extremely vulnerable to disastrous situations such as earthquakes. Failures in the electrical energy supply alone cause not only suspension of the drinking water supply but also in sump pumps for residential sewage. This requires special care in the maintenance of auxiliary electric generating plants. Due to the telloric movements that occurred on September 19th and 20th, 1985, these systems suffered considerable damage.

The hydraulic system was broken causing deficiencies in the supply of services. The failures occurred in the installations of the lowlands of the city, especially in the lake beds of Lake Texcoco and Lake Chalco. The installations in the west and a portion of the south of the city had practically no problems.

The earthquakes caused fractures in the aqueducts of the south west of the city, in the San Luis, Tulyehualco, Chalco and Tecomitl branches, which prevented a flow of 7,600 liters per second from being supplied, thus affecting the precincts located in the southwest and center of the city.

The main failures in these reinforced concrete aqueducts were the rupture and separation of pipe joints. The damage was repaired by substituting complete lengths which had serious fractures in the bell and spigot and by placing tie plates on the damaged joints.

By the end of October, more than a month later, a flow of 7,100 liters per second had been re-established.

In the primary network, 167 leaks were repaired in asbestos-cement and reinforced concrete pipes with diameters that varied from 20 to 48 inches. The failures were due to transverse fractures, the rupture of joints and fissures in special parts.

In the secondary network, 7,220 leaks were repaired. These leaks were caused by the rupture of special parts made of cast iron in the valve boxes, by the changes of flow direction due to clogging, by the penetration of some pipes into others, transverse fractures and breakdowns of couplings connecting right angles.

By the 30th of October, scarcely 40 days after the earthquakes, the remainder of the Chalco-Xochimilco aqueduct began operation, which had suffered 28 fractures, thereby normalizing the drinking water supply of the Federal District. Since that date service has been maintained in 16 political districts at a level similar to that before the earthquakes.

The water commission of the Valley of Mexico contributed with an additional flow of 1,734 liters per second from the Cutzamala system, which alleviated the need in various areas of the city.

Six hundred and eleven (611) million liters of water were supplied without charge through water trucks with as many as 465 trucks available provided by various states of the Republic, private enterprises, state departments, precincts of the Federal District and the Department of Construction and Hydraulic Operations. Furthermore, 715,000 plastic bags with one liter of drinking water were distributed. Eighty-nine (89) portable rubber tanks each of 11,000 liter capacity were installed mainly in the precincts of Iztaplapa, Cuauhtemoc, Iztacalco, Venustiano Carranza and Benito Juarez, supplied daily by tank trucks.

Regarding the quality control of water, 59,400 tests were made from September 19th to November 15th, 1985, to determine residual chlorine and bacteria analysis. In less than two months more tests were made than the annually scheduled 40,000 tests in the Federal District. This testing intensity has been scheduled to be maintained during 1986.

The drainage system suffered serious damages in the Piedad River (Miquel Aleman expressway), the Churubusco River, the central, eastern, west central and western deep drainage system. (Mexico City has several systems: surface, mid depth and one at the very bottom referred to as the deep drain.)

The Piedad River has separated from its connections at a length of 6,500 meters where fractured sections were repaired by caulking and restoration with concrete. The proposed integral solution is to internally line the aqueduct with reinforced concrete.

In the Churubusco River the damages that occurred between Avenue Universidad and Avenue Cinco were repaired. The major break which occurred at the intersection of Avenue Pantitlan was satisfactorily repaired in short time despite the technical and operational difficulties of the aqueduct.

The aeration pond of San Luis Tlaxiatmalco has longitudinal cracks on the bottom and in the lining of the sides. It's repair is being meticulously studied in order to avoid the contamination of water bearing strata.

The primary network, the intercepting sewer of the southern towns, suffered various fractures throughout its length, as well as various intercepting sewers that discharge in the large wasteway drain, whose main problem was the deformation due to differential settlements caused by the earthquakes.

Some wastewater pumping plants show cracks in the sump pumps which will be solved by placing a second lining in the sump.

In the deep drains, storm tanks, and intercepting sewers had minor damage.

In the residual water treatment system 50 pipe leaks were repaired in the districts of Iztapalapa, Venustiano Carranza and Benito Juarez which were checked for damages.

At the Department of Construction and Hydraulic Operation, existing data banks are being worked on to obtain curves of equal depth as caused by the earthquake.

The piezometric configuration of the aquifers of the metropolitan area is being updated in order to know its changes and levels. At present, with the participation of other offices, the system design standards and the manufacturing standards of drinking water and sewage pipe in seismic zones are being reviewed and by analyzing the possibility of using flexible joints which allow better for displacement and major deflection than the present components.

Works of the Department of Public Works and Housing and its Emergency Planning Commission

During the emergency stage, attention was given to 285 cases of damage with approximately 850 heavy machinery, 1,500 lighter machinery, and 15,000 men.

Priorities were to demolish, clean up of debris produced by collapsed buildings and to reestablish road service of the main avenues of the city.

Once cleanup work was concluded, parks were constructed on the former sites of crumbled buildings, and this with the budget and personnel from the affected geopolitical districts.

The Department of Public Works and Housing performed 2,679 expert appraisals (inspections) and 783 non-expert appraisals of structurally damaged buildings.

The Traffic and Urban Transportation Commission of the Department of the Federal District (COVITUR) performed 10,500 building inspections to help the population in ascertaining safety.

During the month of October, a few days after the earthquake, the Emergency Planning Commission was created under the Department of Public Works to coordinate and control immediate demolition work ordered by official

appraisers   (inspectors).   Also,   a General Coordination
Office for the Reconstruction Program of Schools in the
Federal District of Mexico was created and started operation
on October 15th.

With regard to the damage inflicted on roads directly
caused by the earthquake and by collapsed buildings and the
use of heavy machinery for the clean up of debris and for
demolition operations, 65 damaged areas were repaired in 13
avenues with the heaviest traffic as follows:

Roads	Repair Work
1. Eje 1 Pte.	8
2. Eje Central	7
3. Avenue 20 de Noviembre	2
4. Avenue Juarez	4
5. Eje 2 Pte. Monterrey	5
6. Eje 4 Sur Xola	3
7. Paseos de la Reforma	2
8. Calzada de Tlalpan	5
9. Calzada Jose Ma. Pino Suarez	4
10. Avenue de los Insurgentes	7
11. Avenue Fray Servando Teresa de Mier	7
12. Avenue Chapultepec	5
13. Avenue Jose Ma. Izazaga	6
TOTAL	65

Repair work was performed in the evening hours from 10 p.m.
to 5 a.m.

The regular program for pavement reconstruction was
modified and a new emergency program was created on November
11th ending December 31st, 1985.

Works of the Building Control Commission

The Building Control Commission was created to enforce
the technical codes of buildings of 5 or more stories while
construction of buildings of 4 stories or less were in the
charge of political precincts.

The Building Control Commission is responsible for
building permits, for major and minor repair permits and the
authorization of partial or total demolition of buildings
under their control.

The control of real estate registration procedures and
reporting of repair and demolition work is maintained with a
computer system.

Based on the records up to June 30th, 1986, the following relation exists:

Situation	Number of Buildings
Restored	47
Demolished	106
Repaired	169
In demolition	77
In repair	348
Without attention	499
No specifics	226
TOTAL	1,472

These records were tabulated since October 1985.

Special attention was paid to major repair work and partial demolition in order to ascertain the necessary stability of structures and to attain a high degree of confidence in the buildings.

Highly prestigious technical enterprises have been contracted, professionals in structural analysis, to perform technical revisions and judgments of buildings and to examine appraisals presented by owners.

The works of the Metro deserve special recognition which suffered no damage in spite of the harmful characteristics of the earthquakes.

The surface lines, the elevated lines, underground caisson lines and deep tunnel lines were undamaged which demonstrates the excellence of their design and construction.

Operation was only suspended for the necessary time required for a detailed inspection.

The surface lines and underground caisson lines 1,2,3 and 5 with a total operating length of 69.77 kilometers, suffered no structural damage that interfered with its proper operation and even in the Pino Suarez transfer station for Lines 1 and 2, no damages were suffered despite the total collapse of a 20-story building above the station and the caisson of Line 2.

The movements registered after the earthquakes in the elevated Line 4 with a length of 10.7 kilometers, were manifested in the sudden sinking of some load bearing supports which sank between 4 and 10 millimeters, a magnitude which is considered very small and which in no way has affected the operation of the Metro. Since the movements occurring to date are faithfully following the theoretical behavior invisioned by the movement graphs available to date, it can be established that the magnitude of the sinking developed in each of the supports is within the foreseen parameters and very close to its stabilization. The differential movement that occurred between two consecutive supports does not exceed the maximum permissible limit of 4 centimeters which was a premise of the project.

The elevated portion of Metro Line 9, presently under construction, was based on the project design of Line 4 and is using the most advanced technological procedures in the world in civil engineering. Among the advances we can mention that the prefabrication of very thin beams, covering very large spans in the order of 40 meters, has been achieved. The supports for the beams have been designed with a thick neoprene pad sandwiched between metal plates, which absorb the longitudinal sliding in the support with Teflon plates.

Despite Mexico City having a very unstable subsoil with a high moisture content, the differential sinkings have been controlled with foundation systems based on friction piles and concrete slab footings.

Conclusion

The impartial and enterprising collaboration of the citizenship in the tragedy resulting from the earthquake, praises the country of Mexico and the generous aid received from Mexicans as well as foreigners.

This demonstrates that only with the participation of citizens have we been able to realize our goals. This great city has been built up with the tenacious strength and work of everyone. Its bright future in is the will of all. Let's do it.

SUBJECT INDEX

Page number refers to first page of paper.

Acceleration, 96
Accelerograms, 19, 33
Analytical techniques, 148

Bracing, 426
Bridges, 368
Building codes, 264, 440, 455
Buildings, 55, 70, 217

Case reports, 396
Communication systems, 368
Concrete, reinforced, 233, 255, 279, 328, 426
Concrete structures, 233, 279, 308, 426
Construction, 463

Dam failure, 134
Damage assessment, 70, 119, 409
Damage estimation, 217
Damage patterns, 55, 70
Data collection, 19
Deep foundations, 78
Deformation, 264
Design criteria, 204
Drift, 279
Dynamic analysis, 233
Dynamic response, 148, 193

Earthquake damage, 178
Earthquake engineering, 33
Earthquake magnitude scale, 96, 440
Earthquake resistant structures, 255
Earthquakes, 1
Embankment stability, 134

Foundation performance, 350
Foundation settlement, 178
Foundations, 119, 193, 204, 264
Frames, 279, 328

Government agencies, 463
Ground motion, 7, 55, 96, 148, 264, 328

Highways, 368

Industrial plants, 381
Infrastructure, 368
Instrumentation, 19
Internatioal compacts, 1

Laboratory tests, 328
Lateral loads, 308
Liquefaction, 119

Mathematical models, 396
Mexico, 1, 33

Pile foundations, 78
Piles, 204
Plates, 255
Powerplants, 381
Public works, 463

Railroads, 368
Rehabilitation, 396
Repairing, 426
Research, 1
Retrofitting, 409

Seismic design, 204, 455
Seismic response, 134, 193, 409
Seismic studies, 7
Seismology, 33
Settlement analysis, 178
Shallow foundations, 78
Shoring, 426
Site evaluation, 96
Soil conditions, 148, 163, 193, 350
Soils, 148
Soil-structure interaction, 163, 193, 440
Statistics, 70
Steel frames, 255
Steel structures, 350, 409
Stiffening, 396
Stratigraphy, 78
Structural analysis, 396
Structural behavior, 119, 308, 350
Structural design, 455
Structural response, 193, 217, 440
Subsidence, 119
Subsurface investigations, 119

Technology transfer, 33
Three-dimensional analysis, 233, 396
Torsion, 264
Transportation systems, 368

Underground structures, 78
Underpinning, 204
United States, 33
Urban development, 7

Vibration tests, 233

Water pipelines, 364
Water supply systems, 364
Wave propagation, 148

AUTHOR INDEX

Page number refers to first page of paper.

Anderson, John G., 33

Bertero, Vitelmo V., 264
Bodin, Paul, 33
Borja-Navarrete, Gilberto, 70
Brune, James N., 33

Castaneda Narvaes, Carlos E., 463
Celebi, Mehmet, 217
Corley, W. G., 328

de Buen, Oscar, 455
del Valle-Calderón, Enrique, 70
Diaz-Canales, Manuel, 70

Eder, S. J., 381

Fossas R., Fernando, 255

Ghosh, S. K., 328
Girault D., Pablo, 178
González-Valencia, Francisco, 134
Gutiérrez, Carlos, 119

Hanson, Robert, 350
Housner, George W., 1

Iglesias, Jesus, 426

Kobayashi, Hiroyoshi, 55
Krinitzky, Ellis L., 96

Lee, Gary M., 364
Lopez, Ricardo R., 279

Marsal, Raúl J., 78

Martin, Ignacio, 396
Martínez-Romero, Enrique, 409
Meli, Roberto, 308
Mena, Enrique, 19, 33
Midorikawa, Saburoh, 55

Norena Casado, Francisco, 463

Onate, Mario, 33

Prince, Jorge, 33, 217

Quaas, Roberto, 19, 33

Reséndiz, Daniel, 193
Rodriquez Cuevas, Ing. Neftali, 233
Roesset, J. M., 193
Romo, Miguel P., 148
Rosenblueth, Emilio, 440

Santoyo, Enrique, 119
Scawthorn, Charles, 217
Seed, H. Bolton, 148
Seo, Kazuoh, 55
Singh, S. K., 7
Singh, Shri Krishna, 33
Sozen, Mete A., 279
Stone, William C., 233
Suárez, G., 7
Swan, S. W., 381

Tamez, Enrique, 204

Vargas-Gómez, Froylán, 368
Vázquez-Vera, Alejandro, 70

Whitman, Robert V., 163